Tokyo

John Ashburne
Chris Rowthorn

D1008087

LONELY PLANET PUBLICATIONS
Melbourne • Oakland • London • Paris

Tokyo
4th edition – September 2001
First published – March 1993

Published by
Lonely Planet Publications Pty Ltd ABN 36 005 607 983
90 Maribyrnong St, Footscray, Victoria 3011, Australia

Lonely Planet Offices
Australia Locked Bag 1, Footscray, Victoria 3011
USA 150 Linden St, Oakland, CA 94607
UK 10a Spring Place, London NW5 3BH
France 1 rue du Dahomey, 75011 Paris

Photographs
Many of the images in this guide are available for licensing from
Lonely Planet Images.
W www.lonelyplanetimages.com

Front cover photograph
Giant screen TV, Tokyo, Japan (Eric L Wheater)

Map section title page photograph
Layered roads, Tokyo, Japan (John Hay)

(handwritten notes, left column):
Infiniti is what's next.
A more evolved automobile
Driving has evolved
Welcome to Infiniti
Imagine. Infiniti.
The most interesting car on the road.
A highly evolved automobile.
Highly evolved.
Correct Spirit

(handwritten notes, right column):
Designed like no other car on the road
Making the road more beautiful
The new standard in design
* Designed to Move.
Experience. Infiniti
A friendly machine.
On the vanguard of luxury.

ISBN 1 74059 059 7

text & maps © Lonely Planet Publications Pty Ltd 2001
photos © photographers as indicated 2001
Tokyo Subway Network reproduced by kind permission of Teito Rapid
Transit Authority.

Printed by Craft Print International Ltd, Singapore

Contents – Text

Contents – Maps

FACTS ABOUT TOKYO

GETTING THERE & AWAY

EXCURSIONS

COLOUR MAP SECTION

MAP LEGEND   back page

The Authors

John Ashburne

John Ashburne grew up in Yorkshire, flirted with English Literature and Education at Durham and Cambridge Universities, and worked as a private tutor in the Caribbean. Thereafter he attempted office work with Robert Maxwell's publishing company in Oxford, fleeing two seconds ahead of his dismissal notice, ending up in the rural hinterlands of Japan. Fourteen years later he resides in Kyoto, where he roots out noodle restaurants, when he's not off to Vietnam, Cambodia or Italy – in search of more noodle restaurants. He is author of several books on Japan, and twice winner of the Mazda International Photo Contest. As well as *Tokyo* he has authored Lonely Planet's *Japan*, *World Food: Japan* and *Tokyo Condensed*.

Chris Rowthorn

Chris was born in England and grew up in the USA. Since 1992 he's been based in Kyoto. He's worked on a total of nine books for Lonely Planet, including *Japan*, *Malaysia, Singapore & Brunei*, *Hiking in Japan* and *Read This First: Asia & India*. When he's not on the road for Lonely Planet, Chris enjoys trekking in Nepal, diving in Thailand and relaxing in Japanese hot springs.

FROM THE AUTHOR
From John

Zillions of thanks, as ever, to Sasha. Also endless *arigatos* to Yuka Takahashi of the TCVB; Yoko Tatsumi of JNTO; Wes Smith; Lauren Shannon; Philip Beech; Barbara Stein, Michiyo Houser & the Friends World students; Chris Rowthorn & Mason Florence; and to Conner Gorry, for a timely reminder that the Ueno station toilets, fearsome as they are, ain't got nuthin' on rural Bolivia.

This Book

The first two editions of *Tokyo* were written by Chris Taylor, with Chris Rowthorn taking over for the 3rd edition. John Ashburne has built on the work of Chris and Chris to update this 4th edition.

FROM THE PUBLISHER
The production of this edition of *Tokyo* was coordinated by Chris Tsismetzis (cartography and design) and Errol Hunt (editing). Chris was assisted with mapping by Meredith Mail and Chris Love, and with design by Barbara 'the caption queen' Benson. A heroic band of editors stepped in to help Errol: Michael Day, Kyla Gillzan, Anastasia Safioleas, Kim Hutchins and Linda Suttie. Thanks dudes!

The Language chapter was written and formatted by Quentin Frayne and Emma Koch. Yoshi 'the kanji king' Abe, assisted with Japanese script used throughout this book. Matt King coordinated illustrations and Val Tellini and Glenn Beanland coordinated images. Mark Germanchis assisted with tricky layout issues.

Clint Curé (CC) drew the new cartoons – including 'Walking Dude', your friendly companion on Tokyo walking tours. We also used cartoons and illustrations by Mic Looby (ML), Margie Jung (MJ) and Lonely Planet Publications (LPP). Chris Tsismetzis drew the chapter ends.

The whole process was overseen by Meredith Mail (design) and Jocelyn Harewood (editing). Chris Love did the final artwork check.

ARIGATŌ GOZAIMASU (THANKS)
Lonely Planet would like to thank the following readers for sending us their anecdotes, suggestions and recommendations:

Graeme Anshaw, Nicole Bird, Kim Blick, Peder Christensen, Artur Correia, Patrick Courtenay, Pamela De Mark, David Deng, Harold Dodd, Margaret Eveleigh, Tim Eyre, Doug Fischer, Ulrich Fischer, Marc L Fontaine, Jarrod Hector, Leigh Hermann, Miynki Ishii, Wendy Jonas, Andrew Jones, Ivo Keel, Gene Klein, Taeko Kobayashi, Paul Lufkin, Reto Maccioni, Alfred MacRae, Ryu Makoto, Desiree Mensink, Boye Lafayette De Mente, Simon Merry, Valerie Moffat, Tom Munoz Je, Linda Nagy, Dennis Nielsen, John O'Doherty, Jane Perkins, Peter Phillips, Joe Poconto, Tom Riddle, Yves Rosiers, Grant Rule, Jo Rumble, Ian Satherley, Jon Sayers, Connie Schmollinger, Ged Shimokawa Kelly, Eduardo Spaccasassi, Cheryl & Frank Stearn, Clare Stringer, Hans ter Horst, Kelly Thorpe, Eric van der Palen, Hans van der Veen, Sarah Varela, Kees Verloop, Tim Walker, Sandy Walters, Richard Weber, Peggy Weymouth, Alex Williams

Foreword

ABOUT LONELY PLANET GUIDEBOOKS
The story begins with a classic travel adventure: Tony and Maureen Wheeler's 1972 journey across Europe and Asia to Australia. Useful information about the overland trail did not exist at that time, so Tony and Maureen published the first Lonely Planet guidebook to meet a growing need.

From a kitchen table, then from a tiny office in Melbourne (Australia), Lonely Planet has become the largest independent travel publisher in the world, an international company with offices in Melbourne, Oakland (USA), London (UK) and Paris (France).

Today Lonely Planet guidebooks cover the globe. There is an ever-growing list of books and there's information in a variety of forms and media. Some things haven't changed. The main aim is still to help make it possible for adventurous travellers to get out there – to explore and better understand the world.

At Lonely Planet we believe travellers can make a positive contribution to the countries they visit – if they respect their host communities and spend their money wisely. Since 1986 a percentage of the income from each book has been donated to aid projects and human rights campaigns.

Updates Lonely Planet thoroughly updates each guidebook as often as possible. This usually means there are around two years between editions, although for more unusual or more stable destinations the gap can be longer. Check the imprint page (following the colour map at the beginning of the book) for publication dates.

Between editions up-to-date information is available in two free newsletters – the paper *Planet Talk* and email *Comet* (to subscribe, contact any Lonely Planet office) – and on our Web site at www.lonelyplanet.com. The *Upgrades* section of the Web site covers a number of important and volatile destinations and is regularly updated by Lonely Planet authors. *Scoop* covers news and current affairs relevant to travellers. And, lastly, the *Thorn Tree* bulletin board and *Postcards* section of the site carry unverified, but fascinating, reports from travellers.

Correspondence The process of creating new editions begins with the letters, postcards and emails received from travellers. This correspondence often includes suggestions, criticisms and comments about the current editions. Interesting excerpts are immediately passed on via newsletters and the Web site, and everything goes to our authors to be verified when they're researching on the road. We're keen to get more feedback from organisations or individuals who represent communities visited by travellers.

Lonely Planet gathers information for everyone who's curious about the planet – and especially for those who explore it first-hand. Through guidebooks, phrasebooks, activity guides, maps, literature, newsletters, image library, TV series and Web site we act as an information exchange for a worldwide community of travellers.

Research Authors aim to gather sufficient practical information to enable travellers to make informed choices and to make the mechanics of a journey run smoothly. They also research historical and cultural background to help enrich the travel experience and allow travellers to understand and respond appropriately to cultural and environmental issues.

Authors don't stay in every hotel because that would mean spending a couple of months in each medium-sized city and, no, they don't eat at every restaurant because that would mean stretching belts beyond capacity. They do visit hotels and restaurants to check standards and prices, but feedback based on readers' direct experiences can be very helpful.

Many of our authors work undercover, others aren't so secretive. None of them accept freebies in exchange for positive write-ups. And none of our guidebooks contain any advertising.

Production Authors submit their raw manuscripts and maps to offices in Australia, USA, UK or France. Editors and cartographers – all experienced travellers themselves – then begin the process of assembling the pieces. When the book finally hits the shops, some things are already out of date, we start getting feedback from readers and the process begins again ...

WARNING & REQUEST

Things change – prices go up, schedules change, good places go bad and bad places go bankrupt – nothing stays the same. So, if you find things better or worse, recently opened or long since closed, please tell us and help make the next edition even more accurate and useful. We genuinely value all the feedback we receive. A well travelled team reads and acknowledges every letter, postcard and email and ensures that every morsel of information finds its way to the appropriate authors, editors and cartographers for verification.

Everyone who writes to us will find their name in the next edition of the appropriate guidebook. They will also receive the latest issue of *Planet Talk*, our quarterly printed newsletter, or *Comet*, our monthly email newsletter. Subscriptions to both newsletters are free. The very best contributions will be rewarded with a free guidebook.

Excerpts from your correspondence may appear in new editions of Lonely Planet guidebooks, the Lonely Planet Web site, *Planet Talk* or *Comet*, so please let us know if you *don't* want your letter published or your name acknowledged.

Send all correspondence to the Lonely Planet office closest to you:

Australia: Locked Bag 1, Footscray, Victoria 3011
USA: 150 Linden St, Oakland, CA 94607
UK: 10A Spring Place, London NW5 3BH
France: 1 rue du Dahomey, 75011 Paris

Or email us at: talk2us@lonelyplanet.com.au

For news, views and updates see our Web site: www.lonelyplanet.com

HOW TO USE A LONELY PLANET GUIDEBOOK

The best way to use a Lonely Planet guidebook is any way you choose. At Lonely Planet we believe the most memorable travel experiences are often those that are unexpected, and the finest discoveries are those you make yourself. Guidebooks are not intended to be used as if they provide a detailed set of infallible instructions!

Contents All Lonely Planet guidebooks follow roughly the same format. The Facts about the Destination chapters or sections give background information ranging from history to weather. Facts for the Visitor gives practical information on issues like visas and health. Getting There & Away gives a brief starting point for researching travel to and from the destination. Getting Around gives an overview of the transport options when you arrive.

The peculiar demands of each destination determine how subsequent chapters are broken up, but some things remain constant. We always start with background, then proceed to sights, places to stay, places to eat, entertainment, getting there and away, and getting around information – in that order.

Heading Hierarchy Lonely Planet headings are used in a strict hierarchical structure that can be visualised as a set of Russian dolls. Each heading (and its following text) is encompassed by any preceding heading that is higher on the hierarchical ladder.

Entry Points We do not assume guidebooks will be read from beginning to end, but that people will dip into them. The traditional entry points are the list of contents and the index. In addition, however, some books have a complete list of maps and an index map illustrating map coverage.

There may also be a colour map that shows highlights. These highlights are dealt with in greater detail in the Facts for the Visitor chapter, along with planning questions and suggested itineraries. Each chapter covering a geographical region usually begins with a locator map and another list of highlights. Once you find something of interest in a list of highlights, turn to the index.

Maps Maps play a crucial role in Lonely Planet guidebooks and include a huge amount of information. A legend is printed on the back page. We seek to have complete consistency between maps and text, and to have every important place in the text captured on a map. Map key numbers usually start in the top left corner.

Although inclusion in a guidebook usually implies a recommendation we cannot list every good place. Exclusion does not necessarily imply criticism. In fact there are a number of reasons why we might exclude a place – sometimes it is simply inappropriate to encourage an influx of travellers.

Introduction

Tokyo, like all great cities, is a conundrum, a riddle of contradictions that springs from tensions between large-scale ugliness and meticulous detail; the frantic rhythms of 20th-century consumer culture and the still, quiet moments that are the legacy of other, older traditions. It is a creative behemoth, inevitably reinventing, re-creating, resolving itself. It is chaos at the centre. It's a meteoric speedball that doesn't give a damn. It may well be the perfect metaphor for the globe as it spins and wobbles off course into the 21st century.

Naturally, it's a lot of fun.

Tokyo is the nesting place of both Japan Inc and the lineages of the old town of Edo. Reposing by fashionable Ginza and administrative Nihombashi is the Imperial Palace, with its gardens, its closeted Imperial dynasty, and photogenic views. In the heart of Akasaka, surrounded by world-class hotels, trendy boutiques and eateries, is Hie-jinja. The central areas of Ueno and Asakusa are home to splendid museums and to bustling Sensō-ji, possibly Japan's liveliest Buddhist temple. And just two hours from Tokyo by train are the historic towns of Kamakura and Nikkō, and the scenic regions of Hakone and Mt Fuji.

While Tokyo sports some of the world's biggest and most lavish department stores, the average Tokyo suburb hasn't fallen prey (just yet) to supermarket culture – the streets are lined with tiny specialist shops and restaurants, most of which stay open late into the night. Near soaring office blocks are entertainment quarters – mazes of narrow alleys blazing with neon by night, offering intoxicating escape from the work regimen that is the lot of Tokyo's surging crowds of office workers. And in the shadow of the overhead expressways exist pockets of another Tokyo: an old wooden house, a Japanese inn, an old lady in *kimono* and *geta* slippers sweeping the pavement outside her home with a straw broom.

What confronts the visitor above all is Tokyo's sheer level of energy. On the busy train lines, even late on a Monday night, it's standing room only. The crowds carry you through an auditory assault, from ghostly train announcements and sing-song instructions on escalators to blasting shop jingles and the digitised melodies of traffic lights and vending machines.

Tokyo jumps out at you unexpectedly on a crowded street: the woman dressed in kimono buying a hamburger at McDonald's, the Buddhist monk with an alms bowl poised serenely in the midst of jostling shoppers in Ginza. Look closely – the monk's shock-proof watch sports an altimeter.

Tokyo is a living city. It may offer the visitor some splendid sights, but it is less a collection of sights than a total experience, the urban explorer's dream.

Facts about Tokyo

HISTORY

When the first European visitors, Por-tuguese traders, came to Japan in the 16th century, Tokyo was an unlikely destination. The area then known as Edo was a sizeable fishing town and even had an abandoned castle, but there was little to indicate that Edo would one day grow to become the capital of Japan and one of the world's major cities. Strangely enough, however, the Portuguese visitors were instrumental in the events that led to Edo usurping Kyoto as Japan's traditional seat of imperial power and becoming Tokyo. Some three centuries after the first Western influx, when Com-modore Matthew Perry of the US Navy showed up with gunships and demands that the country open its doors to commerce with the outside world, it was to the erst-while fishing town of Edo that he came.

Before Edo

Shintō, Japan's native religion, had its origin in the Yayoi period (300 BC to AD 300), when wet-rice farming techniques were in-troduced from Korea. By AD 300, Japan was already, more or less, a unified nation, under the Yamato clan, who claimed a handy direct descent from the sun goddess Amaterasu. It was they who introduced the title of *Tenno* (emperor), around the 5th century. But the most important event in the early history of Japan was the arrival of Buddhism in the 6th century via China and Korea.

Buddhism brought a highly evolved sys-tem of metaphysics, codes of law and the Chinese writing system, a conduit for the principles of Confucian statecraft. By the 8th century, however, the Buddhist clerical bureaucracy had become vast, threatening the authority of the imperial administration. The emperor responded by relocating the capital from Nara and establishing a new seat of imperial power at Heian (modern-day Kyoto). Kyoto was, by and large, to serve as the imperial capital until the Meiji Restoration and Tokyo's foundation as

Japan's capital. The one interruption came when Minamoto Yoritomo defeated the rul-ing Taira clan and established the first shō-gunate in Kamakura in 1180. He ruled a military government there until 1333, when he was toppled by a rebellion and official power reverted to Kyoto.

Even from Kyoto's early days, a warrior *samurai* class in the employ of feudal lords (*daimyō*) was emerging. Much of Japan's subsequent history was a record of struggles for power among the daimyō while the em-peror mostly watched impotently from the haven of Kyoto's Imperial Palace.

By the time the Portuguese arrived in 1543, Japan was a divided realm of feudal fiefs. One of the most powerful daimyō, Oda Nobunaga, was quick to see how the Portuguese might have a part to play in his own ambitious plans. He saw Christianity as a potential weapon against the power of the Buddhist clergy and made ample use of another import brought by the God-fearing Portuguese – firearms. By the time he was assassinated in 1581, Nobunaga had united much of central Japan. He was succeeded by Toyotomi Hideyoshi, who continued unification but looked less favourably on the growing Christian movement, subject-ing it to systematic persecution.

Hideyoshi's power was briefly contested by Tokugawa Ieyasu, son of a minor lord who had been allied to Nobunaga. After a brief struggle for power, Ieyasu agreed to a truce with Hideyoshi; in return, Hideyoshi granted him eight provinces of eastern Japan, including all of the Kantō region. While Hideyoshi intended this as a move to weaken Ieyasu by separating him from his ancestral homeland, the young Ieyasu looked upon the gift of land as an opportu-nity to strengthen his power. He set about reclaiming his homeland and turning Edo into a real city.

When Hideyoshi died in 1598, power passed to his son, Hideyori. However, Ieyasu had been busily scheming to secure the shōgunate for himself and soon went to war against those loyal to Hideyori. Ieyasu finally defeated Hideyori and his supporters at the Battle of Sekigahara in 1600, moving him into a position of supreme power. He chose Edo as his permanent base and thus began 250 years of Tokugawa rule.

Tokugawa Edo

Tokugawa Ieyasu was appointed *shōgun* (military administrator) in 1603 by the emperor. One of the most important acts of the Tokugawa regime in its quest to achieve total control of the country was to implement the *sankin kōtai* system. This demanded that all daimyō throughout Japan spend at least one year out of two in Edo. Their wives and children were to remain in Edo. This dislocating ransom policy made it difficult for ambitious daimyō to usurp the Tokugawas.

Society was made rigidly hierarchical, comprising (in descending order of importance) the nobility, who had nominal power; the daimyō and their samurai; the farmers; and finally the artisans and merchants. Class dress, living quarters and even manner of speech were all strictly codified, and inter-class movement prohibited.

When Ieyasu died in 1616, his ashes were briefly laid to rest in Chūbu before being moved to Nikkō. Generations of Tokugawas made improvements to his shrine, transforming it into one of the grandest in all Japan.

In 1638, concerned that missionaries were gaining too much power, Ieyasu's grandson, Tokugawa Iemitsu, massacred a number of Kyūshū Christians and closed the country to almost all foreign trade. This radical isolation policy, known as *sakoku*, was to remove Japan from the world stage for nearly three centuries.

These sudden changes led to the rapid growth of the small town of Edo. By the early 17th century the population had grown to more than one million, making it the largest city in the world. Meanwhile, the caste-like society imposed by Tokugawa rule divided Edo into a high city (Yamanote) region and a low city (Shitamachi) region.

The higher Yamanote (literally, hand of the mountains) area was home to daimyō and their samurai, while the lower orders of Edo society were forced into the low-lying Shitamachi area.

Shitamachi residents lived in squalid conditions, usually in flimsy wooden structures with earthen floors. Great conflagrations often swept across these shantytowns. These fires were known to locals as *Edo no hana*, or flowers of Edo. The cocky bravura of the expression sums up the spirit of Shitamachi – living under circumstances of great privation and in accordance with a social order set by the Tokugawa regime, Shitamachi produced a flourishing culture that thumbed its nose at social hardships and the strictures of the shōgunate. Today, the best glimpses we have in to that time come from ukiyo-e prints (see the Fine Arts section, later in this chapter). They reveal a world where money meant more than rank, actors and artists were the arbiters of style, and prostitutes elevated their accomplishments to a level matching those of the ladies of nobility.

Another feature of Edo that has left its mark on today's Tokyo was the division of the city into towns *(machi)* according to profession. Even today it is possible to stumble across small enclaves that specialise in particular wares. Most famous are Jimbōchō, the bookshop area; Kappabashi, with its plastic food and kitchen supplies; Asakusabashi, with its toy shops; and Akihabara, which now specialises in electronics, but in the past has been a bicycle retailing area, an area specialising in domestic household goods and a freight yard.

Tokyo Rising

The turning point for the city of Edo, indeed for all of Japan, was the arrival of Commodore Matthew Perry's armada of 'black ships' at Edo-wan (now known as Tokyo Bay) in 1853. Perry's US Navy expedition demanded that Japan open to foreign trade. Other Western powers were quick to follow the US in demanding the Japanese open treaty ports and end the isolation policy. The coming of Westerners heralded a far-reaching social revolution against which the antiquated Tokugawa regime was power-less. In 1867–68, faced with wide-scale antigovernment feeling and accusations that the regime had failed to prepare Japan for the threat of the West, the last Tokugawa shōgun resigned and power reverted to Emperor Meiji.

The Meiji Restoration was not an entirely peaceful handover of power. In Edo some 2000 Tokugawa loyalists put up a futile last-ditch resistance to the imperial forces in the brief Battle of Ueno. The struggle took place around Kanei-ji, which, along with Zōjō-ji, was one of Edo's two mortuary temples for the Tokugawa shōgunate.

In 1868 the emperor moved the seat of imperial power from Kyoto to Edo, renaming the city Tokyo (eastern capital) in the process. In some ways it was less a restoration than a revolution. The Japanese underwent a crash course in industrialisation and militarisation, and by 1889 the country had instituted a Western-style constitution. In remarkably little time Japan achieved military victories over China (1894–95) and Russia (1904–5) and embarked on modern, Western-style empire building, from the annexation of Taiwan (1895), then Korea (1910) and Micronesia (1914).

Nationalists were also transforming Shintō into a jingoistic state religion. Seen as a corrupting foreign influence, Buddhism suffered badly – many valuable artefacts and temples were destroyed, and the common people were urged to place their faith in the pure religion of 'State Shintō'.

During the Meiji period, changes that were taking place all over Japan could be seen most prominently in the country's new capital city. Tokyo's rapid industrialisation, uniting around the nascent *zaibatsu* (huge industrial and trading combines), drew job seekers from around Japan, causing the population to grow rapidly. Western-style buildings began to spring up in fashionable areas such as Ginza, and in the 1880s electric lighting was introduced. However, if the Meiji Restoration sounded the death knell for old Edo, there were two more events that were to erase most traces of the old city.

Tokyo Disasters

The Great Kantō Earthquake struck at noon on 1 September 1923. It was less the earthquake itself than the subsequent fires, lasting some 40 hours, that laid waste to the city. A quarter of the quake's 142,000 fatalities occurred in one savage firestorm that swept through a clothing depot.

In true Edo style, reconstruction began almost immediately. The spirit in which this was undertaken is perhaps best summed up by Edward Seidensticker. He observed that it was popular wisdom that any business which did not resume trading within three days of being burnt out did not have a future. Opportunities were lost in reconstructing the city – streets might have been widened and the capital transformed into something more of a showcase. As it was, Tokyoites were given a second opportunity.

From the accession of Emperor Hirohito and the initiation of the Shōwa period in 1926, Japanese society was marked by a quickening tide of nationalist fervour. In 1931 the Japanese invaded Manchuria, and in 1937 embarked on full-scale hostilities with China. By 1940 a tripartite pact with Germany and Italy had been signed and a new order for all of Asia formulated: the 'Greater Asia Co-Prosperity Sphere'. On 7 December 1941 the Japanese attacked Pearl Harbor and thus the US, their principal rival in the Asia-Pacific region.

Despite initial successes, the war was disastrous for Japan. The earliest bombing raids on Tokyo took place on 18 April 1942, when B-25 bombers carried out a bombing and strafing raid on the city, with 364 casualties. Much worse was to come. Incendiary bombing commenced in March 1944, notably on the nights of the 9th and 10th, when some two-fifths of the city, mainly in the Shitamachi area, went up in smoke and 70,000 to 80,000 lives were lost. The same raids destroyed Asakusa's Sensō-ji, and later raids destroyed Meiji-jingū. By the time Emperor Hirohito made his famous address to the Japanese people on 15 August 1945, much of Tokyo had been decimated and sections of it almost completely depopulated as surely as if it had shared the same fate (atomic-bomb explosions) as Hiroshima and Nagasaki.

Post-War Years

Tokyo's phoenix-like rise from the ashes of WWII and its emergence as a major global city is something of a miracle. Once again, Tokyoites did not take the devastation as an opportunity to redesign their city, but rebuilt where the old had once stood.

During the US occupation in the early post-war years, Tokyo was something of a honky-tonk town. Now-respectable areas such as Yūrakuchō were the haunt of the so-called *pan-pan* girls, and areas such as Ikebukuro and Ueno had thriving black-market zones. The remains of Ueno's black market can be seen in the Ameyoko Arcade, which is still a lively market, though there is no longer anything very black about it.

By 1951, with a boom in Japanese profits arising from the Korean War, Tokyo, especially the central business district, was being rapidly rebuilt, and the subway began to take on its present form. The city has never looked back. From the postwar years to the present, Tokyo has continually reconstructed itself.

During the 1960s and '70s, Tokyo re-emerged as one of the centres of growing Asian nationalism (the first phase was in the 1910s and '20s). Increasing numbers of Asian students have come to Tokyo, taking home with them new ideas about Asia's role in the postwar world.

One of Tokyo's proudest moments came when it hosted the 1964 summer Olympics, and in preparation the city embarked on a frenzy of construction unequalled in its history. Many Japanese see this time as a turning point in the nation's history, the moment when Japan finally recovered from the devastation of WWII to emerge as a major player in the modern world economy.

Construction and modernisation continued at a breakneck pace through the '70s, with the interruption of two Middle East oil crises, to reach a peak in the late '80s, when wildly inflated real estate prices and stock speculation fuelled what is now known as the 'bubble economy'. When the bubble burst in

The Uyoku

Since the end of WWII, right-wing and nationalist sentiments have generally taken a back seat to moderate political views or outright apathy. However, there remain pockets of right-wing sentiment. These are most visible to the visitor in the form of sinister black buses and vans, which ply the streets of big cities blaring patriotic Japanese songs (which unfortunately always sound like the TV theme songs for kids manga cartoons) at ear-splitting volume. These vehicles represent the propaganda arm of the *uyoku*, far-right political parties and organisations.

While rather alarming at first sight, uyoku buses and their occupants pose no threat to tourists. Rather, their target is the Japanese public. When not playing music, speakers deliver lengthy diatribes against Japanese politicians or a litany of nationalist sentiments. Their favourite line is 'Revere the Emperor! Expel the Barbarian'. Yes, dear reader, that's you.

Japanese pedestrians studiously ignore black buses blaring 100 decibels of noise. When regular citizens pay them any notice at all, it's usually to dismiss them as cranks.

There is a dark side to the uyoku: they act as a volunteer police force for right and right-leaning politicians, effectively prohibiting criticism of the emperor. This is done by intimidating would-be critics with threats of violence, which are occasionally carried out.

As Japan's economy goes down the tubes, and the Barbarians – most noticeably the US variety – try to pry open Japan's trade markets, the noisy, punch-permed boys in red and black are likely to stay around, either as a bizarre distraction to the serious business of weekend shopping, or as a sobering echo of a darker time in Japanese history.

東京 東京 東京 東京 東京 東京 東京 東京

1989, the economy went into a slump, one from which it has not fully recovered.

In March 1995, members of the Aum Shinrikyō cult released sarin nerve gas on a crowded Tokyo commuter train, killing 12 and injuring 5000. This, together with the

Kōbe earthquake of the same year, signalled the end of Japan's feeling of omnipotence, born of the unlimited successes of the '80s. Now, the city is working to get over its crisis of confidence and shake the seemingly intractable recession.

Having survived mad cults and the burst of the bubble, Tokyo continues to forge ahead. Vast areas of Tokyo Bay have been reclaimed and are now home to international conference centres and business parks, and work is under way to overhaul the already excellent subway system. The city is also attempting a modest 'green revolution'.

Tokyo is above all a singular expression of Japanese modernity, with a concentration of industry, business, higher education, the

TOKYO WARDS (KU)

1	Nerima-ku 練馬区	9	Nakano-ku 中野区	17	Kōtō-ku 江東区
2	Itabashi-ku 板橋区	10	Suginami-ku 杉並区	18	Chūō-ku 中央区
3	Kita-ku 北区	11	Shibuya-ku 渋谷区	19	Minato-ku 港区
4	Adachi-ku 足立区	12	Shinjuku-ku 新宿区	20	Meguro-ku 目黒区
5	Katsushika-ku 葛飾区	13	Chiyoda-ku 千代田区	21	Setagaya-ku 世田谷区
6	Arakawa-ku 荒川区	14	Taitō-ku 台東区	22	Shinagawa-ku 品川区
7	Bunkyō-ku 文京区	15	Sumida-ku 墨田区	23	Ōta-ku 大田区
8	Toshima-ku 豊島区	16	Edogawa-ku 江戸川区		

TOKYO WARDS (KU)

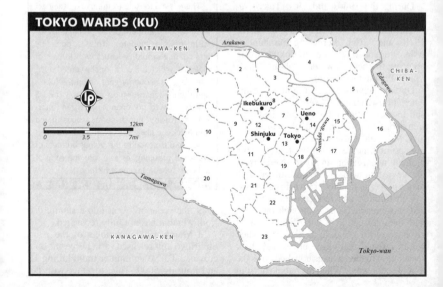

arts and a sheer diversity rarely found in capital cities around the globe.

GEOGRAPHY

Tokyo is situated on the Kantō Plain, on the eastern seaboard of Honshū island, the largest of Japan's four principal islands.

Administratively, Japan is made up of 47 prefectures (usually *ken*). Tokyo Metropolitan prefecture itself comprises 23 wards *(ku)*, 27 cities *(shi)*, one county *(gun)* and four island administrative districts *(shi-chō)*, a total area of 2168 sq km. Tokyo Metropolitan prefecture is bordered by Saitama prefecture to the north, Chiba prefecture to the north-east, Tokyo Bay to the south-east, Yamanashi prefecture to the west and Kanagawa prefecture to the south-west.

The western Yamanote wards lie on the Musashino Plateau, a deposit of volcanic ash from the Fuji-Hakone mountain range. Parts of the eastern Shitamachi area lie beneath sea level and other areas have been built up on reclaimed land in the Tokyo Bay area.

CLIMATE & WHEN TO GO

Like the rest of Japan, the best time to visit Tokyo is spring, from March to May. The cherry blossom season is from early April, when even Tokyo can seem quite beautiful. It's a lively time too, with hordes of revellers heading off to the parks for *hanami* (cherry blossom viewing) parties. Summer is hot and muggy, a time when the overcrowded trains are at their most unbearable. The monsoon season *(tsuyu)*, which usually falls at the beginning of summer in June, can mean four or five days of torrential rain that can play havoc with a tight travel itinerary.

Autumn (September to November) is the next best time to be in Tokyo. Areas like Kamakura and Nikkō are especially beautiful at this time of year. The weather is cool and there's a high proportion of clear days – perfect sightseeing weather. Temperatures occasionally drop below 0°C in winter, but most of the time it's just heavy-overcoat weather. Tokyo generally gets a couple of snowfalls every winter, but they're usually over fairly quickly. Depending on your preferences, the quiet winter can be a more

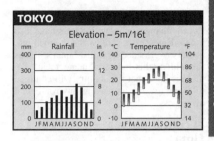

pleasant time to be in Tokyo than the height of summer.

On the whole, it's probably a good idea to avoid visiting Japan during major holidays, in particular Golden Week (29 April to 5 May) and the mid-August O-bon festival. Things close down over New Year as well. However, holidays can be a good time to do some sightseeing in Tokyo, as most of the locals are away and the city becomes a ghost town (well, almost). If your trip includes other parts of Japan, however, try and reschedule it around these national holidays.

ECOLOGY & ENVIRONMENT

Tokyo is one of the cleanest cities in Asia. This was not always the case. Back in the years of helter-skelter economic growth following WWII, Japan was one of the most polluted countries in the world. Since 1967, when Japan's first anti-pollution laws were passed, things have improved immensely.

However, water pollution is still a problem in the rivers of Tokyo and in Tokyo Bay, and air pollution often exceeds government-set levels. Nevertheless, pollution is not a deterrent to exploring the city, as it can be in other Asian metropolises.

The main environmental concern for residents is the shortage of greenery and parks. The average Tokyo resident enjoys a living space of less than 20 square metres, streets and transport facilities are crowded, and it is often a long haul to a real park. Most suburban 'parks' consist of a tiny patch of bare earth with a couple of swings.

There is currently something of a 'green movement' in Japan, centring on recycling, co-op movements, organic food, proper waste-disposal and citizen action groups. Recent changes in recycling laws have also led to decreases in solid waste dumped into already overloaded landfills. Japan still lags far behind other industrial democracies, but there is hope that the country will continue to work toward increasing environmental awareness.

FLORA & FAUNA
Flora
The flora of the Kantō Plain resembles that of some parts of Korea and China. Much of the plain was originally marshland, while areas of higher ground were heavily forested. In today's Tokyo, you will see little evidence of either zone, since both are mostly buried under concrete. Parks are heavily manicured and do not reflect the original flora. Many of them are beautiful, however.

Within easy reach of Tokyo are a number of national parks that give you a better chance to appreciate the natural beauty of Japan. These include Nikkō National Park and Fuji-Hakone-Izu National Park (see the Excursions chapter). Further afield, Minami-Alps National Park presents the visitor with some of Japan's most stunning mountain scenery.

Fauna
You will see little evidence of Japan's wildlife in Tokyo, where pigeons and domestic animals generally hold sway. However national parks are home to some wilder species, including the endemic Japanese macaque (better known in the West as the snow monkey).

In the city, even family pets are routinely treated poorly; dogs are often tied to stakes and left to bark at passers-by. Pets are also regularly abandoned and left to be destroyed by the city authorities. At zoos in Tokyo and elsewhere, the cages and display areas of animals are often cramped and dirty. This does not go unnoticed by the Japanese, who are starting to band together to fight such mistreatment. Contact the Japan Environmental Exchange (☎ 075-5434 9456) for more information.

ECONOMY
Japan's postwar success story has led to certain exaggerated perceptions. While exports are highly visible, they still account for less than 10% of the nation's GNP. Japanese investment in the US is still on a far smaller scale than similar investment by countries such as the UK and Canada.

In just 60 years, Japan has gone from being a defeated empire to the world's largest creditor nation. This can largely be attributed to industriousness, reinvestment in research and development, far-sighted management and production strategies, and the export orientation of the economy.

Yet Japan's domestic economy slouches in the doldrums, and the country continues to endure its worst-ever post-war recession. Both public and private opinion remain gloomy on the possibility of an economic upturn. Pundits continue to talk of *fukeiki* (poor economy) and *ristora* 're-structuring', ie, redundancies. Jobs will continue to be lost, and the jobs crisis facing young graduates is already extending further into the ranks of Japan's mid-career workers.

Meanwhile, the US continues to try to prize open Japan's massively protected, and very lucrative, rice market, and signs of increasing American business investment – Starbucks, Kinko's and Merrill-Lynch on every street corner, convinces everyone that change is in the air.

In one sense, Tokyo's role in this change has been central. Thus, while the rest of the country is still getting used to the idea of multiple careers in one lifetime, loyalty to one's self over one's company, and life online during the Internet 'revolution', in Tokyo these are accepted as givens.

Yet in Nakata-chō the central government, rife with internal squabbling, and unable to find a convincing prime minister, blunders unconvincingly on.

POPULATION & PEOPLE
According to mythology, the origins of the Japanese people stretch back to a time when the world was the pristine playground of the gods. The Japanese are, according to

this scheme, divine in origin, the issue of the sun goddess, Amaterasu Ōmikami.

In more secular terms, Japanese people belong to the Mongoloid group, like Koreans and Han Chinese. Evidence points to Japan as the terminus for waves of immigration from other parts of Asia, Europe, Siberia and even the Polynesian islands of the Pacific.

Around 11.8 million of Japan's more than 123 million people live in metropolitan Tokyo. The city's daytime population is actually much higher – more than 22 million people use Tokyo's transport system every day. The high cost of land and lack of residential space has pushed many Tokyo commuters beyond the suburbs into other cities like Yokohama, Tachikawa and Chiba.

Like the rest of Japan, the population of Tokyo is extremely homogeneous. Recent years have seen a large influx of foreign workers, but nothing to match the scale of immigration found in many major cities around the world. More importantly, foreigners, or *gaikokujin* (literally, outside country person, usually contracted to *gaijin*), in Tokyo are for the most part there temporarily, and the laws conspire to keep it that way.

The largest group of non-Japanese permanent residents in Tokyo are Koreans, who are for outsiders, and for the Japanese, largely an invisible minority. Nonetheless, Koreans who are as 'Japanese' as possible still face discrimination in the workplace and in other aspects of their daily lives.

There are also sizeable populations of Chinese, Filipinos and Iranians in Tokyo, mostly used to fill jobs which socially mobile Japanese are unwilling to do, like construction and factory work. Many of these immigrants, fluent in Japanese, are finding more lucrative employment and some have opened their own businesses, braving the hardships of the long-standing recession.

The Ainu, among the earliest inhabitants of Japan, have been reduced to very small numbers and are today found almost only in communities on Hokkaidō. You're certainly not likely to run into any Ainu in Tokyo, and if you do, the chances are that they will have well and truly integrated into the Japanese mainstream.

You will also come across a surprisingly large homeless population in Tokyo, as well as large numbers of urban poor left behind by the postwar economic boom and bust. Many of these people come from Japan's once 'untouchable class', the *burakumin*, a group that performed labour which the higher classes refused to do, like slaughterhouse work and leather work. While discrimination against those of burakumin ancestry is now illegal, it persists. It is still considered perfectly normal to hire a detective to ferret out any possible traces of burakumin blood in a potential spouse's family tree.

In addition to these disenfranchised classes, there are huge numbers of affluent young people in Tokyo who are so different from their predecessors as to merit the title *shinjinrui* (literally, new human type). The existence of these 'Japanese yuppies' is deeply troubling to older Japanese, who see them as the death knell of traditional ways.

Within Japan, Tokyoites themselves are considered almost a separate species. Many Japanese say that they are aloof, even condescending, but in practice this is rarely the case. To a foreign resident, they are by far the most cosmopolitan of all Japanese, hardly noticing foreigners who in other parts of the country are cause to gape and giggle.

ARTS

The wealth of modern Japan is partly founded on the ability to absorb influences from the outside world and use them to create something distinctly Japanese. The extraordinarily rich art of Japan is founded on very much the same ability. In essence, Japanese art is the result of this ability coupled with a tremendous native technical facility and aesthetic sensitivity.

Until the last century, the main influences on Japanese art came from nearby China and Korea; indeed, the artists themselves were often itinerant artisans from these countries.

Japan also absorbed influences from such distant places as Persia, Afghanistan and even ancient Rome, since China maintained an active trade with these places along the

Geisha were favoured subjects for the practice of *Katachi* – infusing the artistic form with life energy.

Silk Road. Perhaps the most important influence came from India, via China, in the form of Buddhism.

From the Meiji Restoration in 1868, the West also began to exert a powerful influence on Japanese arts. Modern art galleries in Tokyo display influences of major western movements from expressionism to postmodernism.

The artistic traffic has not been all oneway, however. *Ukiyo-e* (pictures from the floating world) prints owe something to Chinese innovations such as multicolour wood-block printing, but are distinctively Japanese in their execution and subject matter. Ukiyo-e caused a sensation among artists in late-19th-century Europe, and were much admired and subtly imitated by major artists like Manet, Gauguin, Van Gogh and Toulouse-Lautrec.

Aesthetics

Outside influences notwithstanding, there is something called 'Japanese aesthetics', however elusive it might be. The Walkman may be as 'essentially Japanese' in its conception and design as tea ceremony: the purpose of both is to create an 'empty', contemplative space.

This artistic focus on space is exemplified in the creation of miniature landscapes, as in the meditative arts of *bonsai*, *bonkei* and *ikebana*. Bonsai miniaturises trees through careful pruning, while bonkei achieves the same with an entire landscape. Ikebana, the art of flower arrangement, is promoted as a requisite skill for the cultivated 'young lady', but again it has a stress on contemplation.

Chanoyu, or tea ceremony, expresses all these peculiarly Japanese qualities. Sen-no-Rikyū (1522–91) transformed tea ceremony into an art form. He believed that using rough and irregular settings and utensils (many of which were from Korea) reflected the asymmetry of an egoless natural world. This was in stark contrast to the delicate designs and stylised perfection of Chinese ceramics.

If the Japanese themselves to define their aesthetic principles, two words from the Zen art of tea would inevitably be used: *wabi* and *sabi*. Sometimes claimed to be beyond the grasp of non-Japanese, these words refer to a kind of rustic simplicity, a sublime quality and understated beauty prized in their art. Japanese also admire art which they describe as *shibui*. This word translates roughly as restrained, quiet and cultivated. Taken together, these three words suggest what the Japanese call beautiful.

But there are also grand public displays that contradict the logic of many 'Japanese' qualities. Nikkō's shrines, for example, are far from understated. They are decorated in a riot of colour, and the deliberate 'mistakes' were not due to an aesthetic of imperfection, but to a fear that the works' perfection would arouse the envy of the gods. But these *are* public displays, often owing much to Chinese influences, and are in a different category to most Japanese art forms.

Gardens

The Japanese are fond of saying that they love nature. It is perhaps more accurate to say that they love a well-tended, thoroughly

LPP

Bonsai (meaning planted in a container) is a Meiji word, though the practice came from China during the Heian period.

'humanised' nature. Nowhere is this more evident than in the Japanese garden, which may at first glance look like raw nature, but is in fact reflectively and meticulously planned down to the last pebble.

There are a few main features that set Japanese gardens apart from those in Europe. Notable among these is a lack of flowers, water fountains and flowing rivers. More importantly, in Japan, every effort is made to harmonise the garden with the living space, as opposed to the European garden, which tends to stretch away from the house and exist very much as a space unto itself.

Fine Arts

Painting The techniques and materials used in the early stages of Japanese painting owed much to Chinese influence. Buddhism also provided Japanese painting with a role as a medium for religious instruction.

Towards the end of the Heian period (AD 794–1185) the emphasis on religious themes painted according to Chinese conventions gave way to a purely Japanese style, *yamato-e*, which covered indigenous subjects, and was frequently used in scroll paintings and on screens.

Ink paintings *(suiboku* or *sumi-e)* made by Chinese Zen artists were introduced to Japan during the Muromachi period (1333–1576) and copied by Japanese artists who produced hanging pictures *(kakemono)*, scrolls *(emaki)*, decorated screens and sliding doors.

The ruling classes demonstrated their opulence and prestige during the Momoyama period (1576–1600) by commissioning artists to use flamboyant colours and copious gold leaf. The most popular themes were those depicting Japanese nature (plants, trees and seasons) or characters from Chinese legends.

Western techniques of painting, including the use of oils, were introduced during the 16th century by the Jesuits.

The Edo period was marked by earnest patronage of a wide range of painting styles. The earlier Kanō school continued to be in demand for the depiction of subjects related to Confucianism, mythical Chinese creatures, or scenes from nature. The Tosa school, whose members followed the yamato-e style of painting, was kept busy with commissions from the nobility to paint scenes from the ancient classics of Japanese literature.

The Rimpa school not only absorbed the style of other schools (Chinese, Kanō and Tosa), but went beyond them to produce strikingly original decorative painting. The Rimpa-school art produced by Tawaraya Sōtatsu, Honami Kōetsu and Ogata Kōrin ranks among the finest of this period.

Calligraphy Known as *shodō* (the way of writing) in Japanese, this is one of Japan's most vital and valued arts, cultivated by nobles, priests and samurai alike, and still studied by Japanese schoolchildren as *shūji*.

Like Japanese writing, the art of shodō was imported from China. In the Heian period, a distinctly Japanese style of shodō evolved called *wayō*. This is more fluid and curved than the purely Chinese style (called *karayō*). The Chinese style remained very popular in Japan even after the Heian period among Zen priests and the literati.

In both Chinese and Japanese shodō there are three types of script. The most common is called *kaisho*, or block-style script. Due to its clarity, this style is favoured in the media and in applications where readability is a must. The second is *gyōsho*, or running hand. Often used in informal correspondence, it is half-cursive and somewhat more difficult to read. The third type is called *sōsho*, or grass hand, and is a truly cursive style. Sōsho abbreviates and links the characters together to create a graceful, flowing effect.

Ukiyo-e If there is one art that Westerners instantly associate with Japan, this is it. The name, 'pictures of the floating world', refers to a Buddhist metaphor for the transience of the human world. The subjects chosen by ukiyo-e artists were characters and scenes from the 'floating world' of the pleasure quarters of Edo, Kyoto and Osaka.

In Europe, the vivid colours, novel composition and flowing lines of these prints sparked a vogue which a French critic dubbed 'Japonisme'. Among the Japanese, however, the prints were hardly given more than passing consideration – millions were produced annually in Edo, often thrown away or used as wrapping paper for pottery.

The reputed founder of ukiyo-e was Iwa Matabei. The genre was later developed by Hishikawa Moronobu, who rose to fame with his illustrations for erotic tales. His wood-block prints of scenes from the entertainment district of Yoshiwara introduced the theme of *bijin-e* (paintings of beautiful women), which later became a standard subject. Early themes also covered scenes from the theatre and the erotic *shunga*. Kitagawa Utamarō is also famed for his bijin-e, which emphasise the erotic and sensual beauty of his subjects. All that is known about Tōshūsai Sharaku is that he produced 145 superb portraits of kabuki actors between 1794 and 1795.

Toward the end of the Edo period, two painters produced outstanding works in this art genre. Katsushika Hokusai was a prolific artist who observed his fellow Edo inhabitants with a keen sense of humour. His most famous works include *manga* (cartoons),

Fugaku Sanjūrokkei (Thirty-Six Views of Mt Fuji) and *Fugaku Hyakukei* (One Hundred Views of Mt Fuji).

Andō Hiroshige followed the lead of Hokusai and specialised in landscapes, although he also created splendid prints of plants and birds. Hiroshige's most celebrated art includes *Tōkaidō Gojūsan-tsugi* (Fifty-Three Stations of the Tōkaidō); *Meisho Edo Hyakukei* (One Hundred Views of Famous Places in Edo); and *Omi Hakkei* (Eight Views of Omi) – Omi is now known as Lake Biwa-ko.

Manga With design, cinema and architecture, cartoons are probably the most recognised of Japan's modern arts. Manga is a catch-all word covering cartoons, magazine and newspaper comic strips, and the comic books seen everywhere – even high art ukiyo-e prints were once a form of manga, evolving with *kibyōshi* (yellow cover) wood blocks used to create adult story books. The great wood-block artist Hokusai coined the word 'manga' by combining the characters for 'frivolous' and 'picture'.

The father of modern manga was Tezuka Osamu, who in the late 1940s began working cinematic effects based on European movies into his cartoons. His adventurous stories quickly became movie-length comic strips – films drawn on paper. What Tezuka started took off in a big way once weekly magazines realised they could boost sales by including manga on their pages.

As a result of Tezuka's innovations, Japanese comics are rarely slim affairs (weekly comics as thick as phone directories are not unusual). Manga's multipanel movements, perspectives bringing the reader into the action, close-ups and curious angles have been belatedly picked up by US comics; many manga also spin off into popular, cutting-edge animation films *(anime)* that can make Disney's look like goofy doodling (to say nothing of the soundtracks). Oshii Mamoru's 1995 anime version of the Masamune Shirow manga *Ghost in the Shell* is a good example; the *Macross* series is another.

The text in manga comics is always in Japanese, but there's usually an English subtitle on the cover announcing whether the particular comic is a 'Lady's Comic', a 'Comic for Business Boys' or even an 'Exciting Comic for Men' (for 'exciting' read 'soft porn'). Japanese censors may prudishly cover the pubic hair in imported porn, but it all hangs out in comic books – peer over a shoulder on the train and you may catch a schoolgirl quietly following the progress of a 2km-long penis as it ravages Tokyo. Even the 'Lady's Comics' can contain a fair bit of sex (check out *Comic Amour*). But manga comics also tackle the straightest of subjects: *jitsuma manga* (practical comics) and *benkyō manga* (study comics) teach everything from high-school subjects to ikebana and international finance.

Crafts Craft workers have always enjoyed the same esteem accorded artists and their works are prized as highly as fine art. Indeed, the distinction between art and craft is artificial in Japan, as many crafts are produced purely as works of art (for example, lacquerware) and many works of art are made to be used in daily life (for example, painted screens).

Girls' Comics

LPP

Unlike in the West, in Japan comics are far from a male preserve: *shōjo manga*, or 'girls' comics', are hugely popular. These have been around since the beginning of the comic movement in Japan, but since the mid-60s have been mainly created by women. Artists like Riyoko Ikeda, Moto Hagio and Keiko Takemiya were pioneers in the art of gender ambiguity, taking on 'male' themes with characters far from stereotypical. Later shōjo manga developed highly influential subgenres defined by (and defining) age groups and outlooks (eg, female expectations in Tokyo and in small cities).

Amateur manga is another area where women more than hold their own in Japan. The two day, semi-annual *Komikku Māketto* (Comic Market) in Tokyo attracts thousands of young women to displays of amateur work by female artists. The theme is mainly brief homoerotic encounters between boys, an interesting twist on popular boys' manga of the mid-80s. These cut-up tales of eroticised violence typify the so-called *yaoi* creed: 'no climax, no purpose, no solutions'.

The appeal for girls of liaisons between boys (lesbian encounters in the genre are rare) is hard to work out: maybe it's the broken taboo or the displaced purity of fated attraction that sells (it sold less well for novelist Yukio Mishima). Certainly the purity is unsullied by politics. Some gay activists have criticised the absence of social messages in yaoi manga – which, defenders insist, is exactly the point.

Some visitors are genuinely shocked by manga's often explicit content. Others tut-tut its sexual violence, while titillating with accounts of manga's 'dark side' and Japan's 'social repression'. But it's doubtful morality or psychology tell us much about the art, let alone the appeal, of these comics. A crash course in Japanese aesthetics – where extremes can be pushed to create an 'empty' space for a hidden event to occur – might be a start. So would asking the girls themselves.

Those interested in manga in all its forms can join the crowds perusing recent issues in bookshops. Many smaller hotels, hostels and ryokan have stacks of old issues for their guests' amusement. *Dreamland Japan – Writings on Modern Manga* by Frederik Schodt (1996) is a good introduction; the Internet offers hundreds of additional resources.

Russ Kerr

東京 東京 東京 東京 東京 東京 東京 東京 東京 東京 東京 東京 東京 東京 東京

Ceramics & Pottery Ceramic art in Japan is usually said to have begun with the introduction of Chinese techniques and the founding of a kiln in 1242 at Seto (Aichi prefecture) by Tōshirō. The Japanese term for pottery and porcelain, *setomono* (literally, things from Seto), even derives from this ceramic centre, which is still thriving.

The popularity of tea ceremony in the 16th century stimulated developments in ceramics. The great tea masters Furuta Oribe and Sen-no-Rikyū promoted the production of exquisite Oribe and Shino wares in Gifu prefecture. Hideyoshi allowed the master potter Chōjiro to embellish the tea bowls he created with the character *raku* (enjoyment), the beginning of Kyoto's famous *raku-yaki* style of pottery. Tea bowls became highly prized objects commanding stupendous prices. Even today, connoisseurs happily shell out as much as US$30,000 for the right tea bowl.

There are more than 100 pottery centres in Japan, producing everything from exclusive tea utensils to souvenir badges *(tanuki)*. Department stores regularly organise exhibitions of ceramics. Master potters are revered – the finest are designated 'Living National Treasures'.

Lacquerware Known in Japan as *shikki*, lacquerware is made using sap from the lacquer tree *(urushi)*. Once it is hardened, lacquer becomes inert and extraordinarily durable. The most common colour of lacquer is amber or brown, but additives have been used to produce violet, blue and even white lacquer.

Japanese artisans have devised various ways to further enhance the beauty of lacquer. The most common method is called *maki-e*, which was developed in the 8th century. Here, silver and gold powders are sprinkled on to the liquid lacquer to form a picture. After the lacquer dries, another coat of lacquer is applied to seal the picture. The final effect is often dazzling and some of the better pieces of maki-e lacquerware are now 'National Treasures'.

Washi In the Heian era, handmade paper *(washi)* was highly prized by the Kyoto court for writing poetry and diaries. Colours were added to produce patterns – even silver and gold leaf were used to create highlights. Paper was sometimes made specially to accentuate the sentiments of a particular poem. Washi continued to be made in large quantities until the introduction of Western paper in the 1870s. Recently, washi has enjoyed a revival, and a large variety of colourful, patterned paper is available in speciality stores.

Textiles Textiles have always played an important role in Japan, since the fabric of one's kimono was a ready indication of one's place in the social order. Until the introduction of cotton in the 16th century, Japanese textiles were made mostly of bast fibres or silk. Of all textiles, intricately embroidered brocades have always been the most highly prized, but sumptuary laws imposed on the merchant class in the Edo period prohibited the wearing of such kimonos. To circumvent these laws, new techniques of kimono decoration were devised, most importantly *yūzen* dyeing. Here, rice paste is applied to the fabric like a stencil to prevent a colour from bleeding onto other areas of the fabric. By repeatedly changing the pattern of the rice paste, complex designs can be achieved.

Carpentry It has been said that jade is the perfect medium for the expression of the Chinese artistic genius. Likewise, wood may be the perfect medium for Japanese artistry. Perhaps nowhere else has the art of joinery been lifted to such levels as it has in Japan.

This genius translates well into the art of cabinet-making. Particularly prized by collectors of Japanese antiques are chests called *tansu*. Perhaps the most prized of these is the *kaidan dansu*, so named because it resembles a flight of stairs (kaidan means stairs). These are becoming increasingly difficult to find – determined hunting at flea markets and antique stores will still yield a few good pieces, but don't expect any bargains.

Dolls Two festivals celebrate Japan's long love affair with dolls: Hina Matsuri (Doll

Festival), when girls display *hina ningyō* dolls; and Children's Day, when boys and girls show special dolls.

Some common dolls are *daruma*, which are based on the figure of Bodhidharma, who brought Buddhism to China from India; *gosho ningyō*, chubby plaster dolls sometimes dressed as figures in nō dramas; *Kyō ningyō*, elaborate dolls made in Kyoto, dressed in fine brocade fabrics; *kiku ningyō*, large dolls covered in real chrysanthemum flowers; and *ishō ningyō*, a general term for elaborately costumed dolls, sometimes based on kabuki characters.

Kites Japanese kites were originally linked to Shintō rites and flown with messages to the gods and spirits. Historically, kites also have a military connection in Japan as bearers of signals.

With the emergence of Edo as a major city, kite-flying gained a popular appeal. Woodblock prints from the Edo period often depict the Edo skyline jostling with swooping paper kites. The Edo period established a repertoire of kite designs that are still in demand.

The most popular depicts a warrior hero from Japanese history or legend. Also favoured is a daruma design, based on the spherical dolls of the same name. Other designs depict birds or insects, especially the cicada.

Bamboo Crafts Japanese bamboo baskets are among the finest in the world and are amazing in their complexity and delicacy (as well as their price). Ladles and whisks used in tea ceremony are also made of bamboo, and make attractive souvenirs. Be careful when buying bamboo crafts in Japan, as many are not Japanese at all, but cheap imitations imported from China.

Bonsai & Bonkei A skill imported from China during the Kamakura era (1185–1333), bonsai is the dwarfing of trees or the miniaturisation of nature. Some bonsai have been handed down over generations and have become extremely valuable. Bonkei is the

art of reproducing nature on a small tray using moss, clay, sand etc.

Flower Arrangement Ikebana stems from the 15th century, and can be grouped into four main styles: *rikka* (standing flowers); *nageire* (throwing-in); *shōkai* (living); and *moribana* (heaped). There are several thousand different schools at present, the top three of which are Ikenobō, Ōhara and Sōgetsu. However, the schools all share one aim: to arrange flowers to represent heaven, earth and humanity. Ikebana displays were first used as part of tea ceremony, but can now be found in homes in *tokonoma* (the alcove for displays), and even in large hotels.

Ikebana is also a lucrative business – its schools have millions of students, including many young women who view proficiency in the art as a means to improve their marriage prospects.

Tea Ceremony

Known as chanoyu or *chadō* (the way of tea), the ritual drinking of tea dates back to the Nara period (710–94), when it was used by meditating Buddhist monks to promote alertness. By the 14th century, it had developed into a highly elaborate and expensive pursuit for the aristocracy.

The turning point took place in the 16th century, when Sen-no-Rikyū eschewed opulence and established a more elemental aesthetic. Other tea masters took different approaches, and today tea ceremony can be divided into three major schools: Urasenke, Omotesenke, and Musha-no-kojisenke.

The traditional setting is a thatched teahouse set in a landscaped garden. Tea preparation and drinking follows a highly stylised etiquette, and the mental discipline involved was once essential to the training of a samurai. Novices tend to find it fatiguing, and connoisseurs maintain that full appreciation of the art takes years of reflection.

Performing Arts

The two most famous Japanese theatrical traditions are *kabuki* and *nō*. Both are fascinating, but without a great deal of prior study, don't expect to understand much of the proceedings. This is not a major problem, as both forms work well as spectacle; in any case, even native Japanese speakers have difficulty understanding the archaic Japanese used in traditional theatre. Fortunately, some theatres in Tokyo have programs with a synopsis of the play in English, and headphones are sometimes available for a commentary in English.

Kabuki The origins of kabuki lie in the early 17th century, when it was known as *kabuki odori* (loosely, avant-garde dance). Its first exponent was a maiden of Izumo Taisha Shrine who led a troupe of women dancers to raise funds for the shrine. It quickly caught on and was soon being performed with prostitutes in the lead roles. With performances plumbing ever greater depths of lewdness, the Tokugawa regime banned women from kabuki. They were promptly replaced with attractive young men of no less availability. The exasperated authorities issued another decree, this time commanding that kabuki roles be taken by older men.

Kabuki is a blend of music, dance, mime and spectacular staging and costuming.

This move had a profound effect on kabuki. The roles played by these older male actors required greater artistry to be brought off credibly. The result was that, while remaining a popular art form expressing popular themes, kabuki became a serious art, with its more famous practitioners becoming the stuff of which legends are made.

Kabuki is the theatre of spectacle, of larger-than-life gestures, and as such employs opulent sets, a boom-crash orchestra and a ramp through the audience that allows important actors to get the most mileage out of their melodramatic entrances and exits. Kabuki mostly deals with feudal tragedies of divided loyalties and of the struggle between duty and inner feelings (eg, love suicides).

Unlike conventional Western theatre, the playwright is not the applauded champion in kabuki. The play is merely a vehicle for the performance of the actor; he is remembered long after the writer who put the words in his mouth is forgotten.

Nō Even older than kabuki, nō dates back some 600 years. It seems to have evolved as a cross between Shintō-related dance and mime traditions, and dance forms from elsewhere in Asia. It was adopted as a courtly performing art, and underwent numerous refinements. Unlike the spectacle of kabuki, the power of nō lies in understatement – subtle masks and the stark emptiness of the sets direct all attention to the performers.

Two performers alone are vital to nō presentation – the one who watches *(waki)* and the one who acts *(shite)*. As nō is a theatre of masks, it is the role of the one who watches to, as it were, unmask the one who acts. The shite is not who he or she seems, but is usually a ghost whose spirit has lingered on because of a past tragedy. The unmasking gives way to the second act, in which the shite dances a re-enactment of the tragedy, and reveals his or her true identity.

Whether this is a liberation from, or a sorrowful celebration of, the lingering pain of the tragedy partly depends on whether the story is a happy one or not. It also depends on how you interpret the sometimes quite bizarre but nevertheless spell-binding proceedings of the nō performance.

Kyōgen This comic drama evolved hand in hand with nō. It first served as an interlude, but came to stand on its own and is now more often performed between two different nō plays. Unlike the heavily symbolic nō, kyōgen draws on the everyday world for its subjects and is acted in colloquial Japanese. The subjects of its satire are often samurai, depraved priests and faithless women. Performers are without masks and a chorus or chants is used.

Rakugo *Rakugo* (the dropped word) is a comic narrative dating back to the late 16th century.

It is delivered by a solitary performer seated on a cushion in the centre of a propless stage, with rare musical flourishes provided by offstage instruments such as drums, a *shamisen* (three-stringed instrument) or a flute. Like kabuki, where the performer reigns supreme, the prestige of rakugo artists lies not with the stories they tell but how they tell them.

Bunraku Developed in the Edo period, *bunraku* is Japan's unique puppet theatre, using puppets that are a half to two-thirds life-size, operated by three puppeteers, who remain visible to the audience. A narrator tells the story and provides the voices for characters; music comes from a shamisen.

Butō This experimental dance was born in the '60s and has received a fair amount of international attention and acclaim. Butō dancers perform nearly nude, wearing only loincloths and body paint. Movement is slow, drawn-out and occasionally grotesque, intended to express emotions in the most elemental, direct way possible.

Music
Ancient Music *Gagaku* is the 'elegant' music of the imperial court. Gagaku flourished between the 8th and 12th centuries, then fell out of favour until the renewed

The *koto* is still an essential *geisha* accessory.

interest in 'national' traditions during the Meiji period.

Nowadays, a gagaku ensemble usually consists of 16 players performing on drums, stringed instruments such as the *biwa* (lute) and *koto* (plucked zither), and wind instruments like the *hichiriki* (Japanese oboe) and various types of flute.

Traditional Japanese Instruments The shamisen is a three-stringed instrument resembling a banjo with an extended neck. It was very popular during the Edo period, and is still used as formal accompaniment in Japanese theatre (kabuki and bunraku). The ability to perform on the shamisen remains one of the essential skills of a *geisha*.

The koto is a type of plucked zither originally based on a Chinese instrument. The koto gradually increased the number of strings from five to 13. Koto schools still operate, often catering to young women.

The biwa, which resembles a lute, was played by travelling musicians, often blind, who recited Buddhist sutras to the accompaniment of the instrument. Although biwa ballads came into vogue during the 16th century, the instrument later fell out of favour. More recently, composer Takemitsu Tōru has found a new niche for the biwa in a Western orchestra.

The *shakuhachi* is a wind instrument imported from China in the 7th century. It was popularised by wandering Komosō monks in the 16th and 17th centuries, who played it as they walked alone through the woods. Even today, the sound of the shakuhachi conjures for the Japanese an image of lonely monks and dark forests.

Taiko refers to any of a number of large Japanese drums often played at festivals or in parades. The drummers who perform this music train year-round to endure the rigours of playing these enormous drums.

Modern Music Japan has the second largest domestic record market in the world, and you can meet fans of everything and everybody from Bach fugues to acid jazz, from Ry Cooder to Marilyn Manson. Even if you don't speak any Japanese, you can at least sit around with young Japanese and swap the names of bands you like.

The local scene is dominated by the *aidoru*, or idol singer. Generally untalented, idols enjoy a popularity generated largely through media appearances and are centred on a cute, girl-next-door image. Idols are so interchangeable that a completely computer-generated aidoru made the charts in 1997.

Almost every Western musical form and trend has produced Japanese imitators, but not much Japanese music makes the Western big time. Exceptions are artists like Kitarō and Sakamoto Ryūichi, a former member of Yellow Magic Orchestra. Though little known in his own country, one musician held in high esteem by many Western musicians is Kina Shōkichi, a major force in the popularisation of indigenous Okinawan music. His electric-traditional crossovers make for fascinating, often haunting listening.

Literature

Japan's first real literary works, the *Kojiki* (Records of Ancient Matters) and *Nihon*

Shoki (Chronicle of Japan), were written in the 8th century in emulation of Chinese historical accounts. It was only during times of relative isolation from the mainland that Japanese literature developed its own voice.

Much of what became Japanese literature was first written by women, since men wrote in Chinese characters, while women wrote in the once lowly Japanese script *(hiragana)*. Among these early authors is Lady Murasaki Shikibu, who wrote one of Japan's classics: *The Tale of Genji*. This lengthy novel documents the intrigues and romances of early Japanese court life.

The Narrow Road to the Deep North is a travel gem by the revered poet Matsuo Bashō. *Kokoro*, by Natsume Sōseki, is an early modern classic depicting the conflict between old and new Japan.

Tanizaki Junichirō's *The Makioka Sisters* (1957) is a famous family chronicle that has been likened to a modern-day *The Tale of Genji*. Ibuse Masuji's *Black Rain* (1969) is a response to Japan's defeat in WWII.

Snow Country, by Kawabata Yasunari, is a famous story set in Japan's north. Mishima Yukio's *The Golden Pavilion* (one-fourth of a brilliant tetralogy) uses the burning of Kyoto's Kinkaku-ji Temple in 1950 as an occasion for a meditation on philosophy, sexuality and nihilism. Abe Kōbō's *Woman in the Dunes* is a haunting tale by one of Japan's best avant-garde writers.

Murakami Ryū's *Almost Transparent Blue* is strictly sex and drugs and was a blockbuster in the '70s. Murakami Haruki is the bestselling author of nonconformist works like *A Wild Sheep Chase* and *The Wind-Up Bird Chronicle*.

Nobel laureate Oe Kenzaburo's *A Personal Matter* is a good introduction to the modern literary scene.

Film

Motion pictures were first imported from the West in 1896 and, characteristically, Japan was making its own by 1899. Until the advent of talkies, dialogue and general explanation of what was going on was provided by the *benshi*, a live commentator. As in live Japanese theatre, the performance of the benshi quickly became as important a part of the cinematic experience as the film itself.

Japanese films were initially cinematic versions of traditional theatre, but the 1923 earthquake prompted a split between period films, or *jidaigeki*, and new *gendaigeki* films, which followed modern themes. The more realistic storylines of the new films soon influenced traditional ones, hence the *shin jidaigeki*, or new period films. During this era, samurai themes became an enduring staple of Japanese cinema.

The '50s are generally considered the golden age of Japanese cinema. Directors like Kurosawa Akira led Japanese cinema on to the world stage when his *Rashōmon* (1950) took top prize at the Venice Film Festival in 1951. Kurosawa soon emerged as Japan's most influential director. His classic 1954 film *Shichinin-no-Samurai* (Seven Samurai) gained the ultimate accolade when it was shamelessly ripped off by the Hollywood blockbuster *The Magnificent Seven*. Other Kurosawa classics include *Yōjimbō* (1961), the tale of a masterless samurai who single-handedly cleans up a small town bedevilled by two warring gangs; and *Ran* (1985), a gorgeous epic historical film. Kurosawa's recent work, like 1990's *Yume* (Dreams) and *Madadoyo* (1993), has not been as well received in the West.

Itami Jūzō's *Tampopo* (1985) is a wonderful comedy about sex and food – 'Zen and the art of noodle making', as one critic described it. In the '70s and '80s Japanese cinema retreated before the onslaught of international movie making, but some independent Japanese films have had recent art-house success abroad.

Sumō

Sumō was originally performed in Shintō shrines as a form of divination, but was already popular as a sport in the 6th century. The rules are simple: the victor causes any part of his opponent's body other than his feet to touch the ground inside the ring *(dōyo)*, or pushes him outside the ring. There are no rounds – often it is all over in a matter of seconds – and there are no weight classes: they are all *big*.

Sumō's origins remain in the shrine-like roof over the ring and in the brightly attired wizard-like figure of the referee, or *gyōji*. The gyōji comes complete with a dagger which he once might have used to commit ritual suicide if he made a bad decision. Another Shintō feature is the purifying scattering of salt into the ring.

Although sumō wrestlers look like enormous flabby infants, their physiques are actually the products of long and intensive training. Part of this is eating big. *Chankonabe*, a special stew with weight-accruing properties, is a staple of the sumō diet. But the rest of the training is very physical, and all that flab conceals a lot of muscle.

Apart from upholding Shintō values, a successful sumō, particularly one who joins the top 50 in *sekitori* status, will have fame and a very comfortable living. Those who reach grand champion, or *yokozuna*, status are made for life and often achieve a kind of cult status during their careers. And for those who don't succeed? Well, it's off to weight watchers and perhaps a career as a furniture removalist.

See Sumō under Spectator Sports in the Entertainment chapter.

SOCIETY & CONDUCT

While Japan is quick to adopt technical innovations from abroad, the country is quite reluctant to abandon its traditional ways of doing things. For the visitor, this means that some things may come as quite a surprise, and others may appear quite puzzling, even downright incomprehensible.

The Group

One of the most widely disseminated ideas regarding the Japanese is the priority of the group over the individual. Loyal workers bellowing the company anthem and attending collective exercise sessions have become a motif almost as powerful as Mt Fuji in calling to mind the Land of the Rising Sun.

It's easy to see the business-suited crowds jostling on train platforms as so many ant-like members of a collectivist society that has rigorously suppressed individuality. If this starts to happen, remember that in some senses the Japanese are no less individual than their Western counterparts. The difference is that while individual concerns have a place in the lives of the Japanese, their principal orientation remains that of the group, without which the individual has no meaning.

There is a creative, sometimes tragic, tension between *honne*, personal views, and *tatemae*, the views demanded by one's position in the group. The group emphasis gives rise to the important *uchi* (inside) and *soto* (outside) distinction. All things are either inside or outside. Relationships, for example, are generally restricted to those inside the groups to which they belong.

The inside-outside distinction is hardly unique to Japan; it's just that in Japan being inside a group makes such special demands on the individual. Perhaps foreigners who have spent many years in Japan learning the language and who finally throw up their hands in despair, complaining 'you just can't get inside this culture', should remember that to be 'inside' in Japan is to surrender the self to the priorities of the group – and not many outsiders are willing or able to do that.

Men & Women

Japan may be a modern society in many respects, but don't look for the same level of equality between the genders that you may expect in your own country. As with nearly everything else in Japan, male-female roles and social relationships are strictly codified. Although this is changing, it's definitely doing so at a much slower pace than in the West. Part of the reason is that 'feminism' is a Western import and in a Japanese context tends to have a different resonance than it does in its culture of origin.

Japanese women, like women in other parts of the world, are subordinate to men in public life. However, both sexes have their spheres of influence, domains in which they wield power. Basically women are *uchi-no* (of the inside) and men are *soto-no* (of the outside). Woman's domain is the home, and here she will take care of all decisions related to the daily running of

domestic affairs. In the public world it is principally the role of women to listen, to cater to male needs and often to serve as vents for male frustrations – *uchi* (inside) is the place for emotions too.

The codification of men's and women's roles translates over to the marriage market, which has an impact on women's career options – it is widely perceived that they should be married by their mid-20s, and married women are expected to resign from their work. However, there's been a rise in the number of women willing to cast aside expectations, travel and pursue a career, even if it jeopardises their chances for marriage. Indeed, the present generation has been called *mukekkon* (no-marriage), because so many people are simply not getting married or are putting it off until much later than before.

However, Japan still has a long way to go before any real gender equality exists in terms of equal pay, job promotion and representation in management and government.

Meeting the Japanese

The Japanese have a reputation as being hard to get to know, but even on a short visit to Tokyo there are opportunities to meet them. Perhaps the easiest are those in a more formal setting, such as the conversation lounge or via the home visit system (see the Home Visit System entry in the Facts for the Visitor chapter). Alternatively, just going out for a drink somewhere usually gives you an opportunity to meet locals in a more relaxed setting. Generally all it takes is a smile and a nod to be brought in to a conversation.

The Japanese are generally a shy people (unless they've been drinking), relatively unused to mixing with foreigners and fearful of upsetting situational harmony with embarrassing mistakes. Especially when asking directions, try to appear calm and relaxed, and smile as you do so.

Etiquette

In rule-bound Japan social interaction is cluttered with a wide range of dos and don'ts. The good news is that with a bit of sensitivity most of it is easy to pick up and Japanese are generally very tolerant when it comes to foreigners. The times are also changing in Japan, and young people tend to be a lot less scrupulous about traditional rules – among themselves and with foreigners at least.

Bowing Most young people and businessmen are accustomed to shaking hands, but the bow is still the traditional mark of respect for greetings and leave takings. The depth of a bow is an index of status: when bowing with your boss, for example, your bow should be the deeper of two. As a visiting foreigner, an inclination of the waist and a bob of the head will do the trick.

Business Cards *Meishi* (business cards) carry much more weight in Japan than they do in the West. Information about a person's status can be obtained from a business card, and they are ritually exchanged on first meetings. It's good form to accept cards with both hands and examine them before tucking them away into your purse or wallet. Don't write on a card that someone has given you, at least not in their presence.

Direct Speech Unlike most Westerners, the Japanese do not make a virtue of being direct. People tend to feel their way around problems and sound out things in ways that to many foreigners seem impossibly vague, but actually aim to preserve harmony and avoid 'loss of face' – for you as much as for them. Thus, forceful and contrary opinions will be seen as embarrassingly vulgar and will more likely elicit a nervous giggle than a candid exchange of views.

Giving & Taking Debt and obligation *(giri)* are a social currency in Japan and incurring either should not be done lightly by the visitor. What may strike you as a simple request or favour may assume far greater significance in the eyes of your Japanese counterpart. Nowhere is this more apparent than in the almost sacred ritual of gift giving. Gifts in Japan are used as thanks for favours done, a means to get things done,

guarantees of continued favour and as just plain gifts.

A gift given demands at some point one in return. Keep this in mind when making visits of any kind, particularly to a Japanese home. If you need to pick up a gift at the last minute, there are plenty of stores in the bigger train stations just for this purpose. Also, if you are offered a gift by Japanese, it is polite to put up a brief resistance.

At Home It is usual to sit on the floor at home. Japanese sit with their feet tucked under them in a slouched-back kneeling position, and unless you've had a lifetime of training, it quickly becomes excruciating. Stretching out your legs discreetly is OK, but be careful not to point your feet at anyone.

Before you step into a Japanese home, slip off your shoes and exchange them for a pair of the slippers provided. This also applies at some public buildings, temples, shrines and traditional restaurants. These slippers can be worn everywhere inside except the bathroom, where you will have to switch to the special bathroom slippers. In any room where there is a *tatami* (straw mat) floor, it is usual to go barefoot or in socks.

In Public When outdoors it is bad form to stroll around eating (the exception is ice cream, which as everyone knows is an ambulatory foodstuff). Blowing your nose in public is definitely out. The done thing is a stoic and noisy sniffle maintained until you find somewhere private to do your business. Urinating in public (for men at least), on the other hand, is socially acceptable provided you have been drinking. In fact, drinking in general seems to provide a ticket to freedom from much Japanese social etiquette.

RELIGION

The term religion can be misleading when it is applied to Japan. In Christian and Islamic cultures, religion is connected to the idea of an exclusive faith. However, religions in Japan tend to mingle and find expression in different facets of daily life – Shintō, Buddhism, Confucianism and even Christianity (eg, in wedding ceremonies) all play a role in Japanese society.

Shintō

Shintō is an indigenous religion that gained its name, 'the way of the gods', to distinguish it from Buddhism, a later arrival. It grew out of an awe of nature, including the sun, water, rock formations, trees and even sound. All of these things were believed to have their god *(kami)*, giving rise to a complex pantheon of gods and a rich mythology, including an account of the nation's birth from the land of the gods. Certain sites were considered to be particularly sacred, and shrines were erected on these places. Purification with water (to bring one closer to the kami) before entering such sacred domains is an important Shintō ritual.

Shintō shrines are generally far more serene places than Buddhist temples, though you will often find both almost next door to each other. Compare the solemnity of Meiji-jingū and Yasukuni-jinja shrines with the bawdy carnival atmosphere that prevails at the Buddhist Sensō-ji Temple in Asakusa.

In daily life, Shintō functions less as a religion and more as a custom, with visits to a shrine used to mark important days in the Japanese calendar. At midnight on New Year's eve and on the following morning, families head to the local shrine to pray for good luck in the coming year in a custom known as *hatsumōde* (first shrine visit). A visit to a shrine is also used to mark the coming of age, the birth of a baby or the union of marriage. In a sense, the Japanese view Shintō, and Shintō shrines, as insurance – a touchstone to insure safe passage through the world. They see Buddhism as more intimately related to the soul and their passage into the next world. Thus, Japanese people often remark, 'Shintō is for when you're born, Buddhism is for when you die'.

The postwar separation of religion and state has been challenged by the controversial Yasukuni-jinja, which enshrines Japan's war dead and is regularly visited by politicians. As far as most Japanese people are concerned, however, there appears to be little regret that Shintō has reverted to its previous role as a guarantor of safe passage through daily life.

Buddhism

Siddhartha Gautama, the Indian prince who became the Buddha, based his teaching largely on karma *(innen* in Japanese), a radical conception of cause and effect. Buddha observed that life is 'suffering' *(duhkha* in Sanskrit, a sort of background discontent made comfortable by the illusions of ego), and that the cause of this suffering is desire. Desire exists because of an illusory split between the self and the world – we chase after a unity that the very concepts 'I' and 'we' deny.

Thus, desire expresses itself in more than simply the sensual; indeed, the totality of what we call existence is desire. The concept of nirvana, or enlightenment, then, is not a blissful paradise but an extinction of desire, an exit from *samsara* (a Sanskrit term), the wheel of suffering.

Buddhism in Japan, as in China, belongs to the Mahayana (greater vehicle) school, and has fissured into a great number of smaller schools of thought, the most famous of which in the outside world is Zen. Zen takes its name from the Chinese Ch'an, which is in turn from the Sanskrit *dhyana*, meaning meditation. Two major Zen schools are Rinzai and Sōtō; both stress meditation, but Rinzai also employs *koan* (illogical riddles) to break the mind's dependence on fixed structures of thought.

Buddhism's relations with Shintō have produced a distinctive result – Buddhism has become a salvation religion of sorts. Traditionally the soul *(tama)* left the body at death, but continued to watch over the fortunes of the family. *Hotoke*, the word for a departed soul, also happens to mean a Buddha or enlightened being; thus, Buddhism in Japan has become associated with 'life after death'. In the popular mind, Buddhist 'saints' (usually Bodhisattvas – those who have postponed enlightenment in order to help others along the same path) have also become figures to be appealed to for help in this life.

Add to this the popularity of Pure Land Buddhism (which uses invocation of Amida

Visiting a Temple or Shrine

Visitors to Japan are often nervous about committing some dreadful faux pas at a temple or shrine. Relax – as with most other aspects of their lives, the Japanese are not particularly rigid in these matters and certainly wouldn't judge a foreign visitor for not adhering to ritual patterns. As with nearly everything else, if you simply adhere to what would be good manners in your own country, you will almost never commit offence.

Shrines

Just past the *torii* (gate) is a trough of water *(chōzuya)* with long-handled ladles perched on a rack *(hishaku)* above. This is for purifying yourself before entering the sacred precincts of the shrine. Some Japanese do forego this ritual and head directly for the main hall. If you choose to purify yourself, however, take a ladle, fill it with fresh water from the spigot, pour some over one hand, transfer the spoon and pour water over the other hand, then pour a little water into a cupped hand and rinse your mouth, spitting the water on to the ground beside the trough (not into the trough).

Once you've purified yourself, head to the *haiden* (hall of worship), which sits in front of the *honden* (main hall) enshrining the god of the shrine *(kami)*. Here you'll find a thick rope hanging from a gong, in front of which is an offerings box. Toss a coin into the box, ring the gong by pulling on the rope (to summon the deity), pray, then clap your hands twice, bow and then back away from the shrine. Some Japanese believe that a ¥5 coin is the best for an offering at a temple or shrine, and that the luck engendered by the offering of a ¥10 coin will come further in the future (since 10 can be pronounced 'tō' in Japanese, which also means 'far').

Amulets are sold, usually for ¥100 or ¥200, at the shrine office near the worship hall. Finally, if photography is forbidden at a shrine, it will be posted as such; otherwise, it is permitted and you should simply use your discretion when taking pictures so as not to interfere with other visitors.

Temples

Unless the temple contains a shrine, you will not have to purify yourself before entry. The place of worship in a temple is in the *hondō*, which usually contains a Buddhist altar and one or more Buddha images. Entry is usually free; otherwise admission is around ¥500. The standard practice is to toss some change into the offerings box, which sits in front of the altar, step back, place one's hands together, pray, then bow to the altar before backing away.

Most temples sell *omikuji* (fortunes written on little slips of paper). These usually cost ¥100. You either pay an attendant or place the money in an honour-system box. Fortunes are dispensed randomly from a special box containing sticks with different numbers written on their ends. Shake the box until one stick drops out of a hole in its top. Take this to the attendant and you will be given a fortune matching the number on the stick. This will be written in Japanese under one of four general headings: *dai-kitchi* (big luck), *kitchi* (luck), *sho-kitchi* (small luck) and *kyō* (bad luck). Kitchi is considered best – your luck is good, but getting better – whereas dai-kitchi implies that it's all downhill from here. Sho-kitchi is moderately grim, and kyō is the worst. You can always ask a Japanese to read your fortune for you. Once you've read it, fold the fortune and tie it to a nearby tree branch so that the wind can disperse the bad luck (there's always a tree nearby festooned with white fortunes).

You can also purchase amulets called *omamori* at temples. These usually cost a few hundred yen and come in a variety of shapes and sizes, the most common of which is a piece of fabric bearing the temple's name enclosed in a plastic case. Some temples have omamori for specific things like traffic safety, good health and academic success. Hello Kitty omamori are currently all the rage.

Finally, photography is usually permitted inside the smaller, local temples, but not in larger, fee-charging places.

Buddha's name as a salvation device) and the result is that Buddhism, with some crucial differences, provides spiritual help for the average person in much the same way popular Christianity does in the West. This is perhaps best embodied by the most popular Japanese Bodhisattva, Jizō, who looks after travellers and children. Stone Jizō statues can be found all over Japan, and many temples have row upon row of them.

Confucianism
Confucianism began in China and made its way to Japan via Korea in the 5th century. However, its principles have had much less effect on Japan than on either neighbour. Central to Confucius' thought is the harmony of 'heaven, earth and humanity', an ideal reflected in the Japanese art of ikebana. These can best be harmonised by the 'upright man' (*Chunzi* in Chinese), who upholds the patriarchal 'five relations'.

Quotes from the *Analects* (the collected sayings of Confucius) are sometimes used in formal speeches, and remnants of Confucianism can be seen in such things as the rigidly hierarchical structure of Japanese companies, respect for elders and strictures to care for one's parents in their old age. The close family structure and tight web of social obligations all reflect a Confucian influence, though few Japanese would mention Confucianism as a guiding principle in their lives.

Christianity
The first Christian missionary to reach Japan was the Jesuit Francis Xavier in 1549. Others followed briskly in his footsteps and by the turn of the 16th century there were some 300,000 Japanese converts – Franciscans and Jesuits came into conflict several times over the rights to these souls.

After a period of supression, during the Tokugawa era, Christianity enjoyed a resurgence during the Meiji Restoration, but was again officially discouraged during WWII. Today there are about 1.1 million Japanese Christians, slightly less than 1% of the total population. Protestants slightly outnumber Catholics.

Religious Services
The following places of worship offer services in English. Catholic services are held at St Anselm's Benedictine Church (☎ 03-3491 6966) in Meguro and at St Ignatius Church (☎ 3263 4584) in Kōjimachi. St Alban's (☎ 3431 8534) in Kamiyachō has Anglican services on Sunday, as do the Tokyo Baptist Church (☎ 3461 8425) in Shibuya and the Tokyo Union Church (☎ 3400 0047) in Omote-sandō.

The Islamic Center of Japan (☎ 3404 6411) has Friday prayer at its Arabic Islamic Institute in Setagaya. The Japan Islamic Congress Majid (☎ 3205 1313) has call to prayer five times daily at the congress centre in Shinjuku.

Other religious groups that can be found in Tokyo include the Jewish Community of Japan (☎ 3400 2559) and the Tokyo Bahai'i Center (☎ 3209 7521).

J-Select magazine has detailed listings of other faiths.

For general Buddhist services in English, Hongan-ji in Tsukiji has a sermon in English on the second and fourth Sunday of every month at 5pm. For more on Zen lectures and meditation sessions, see the Activities section in the Things to See & Do chapter.

LANGUAGE
Visitors to Tokyo shouldn't have too many language problems. Lots of people speak English, and there are quite a few English signs. The main issue is the writing system, which uses three different scripts (the most difficult of which is *kanji*). See the Language chapter at the end of this book for useful Japanese words and phrases. You'll also find helpful kanji in the boxed texts 'Useful Kanji' in the Getting Around chapter; 'Words & Sights' in the Things to See & Do chapter; 'Useful Japanese' in the Places to Stay chapter; and the special section 'Japanese Food & Drinks'.

Tokyo International Forum

Japanese telephone booth

'Tokyo Big Sight' – aka Tokyo International Exhibition Centre

Eiffel envy – Tokyo Tower

Metropolitan Gov't Offices

Asakusa's 'golden turd' apparently represents the froth on a beer.

Ginza Street clock tower

The red lions of Taiyūin-byō shrine at Nikkō

The entrance to Meiji-jingū shrine

Taxis outside Tokyo train station

Kiyōmizu Kannon-dō temple in Ueno-kōen park

TOKYO ARCHITECTURE

Much of Tokyo may resemble the set of an old Godzilla movie, but if you know where to look, the city offers some amazing architectural experiments. Some work, some don't, but they're all worth a look.

The architecture of Tokyo can be loosely divided into three periods: surviving Edo structures, buildings of the Meiji era (1868–1945) and modern architecture. Almost nothing of Edo architecture has survived the calamities of the 20th century. The Imperial Palace is a reconstruction on the site of the old Edo-jō. Very few Edo-style wooden homes still exist, though occasionally they pop up (the area between Nippori and Ueno is a good place to look), sandwiched between 'mansion' apartment blocks. The best place to seek out traditional temples and shrines is not Tokyo itself but the areas of Kamakura and Nikkō. In Tokyo, however, it is worth visiting some of the old Edo gardens such as Hama Rikyū Detached Palace Garden, Koishikawa Kōraku-en and Rikugi-en for their beautifully restored gardens and traditional teahouses.

The Meiji Restoration saw a large-scale invasion of Western architectural forms. Examples can be seen in buildings such as the Akasaka Detached Palace and the 'imperial-style' Tokyo station. An early (somewhat overstated) example of a mixed Japanese-Western style can be seen in the Kabuki-za Theatre in Ginza.

Right: Happily, there's more to the Tokyo cityscape than Western-derived 'New International Style' buildings and rooftop boxes. MARTIN MOOS

Shrines

Shrines are the places of worship in Shintō. The first shrines were simply places of natural significance, like waterfalls and mountains, delineated with a special rope called a shimenawa. From this rope evolved the use of fences and eventually special gates (torii), which remain today as the most obvious feature of shrines.

Shrine buildings themselves probably evolved from rice storehouses used in pre-Buddhist Japan, and many of their now ornamental features were once functional. The main building of the shrine is the *honden*, which enshrines the *kami* (god) of the shrine. This can never be entered by laymen and only occasionally by Shintō priests. In front of the honden is the *haiden*, or hall of worship, which is used for worship and offertory. In smaller shrines, these two are often joined together under one roof.

Jinja & Ji

The difference between a *jinja* (temple) and a *ji* (shrine) is blurred.

The oldest shrines were built in a purely Japanese style, but after the introduction of Buddhism, shrine buildings started to incorporate elements of temple architecture – and vice versa, eg, some temple precincts have torii to mark the site's guardian kami. Also, shrines may have what appears to be a temple's equivalent of a torii, the *sanmon* or *niōmon* (a heavy gateway with tiled roof and two ferocious-looking guardian *niō* figures). As open centres of spiritual power coexisting in a syncretic culture, it's not surprising shrines and temples exchange many features.

Temples

Along with the religion itself, Japan imported from Korea and China the architecture used in Buddhist temples. While some differences exist between the temples of Japan's various schools of Buddhism, most temple compounds contain the following basic structures:

CHRIS MELLOR

Left: Zojo-ji temple near Tokyo Tower. The roof detail shows the chrysanthemum, Japan's national emblem.

Pagoda This is a tower-like structure based on the Indian stupa, which is believed to house a relic of the historical Buddha. While these were the focal point of early Japanese temples, in later temples they are often relegated to the periphery.

Kondō or Hondō This is the main hall of the temple and is often found at the centre of the compound. Housed within this structure are the main images of the Buddha as well as other elements of a Buddhist altar. This is where worship takes place, and lay people are sometimes excluded from entry on all but special occasions.

Kōdō This is the lecture hall, where monks gather to study and recite scriptures. It is often beside the main hall.

Mon This means 'gate' and refers to both the large outer gate of the temple *(daimon)* and the smaller inner gate *(chūmon)*. Housed within these gates you will sometimes find two niō, whose role it is to fend off evil and remind visitors to enter with a pure mind.

Kyōzō This is the sutra repository, which is used to store the sacred scriptures of the temple. Often built in the shape of a log cabin on stilts, this structure is designed to maintain a constant internal temperature to guard the sutras against decay.

Other Structures On the periphery of the compound you will also find the monk's daily living areas, like the dining hall and the dormitory. Of course, now that many temples are operated as business concerns, you will also find a temple office.

Modern Architecture

Shrines and temples the city may more or less preserve, but in Tokyo real value has always reposed in land, not buildings. Architecture tends to be utilitarian, designed to be replaced after a couple of decades of use, but there are some fabulous structures scattered across town.

The overwhelming architectural feature of the city is the Tokyo Metropolitan Expressway – 220km of it girds the city. For most of us it is such an eyesore that it tends to get overlooked. But as Noriyuki Tajima points out in his wonderful pocket guide *Tokyo – A Guide to Recent Architecture*, 'The scale and monumentality, weight and strength of the expressway – like ancient Roman city walls – easily overwhelms any of the city's buildings, and striking contrasts are formed against its backdrop.' Take a look at how the expressway interacts with street scenes in central Tokyo (particularly Yūraku-chō and Nihombashi) and you'll see what he means.

The most famous of Japan's home-grown architects is Tange Kenzō. His Tokyo Metropolitan Government Offices in Shinjuku may look sinister (and have been criticised as totalitarian), but they are a remarkable achievement and pull in large numbers of visitors daily (around 6000).

Those with an interest in Tange's work should also look out for the United Nations University, close to Omotesandō subway station.

Peter Eisenman has made some avant-garde contributions to Tokyo's urban landscape. The NC building is perhaps the most interesting. It embodies the movement of tectonic plates and the transient nature of Tokyo architecture. The result is a structure caught in the moment of collapse, all angles at odds with each other, as if you'd given a child a felt tip and asked them to design a building. The NC building is close to Shin-Koiwa station on the JR Sōbu line.

In central Tokyo, the Tokyo International Forum was the product of an international competition. The result is a glass and steel ocean liner with a miracle of a hall – pedestrian walkways are planned to link Yūraku-chō and Tokyo stations via the forum. The new Edo-Tokyo Museum in Ryōgoku is a bizarre structure that you can't help but marvel at, particularly as you stand in the sprawling plaza that surrounds it – the Star Wars connotations seem to strike everyone.

Visitors to Asakusa in search of 'lost Japan' might pause and take a look at the Super Dry Hall, an eccentric Philippe Starck design that celebrates Asahi beer with an upside-down building and what looks to be a golden turd on its bottom (head) – the 'golden flame' represents the frothy head of a beer. The interior is as remarkable as the exterior.

In recent years, the Tokyo Bay/Daiba areas have seen a boom in experimental architecture. Buildings like the Fuji Television Broadcast Center and the Tokyo Big Sight international conference hall are examples of architectural exuberance given free reign; both are must-sees. Crowded Tokyo has also seen a small revolution in the use of interior space. The Metropolitan Art Space and Toyota Amlux buildings in Ikebukuro and the Spiral building in Aoyama are all good examples. Shibuya is a good area to scout for architectural highlights, notably the Bunkamura, Humax Pavilion and Shibuya Beam.

JOHN ASHBURNE

Left: Tokyo, Odaiba, Fuji TV Building

Facts for the Visitor

ORIENTATION

Tokyo is a vast conurbation spreading out across the Kantō Plain from Tokyo Bay. Nevertheless, for visitors nearly everything of interest lies either on or within the Japan Railways (JR) Yamanote line, the rail loop that circles central Tokyo. In Edo times, Yamanote was the name of Tokyo's 'high city', the estates and residences of feudal barons, the military aristocracy and other members of elite Edo society in the hilly regions of Edo. Shitamachi, or 'low city', was home to the working classes, merchants and artisans.

The high/low distinction persists, though Shitamachi now generally refers to the slightly down-at-the-heels atmosphere that lingers in the markets and backstreets of Ueno and Asakusa, while Yamanote is basically any place which doesn't fit this description, meaning most of modern Tokyo.

One confusing aspect of Tokyo is its lack of a main centre. While most cities are built around a central area which gradually tapers off to distant suburbs, Tokyo has several large urban hubs, most of which are located on the Yamanote line. The main financial and commercial districts can be found in the areas around Tokyo station. Nearby, the Imperial Palace is perhaps the spiritual centre of Tokyo and sits in the middle of the rough circle formed by the Yamanote loop line. Government buildings can be found to the west of these areas in Kasumigaseki and Akasaka, while the city government offices are located still further west in Shinjuku. Shopping districts are spread all over the city, and each major stop on the Yamanote line is surrounded by a booming mercantile zone.

Essential for finding your way around Tokyo is a good map. One complication is the lack of street names; the few large ones that are named end in *dōri* (avenue or road). If you're going to do any exploring, you're going to be riding the city's subways and the JR rail system, both of which are excellent. The JR Yamanote line does an above-

ground loop that takes you through most of the important centres of the city. Buying a ticket to the next station for ¥130 doesn't stop you going the long way around, if you want to city-watch on the way.

Surrounding central Tokyo are sprawling, uninteresting urban zones made up mostly of homes, small businesses and factories. Once you pass through these areas, you finally reach the pleasant greenery of northwestern Saitama, Gunma and Yamanashi.

To the south, the bay-side city of Yokohama works hard to escape its image as just another Tokyo suburb. It is home to large international conference halls and the headquarters of some of Japan's large businesses.

MAPS

Visitors to Tokyo should get a copy of the *Tourist Map of Tokyo*, available from the Tourist Information Center (TIC) either near Tokyo station or in Narita airport. This excellent, free map provides a good overall view of the city. More detailed is Kodansha's *New Tokyo Bilingual Atlas* available at Tokyo's larger bookshops. You can also pick up a free copy of the TRTA subway authority's *Subways in Tokyo* map, which also has English-language explanations on buying tickets and special deals. For a more comprehensive guide to Tokyo transportation, see Kodansha's *Rail and Road Atlas*. Bus maps of the city are also available (see Bus in the Getting Around chapter).

If you read *kanji* (Japanese script), Shobunsha maps and Rurubu guides are probably the best and are available at most of Tokyo's bookshops. For detailed maps of Tokyo's train lines and stations, *Chikatetsu Benri Gaido* is a handy resource; anyone moving to the city should certainly grab a copy.

There is very little in the way of maps for Japanese cities available outside Japan; the above-mentioned *New Tokyo Bilingual Atlas* is probably the best bet.

Japanese Addresses

In Tokyo, as in the rest of Japan, finding a place from its address can be a near impossibility, even for the Japanese. The usual process is to ask directions (even taxi drivers often have to do this). Businesses often include a small map in their advertisements or on their business cards to show their location. Having the address written in Japanese is also a great help.

Off the main roads, there are very few streets with names. Addresses work by narrowing down the location of a building to a number within an area of a few blocks. Unlike English addresses, they work from top to bottom. Thus, Tokyo would be indicated first, followed by the *ku* (ward), then the *chō* or *machi* (loosely, suburb) and then the *chōme*, which is an area of just a couple of blocks. Numbers for the building and chōme are frequently condensed into two or three numbers, as in 1-10-5 Akasaka, where 1 is the chōme and 10-5 indicates the location of the building. But beware: this can also be written in a different order – 10-5 Akasaka, 1 chōme – and mean exactly the same. It can all be awfully frustrating at times.

One good way the Japanese avoid these complicated addresses is to refer to major landmarks, often railway stations. People will often ask you which train line and station you will take, then they'll tell you which station exit *(deguchi)* to use. From here, they'll give you directions based on local landmarks like police boxes, parks, stores and the number of streets you must cross. Stores such as Starbucks, McDonalds, and Kinkos, with their prominent English signboards make good reference points.

Thus, before going to an unfamiliar address, see if you can get a map drawn for you. If all else fails, try 'Mukai ni kite itadakemasu ka?', which means 'Can you come meet me?'. But then of course you'll have to explain where you are...

東京 東京 東京 東京 東京 東京 東京 東京 東京 東京 東京 東京 東京 東京

TOURIST OFFICES

The Japan National Tourist Organization (JNTO), with both Japanese and overseas offices, is the government agency dealing with tourism promotion and travel inquiries (about Tokyo and the rest of Japan). It also produces a great deal of literature.

Tourist Information Centers (TIC)

JNTO operates three Tourist Information Centers (TIC) in the Tokyo area – in the arrivals wing of terminals 1 and 2, Narita airport (☎ 0476-34 6251), open from 9am to 8pm daily; and on the 10th floor of the Tomen Building (☎ 3201 3331) near Tokyo station, it's open weekdays from 9am to 5pm, and until noon on Saturday. TIC offices will make accommodation reservations, but only for hotels and *ryokan* (traditional Japanese inns) that are members of the Welcome Inn group.

The Tokyo TIC offers Teletour (☎ 3201 2911), which is a round-the-clock taped information service about current events in town. JNTO also runs Goodwill Guides, a volunteer program with some 30,000 members (identified by a blue-and-white badge with a dove and globe logo).

The Tokyo TIC address is B1F, Tokyo International Forum, 3-5-1 Marunouchi, Chiyoda-ku, Tokyo 100. Exit the Marunouchi side of Tokyo station, turn left in front of the central post office and walk parallel to the JR tracks for about 200m. The Tokyo International Forum is the spectacular large glass building in front of you; the TIC is in the basement to the right of the escalator.

Information counters are easy to spot.

CHRIS ROWTHORN

The office has pamphlets on everything from *ikebana* clubs to factory tours – as a starter, pick up copies of the *Tourist Map of Tokyo* and magazines such as *Tokyo City Guide*, *City Life* or *Nippon View*. The latter have good events listings

Telephone Services

JNTO operates a Japan Travel-Phone service for visitors to the Tokyo region. English-speaking travel experts can be contacted from 9am to 5pm daily on ☎ 3201 3331, or toll-free outside Tokyo on ☎ 0088-224 800 or ☎ 0120-444 800 from any green or grey public phone.

Other Information Offices

The Tokyo city government operates two English-speaking information offices (open from 9am to 6pm, closed Sunday and public holidays) at the JR Shinjuku station (Map 3): one office is on the east side of the station, on the ground floor near the My City exit; and the other office is on the station's west side to the right of the Keiō line entrance.

The major tourist sights around Tokyo also have information offices *(annai-jo)* with brochures and maps, and are able to help with finding accommodation. However, the staff may not always speak good English. If you would like a licenced, professional tourist guide, ask at the TIC, or phone the Japan Guide Association (☎ 3213 2706).

For information on JR services into and out of Tokyo, see Train in the Getting There & Away chapter.

JNTO Offices Overseas

Overseas offices of JNTO include:

Australia (☎ 02-9232 4522, fax 9232 1494)
Level 33, Chifley Tower, 2 Chifley Square, Sydney, NSW 2000
Canada (☎ 416-366 7140, fax 366 4530) 165 University Ave, Toronto, Ontario M5H 3B8
France (☎ 01 42 96 20 29, fax 01 40 20 92 79) 4–8 rue Sainte-Anne, 75001 Paris
Germany (☎ 069-20353, fax 284281) Kaiserstrasse 11, 60311 Frankfurt am Main 1
Hong Kong (☎ 2968 5688, fax 2968 1722) Suite 3704–05, 37/F, Dorset House, Taikoo Place, Quarry Bay, Hong Kong

South Korea (☎ 02-732 7252, fax 732 7527)
10th Floor, Press Center Bldg, 25 Taepyongno 1-ga, Chung-gu, Seoul
Thailand (☎ 02-233 5108, fax 236 8356) Wall Street Tower Bldg, 33/61, Suriwong Rd, Bangkok 10500
UK (☎ 020-7734 9638, fax 7734 4290) 20 Saville Row, London
USA
Chicago: (☎ 312-222 0874, fax 222 0876) Suite 770, 401 North Michigan Ave, IL 60611
Los Angeles: (☎ 213-623 1952, fax 623 6301) Suite 1611, 624 South Grand Ave, CA 90017
New York: (☎ 212-757 5640, fax 307 6754) Suite 1250, One Rockefeller Plaza, NY 10020
San Francisco: (☎ 415-989 7140, fax 398 5461) Suite 601, 360 Post St, CA 94108

TRAVEL AGENTS

Four well established agents where English is spoken are:

Across Traveller's Bureau (☎ 03-3340 6741) Shinjuku, (☎ 5391 2871) Ikebukuro
Just Travel (☎ 3362 3441) Takadanobaba
No 1 Travel (☎ 3200 8871) Shinjuku, (☎ 3770 1381) Shibuya, (☎ 3986 4291) Ikebukuro, (☎ 045-322 1701) Yokohama
STA Travel (☎ 5269 0751) Yotsuya, (☎ 5485 8380) Shibuya, (☎ 5391 2922) Ikebukuro

Perhaps the cheapest of the four is No 1 Travel, whose Shinjuku branch (Map 3) is conveniently located on Yasukuni-dōri, about five minutes from Shinjuku station.

Some theatre ticket outlets are also able to provide discounted tickets for domestic air flights and shinkansen journeys. A good place to try is Ikari (☎ 3407 3554), opposite Shibuya post office (Map 4) on the 3rd floor of the Gloria Shibuya building.

DOCUMENTS
Visas

Tourists and business visitors of many nationalities are not required to obtain visas if staying in Japan for 90 days or less. (Visits involving employment require an appropriate visa.)

Citizens of some countries, including Germany, Ireland and the UK will be granted a standard 90-day stay at the airport when they arrive (they have to apply for an extension if they want to stay longer; see Visa Extensions).

Citizens of the USA, Canada, Australia and New Zealand are also granted a 90-day stay at the airport but they have to leave Japan if they want to extend it.

Visitors from most other countries must acquire a visa before coming to Japan. This is usually issued free, but passport photographs are required, and a return or onward ticket must be shown. Visas are valid for 90 days.

Check out W www.mofa.go.jp/j_info/visit/visa/ for the whole (painfully long) story.

Working-Holiday Visas Australian, Canadian, French, German and New Zealand citizens between the ages of 18 and 30 (25 for UK citizens) can apply for a working-holiday visa. This visa allows a six-month stay and two six-month extensions. Its aim is to enable young people to travel extensively during their stay, so employment is supposed to be part-time or temporary, although in practice many people work full time.

A working-holiday visa is much easier to obtain than a working visa and is popular with Japanese employers, as it can save them a lot of inconvenience. Applicants must apply for the visa in their own countries and have the equivalent of A$2500 in funds and an onward ticket.

Working Visas It's a lot harder to get a visa to work in Japan than it once was – requirements have become stricter. In theory, working visas must be arranged outside Japan, but some people *do* manage to arrange them in Japan, then pick them up outside the country (Korea is a nearby favourite). If you can find an employer to sponsor you, and have all your paperwork in order, you will be issued a Certificate of Eligibility. Once you get this, it is necessary to leave the country with the certificate and apply for a working visa at a foreign visa office.

Visa Extensions It has also become quite difficult to extend visas. With the exception of nationals of the few countries whose reciprocal visa exemptions allow for stays of six months, 90 days is the limit for most people. If you do apply you should provide two copies of an Application for Extension of Stay (available at the Tokyo Immigration Bureau), a letter stating reasons for the extension, supporting documentation and your passport. There is a processing fee of ¥4000.

You can get around the extension problem by briefly leaving – usually people go to Hong Kong, Seoul or Bangkok – then re-entering on a new 90-day visa issued at the airport. However, this is risky. If immigration officials suspect you are working illegally you may be detained at the airport and sent home at your own expense.

The Tokyo Immigration Bureau (Map 8) has a visa information line (☎ 3213 8523/7) where questions about visas can be answered in English (open weekdays from 9.30am to noon and 1pm to 4 pm). From Ōtemachi subway station on the Chiyoda line, exit C2, cross the street at the corner and turn left. Walk past the Japan Development building; the immigration office is the next on your right.

Alien Registration Card

Anyone, including tourists, who stays more than 90 days must get an Alien Registration Card *(Gaikokujin Toroku Shomeisho)*. The card can be obtained at the municipal office of the city, town or ward in which you're living, but moving to another area requires that you re-register within 14 days. To register, you need your passport, an application form and two passport-size photographs.

You must carry your Alien Registration Card at all times, as the police can stop you and ask to see it. If you don't have it, you will be taken to the station and will have to wait there until someone fetches it for you.

Travel Insurance

A travel-insurance policy to cover theft, property loss and medical problems is a wise idea. With such a wide variety of policies available, it may be best to consult your travel agent. Some policies offer a choice of lower and higher medical-expense options; choose the high-cost option for Japan. The international student travel policies handled by STA Travel or other student-travel organisations are usually good value.

When you buy your policy, always read the fine print. Some policies exclude 'dangerous activities' and their idea of dangerous might inlude activities as tame as scuba diving and motorcycling. If you plan on motorcycling in Japan, check that your policy covers you. Keep all documentation of any medical treatment that you receive, as these will be required when making a claim later on.

Driving Licence
Those planning on driving in Tokyo (really not recommended) should come prepared with an International Driving Permit (with your regular licence as a backup). If you have this, renting a car is no problem – finding somewhere to park is another matter.

Hostelling International Card
You can organise international youth hostel membership before you leave home or do it in Tokyo. Either join at one of the hostels or contact Japan Youth Hostels Inc (☎ 3269 5831) – there are offices scattered around Tokyo.

Student & Youth Cards
A valid international student card will win you discounts on entry fees to some sights in Tokyo and sometimes discounted prices on long-distance train travel.

EMBASSIES & CONSULATES
Japanese Embassies Abroad
Australia
Embassy: (☎ 02-6273 3244) 112 Empire Circuit, Yarralumla, Canberra, ACT 2600
Consulate in Brisbane: (☎ 07-3221 5188)
Consulate in Melbourne: (☎ 03-9639 3244)
Consulate in Perth: (☎ 08-9321 7816)
Consulate in Sydney: (☎ 02-9231 3455)
Canada
Embassy: (☎ 613-241 8541) 255 Sussex Drive, Ottawa, Ontario K1N 9E6
Consulate in Edmonton: (☎ 403-422 3752)
Consulate in Montreal: (☎ 514-866 3429)
Consulate in Toronto: (☎ 416-363 7038)
Consulate in Vancouver: (☎ 604-684 5868)

France (☎ 01 48 88 62 00) 7 Ave Hoche, 75008 Paris
Germany (☎ 0228-81910) Godesberger Allee 102–104, 53175 Bonn
Hong Kong (☎ 852-2522 1184) 47th Floor, One Exchange Square, 8 Connaught Place, Central
Ireland (☎ 1-269 4033) Nutley Building, Merrion Centre, Nutley Lane, Dublin 4
Netherlands (☎ 346 9544) Tobias Asserláan 2, The Hague 2517KC
New Zealand
Embassy: (☎ 04-473 1540) 7th Floor, Norwich Insurance House, 3–11 Hunter St, Wellington1
Consulate: Auckland (☎ 09-303 4106)
South Korea (☎ 822-739 7400) 9th floor, Kyobo Bldg, Chongro 1-KA, Chongro-ku, Seoul
Thailand (☎ 02-252 6151) 1674 New Petchburi Rd, Bangkok 10310
UK (☎ 020-7465 6500) 101–104, Piccadilly, London W1V 9FN
USA
Embassy: (☎ 202-238 6700) 2520 Massachusetts Ave NW, Washington, DC 20008-2869
Consulate in Atlanta: (☎ 404-892 2700)
Consulate in Boston: (☎ 617-973 9772)
Consulate in Chicago: (☎ 312-280 0400)
Consulate in Houston: (☎ 713-652 2977)
Consulate in Los Angeles: (☎ 213-617 6700)
Consulate in New Orleans: (☎ 504-529 2101)
Consulate in New York: (☎ 212-371 8222)
Consulate in Portland: (☎ 503-221 1811)
Consulate in San Francisco: (☎ 415-777 3533)

Foreign Embassies in Tokyo
Most countries have embassies in Tokyo. Call them to confirm opening times. (You'll find that visas are generally more expensive in Japan than in neighbouring countries.)

Australia (☎ 5232 4111, fax 5232 4149) 2-1-14 Mita, Minato-ku; Map 1
Canada (☎ 5412 6200, fax 5412 6302) 7-3-38 Akasaka, Minato-ku; Map 4
China (☎ 3403 3380) 3-4-33 Moto-Azabu, Minato-ku
France (☎ 5420 8800, fax 5420 8921) 4-11-44 Minami-Azabu, Minato-ku; Map 1
Germany (☎ 3473 0151, fax 3473 4243) 4-5-10 Minami-Azabu, Minato-ku; Map 1
India (☎ 3262 2391, fax 3234 4866) 2-2-11 Kudan-Minami, Chiyoda-ku; Map 8
Indonesia (☎ 3441 4201, fax 3447 1697) 5-2-9 Higashi-Gotanda, Shinagawa-ku

Ireland (☎ 3263 0695, fax 3265 2275) 2-10-7 Kōjimachi, Chiyoda-ku; Map 8

Israel (☎ 3264 0911, fax 3264 0832) 3 Nibanchō, Chiyoda-ku

Malaysia (☎ 3476 3840, fax 3476 4971) 20-16 Nampeidaichō, Shibuya-ku; Map 1

Netherlands (☎ 5401 0411, fax 5401 0411) 3-6-3 Shiba-kōen, Minato-ku; Map 7

New Zealand (☎ 3467 2271, fax 3467 2278, e nzemb@gol.com) 20-40 Kamiyamachō, Shibuya-ku; Map 1

Pakistan (☎ 3454 4861, fax 3457 0341, e eptufail@iac.co.jp) 2-14-9 Moto-Azabu, Minato-ku

Philippines (☎ 3496 2731) 11-24 Nanpei-daichō, Shibuya-ku

Russia (☎ 3583 4224, fax 3505 0593) 2-1-1 Azabudai, Minato-ku

Singapore (☎ 3586 9111, fax 3224 6480) 5-12-3 Roppongi, Minato-ku; Map 4

South Korea (☎ 3452 7611, fax 3455 2018) 1-2-5 Minami-Azabu, Minato-ku; Map 1

Sri Lanka (☎ 3585 7431, fax 3440 6914) 2-1-54 Takanawa, Minato Ku

Taiwan (Taipei Economic & Cultural Representative Office in Japan; ☎ 3280 7800, fax 3280 7929) 5-20-2 Shirogane-dai, Minato-ku

Thailand (☎ 3441 1386, fax 3442 6750) 3-14-6 Kami-Osaki, Shinagawa-ku

UK (☎ 0990 61 2005, fax 5275 0346) 1 Ichibanchō, Chiyoda-ku; Map 8

USA (☎ 3224 5000) 1-10-5 Akasaka, Minato-ku; Map 7

CUSTOMS

Duty-free allowances include 400 cigarettes, 500g of tobacco, 100 cigars, three 760mL bottles of alcohol, 57g of perfume, and gifts and souvenirs up to the value of ¥200,000. Liquor is not cheap in Japan, so it's worth bringing some for yourself or as a gift. It is likely that anything slightly pornographic will be confiscated at the airport. Be warned that the penalties for importing drugs are very severe.

There are no limits on the import of foreign or Japanese currency. Export of foreign currency is also unlimited, but there is a ¥5 million limit for Japanese currency.

MONEY
Costs

Tokyo is the most expensive city in Asia, if not the world, but this isn't an insuperable barrier to an enjoyable trip. There are always cheaper options in Tokyo – it's just a matter of seeking them out. A cup of coffee can indeed cost ¥600 or more, but the many chain outfits charge ¥170. If you want coffee, not a break in a coffee shop, it's ¥120 from an ever-present vending machine.

A rock-bottom daily budget – ¥3200 for a dorm bed, ¥2000 for modest meals, ¥1500 for transport, ¥2000 for incidentals – means you're looking at nearly ¥9000 a day. You may well spend more – a budget business hotel is ¥7000 to ¥10,000 a night.

Food costs can be kept down by taking set meals. 'Morning service' (*mōningu sābisu* or *setto*) in most coffee shops is around ¥400. Set meals at lunch (*teishoku*) are ¥800; cheap noodles are ¥500 and *bentō* (boxed lunch) costs around ¥600. For dinner, a set course or a single order is about ¥900. An evening meal and beer in an *izakaya*, or traditional pub, is around ¥3000. Youth hostels charge around ¥450 for a Japanese breakfast and ¥800 for dinner.

Other prices include: museum admission (¥400 to ¥1000), movie ticket (¥1600 to ¥2000), foreign magazines (¥800 to ¥1200), local English newspapers (¥120 to ¥160), 36-exposure colour film, no processing (¥420), orange juice at a coffee shop (¥450), average cocktail (¥800 to ¥1000), shirt dry-cleaning (¥200) and packet of cigarettes (¥230 to ¥300).

Transport can be expensive. Transport passes are available (see the Getting Around chapter), but a Japan Rail Pass won't be worthwhile unless you are travelling to other parts of Japan. For *shinkansen* (bullet train) trips and domestic flights, discounted tickets are available at some theatre ticketing outlets (see the Travel Agents section in the Getting There & Away chapter). Only use taxis as a last resort – too slow and too expensive.

Carrying Money

The Japanese are used to a safe society and often carry around wads of cash. You can too, but take the usual precautions. Travellers cheques are the safest and most practical way to carry large amounts of money.

Cash

Cold hard yen is the way to pay in Japan. While credit cards are becoming more common in Tokyo, cash is still much more widely used, and travellers cheques are rarely accepted as payment.

Travellers Cheques

US dollar cheques are preferable; other major currencies are acceptable. Travellers cheques can be changed at almost any bank, at many department stores and at some hotels (middle and top-end hotels will usually change them – small business hotels usually will not). Do not expect to pay with them in restaurants, stores or hotels (there are some exceptions to this, usually at top-end places).

You can also buy travellers cheques in Japan – with cash at almost any major bank, and with credit cards at the offices listed under Credit Cards, following.

ATMs

In the wake of the G5 summit in Miyazaki and Okinawa, several hundred post-offices across the nation are now geared to accept foreign-issued cash or credit cards, with more coming online during 2001–02. In theory this means you'll be able to withdraw cash at any post-office. However, as operating instructions for this specialised transaction may only be in Japanese, it's good to visit at hours when the counter is open (usually 9am to 5pm).

In addition some banks and department stores have 'Global ATM' machines that accept most foreign-issued cards (Visa, MasterCard and Cirrus being the most common). These are distinguished by the wide range of accepted credit cards pictured next to their operating instructions. In Shinjuku, try the Global ATM on the 7th floor of Keiō department store (Map 3); in Ginza, look outside the Yūrakuchō Mullion building (Map 7) next to Sumitomo bank. You need your four-digit personal identification number (PIN) to get a cash advance with a credit or cash card. Most Sumitomo bank offices will give cash advances to Visa card holders. More information on ATMs that

accept your cards can be obtained from the Tokyo offices directly. Their numbers are listed below.

Most of the ATMs designed to accept foreign-issued cards have English instructions. On standard Japanese machines, you will have to be able to read Japanese kanji or ask someone for assistance.

Credit Cards

MasterCard and Visa are the most widely accepted, followed by American Express and Diners Club. Almost all top-end and some middle-range hotels accept credit cards, but most cheaper hotels, youth hostels and ryokan do not. Mid-range and top-end restaurants catering to foreigners generally accept credit cards. The big department stores and pricier small stores usually accept cards, but most regular shops do not. JR and private train lines don't take them. Never assume that a place accepts credit cards; check beforehand. In general, it is better to carry plenty of cash in Japan than to be reliant on credit cards.

The main card offices in Tokyo are:

American Express (☎ 3220 6100, toll-free 24-hours ☎ 0120 020 120) Ogikubo Head Office, American Express Tower, 4-30-16 Ogikubo, Suginami-ku
Diners Club (☎ 3499 1311, emergency ☎ 3797 7311, after hours ☎ 3499 1181) Senshu Building, 1-13-7 Shibuya, Shibuya-ku
JCB Card (☎ 3294 8111) 1-6 Kanda Suragadai, Chiyoda-ku
MasterCard (☎ 5350 8051, emergency ☎ 0031 11 3886) Dai Tokyo Kasai Shinjuku Building, 16F, 3-25-3, Yoyogi, Shibuya-ku
Visa (☎ 5251 0633; emergency ☎ 0120 133 173) Imperial Tower, 11F, 1-1-1 Uchisaiwai-chō, Chiyoda-ku

Currency

The currency in Japan is the yen (¥). Banknotes and coins are easily identifiable; there are ¥1, ¥5, ¥10, ¥50, ¥100 and ¥500 coins; and ¥1000, ¥2000, ¥5000 and ¥10,000 notes. The ¥1 coin is of lightweight aluminium; ¥5 and ¥50 coins have a hole in the middle. Recently issued ¥500 coins cannot be used in most vending machines.

Exchange Rates

As this book went to production, exchange rates were:

country	unit		Yen
Australia	A$1	=	¥60
Canada	C$1	=	¥77
Germany	DM1	=	¥57
Hong Kong	HK$1	=	¥15
New Zealand	NZ$1	=	¥50
Singapore	S$1	=	¥68
UK	UK£1	=	¥175
USA	US$1	=	¥120

Changing Money

You can change cash or travellers cheques at an 'Authorised Foreign Exchange Bank' (signs will always be displayed in English) or at some large hotels and stores. Some post offices now exchange money – look for the 'Authorised Foreign Exchange' sign. Although the Korean and Taiwanese currencies have recently become easier to change, it is still wise to change them into US dollars or yen before you arrive in Japan.

Banking Hours

Banks are open Monday to Friday from 9am to 3pm, closed on weekends and national holidays. Banking procedures can be time-consuming. If you're caught cashless outside regular banking hours, you can try a large department store or major hotel. The Shinjuku branches of Isetan and Keiō department stores (Map 3), as well as Seibu Loft (Map 2) in Ikebukuro, on the 7th floor, will change travellers cheques. The Tokyo-Mitsubishi Bank's Shibuya branch (☎ 3610 7000) also has an after-hours exchange service until 6pm daily; it's on Meiji-dōri on the south-east side of the station.

Money Transfers

If you are having money sent to a bank in Japan, make sure you know *exactly* where the funds are going: the bank, branch and location. Telex or telegram transfers are much faster, though more expensive, than mail transfers. A credit-card cash advance is a worthwhile alternative.

Bank & Post Office Accounts

If you open a savings account at one of the major banks, you'll receive a savings book and a cash card which allows you to draw cash at any branch or from an ATM. Just say 'futsū chokin' (general deposit), and this should get the ball rolling.

One easy option is to open a post office savings account *(yūbin chokin)*; this allows you to withdraw funds from any post office (the smallest towns in Japan might not have a bank but they all have a post office). If you go to the Tokyo central post office to set up your account you'll get English-language assistance.

For a US-dollar account, higher interest rates and 24-hour ATM service, contact Citibank (☎ 0120-223 773), which has several branches in Tokyo.

Tipping & Bargaining

Nobody in Tokyo expects a tip – which reduces costs so it's best to keep it that way. However, if your maid at a ryokan has given fairy godmother service, you can leave her a small present. If you give cash, the polite way is to place it in an envelope.

Fixed prices prevail in Japan. Akihabara's 'Electric Town' is one exception – most big electronics stores there will give 10% discounts. Don't haggle; a polite request is all that is required. Some flea market vendors are open to bargaining, some won't even consider it; just ask politely.

Taxes & Refunds

Japan has a 5% consumer tax. If you eat at expensive restaurants and sleep in luxury, you will also encounter a service charge which varies from 10% to 15%. A local tax of 3% is added for restaurant bills exceeding ¥5000 or for hotel bills over ¥10,000 (you can ask for separate bills to avoid this). At *onsen* (hot-spring) resorts, a separate onsen tax applies. This is usually 3% and applies at cheap accommodation, even youth hostels.

Those travelling on a tourist visa can avoid the 5% consumption tax on purchases at major department stores and at duty-free stores like LAOX in Akihabara.

For a refund on general purchases, check first that the department store has a service desk for tax refunds. Take the purchase, receipt and your passport to the service desk for an immediate refund.

DOING BUSINESS

Those who come to Tokyo to do business will find a wide range of support services available. With deregulation plans and the Japanese consumer trend away from overpriced goods marketed by domestic giants, things may improve for foreign businesses.

Business Services

Whether you want a good serviced office to kick-start operations in Tokyo or a printing firm to run off a few extra *meishi* (business cards), you'll find plenty of suppliers.

If you're on a tight schedule, it's best to make inquiries before you leave home, particularly if you require interpreting or want to prepare some translated materials. Consult the Japan desk of your government's trade organisation or an overseas office of the Japan External Trade Organization (JETRO), the import-promotion agency of the Japanese government.

Once in Japan, your main allies are your national chamber of commerce and JETRO. The Tokyo JETRO Business Support Center (☎ 5562 3131, fax 5562 3100) is in the Akasaka Twin Tower building (Map 7) at 2-17-22 Akasaka, Minato-ku, Tokyo 107. It offers free office space and meeting rooms, free consultancy and a good library of English-language information about doing business in Japan. In order to use JETRO's services, your company must be registered in your home country and you must apply through the JETRO office in that country. Businesses of any size are welcome, but JETRO does not provide services to PR firms, service industries, banks or newspapers. There are also JETRO Business Support Centers in Yokohama (☎ 045-451 9071).

Kimi Information Center (Map 2; ☎ 3986 1604) in Ikebukuro offers a range of business services. Larger hotels also offer business support services, even to non-guests.

Some foreign chambers of commerce in Tokyo are:

American Chamber of Commerce (☎ 3436 1446) Bridgestone Bldg, 3-25-2 Toranomon, Minato-ku 105

Australian & New Zealand Chamber of Commerce (☎ 3201 2592) CPO Box 1096, 100-91

British Chamber of Commerce in Japan (☎ 3267 1903) Kenkyusha Eigo Center Bldg, 1-2 Kagurazaka, Shinjuku-ku 162

Canadian Chamber of Commerce (☎ 3224 7825) Shelzrene Bldg, 7-4-7 Akasaka, Minato-ku 107

French Chamber of Commerce and Industry in Japan (☎ 3288 9558) Iida Bldg, 5-5 Rokuban-chō, Chiyoda-ku 102

German Chamber of Commerce and Industry in Japan (☎ 5276 8733) KS Bldg, 2 Banchi Sanban-chō, Chiyoda-ku 102

Helpful Japanese and Tokyo government organisations include:

Foreign Investment in Japan Development Corp (☎ 3224 1203) Akasaka Twin Tower Bldg, 2-17-22 Akasaka, Minato-ku 107

Industrial Structure Improvement Fund, Import and Investment Promotion Division (☎ 3241 6283) Kaigin Bldg, 1-9-1 Ōtemachi, Chiyoda-ku 100

Japan Chamber of Commerce and Industry, International Division (☎ 3216 6497) Tosho Bldg, 3-2-2 Marunouchi, Chiyoda-ku 100

Ministry of International Trade and Industry, International Business Affairs Division (☎ 3501 6623) 1-3-1 Kasumigaseki, Chiyoda-ku 100

There are no trade banks as such in Japan, but the bigger Japanese banks have international sections. Some larger Japanese bank head offices are:

Fuji Bank (☎ 3216 2211) 1-5-5 Ōtemachi, Chiyoda-ku

Tokyo-Mitsubishi Bank (☎ 3240 1111) 2-7-1 Marunouchi, Chiyoda-ku; Map 8

POST & COMMUNICATIONS
Post

The symbol for post offices is a white-and-red 'T' with a bar across the top. Red mailboxes are for ordinary mail and blue ones are special delivery. The Japanese postal system is reliable and efficient.

The airmail rate for postcards is ¥70 to any overseas destination; aerograms cost ¥90. Letters under 25g are ¥90 to other countries within Asia; ¥110 to North America, Europe or Oceania (including Australia and New Zealand); and ¥120 to Africa and South America.

Sending parcels overseas from Japan can be as much as 30% cheaper than airmail with Surface Airlift (SAL), and only takes a week longer. Post offices conveniently sell different-sized cardboard boxes, which allows you to pack and send on the spot. Larger department stores can also arrange international postage.

District post offices in and around Tokyo (the main post office in a ward, or *ku)* are normally open from 9am to 7pm on weekdays, to 3pm on Saturday, closed on Sunday and public holidays (some larger district offices are open to 12.30pm on Sunday and public holidays). Local post offices are open from 9am to 5pm on weekdays, closed weekends and public holidays. There are after-hours windows at some district offices; the one at Tokyo's central post office is open 24 hours a day.

Tokyo central post office (Map 8; ☎ 3284 9539) is on the Marunouchi side of Tokyo station, across the street slightly south of the main station building. The Yokohama central post office (☎ 045-461 1385) is on the south-east side of Yokohama station, opposite JR East offices.

For sending and receiving international mail, see the Tokyo international post office information in the following Receiving Mail section.

Mail can be sent to Japan, from Japan or within Japan when addressed in roman script *(romaji)* but it should, of course, be written as clearly as possible.

Receiving Mail In Tokyo, have your mail sent to the main international post office, as this office is familiar with the concept of poste restante. Have it addressed as follows:

SURNAME, First Name
Poste Restante, Tokyo International Post Office
2-3-3 Ōtemachi, Chiyoda-ku, Tokyo

To get to the Tokyo international post office (Map 8; ☎ 3241 4891), take the A4 exit of Ōtemachi subway station. The post office will hold mail for 30 days. Hours are 9am to 7pm weekdays, to 5pm Saturday, to noon Sunday and national holidays.

American Express will hold mail for its card holders or users of American Express travellers cheques. Normally, mail will be held for 30 days only unless marked 'Please hold for arrival'.

Some embassies will hold mail for their nationals – check before you depart. Hotels and youth hostels are another possibility.

Courier Services International couriers operate in Japan, but you can also use the EMS service *(kokusai ekisupuresu)* available at all post offices, though you need an EMS number to access it. EMS is usually as cheap as, and can be faster than, international shippers like Federal Express (☎ 0120-003 200), Nippon Express (☎ 3572 4305) and the Overseas Courier Service (☎ 5476 8106).

Japan also has an excellent system of private domestic carriers, such as Yamato Takyūbin (☎ 3798 5131), which can deliver documents and parcels door-to-door around the country, usually overnight. Bring your package to a convenience store like Lawson's and send it from there (the clerks can help you fill out the forms and explain payment). It's cheap – often less than ¥1500 for a small package.

Telephone

The Japanese public telephone system is very well developed and there are many public phones (which are rarely vandalised). Services within Japan are principally handled by Nippon Telegraph and Telephone Corporation (NTT).

Local calls cost ¥10 for three minutes; long-distance or overseas calls require a handful of coins. Unused ¥10 coins are returned after a call, but change is *not* given for ¥100 coins. Most pay phones will also

Japan Area Codes

The country code for Japan is ☎ 81. Tokyo's area code is ☎ 03 (the area code is not used if dialling a Tokyo number from within Tokyo).

Below are area codes for some main cities and tourist areas:

Fukuoka	092
Hakone	0460
Hiroshima	082
Kamakura	0467
Kyoto	075
Matsuyama	0899
Nagasaki	0958
Nagoya	052
Narita	0476
Nikkō	0288
Osaka	06
Sapporo	011
Sendai	022
Shimoda	0588
Yokohama	045

You do not dial an area code's first 0 if dialling from overseas. For example dialling the number ☎ 555 555 in Tokyo from overseas you would dial your international access number followed by ☎ 81-3-555 555.

東京 東京 東京 東京 東京 東京 東京

accept prepaid phone cards (*terefon kādo*) in denominations of ¥500 and ¥1000. The cards are readily available from vending machines and convenience stores.

International Calls Rates have become more competitive, as Kokusai Denshin Denwa (KDD) now operates alongside the newer International Telecom Japan (ITJ) and International Digital Communication (IDC).

Paid and reverse-charge (collect) overseas calls can be made from grey ISDN phones and green phones that have a gold metal plate around the buttons. These are usually found in phone booths marked 'International & Domestic Card/Coin Phone'. You can't make international calls from the green phones (although you can make

operator-assisted calls). In hotel lobbies and airports, you will also find KDD 'Credit Phones', which allow you to make international calls with credit cards issued outside Japan. In some youth hostels and 'gaijin houses' you will also find pink coin-only phones from which you cannot make international calls (though you can receive them).

Calls are charged by the unit (no three-minute minimum), each of which is six seconds, so if you've not got much to say you could phone home for just ¥100.

You save money by dialling late at night. Economy rates with a discount of 20% apply from 7pm to 11pm, Monday to Friday, and all day to 11pm on weekends and holidays. From 11pm to 8am a discount rate brings the price of international calls down by 40%. It is also cheaper to make domestic calls by dialling outside the standard hours.

To place an international call through the operator, dial ☎ 0051 – international operators all seem to speak English. To make the call yourself, dial ☎ 001 (KDD), ☎ 0041 (ITJ) or ☎ 0061 (IDC) – there's very little difference in their rates – then the international country code, the local code and the number.

Another option is to dial ☎ 0039 for home country direct, which takes you straight through to a local operator in the country dialled (your home country direct code can be found in phone books or by calling ☎ 0051). You can then make a reverse-charge call or a credit-card call with a telephone credit card valid in that country. In some hotels or other tourist locations, you may find a home country direct phone where you simply press the button labelled USA, UK, Canada etc, to be put through to your operator. You need to arrange the home country direct service with your home telephone company before you leave for Japan.

Directory Assistance Dial ☎ 104 for local directory assistance, or for assistance in English ring ☎ 0120 364 463 (9am to 5pm weekdays). For international directory assistance dial ☎ 0057. An English telephone directory is available in *City Source*. It is free, and available at any NTT office or the Tokyo TIC. To place a domestic reverse-charge call, dial ☎ 106. For orders and inquiries about having a phone installed, ring the NTT English Service Section on ☎ 0120-364 463, toll-free.

eKno Communication Service Lonely Planet's eKno global communication service provides low-cost international calls (for local calls you're usually better off with a local phonecard). eKno also offers free messaging services, email, travel information and an online travel vault, where you can securely store all your important documents. You can join online at Ⓦ www .ekno.lonelyplanet.com, where you will find the local-access numbers for the 24-hour customer-service centre (in Japan call ☎ 0053-116 0057). Once you have joined, always check the eKno Web site for the latest access numbers for each country and updates on new features.

Fax, Telegram & Email
Fax Getting access to fax services in Tokyo can be difficult. If you're staying in a major hotel, you should have no problem. For those in more downmarket digs, the branches of KDD in Shinjuku (Map 3; ☎ 3347 5000) and Ōtemachi (☎ 3275 4343) can receive and send international faxes from 9am to 5pm, Monday to Friday (closed on holidays). The Shinjuku branch is on the station's west side; the Ōtemachi branch is next to the C1 exit of Ōtemachi subway station.

Alpha Corporation, on the 1st floor of Shinjuku's Hilton Tokyo (Map 3; ☎ 3343 2575) and in the Akasaka Tōkyū Hotel (Map 7; ☎ 3580 1991), offers fax services. Kimi Information Center (Map 2; ☎ 3986 1604) in Ikebukuro will both receive and send faxes.

Kinko's, the US-based office-service company, offers 24-hour fax sending and receiving (and Internet access) at its outlets currently springing up throughout Tokyo. There are handy branches in Ueno (☎ 5246 9811), Kanda (☎ 3251 7677), Ebisu (☎ 5795 1485), Yaesu (☎ 3278 3911) and Ikebukuro (☎ 5979 5171).

Telegrams For international information, ring ☎ 3344 5151 (some English is spoken) or go to the KDD offices mentioned under Fax, earlier. Prices are steep for international telegrams, and they aren't quick. For domestic telegrams in English, you can also go to any major NTT office, eg, the Marunouchi head office (☎ 5001 3300).

Email Compuserve, America Online and IBM subscribers can pick up their email via local numbers in Japan. Check with your server before coming to Japan for local access numbers. Phone jacks in Japan are the same seven-pin type used in America. Many of the grey IDD public telephones in Japan have a jack that will allow you to log on.

INTERNET RESOURCES
Though the Internet was slow in coming to Japan, the country is scrambling to catch up, and there is currently a wealth of information about Japan available online.

J-Pop (Ⓦ www.jpop-mp3.com) Japanese popular-music Web site complete with MP3 downloads
JNTO (Ⓦ www.jnto.go.jp)
TELLNET (Ⓦ www.majic.co.jp) Put up by the folks at Tokyo English Lifeline, this site has 1200 pages of free information on living in Japan.
Tokyo Q (Ⓦ tokyoq.com) This is a large, inventive and useful Tokyo entertainment resource.
Shift Japan E-zine (Ⓦ www.shift.jp.org) Fashion, lifestyle and design
UK Anime Net (Ⓦ www.uk-anime.net) Japanese animation including manga
Sake World (Ⓦ www.sake-world.com) Want to sound knowledgeable when you're offered *sake* in a restaurant? All you ever needed to know about the famous alcoholic beverage is right here!
Soccerphile (Ⓦ www.soccerphile.com) Information about the FIFA World Cup to be played in Japan and South Korea in 2002

See Gay & Lesbian Travellers, later in this chapter, for some gay-friendly Web sites.

Lonely Planet Online
While you're holding a copy of Lonely Planet's latest 'treeware' for Tokyo, check out the latest travel news, views, Upgrades and more for destinations in Japan, the rest of Asia and the globe at LP's award-winning

Practising *tai chi* at Shinjuku-gyoen garden

Colourful *sumō* banners

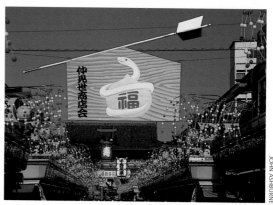
Famous Sensō-ji temple – 2001 was the Year of the Snake

Street art – Japanese style

MARTIN MOOS

CHRIS MELLOR

Trendy Ginza Street at night

MARTIN MOOS

Escalator to subway

MICHAEL TAYLOR

Station master – all aboard!

Nakamise-dōri – a shopping street in the Sensō-ji temple precinct

JOHN McINNES

Rainbow Bridge across Tokyo Bay – at night from Ōdaiba

Tokyo's Internet Cafes

Internet cafes haven't taken Tokyo by storm, but there are a good number of places where you can get online and have a coffee.

Las Chicas (Map 4; ☎ 3407 6863), in Aoyama, has a single Mac that diners can use for free, as does Kiss (Map 4; ☎ 3401 8165).

Pulse Point (☎ 3289 0132), on the 4th floor of Ginza's Sony building (Map 7), has bagels with Macs or IBMs – the cost is ¥500 for 30 minutes. Koinomori (☎ 5568 0269) is a simple place which charges ¥250 for 30 minutes. It's on the 9th floor of the Palais Ginza building, between the Sakura bank and Matsuzakaya department store (Map 7).

Gaiax Cafe (☎ 5332 9201), next to the Star Hotel in West Shinjuku (Map 3) is a comfortable space with dozens of Macs and PCs. It's ¥390 for 30 minutes, or ¥240 if you join their video-chat membership.

Some no-frills options in Roppongi are at Manga Hiroba (☎ 3497 1751) oppposite Hub 2, ¥380 for 1 hour, and at NetCafe Seishido on the 3rd floor of the Seishido buiding at Roppongi crossing.

Click On (☎ 5489 2282) is a small place in Dōgen-zaka on the 5th floor of the Koike building. It's ¥500 for 30 minutes.

東京 東京 東京 東京 東京 東京 東京

Web site (Ⓦ www.lonelyplanet.com). Features include photo galleries, cyber-postcards, travel literature and the Thorn Tree, a lively discussion board. Free online Upgrades for the *Japan* guide are posted every six months.

BOOKS

Tokyo has a number of bookshops with excellent selections of books. Most of the following books should be available in Tokyo, usually in paperback.

Lonely Planet

For trips further afield in Japan and the region, Lonely Planet's *Japan*, *Kyoto* and *North-East Asia* guides contain all the travel detail you'll need.

Lonely Planet also publishes a guide to *Hiking in Japan*, which includes a chapter on walks around Tokyo; *Read this First Asia & India*, an introduction to travel in the region; and the *Japanese phrasebook*.

If you have a Palm OS hand-held device, you might also be interested in the maps and text available on Lonely Planet's City-Sync *Tokyo* (see Ⓦ www.citysync.com for more information). Using CitySync you can quickly search, sort and bookmark hundreds of restaurants, hotels, clubs and more – all pinpointed on scrollable street maps.

Alex Kerr's *Lost Japan* recounts both the dangers facing modern Japan and the author's fascinating experiences in the country.

Guidebooks

Guidebooks to Tokyo come and go quickly, but a few specialised guidebooks are good supplements to the book you have in your hands. Gourmets should look for the *Tokyo Restaurant Guide* by John Kennerdell.

Serious nightlife addicts could seek the *Tokyo Nightlife Guide* by the folks at *Tokyo Journal*.

Tokyo Museums – A Complete Guide by Thomas & Ellen Flannigan is what its title suggests. *Tokyo for Free*, by Susan Pompian, lists hundreds of no-cost activities in the city.

Old Tokyo – Walks in the City of the Shogun by Enbutsu Sumiko is a helpful walking guide to Tokyo's lingering past. Her *The Sumida Crisscross – Tokyo River Walks* is excellent.

Gary Walters' *Day Walks Near Tokyo* covers 25 accessible countryside trails. John Carroll's *Trails of Two Cities* outlines walks around Yokohama and Kamakura.

Culture & Society

Look for the brilliant *Outnation – A Search for the Soul of Japan* by Jonathan Rauch. *In the Realm of the Dying Emperor* by Norma Field is a thoughtful and beautifully written assault on views of Japanese society as both monolithic and de-individualising. Karl Taro Greenfield attempts the same in his racy *Speed Tribes – Children of the Japanese Bubble*.

Tokyo's Bookshops

The English-language sections of several of the larger Tokyo bookshops would put entire bookshops in many English-speaking cities to shame.

The main bookshop area in Tokyo is Jimbōchō (Map 8), and although most of the bookshops there cater only to those who read Japanese, there are a couple of foreign-language bookshops. The best among these is Kitazawa Shoten (☎ 3263 0011), open Monday to Saturday from 10am to 6pm, which has an excellent academic selection on the ground floor and second-hand books on the 2nd floor. It's on Yasukuni-dōri opposite Fuji Bank.

For a decent selection of English books, many of them titles on Japan, Asia and arts and culture, take a look in Tuttle Books (☎ 3291 7071), open from 10.30am to 7pm, Sunday until 6pm, and Isseidō (☎ 3292 0071), open from 10am to 6.30pm, closed Sunday.

One of Japan's better bookshop chains, Kinokuniya has two branches in Shinjuku (Map 3). The old branch on Shinjuku-dōri (☎ 3354 0131), open from 10am to 8pm, has a good selection of English-language fiction and general titles on the 7th floor, including an extensive selection of books and other aids for learning Japanese. It's closed on the third Wednesday of the month. The new Kinokuniya branch (☎ 5361 3301), open from 10am to 8pm, in the annex of the Takashimaya Times Square complex has one of the largest selections of English-language books in Tokyo (on the 6th floor).

Maruzen (Map 8; ☎ 3272 7211), open from 10am to 7pm, in Nihombashi near Ginza has a collection of books almost equal to Kinokuniya's, and it is always a lot quieter. This is Japan's oldest Western bookshop, established in 1869. English-language books are on the 2nd floor. It also has a limited selection of French-language magazines, books and newspapers. It's closed on Sunday.

The 3rd floor of Jena (Map 7; ☎ 3571 2980), open from 10.30am to 8.30pm, in Ginza doesn't have the range of some other foreign-language bookshops, but it does have a good selection of fiction and art books, and it stocks a large number of newspapers and magazines. It's closed on public holidays.

Just south of Tokyo station, Yaesu Book Centre (Map 7; ☎ 3281 1811), open from 10am to 9pm, Sunday to 6pm, has a good selection of English-language books as well as some French and German titles.

The best selection of used English-language books is in Ebisu (Map 5) at Good Day Books (☎ 5421 0957); open from 11am to 8pm, Sunday to 6pm, closed Tuesday. In addition to a wide range of paperbacks, there are some hardcover books and magazines. It also accepts books for exchange, and (very) occasionally will purchase used books. It's closed Tuesday.

For business reading, you can try the bookshops at JETRO (Map 7; ☎ 3582 5522), open weekdays from 9am to 5pm, in Toranomon; and on the 6th floor of the huge Keizai Kōhō Center (☎ 3201 1415), open weekdays from 9am to 5pm, in Ōtemachi (Map 8) – take exit E2 or C7 of Ōtemachi subway station.

The Government Publication Service Center (☎ 3504 3885), open weekdays from 9am to 5pm, in Kasumigaseki (Map 7) also sells Japanese and bilingual official publications. Take exit A9 from Kasumigaseki station, and it's in front of the Ministry of Agriculture, Forestry and Fisheries annex. There's also a branch in Ōtemachi.

Bojinsha (☎ 3239 8673), open from 10am to 7pm, closed on Sunday, is a small but well-stocked bookshop on the 2nd floor of the Kōjimachi New Yahiko building on the east side of Yotsuya JR and subway stations (north of Akasaka). It is an excellent place to pick up texts or AV tools for anyone wanting to learn or teach the Japanese language.

Tower Records' main Shibuya store (☎ 3496 3661), open 10am to 11pm, has a good selection of English books and magazines, and probably the city's best selection of imported music publications on its 7th floor. It's next to the Yamanote railway tracks, north-east of Shibuya station, behind the Marui main store.

Max Danger – The Adventures of an Ex-Pat in Tokyo commands a loyal following. Another light but illuminating read is *You Gotta Have Wa* by Robert Whiting.

Recently updated, *The Japanese Today* by Edwin O Reischauer has long been a standard textbook and is a must-read. *Appreciations of Japanese Culture* by Donald Keane is an eclectic collection of essays by a renowned scholar of Japanese culture.

Angry White Pajamas is adventurer-writer Robert Twigger's account of his year-long *aikido* stint with the Tokyo Riot Police.

History

For a fascinating history of Tokyo from 1867 to 1923, look for Edward Seidensticker's *Low City, High City*. His *Tokyo Rising – The City Since the Great Earthquake* continues the story.

Lafcadio Hearn lived in Meiji Tokyo and wrote many books and essays. Hearn's *Writings from Japan* includes some of his best work. Paul Waley's *Tokyo – City of Stories* is a contemporary attempt at Hearn.

Religion

Good primers include *Japanese Religion – A Cultural Perspective* by Robert S Elwood & Richard Pilgrim, and *Religions of Japan – Many Traditions within One Sacred Way* by H Byron Earhart.

Probably the best introduction to Zen is *Zen and Japanese Culture* by Daisetzu T Suzuki. Peter Matthiessen gives a personal account of his Zen experiences in *Nine Headed Dragon River*.

Business

There is a mountain of tomes purporting to unlock the secrets of Japanese business. *The Art of Japanese Management – Applications for American Executives* has been around for a while, but is still a good introduction.

For nuts-and-bolts information there's the *Japan Company Handbook* (published by Toyo Keizai) detailing listed companies. *Nippon* (JETRO) is an annual statistical publication. Other annual publications include *Survey of Japanese Corporations Overseas* (Toyo Keizai), *Japan Trade Directory* (JETRO), *Japan Economic Almanac* (The Nikkei Weekly) and *Japan: An International Comparison* (Keizai Kōhō Center, or Japan Institute for Social and Economic Affairs).

Practical guides include *Setting Up an Office in Japan* (American Chamber of Commerce in Japan, 1993), *Setting Up and Operating a Business in Japan* by Helene Thian (Tuttle, 1990), and *Setting Up Enterprises in Japan – Guidelines on Investment, Taxation and Legal Regulations* (JETRO, 1993). JETRO's *Investment Japan – A Directory of Institutions and Firms Offering Assistance to People Seeking to Set Up a Business in Japan* is a comprehensive listing of useful contacts across all industries. The *Japan Yellow Pages* is published by Japan Yellow Pages Ltd (☎ 3239 3501).

Language

One of the best colloquial textbooks is *An Introduction to Modern Japanese*, available with an expensive set of tapes. *Japanese for Busy People* comes in several volumes and is also a popular textbook and tape series.

You can impress your Japanese friends with little gems culled from books as diverse as *How to Sound Intelligent in Japanese* by Charles de Wolf and *Japanese Street Slang* by Peter Constantine. Of course, it would be sensible to get the basics of Japanese grammar down before you try quoting Sartre to the local convenience store worker. Those seeking to be bilingual from the waist down should peruse the perennial best-seller *Making Out in Japanese* by Todd and Erika Geers.

For a guide to street-wise *kanji*, a copy of *Reading Japanese Signs* is indispensable. For a more systematic approach to kanji, one of the best books around is *Kanji in Context*. If you want a reference book, Hadaminsky & Spahn's *Kanji & Kana* is without peer for clarity and ease of use.

Fiction

See Arts in the Facts about Tokyo chapter for accessible examples of Japan's rich literary heritage.

NEWSPAPERS & MAGAZINES
Newspapers
There are two widely available local English newspapers: the *Japan Times* and the *Yomiuri Daily* and, as this book goes to production, a collaboration between the *Asahi Newspaper* and *International Herald Tribune* is in the planning stage. The *Japan Times* is popular for its classified section – Monday is the day to check for employment. The *Yomiuri Daily* has a 'View from Europe' section culled from Britain's *Independent* and a 'World Report' from the *Los Angeles Times*. For business news, try *Business Tokyo* and *Nikkei Weekly*. Overseas papers and magazines are available at major foreign-language bookshops.

Magazines
Tokyo has several English-language magazines covering local events, entertainment and cultural listings. The *Tokyo Journal* is worth the ¥600 for its listings of movies, plays, concerts, art exhibitions and unclassifiable 'events'. It is available at bookshops with English-language sections.

Tokyo Classified is a free weekly magazine with classifieds and some news of restaurants, bars and upcoming events. It can be found at record stores like Virgin and Tower, and some bigger bookshops. More widely available is *Pia*, a Japanese-language 'what's-on' publication.

Free information magazines are available at hotels, TIC offices and Narita airport. These include *Tokyo Classified*, *City Life News Tokyo* and *The Nippon View*. The weekly *Tokyo Weekender* is similar.

If you're studying Japanese, articles in the *Hiragana Times* are in English and Japanese, and the kanji includes *furigana* (script used to give pronunciation for kanji) readings.

RADIO & TV
Radio
InterFM on 76.1MHz FM was created in 1996 to serve the needs of Tokyo's large foreign population. The station broadcasts news and daily-life information mainly in English, but also in seven other languages, including Spanish and Chinese. The music is also more cosmopolitan than most other stations. You can also tune into the US armed services' Far East Network (FEN; 810kHz AM).

TV
Unlike radio (where DJs often throw in some English), most TV is Japanese-only. In any case, it's mostly inane variety shows. It's worth watching a bit as a window into the culture, but you're unlikely to get addicted.

TVs can be fitted with an adaptor so that certain English-language programs and movies can be received in either Japanese or English. The Japan Broadcasting Corporation (NHK) has a nightly bilingual news report, though it is rarely very informative. The better hotels do have English-language satellite services, including BBC and CNN.

PHOTOGRAPHY & VIDEO
Film & Equipment
The Japanese are a nation of photographers – no social occasion is complete without a few snaps and an exchange of the photos, so photographic gear is easy to come by.

A 36-exposure colour print film, no processing, costs about ¥420, slide film from ¥800 to ¥980 (Kodachrome 64 slide film about ¥950). Disposable cameras are even sold from vending machines (¥1500 to ¥2000); more expensive ones have a built-in flash.

You can also pick up disposable 3D cameras. The effect is more jarring than pleasing, but they're great for those souvenir shots of you giving Tokyo Tower the Godzilla treatment.

Japan uses the American NTSC standard for video. If you are using PAL or SECAM, bring your own video cartridges with you. It is possible to buy video cameras in Tokyo that switch between the standards.

Processing
Processing print film is fast and economical in Tokyo, although the standards vary. Prices range from ¥1000 to ¥2000 for a 36-exposure roll of film, depending upon the shop and the brand of film (Japanese Fuji film is usually the cheapest). One photo

chain to look out for is Yellow Camera, which offers 90-minute processing. When you hand in the film, you will be asked 'O-isogi desu ka?' ('Are you in a hurry?'); if you can wait overnight (the cheaper option) a simple 'no' will suffice.

Kodachrome slide film can only be processed by the Imagica Kodak depot in Ginza. The processing is fast (24 hours) and the results are good. There is no problem honouring prepaid Kodachrome film.

Photo Etiquette

Japan is an extremely photo-literate country, and every household owns at least one camera. Asking 'Shashin totte ii desu ka?' (Can I take your photo?) is unlikely to cause offence, except to shy types and mobsters. The Harajuku youths positively revel in the attention. If you make Japanese friends, it is considered extremely polite to give (or mail) them prints – even more-so if you include a copy for each person in the picture. Well, the flattering ones at least.

TIME

Japan is in one time zone, nine hours ahead of Greenwich Mean Time (GMT). Daylight-saving time is not used in Japan.

In train stations, bus stations and airports, a 24-hour clock is used, eg, 5pm is 17.00 and midnight is 24.00.

ELECTRICITY

The Japanese electricity supply is at 100V AC, an odd voltage found almost nowhere else in the world. Furthermore, Tokyo and eastern Japan are on a frequency of 50Hz (50 cycles), and western Japan (including Nagoya, Kyoto and Osaka) is on 60Hz.

Most North American electrical items, designed to run at 110V AC, will function reasonably well in Japan. However, some items require a certain frequency as well as a certain voltage – so, for example, some North American clocks (designed to run at 60Hz) will not operate correctly in Tokyo and eastern Japan (50Hz).

The plugs are flat with two pins, identical to US and Canadian plugs.

LAUNDRY

Most hotels, mid-range and up, have laundry services. Or there's the coin laundry, something of an institution in suburban Japan, but nonexistent in central Tokyo. If you are at a budget ryokan, ask the staff for the nearest laundry *(koin randorii)*. Costs range from ¥200 to ¥300 for a load (some places have extra-large machines for ¥500) and ¥100 for 10 minutes of drying time. Note that some washing machines in koin randorii automatically add detergent, a feature which may or may not be indicated in English. You can always ask someone, 'Sekken irimasu ka?' ('Is soap necessary?'). If you need soap, there are usually on-site machines selling small bags for ¥100 (some of these also make change of ¥1000 notes).

Dry cleaners *(kuriningu-yasan)* are in almost every neighbourhood. The standards are high and some offer rush service. It costs about ¥200 for a basic business shirt. You may be asked, 'Norizuke shiage shimashō ka?' ('Do you want it starched?').

Hotel laundry service is available, though, not surprisingly, it costs significantly more than doing it yourself.

WEIGHTS & MEASURES

Japan uses the metric system. One exception is the unit used for the size of rooms, which are measured in *jō*, or *tatami* mats. In Tokyo (the size differs across Japan) a tatami measures 1.76m by 0.88m.

HEALTH

Travel health depends on your pre-departure preparations, your day-to-day health care and how you handle any medical problem or emergency that develops. However, looking after your health in Tokyo should pose few problems, since hygiene standards are high and medical facilities are widely available, though expensive.

No immunisations are required for Japan, but it's wise to keep up to date with tetanus, diphtheria and polio shots (boosters are recommended every 10 years). Tap water is safe to drink and the food is almost uniformly prepared with high standards of hygiene. It is advisable to take out some health insurance – see Travel Insurance under Documents earlier in this chapter.

Those who would like an in-depth look at health issues in Japan and advice on what to do if you get sick in the country may want to pick up a copy of Meredith Maruyama's *Japan Health Handbook* (December Books, 1997). For more general information, check out Lonely Planet's *Healthy Travel Asia & India*.

A small medical kit is a good thing to carry (see the boxed text), even though most items are readily available in Japan. If you wear glasses it's a good idea to bring a spare pair and your prescription. If you require a particular medication, take an adequate supply as it may not be available locally. Take the prescription with the generic rather than the brand name, which may be unavailable, as it will make getting replacements easier. It's wise to have the prescription with you to show you legally use the medication.

Pharmacies *(kusuriya* or *yakkyoku)* have a good selection of drugs, both Western and Chinese herbal *(kanpō yaku)*. You can usually spot a pharmacy by the stacks of medicinal products in the windows and the pharmacy symbol (a green cross). Most are open standard business hours, though some in nightlife districts and big train stations may stay open until midnight.

Be warned – most pharmacy products are labelled in Japanese. Those who want to know exactly what they're taking should go to the American Pharmacy in Ginza (see Medical Assistance, following).

Although oral contraceptives are available from clinics specialising in medical care for foreigners, it is preferable to bring adequate supplies with you. Condoms are widely available, but visitors are advised to bring their own or buy a foreign brand from the American Pharmacy.

Medical Assistance

The TIC has lists of English-speaking hospitals and doctors in Tokyo. Dental care is widely available, although at steep prices. If you need a medicine not readily available in local pharmacies, try the American Pharmacy (Map 7; ☎ 3271 4034) close to the TIC. Oddly, most drugs in Japan are supplied not by pharmacies but by doctors. Critics say that as a result, doctors tend to over-prescribe and choose the most expensive drugs.

You may want to call the Tokyo Medical Information Service (☎ 5285 8181) for

---

Medical Kit Check List

Following is a list of items to consider including in your medical kit – consult your pharmacist for brands available in your country.

☐ **Aspirin or paracetamol (acetaminophen in the USA)** – for pain or fever

☐ **Antihistamine** – for allergies, eg, hay fever; to ease the itch from insect bites or stings; and to prevent motion sickness

☐ **Cold and flu tablets, throat lozenges and nasal decongestant**

☐ **Multivitamins** – consider for long trips, when dietary vitamin intake may be inadequate

☐ **Antibiotics** – consider including these if you're travelling well off the beaten track; see your doctor, as they must be prescribed, and carry the prescription with you

☐ **Loperamide or diphenoxylate** – 'blockers' for diarrhoea

☐ **Prochlorperazine or metaclopramide** – for nausea and vomiting

☐ **Rehydration mixture** – to prevent dehydration, which may occur, for example, during bouts of diarrhoea; particularly important when travelling with children

☐ **Insect repellent, sunscreen, lip balm and eye drops**

☐ **Calamine lotion, sting relief spray or aloe vera** – to ease irritation from sunburn and insect bites or stings

☐ **Antifungal cream or powder** – for fungal skin infections and thrush

☐ **Antiseptic (such as povidone-iodine)** – for cuts and grazes

☐ **Bandages, Band-Aids (plasters) and other wound dressings**

☐ **Water purification tablets or iodine**

☐ **Scissors, tweezers and a thermometer** – note that mercury thermometers are prohibited by airlines

---

advice about which hospital or clinic can best address your needs. They also provide telephone interpretation if a language barrier would prevent you from receiving emergency care. The service operates for non-emergency cases on weekdays from 9am to 8pm. For emergency cases, you can call weekdays from 7am to 10pm, on weekends from 9am to 10pm. In addition to English, there are also staff on hand who can speak Spanish, Thai, Korean and Chinese.

The Association of Medical Doctors for Asia International Medical Information Center (☎ 5285 8088) is a similar service, open on weekdays from 9am to 5pm, closed weekends and public holidays.

If you need medical help in English, the Tokyo Medical and Surgical Clinic (☎ 3436 3028) in Kamiyachō on the Hibiya subway line has foreign doctors. Appointments can be made Monday to Friday from 9am to 4.45pm and until 1pm on Saturday. The International Clinic (☎ 3583 7831) in Roppongi also provides services in English. It is open from 9am to 5pm Monday to Friday, and to noon on Saturday. When making your appointment, be sure to ask for exact directions to get to the clinics. Both clinics are closed Sunday and holidays.

Some other clinics include:

Hibiya Clinic (☎ 3502 2681) open Monday to Friday, 9.30am to noon and 1pm to 5pm; close to Hibiya Park
King Clinic (☎ 3409 0764) open 9am to 4.45pm, closed Saturday and Wednesday afternoon; Harajuku
Ojima Dental Clinic (☎ 3268 8818) open Monday to Friday, 10am to 1pm and 2pm to 6pm; emergency calls also accepted; Shinjuku
Totsuka MT Clinic (☎ 045-862 0050) open 9am to 7pm (to 4pm Sunday); obstetrics, gynaecology, paediatrics; Yokohama

Emergencies

Dial ☎ 110 for police or ☎ 119 for a fire or an ambulance, but English may not be spoken. (Emergency services will usually only react quickly if you speak Japanese.)

For information on your nearest medical treatment centre, you can ring the information desk of the Tokyo Fire Department (☎ 3212 2323); English is spoken. There's also the Tokyo English Lifeline, or TELL (☎ 5721 4347), and Japan Helpline (☎ 0120-461 997), a 24-hour emergency number. Don't clog the line unless you really do have an emergency.

You can also go to a *kōban* (police box) for help in an emergency. These are neighbourhood police stations that can be found on street corners and near railway stations. Kōban have a glass front and a door which is usually left open to the street. You may see some police officers inside; other times they are hidden in the back. Don't visit a kōban unless you have a real problem, as many police look at a visit from a foreigner as a good chance to check their documents, generally waste their time and possibly even to collar a scapegoat.

Counselling & Advice

Adjusting to life in Japan can be tough, but there are several places to turn for help. The TELL phone service (☎ 5721 4347) offers confidential and anonymous help. For longer-term residents, there is also the Foreign Residents Advisory Center (☎ 5320 7744), which is operated by the Tokyo metropolitan government; open weekdays.

TOILETS & PUBLIC BATHS

In Japan you will come across both Western-style and Asian squat toilets. At the latter, the correct position when squatting is facing the hood. Make sure the contents of your pockets don't spill out. Toilet paper isn't always provided, so carry tissues. In homes and ryokan, separate toilet slippers are often provided just inside the door.

Public toilets are almost always free in Japan. The kanji for 'toilet' is お手洗い; for 'men' it is 男; and for 'women' it is 女.

WOMEN TRAVELLERS

By international standards Tokyo is an extremely safe city for women travellers. However, there is a well publicised type of molester known as a *chikan* (masher), who travels packed trains in order to touch female travellers in the close confines of rush-hour

FACTS FOR THE VISITOR

traffic. While Japanese women seem to put up with this or simply move away if possible, another option is to grab the offending hand and shout 'Chikan!'.

Note that some public toilets are not sex-segregated. This does not usually result in any problems, but, if you prefer, there's usually a sex-segregated toilet somewhere nearby.

It is not a good idea to walk in certain areas alone at night. These areas are basically those which *any* solitary traveller would avoid at night – dark alleys, bar districts and the like. If it looks dangerous, go another way.

Hitchhiking is a definite no-go for the solitary female traveller.

GAY & LESBIAN TRAVELLERS

For the traveller, Tokyo is more hip and Westernised than its Asian counterparts when it comes to the gay and lesbian scenes. This doesn't mean it's necessarily easy to break into the local scene – foreigers will find some bars unfriendly – but there is an active international scene that includes clubs, bars, newsletters, support groups etc.

The magazine *Outrageous Tokyo*, which lists gay-friendly associations, clubs and events, is a good starting point. It should be available at HMV in Shibuya and Shinjuku, and at Shinjuku's Virgin Megastore (Map 3).

International (Gay) Friends (☎ 5693 4569; English is spoken) has meetings on the third Saturday of every month. You can write to International (Gay) Friends for more information at IF Passport, CPO Box 180, Tokyo 100-91.

The following Web sites might be of some assistance when you're planning your trip:

Gay Guide to Tokyo 🕢 nobuq.tripod.com/q.html
Gaynet Japan 🕢 www.gnj.or.jp/gaynet/
Gay Scene @ Japan 🕢 members.tripod.co.jp/gsj/
Gay Tokyo 🕢 www.geocities.com/
 WestHollywood/4248/
Planet Rainbow 🕢 www.cyberoz.net/Dorothy/
 planet.RAINBOW/
Utopia 🕢 www.utopia-asia.com

DISABLED TRAVELLERS

Many new buildings have access ramps, traffic lights have speakers playing melodies when it is safe to cross, train platforms have raised dots and lines to provide guidance, but there is much in Tokyo that can be downright dangerous, depending on your disability.

Tokyo's congested rail system is bad enough if you are nimble on your feet. If you are going to travel on a train and need assistance, ask one of the station workers as you enter the station. There are cars on most lines that have areas set aside for those in wheelchairs. Those with other physical disabilities can use one of the seats set aside near the train exits, called *yūsen-zaseki*.

One indispensable guide is *Accessible Tokyo* put out by the Japanese Red Cross (☎ 3438 1311, fax 3432 5507). You can write to them for a copy at Japanese Red Cross Language Service Volunteers c/o Volunteers Division, Japanese Red Cross Society, 1-1-3 Shiba Daimon, Minato-ku, Tokyo 105, Japan.

Some other travel-information sources for the mobility-impaired are:

Access Foundation (☎ 1-516-887 5798) PO
 Box 356, Malverne, NY 11565, USA
Mobility USA (☎ 1-541-343 1284) PO Box
 1076, Eugene, OR 97440, USA
Society for the Advancement of Travel for the
 Handicapped (SATH) (☎ 1-718-858 5483),
 26 Court St, Brooklyn, NY 11242, USA

SENIOR TRAVELLERS

Japan is an excellent place for senior travellers, and Japanese seniors themselves are among the most active travellers in the world.

To qualify for widely available senior discounts, you have to be over 60 or 65, depending upon the place/company. One interesting deal offered by JR for senior couples travelling together is the 'Full Moon Green Pass' which costs (for two people) ¥80,500 for five days, ¥99,900 for a week and ¥124,400 for 12 days. These are on sale at major JR stations from 1 September to 31 May and can be used on consecutive days from 1 October to 31 May, excluding 28 December to 6 January, 21 March to 5 April and 27 April to 6 May (Japanese peak travel periods). These are valid on all JR lines in Japan, including most shinkansen (bullet trains), and entitle you to unlimited travel in Green (1st class) reserved seats and sleeping berths, and the Narita express. To qualify, you must be a married couple whose combined age exceeds 88 (passports can prove this). A ¥5000 discount applies to those over 70.

Japanese domestic airlines (JAS, JAL and ANA) offer senior discounts of about 25% on some flights. For more information, contact the airlines (see the Airlines section in the Getting There & Away chapter).

In addition to travel discounts, you can get discounts on entry fees at most temples, museums and movie theatres.

TOKYO FOR CHILDREN

Tokyo is a relatively easy and safe place to travel with children. One of the few difficulties is the constant attention paid to small children. Otherwise, you will find lots of services, including nappy-changing tables in newer public bathrooms and trains, free child minding at big department stores and widely available discounts for children.

There are a myriad of ways to keep kids amused, and a lot of children's entertainment in Tokyo is so lavish and ingenious that it's fun for accompanying adults too. Just don't start elbowing kids out of the way.

For ideas, see the 'Tokyo with Children' boxed text in the Things to See & Do chapter and Kids' Stuff in the Shopping chapter (for some amazing toy shops).

For general advice on travel with children, pick up Lonely Planet's *Travel with Children* by Maureen Wheeler.

USEFUL ORGANISATIONS
Clubs & Associations

No matter what your interest, there is probably a club or association for it in Tokyo.

English-language telephone directories *City Source* and *Japan Yellow Pages* are valuable resources. Paul Ferguson's *Networking in Tokyo: A Guide to English Speaking Clubs and Societies* and the American

Chamber of Commerce in Japan's *Living in Japan* are useful lifestyle guides.

Embassies and chambers of commerce, along with a myriad of international sister-city and friendship societies, stage activities open to visitors and residents in Tokyo. The embassies send direct mail to anyone who has registered with them, and there are notices in the *Daily Yomiuri*, the *Japan Times* and on Tokyo Q (W tokyoq.com). Also check the *Tokyo Journal* – there's everything from the Breakfast Toastmasters Club to the Japan Tropical Forest Action Network.

Conversation Lounges

Special clubs have been formed to give Japanese the opportunity to meet foreigners (English-speaking ones at least). Activities generally centre around a lounge or coffee shop, entry to which costs foreigners little or nothing – it is the Japanese who pay.

Mickey House (Map 2; ☎ 3209 9686) is an 'English bar' that offers free tea and coffee, reasonably priced beer and food. It is a good place to meet young Japanese as well as long-term *gaijin* residents. Take the Big Box exit of Takadanobaba station and walk straight ahead. Mickey House is on the 4th floor of a building on the left, across the street from Starbucks.

A similar club worth a look is the Corn Popper Club (☎ 3715 4473) in Ebisu.

Home Visit System

The home visit system is publicised in JNTO pamphlets and provides visitors to Tokyo with a chance to spend time with a Japanese family. Visits take place in the evening, and while dinner is not usually served, the hosts will often provide tea and sweets. It is polite to bring a small gift with you.

Home visits can be organised by the Tokyo branch of the Home Visit Service (☎ 3502 1461). There is also a branch in Yokohama (☎ 045-641 5824).

LIBRARIES

Tokyo has quite a few libraries with material in European languages. The British Council (Map 8; ☎ 3235 8031) in Iidabashi has a good collection of books and magazines. It's open from 10am to 8pm, closed weekends. The American Center (☎ 3436 0901) has a library in the Shiba-kōen area (Map 7). The library is open from 10.30am to 6.30pm, closed weekends.

The Japan Foundation Library (Map 1; ☎ 3263 4504) in Kioichō is open only to foreigners and holds some 30,000 English books. It's open from 10am to 5pm, closed Sunday and Monday.

The most extensive library in Tokyo is the National Diet Library (Map 7; ☎ 3581 2331), close to Nagatachō subway station (with a branch in Ueno). It has more than 1.3 million books in Western languages. It's open from 9.30am to 5pm, closed Sunday.

For the World Magazine Gallery, see the Ginza section of the Things to See & Do chapter.

The Bibliotheque de la Maison Franco-Japonaise (☎ 3291 1144) is close to Ochanomizu station; open from 10am to noon and 1pm to 6pm, closed Saturday. The Goethe Institut Tokyo Bibliotek (☎ 3583 7280) is open from noon to 6pm (8pm on Friday), closed on weekends. It's close to Aoyama-itchōme subway station on the Ginza line.

JETRO's head office (Map 7; ☎ 3582 5522) in Toranomon also has an excellent reading library. There are also libraries operated by the Keizai Kōhō Center (☎ 3201 1415) in Ōtemachi, chambers of commerce and embassies.

Other libraries include:

Asia-Africa Library (☎ 0422-44 4640) 5-14-16 Shinkawa, Mitaka-shi
Asian Productivity Organization Library (☎ 3408 7221) 8-4-14 Akasaka, Minato-ku
Institute of Developing Economics Library (☎ 3353 4231) 42 Ichigaya Honmurachō, Shinjuku-ku
Japan Information Center of Science and Technology (JICST) Library (☎ 3976 4141) 2-8-18 Asahichō, Nerima-ku
Japan Textbook Research Center Library (☎ 5606 4311) 1-9-28 Sengoku, Kōtō-ku
Japan-Soviet Library (☎ 3429 8239) 1-11-2 Kyodo, Setagaya-ku
Keidanren (Japan Federation of Economic Organizations) Library (☎ 3279 1411) 1-9-4 Ōtemachi, Chiyoda-ku

Museum of Modern Japanese Literature Library (☎ 3468 4181) 4-3-55 Komaba, Meguro-ku
National Archives (☎ 3214 0621) 3-2 Kitanomaru-kōen, Chiyoda-ku
Tokyo Metropolitan Central Library (☎ 3442 8451) 5-7-13 Minami-Azabu, Minato-ku

CAMPUSES

Tokyo is the educational capital of Japan, and colleges and universities are thick on the ground. It's hard getting into the libraries, but the cafeterias are another story. Finding them's the problem. If this doesn't deter you, here are details for a few of Tokyo's major universities:

Meiji University (☎ 3296 4545) 1-1 Kanda Surugadai, Chiyoda-ku; Map 8
Nihon University (☎ 5275 8000) 4-8-24 Kudan Minami, Chiyoda-ku; Map 8
University of Tokyo (☎ 3812 2111) 7-3-1 Hongo, Bunkyō-ku; Map 9
Waseda University (☎ 3203 4141) 1-104 Totsukamachi, Shinjuku-ku; Map 2

CULTURAL CENTRES

Cultural centres in Tokyo act as a focal point for the national group they represent, and usually have good bulletin boards, events, small libraries and language classes.

The British Council (☎ 3235 8031) 1-2 Kagurazaka, Shinjuku-ku; Map 8
Goethe Institut Tokyo (☎ 3584 3201) 7-5-56 Akasaka, Minato-ku
Institute Franco-Japonais du Tokyo (☎ 5261 3933) 15 Ichigaya Funagawarachō, Shinjuku-ku; Map 8
Sweden Center Japan KK (☎ 3403 1351) 6-11-9 Roppongi, Minato-ku

DANGERS & ANNOYANCES

Tokyo is generally an extremely safe city, though it does have a few annoyances. Air pollution, for which the city used to be famous (to the point of having oxygen vending machines on street corners), has improved a lot, though it can become somewhat dirty during peak hour traffic. You might also find blaring public announcements and loudspeaker advertising annoying.

Though Tokyo is infinitely better than most other Japanese cities in this respect, you may encounter police who treat foreigners as second-class citizens. This is usually not a problem unless you put yourself in the position of having to deal with them – like visiting a kōban (police box), or actually committing an offence.

If passive smoking worries you, a lot of restaurants and coffee shops are going to be uncomfortable. Nonsmoking areas are a lot more common these days, but Tokyo isn't Singapore. If you are intent on finding clear air, John Kennerdell's *Tokyo Restaurant Guide* lists 23 good restaurants where you can enjoy a smoke-free meal.

Lost & Found

One wonderful thing about Tokyo is that lost property is more often than not returned by the finder. If you've left something on a train, in a taxi or at a restaurant, don't give it up as gone for good. For items lost on JR trains and at stations, ring the JR East Infoline (☎ 3423 0111); for TRTA subway trains and stations, ring its Lost & Found Center (☎ 3834 5577); Toei subway trains, stations and buses have a Lost & Found Service Corner (☎ 5600 2020); and for property left in taxis, ring the Tokyo Taxi Kindaika Center (☎ 3648 0300).

Theft

The low incidence of theft and crime in general in Japan is often noted; of course, theft does occur, and its unlikelihood is no reason for carelessness. Airports are reputed to be among the worst places in Japan for pickpockets and other sneak thieves, so take extra care in these places.

Earthquakes

Earthquakes are a risk throughout Japan, but the Tokyo region is particularly prone to them. There is no point in being paranoid, but it is worth checking the emergency exits in your hotel and being aware of earthquake safety procedures. These include turning off anything that might cause a fire, opening a door or window to secure your exit and sheltering in a doorway or under a sturdy

The Big One

Every Tokyo resident's worst fear – the next 'big one' – became an even more tangible threat on 17 January 1995, when Kōbe was devastated by an earthquake that measured 7.2 on the Richter scale. People began to wonder what would happen if a similar or even stronger quake hit sprawling, densely populated Tokyo.

Though almost imperceptible earthquakes happen nearly every day, the last one to give Tokyo a major shakedown was the 1923 'Great Kantō Earthquake'. Although Tokyo is not the city it was in 1923, the prospect of another major quake remains a grim one. Still, earthquake prediction is hardly an exact science, and no-one is sure if Tokyo is overdue for a major quake or not. Whatever the case, the recent Kōbe quake was a reminder to the people of Tokyo and elsewhere in Japan that the mighty geological forces that created their islands are still at work. And the devastation in central Kōbe reminded them that no amount of earthquake preparedness is too much.

東京 東京 東京 東京 東京 東京 東京

table. If an earthquake occurs, NHK will broadcast information and instructions in English on all its TV and radio networks. Tune to Channel 1 on your television, or to NHK (639kHz AM) or FEN (810kHz AM) on your radio.

LEGAL MATTERS

The police are granted extraordinary powers, particularly considering Tokyo is one of the safest societies around. This is fine until you find yourself on the wrong side of the law (or are suspected of being so). If this is the case, it will be an unpleasant experience. Japanese police have the right to detain a suspect without charging them for up to three days, after which a prosecutor can decide to extend this for another 20 days. They can also choose whether to allow you to phone your embassy or lawyer, though you should insist that you will not cooperate in any way until you can make such a call.

Tokyo Blossoms

Tokyo isn't the greenest city in the world, but there are quite a few parks and gardens scattered around, and even a few tree-lined streets.

Autumn Foliage Tokyo's trees are particularly beautiful during the autumn foliage season (koyō), which runs from about mid-October to early November. Look for the maple, which goes through a minor spectrum of yellows and oranges before climaxing in a fiery red. The best spots are:

Koishikawa Kōraku-en (Map 1) North of the central city, with its lovely pond and surrounding gardens, this may be Tokyo's best foliage spot.
Ueno-kōen (Map 9) Famous for its spring cherry blossoms, this park is also a fine foliage spot.
Kitanomaru-kōen (Map 8) Just north of the Imperial Palace, this pleasant park is a great place for an autumn stroll or picnic.
Omote-sandō (Map 4) One of Tokyo's few tree-lined avenues, this is most pleasant on Sunday, when the street is closed to motorised traffic.
Shinjuku-gyoen (Map 3) This spacious garden contains many fine foliage spots, particularly in the Western-style garden.
Yoyogi-kōen (Map 4) With ginko, zelvoka and cherry trees, this is a lovely place for an autumn stroll.
Yasukuni-jinja (Map 8) The tree-lined approach to the shrine is beautiful in October/November.

Plum Blossom Viewing Although overshadowed by their more famous cousins, the cherry blossoms, plum blossoms are still dearly loved by the Japanese as early harbingers of spring. These pink and white blossoms usually start to bud in February and bloom from late February to early March. If it's cold, a stroll under the blossoms will suffice, but if it's warm, bring out a blanket and have a plum blossom party!

東京 東京 東京 東京 東京 東京 東京 東京 東京 東京 東京 東京 東京 東京 東京

Your embassy is the first place you should call if given the chance.

Police will speak almost no English, so you should insist that an interpreter (tsuyakusha) be summoned. Police are legally bound to provide one before proceeding with any questioning. If you speak Japanese, it's best to deny it and stay with your native language.

If you are taken in on a drug offence, get legal representation as soon as possible. Police have been known to use torture in extracting confessions from suspected drug offenders, and having a lawyer will at least make them think twice. Drug laws are very strict – do *not* be tempted in Japan. Other things like public drunkenness, littering and jaywalking are usually ignored.

As a woman dealing with police, sexist treatment is not uncommon. Try not to see police alone, or be left alone with them, and you should let someone know where you are. At the same time, police at kōban (police boxes) are usually friendly, helpful sources of information.

For legal counselling in English and some other languages, call the Human Rights Center Information Line (☎ 3581 2302) from noon to 5pm on weekdays. The Gaikokujin Komarigoto Sōdan (Foreigners' Crisis Consultation) centre (☎ 3503 8484) can provide telephone interpretation with police if needed.

BUSINESS HOURS

Shops are typically open seven days a week from around 10am to 8pm. Department stores close earlier, usually 6.30pm or 7pm, and close one weekday. Department stores close on different days of the week, so that even if, say, Mitsukoshi is closed, Isetan will be open. Large companies usually work a 9am to 5pm five-day week; some also operate on Saturday morning. Public offices also work a 9am to 5pm schedule, and sometimes close for lunch between noon and 1pm.

Tokyo Blossoms

Hanami The climax of spring, and perhaps the most celebrated moment of the Japanese year, is the arrival of the cherry blossoms. This generally occurs some time in April, and the entire nation erupts in cherry blossom mania.

Hanami (cherry-blossom viewing) parties continue through the roughly week-long flowering season, from the earliest buds to the last clinging blossoms. Both daytime parties and moonlit soirees are popular. *Sake* plays an important role, as do singing and dancing (portable *karaoki* machines often appear).

At popular hanami spots the best sites are often taken by people who have camped out overnight for them. But there is always somewhere left to sit, and a stroll in a Tokyo park on a clear spring day through a riot of pink blossoms and boisterous parties is unforgettable.

With over 1000 trees of several varieties, Ueno-kōen (Map 9) is the hanami capital of Japan. A stroll through the frenzied grounds is a chance to see the Japanese at their most uninhibited. Here are some other spots which may yield a little more breathing room:

Shinjuku-gyoen (Map 3) A prime cherry-blossom attraction, this garden has several varieties of cherry trees, including *yaezakura* (double-blossoming cherries).
Yasukuni-jinja (Map 8) There are more than 1000 cherry trees in the grounds of the shrine; check out the cherry trees lining the nearby Imperial Palace moat as well.
Yoyogi-kōen (Map 4) There is plenty of space here to admire the park's 500 or so cherry trees.
Hama Rikyū Onshi-teien (Map 7) There are about 100 cherry trees here, including wild cherry trees. An admission fee keeps the crowds at bay and the rest of the garden is pleasant as well.
Sumida-kōen (Map 9) Located on both banks of the Sumida-gawa river near Asakusa, lots of trees and the river somewhat offset the concrete surroundings of this garden.
Shiba-kōen/Zō-jō-ji (Map 7) About 100 trees are found here, with the temple for a backdrop.

東京 東京 東京 東京 東京 東京 東京 東京 東京 東京 東京 東京 東京 東京 東京 東京

Most government-run attractions (such as major museums) usually open from 9.30am to 4.30pm. Note that most ticket offices close half an hour before actual closing time. Private galleries, such as those in department stores, tend to open later and close later. Typically, restaurants open for three hours at lunch (about 11.30am to 2.30pm) and four or five hours in the evening (6pm to 10.30pm), though there are abundant exceptions. Cheaper, family-run restaurants often stay open from around 11.30am to 11.30pm, particularly those around railway stations.

For bank hours, see Banking Hours under Money, earlier in this chapter.

PUBLIC HOLIDAYS

National holidays are spread across the year, but beware of the three holidays on 29 April, and 3 and 5 May. These make up 'Golden Week', when Japanese are all on international flights or long train and bus journeys, making it very difficult to get around or out of the country. Another difficult time to travel is during O-bon (Festival of the Dead) from 13 to 16 August, when most Japanese try to get back to their home town.

On most public holidays, essential services and stores remain open, and getting around and eating is not a problem. The one major exception is the New Year's holiday period, from 31 December to 2 or 3 January. During this time, about the only places open are convenience stores and fast-food joints; if you don't want to survive on potato chips and fries, make appropriate preparations.

Here is the list of public holidays:

Ganjitsu (New Year's Day)	1 January
Seijin-no-hi (Adult's Day)	15 January
Kenkoku Kinen-bi (National Foundation Day)	11 February
Shunbun-no-hi (Spring Equinox Day)	21 March (approx)

Midori-no-hi (Green Day)	29 April
Kenpo Kinen-bi	
(Constitution Memorial Day)	3 May
Kodomo-no-hi (Children's Day)	5 May
Umi no hi (Marine Day)	20 July
Keiro-no-hi	
(Respect-for-the-Aged Day)	15 September
Shūbun-no-hi	
(Autumn Equinox Day)	23 September (approx)
Taiiku-no-hi (Sports Day)	10 October
Bunka-no-hi (Culture Day)	3 November
Kinrō Kansha-no-hi	
(Labour Thanksgiving Day)	23 November
Tennō Tanjōbi	
(Emperor's Birthday)	23 December

FESTIVALS

The following is a list of the major festivals celebrated in and around Tokyo. There are so many that, no matter when you visit, you're bound to be in time for something. While festivals (*matsuri*) in Japan are usually nonparticipatory affairs, many other special events call for full participation – this often translates as drinking, which reaches its peak during the New Year's and *hanami* (blossom viewing) seasons.

January–February

Ganjitsu (New Year's Day) 1 January; it is customary for Japanese to visit Buddhist and Shintō shrines to pray for luck in the coming year. Go to Meiji-jingū Shrine, Sensō-ji Temple or Yasukuni-jinja Shrine. The day after New Year's Day is one of the two occasions each year when the Imperial Palace is open to the public. Enter the inner gardens by Nijū-bashi between 9am and 3.30pm.

Dezome-shiki 6 January; firemen dressed in Edo-period costumes put on a parade involving acrobatic stunts on top of bamboo ladders. The parade takes place on Chūō-dōri in Harumi from 10am.

Seijin-no-hi (Adult's Day) 15 January; a traditional display of archery is held at Meiji-jingū.

Setsubun 3 or 4 February; held at Zōjō-ji, Kanda-jinja and Sensō-ji. Sensō-ji offers the added attraction of a classical dance.

Hari-kuyō usually early February; a typically quirky Japanese festival held for pins and needles that have been broken in the preceding year. At Sensō-ji, women lay their pins and needles to rest by 'burying' them in tofu and radishes.

Matsuri

The Japanese year is marked by a colourful abundance of festivals, or *matsuri*, and nowhere more so than in Tokyo. Matsuri are an expression of Shintō, and were originally held in farming communities according to the seasonal planting and harvesting of rice. Spring festivals were held to supplicate the local gods (*kami*) and to secure a plentiful harvest. Autumn festivals were held in thanks and celebration of a rich harvest. Summer and winter matsuri were less common, though summer festivals were sometimes held to ward off the natural disasters that could ravage a crop before harvest. Summer matsuri became a more common event with the rise of large urban settlements like Edo, where they were held in the hope of circumventing pestilence and plague.

There are many elements to matsuri. One that is common to nearly all is a boisterous crowd of scantily clad men puffing and heaving beneath the weight of a portable shrine (*mikoshi*). In Tokyo's two-yearly Kanda Festival, 200 mikoshi are paraded through the streets. Apparently the gods also delight in revelry of all kinds, providing an excuse for the swilling of sake, archery contests, horse-riding displays and dancing. The Tōshō-gū Grand Shrine Festival held at Nikkō annually on 17 and 18 May also provides a good opportunity to see these traditional entertainments. In mid-May, earthy Asakusa boasts the boisterous Sanja Matsuri.

Purists might complain that the contemporary urban festivals of Japan have abandoned their traditional origins in favour of an excuse for a huge ceremonial piss-up, yet they are still tremendous fun and wonderfully photogenic.

東京 東京 東京 東京 東京 東京 東京

March–April

Hina Matsuri (Doll Festival) 3 March (main celebration); from mid-February onwards, a doll fair is held in Asakusabashi – check with the TIC for exact details.

Kinryū no Mai 18 March, a dance is held at Sensō-ji to celebrate the discovery of the golden image of Kannon that now rests there. Two or three dances are performed during the day.

Gōhan Shiki 2 April; a rice-harvesting festival held at Rinnō-ji, Nikkō, in which men (in days past, they would have been *samurai* lords) are forced to eat great quantities of rice in a tribute to the bounty supplied by the gods. Sacred dances are also performed by priests as an accompaniment to the ceremonial pig-out.

Hanami (Blossom Viewing) early to mid-April; this is one festival you can't help hearing about if you're in Japan when the blossoms come out.

Kamakura Matsuri second and third Sunday of April; a whole week of celebrations centred around Tsurugaoka Hachiman-gū in Kamakura.

Hana Matsuri (Buddha's Birthday) 8 April; celebrations are held at Buddhist temples all over Japan. In Tokyo, celebrations take place at Sensō-ji and Zōjō-ji, among others.

Jibeta Matsuri 15 April; Kawasaki's famous festival celebrates the vanquishing of a sharp-toothed demon residing in a young maiden, by means of an iron phallus (it's true, really!). The festival starts with a procession, followed by a re-enactment of the forging, and is rounded off with a banquet. The action takes place close to Kawasaki-Taishi station.

Yayoi Matsuri 16–17 April; a procession of portable shrines is held at Futāra-san-jinja in Nikkō.

Ueno Tōshō-gū Taisai 17 April; traditional music and dance at Ueno's Tōshō-gū in memory of Tokugawa Ieyasu.

May–June

Kanda Matsuri mid-May; this festival is held on odd-numbered years on the Saturday and Sunday closest to 15 May, and is a traditional Edo festival that celebrates a Tokugawa battle victory. A whole range of activities takes place at Kanda-jinja.

Kuro-fune Matsuri (Black Ship Festival) 16–18 May; held in Shimoda on the Izu-hantō Peninsula. It commemorates the first landing of American Commodore Perry with parades and fireworks displays.

Tōshō-gū Shrine Grand Festival 17–18 May; Nikkō's most important annual festival, featuring horseback archery and a 1000-strong costumed re-enactment of the delivery of Tokugawa Ieyasu's remains to Nikkō.

Sanja Matsuri third Friday, Saturday and Sunday of May; at Sensō-ji up to 100 *mikoshi* (portable shrines) are carried by participants (many *yakuza*, often sporting tattoos) through the area near the temple.

Sannō-sai 10–16 June; street stalls, traditional music and dancing, and processions of mikoshi are all part of this Edo festival, held at Hie-jinja, near Akasaka-mitsuke subway station.

July–October

Tarai-nori Kyōsō first Sunday of July; held in Itō on Izu-hantō; a race that involves paddling down the Matsukawa in washtubs using rice scoops as oars; what it's in aid of, no-one seems to know.

Tsukudajima Sumiyoshi-jinja Sunday closest to 7 July; a three-yearly festival, with activities centred around the Sumiyoshi-jinja; it includes dragon dances and mikoshi parades.

O-bon 13–15 July; this major festival takes place at a time when, according to Buddhist belief, the dead briefly revisit the earth. Dances are held and lanterns lighted in their memory. In Tokyo *bon odori* dances are held in different locations around town.

Sumida-gawa Hanabi Taikai last Saturday of July; the biggest fireworks display of its kind in Tokyo is held on the Sumida-gawa in Asakusa.

Ashino-ko Kosui Matsuri 31 July; this festival is held at Hakone-jinja in Moto-Hakone, and features fireworks displays over Ashino-ko.

Fukagawa Hachiman Matsuri 15 August; another three-yearly, three-day Edo festival, when foolhardy mikoshi-bearers charge through 8km of frenzied crowds who dash water on them. The action takes place at Tomioka Hachiman-gū, next to Monzennakachō subway station on the Tōzai line.

Hakone Daimonji-yaki Festival 16 August; in Hakone, torches are lit on Mt Myojoga-take so that they form the shape of the kanji character for 'great' or 'large'.

Asakusa Samba Carnival late August (check with the TIC for exact dates); one of Tokyo's most un-Japanese matsuri. Put on by Brazilian-Japanese returnees, it includes a parade down Kaminarimon-dōri by festively (scantily) attired dancers, and attracts a huge crowd.

Hachimangū Matsuri 14–15 September; festivities include a procession of mikoshi, followed by a display of horseback archery on the 16th.

Ningyō-kuyō 25 September; childless couples offer dolls to Kannon in the hope that she will bless them with children. More interesting for spectators is the ceremonial burning by priests of all the dolls that have been held in the temple precinct from the previous year. The ceremony takes place at Kiyomizu-dō in Ueno-kōen from 2pm to 3.30pm.

Furusato Tokyo Matsuri (Metropolitan Citizen's Day) first Saturday and Sunday in October; a wide range of activities is held at different locations around town. In particular, check out Asakusa's Sensō-ji and Ueno-kōen.

Oeshiki 12 October; held in commemoration of Nichiren (1222–82), founder of the Nichiren sect of Buddhism. On that night, people bearing large lanterns and paper flower arrangements make their way to Hommon-ji. The nearest station is Ikegami station on the Tōkyū Ikegami line.

Tōshō-gū Autumn Festival 17 October; in Nikkō, the equestrian archery performance staged during May's Nikkō's grand festival is held again.

Meiji Reidaisai 30 October to 3 November; held at Meiji-jingū in commemoration of the Meiji emperor's birthday. Particularly interesting are displays of horseback archery by riders dressed in traditional clothes. Other events include classical music and dance.

November–December

Hakone Daimyō Gyōretsu 3 November; a re-enactment of a feudal lord's procession by 400 costumed locals; held in Hakone.

Shichi-go-san (Seven-Five-Three Festival) 15 November; as its name suggests, this is for children aged seven, five and three. They make a colourful sight, dressed in traditional clothes and taken to several shrines, notably Meiji-jingū, Yasukuni-jinja and Sannō Hie-jinja.

Gishi-sai 14 December; commemorating the 47 *rōnin* (masterless samurai) who committed *seppuku* (ritual suicide) after avenging the death of their master. The activities involve a parade of warriors to Sengaku-ji – the rōnins' burial place – and a memorial service from 7.30pm.

WORK

Unless you are highly qualified, Japan is not a good place to look for work. Japanese employers have become more discriminating, and the market is increasingly saturated with young hopefuls looking for a bit-part in what's left of the Japanese economic success story. Do your job hunting before you arrive in Japan – foreign professionals are overwhelmingly recruited from overseas. Arriving in Tokyo with a smart suit and an impressive CV is no guarantee against spending a couple of months attending interviews and watching your savings rapidly disappear.

The same is true of English teaching. If you don't have a college or university degree, forget it – you cannot be issued a working visa to teach without one. Even people with MA degrees in Teaching English as a Foreign Language (TEFL) often spend a month or so answering advertisements before they finally get accepted somewhere. If you want to teach in Japan, try getting a placement from your home country.

Besides English, it may be possible to find work if you have teaching experience and credentials for another major language like French, Spanish, German, Chinese or Korean. But as with English, openings are scarce and go only to those with real ability.

Many foreigners work in the entertainment industry as dancers, singers, hostesses and bartenders. The problem with most of these jobs is that they do not qualify you for a working visa, and you are going to have to live with the constant threat of immigration problems. Some skilled workers also find jobs in the construction industry, both as labourers and carpenters, though the present sluggish economy has severely reduced openings. Skilled proofreaders, translators and editors are also in demand in Tokyo, but you can bet that most of the good jobs are taken by those who have been in the city for a long time.

If you aren't dissuaded by all this, the best place to look for employment is in the Monday edition of the *Japan Times*. You can also check the want ads in the *Tokyo Journal* or the *Tokyo Classified*. Unless you plan on working illegally, which some do, you are going to need to get a work visa.

Morning commuters at Shinjuku station

Acres of neon lights

Efficient use of space at a Tokyo capsule hotel

Dazzling neon signs in the Kabukichō red-light district

MICHAEL TAYLOR

Flag on Sumida-gawa boat

MARTIN MOOS

Trainee *sumō* wrestlers ham it up for the camera – Kantō

JOHN HAY

Traditional prayer boards

MARTIN MOOS

Tokyo Tower with the Shinjuku skyscrapers in the background

Getting There & Away

AIR
Airports
Tokyo is serviced by two major airports, Narita and Haneda. All international carriers with the exception of China Airlines fly to/from Narita airport. The bulk of domestic air traffic goes through Haneda. Fortunately, the two airports are connected by a regular bus service. Flights to and from Narita are usually the cheapest way in or out of Japan, but you may find a rare deal to Nagoya, two hours west of Tokyo by *shinkansen* (bullet train) or to Osaka's Kansai international airport (KIX; four hours west of Tokyo by shinkansen) for less. As a rule, Tokyo-bound travellers should fly into Nagoya or Osaka *only* when it means a saving of over ¥30,000, since this is at least what you'd spend on a round-trip train fare to these airports.

For details about Narita and Haneda airports, including check-in procedures and transport, see the Getting Around chapter.

Departure Tax
There is a ¥2040 departure tax at Narita airport, but it is included in the price of your ticket, while all those lucky people flying China Airlines from Haneda airport get out of the country for nothing.

Airline Offices
Following is a list of the major airline offices in Tokyo. All have a 03 prefix except where an alternative prefix is specified:

Aeroflot (☎ 3434 9671) No 2 Matsuda Bldg, 3-4-8 Toranomon, Minato-ku
Air China (☎ 5251 0711) AO1 Bldg, 3-2-7 Akasaka, Minato-ku
Air France (☎ 3475 1511) 1-1-1 Minami Aoyama, Minato-ku
Air India (☎ 3214 1981) Hibiya Park Bldg, 1-8-1 Yūrakuchō, Chiyoda-ku
Air New Zealand (☎ 3287 1641) Shin-Kokusai Bldg, 3-4-1 Marunouchi, Chiyoda-ku
Alitalia (☎ 5166 9111) Tokyo Club Bldg, 3-2-6 Kasumigaseki, Chiyoda-ku

All Nippon Airways (ANA; ☎ 3592 3055, international toll-free ☎ 0120-029 333, domestic toll-free ☎ 0120-029 222) Kasumigaseki Bldg, 3-2-5 Kasumigaseki, Chiyoda-ku
American Airlines (☎ 3214 2111) Nichirei Higashi-Ginza Bldg, 6-19-20 Tsukiji, Chūō-ku
Asiana Airlines (☎ 5572 7664) Ryuen Bldg, 1-3-1 Shiba-kōen, Minato-ku
Austrian Airlines (☎ 3597 6100) Kokusai Shin-Akasaka Bldg, East Tower, 2-14-7 Akasaka, Minato-ku
Biman Bangladesh Airlines (☎ 3502 7922) Kasumigaseki Bldg, 3-2-5 Kasumigaseki, Chiyoda-ku
British Airways (☎ 3222 6801, 3593 8811) Sanshin Bldg, 1-4-1 Yūrakuchō, Chiyoda-ku
Canadian Airlines International (☎ 3281 7426) Hibiya Park Bldg, 1-8-1 Yūrakuchō, Chiyoda-ku
Cathay Pacific Airways (☎ 3504 1531) Tōhō Twin Tower Bldg, 1-5-2 Yūrakuchō, Chiyoda-ku
China Airlines (☎ 3436 1661) Sumitomo Bldg, 1-12-16 Shiba-Daimon, Minato-ku
China Eastern Airlines (☎ 3506 1166) AO1 Bldg, 3-2-7 Akasaka, Minato-ku
Continental Micronesia (☎ 3508 6411) Kokusai Bldg, 3-1-1 Marunouchi, Chiyoda-ku
Delta Air Lines (☎ 5275 7000) Kiochō Bldg, 3-12 Kiochō, Chiyoda-ku
EgyptAir (☎ 3211 4521) Palace Bldg, 1-1-1 Marunouchi, Chiyoda-ku
Finnair (☎ 3222 6801) NK Bldg, 2-14-2 Kōjimachi, Chiyoda-ku
Garuda Indonesia (☎ 3240 6161) Kanzan Kaikan Bldg, 3-2-4 Kasumigaseki, Chiyoda-ku
Iberia (☎ 3578 3555) Ark Mori Bldg, 1-12-32 Akasaka, Minato-ku
Japan Airlines (JAL; international toll-free ☎ 0120-255 931, domestic toll-free ☎ 0120-255 971) Dai-ni Tekko Bldg, 1-8-2 Marunouchi, Chiyoda-ku
Japan Air Systems (JAS; ☎ 045-212 2111, toll-free ☎ 0120-711 283) 4-47 Ōtemachi, Naka-ku, Yokohama
Japan Asia Airways (☎ 5489 5411, toll free ☎ 0120-747 801) Yūrakuchō Denki Bldg, 1-7-1 Yūrakuchō, Chiyoda-ku
KLM-Royal Dutch Airlines (☎ 3216 0771) Yūrakuchō Denki Bldg, 1-7-1 Yūrakuchō, Chiyoda-ku

Korean Air (☎ 5443 3311) Tokyo KAL Bldg, 3-4-15 Shiba, Minato-ku

Lufthansa Airlines (☎ 3578 6777) 3-2-6 Kasumigaseki, Chiyoda-ku

Malaysia Airlines (☎ 3503 5961) Hankyū International Express Bldg, 3-3 Shimbashi, Minato-ku

Northwest Airlines (☎ 3533 6000) Forefront Tower, 3-12-1 Kachidoki, Chūō-ku

Olympic Airways (☎ 3201 0611) Yūrakuchō Denki Bldg, 1-7-1 Yūrakuchō, Chiyoda-ku

Pakistan International Airlines (PIA; ☎ 3216 6511) Hibiya Park Bldg, 1-8-1 Yūrakuchō, Chiyoda-ku

Philippine Airlines (☎ 3580 1571) Hibiya Mitsui Bldg, 1-1-2 Yūrakuchō, Chiyoda-ku

Qantas Airways (☎ 3593 7000) Tokyo Chamber of Commerce Bldg, 3-2-2 Marunouchi, Chiyoda-ku

Sabena (☎ 3585 6151) Address Bldg, 2-2-19 Akasaka, Minato-ku

Scandinavian Airlines (SAS; ☎ 3503 8101) Tōhō Twin Tower Bldg, 1-5-2 Yūrakuchō, Chiyoda-ku

Singapore Airlines (SIA; ☎ 3213 3431) Yūrakuchō Bldg 709, 1-10-1 Yūrakuchō, Chiyoda-ku

Swissair (☎ 3212 1016) Hibiya Park Bldg, 1-8-1 Yūrakuchō, Chiyoda-ku

Thai Airways International (THAI; ☎ 3503 3311) Asahi Seimei Hibiya Bldg, 1-5-1 Yūrakuchō, Chiyoda-ku

United Airlines (☎ 3817 4411, toll-free ☎ 0120-114 466) Kokusai Bldg, 3-1-1 Marunouchi, Chiyoda-ku

Vietnam Airlines (☎ 3508 1481) Toranomon Jitsugyō Kaikan, 1-20-1 Toranomon, Minato-ku

Virgin Atlantic (☎ 3499 8811) 3-13 Yotsuya, Shinjuku-ku

Buying Tickets

Competition has brought Tokyo ticket prices down in recent years. Start your search in the *Tokyo Journal*, the *Japan Times* or the *Daily Yomiuri*, all of which run ads from the big Tokyo travel agents that specialise in selling tickets to foreigners (see the Travel Agents section of the Facts for the Visitor chapter). The prices offered by these agents are the lowest you will find in Japan, and departures from Tokyo are almost always the cheapest.

During the three peak travel periods – Christmas and New Year, Golden Week, and O-bon – ticket prices nearly double (see

the Public Holidays section of the Facts for the Visitor chapter). If you are willing to advance or delay your travel by a day or two to avoid these periods, you can often make considerable savings. If you must fly you'll have to reserve well in advance.

Travel agents in Japan are reliable, and the only way you are likely to get ripped off is by buying a ticket from an individual selling a non-refundable ticket that he or she is unable to use (which is inadvisable anyway, as airlines flying in and out of Tokyo usually check tickets against passports). If you buy a ticket in Japan, you will have to pay a deposit, then pay the balance when you pick up the ticket (Japanese travel agents do not usually issue tickets on the spot).

With your ticket, you will receive a copy of the travel agent's ticket refund policy. Check it before buying your ticket.

Travel agents may want to see your passport when you make a reservation or purchase. This is to ensure that you can enter your intended destination without visa problems.

Travellers with Special Needs

If you have a special need – a broken leg, a wheelchair, a baby, dietary restrictions, fear of flying – let the airline know early so that staff can make arrangements for you. Remind them when you reconfirm your booking (at least 72 hours prior to departure) and again when you check in at the airport.

Airports and airlines can be quite accommodating to passengers in wheelchairs, but they do need advance warning. Most international airports will provide escorts from the check-in desk to the aeroplane, and there should be ramps, lift-accessible toilets and reachable phones. Aircraft toilets, however, are likely to present a problem; travellers should discuss this with the airline at an early stage and, if necessary, with their doctor.

Hearing-impaired travellers can request airport and in-flight announcements to be written down for them.

Children under the age of two travel for 10% of the standard fare (or free on some airlines), as long as they don't occupy a seat. (They don't get a baggage allowance.)

'Skycots' should be provided by the airline if requested in advance; these take children weighing up to 10kg. Children between the ages of two and 12 usually occupy a seat for half to two-thirds of the full fare, and do get a baggage allowance. Strollers can often be taken on as hand luggage.

Guide dogs for the visually impaired will often have to travel in a specially pressurised baggage compartment with other animals, though smaller guide dogs may be admitted to the cabin.

Japanese regulations on the importation of live animals are very strict, and are not waived for guide dogs. Dogs brought from countries in which rabies has been eradicated need not be quarantined, provided their owners can show an exportation certification (*yūshutsu shomeisho*). Dogs arriving from countries in which rabies occurs will be placed in quarantine for up to six months unless their owners can supply an exportation certification, a veterinary examination certification and written proof of rabies vaccination.

USA & Canada

Recent years have seen huge drops in prices for tickets between North America and Japan.

From New York, in the low season, return fares as low as US$650 can be found. Carriers to check include United Airlines, Northwest Airlines, Korean Air, Japan Airlines (JAL) and All Nippon Airways (ANA). From the US west coast, return fares can start from as low as US$450. High-season discount fares will double that figure.

United Airlines is one of the better price bets from the US to Japan; its schedule and routes are hard to beat for convenience, and its frequent flier program is among the best around.

United also has great Japan-USA-Japan tickets which allow you to stop at four destinations in continental USA for as low as ¥80,000, and Japan-USA-Europe-Japan tickets for as low as ¥120,000.

Check the Sunday travel sections of papers like the *Los Angeles Times* or the *New York Times* for travel bargains. Council Travel and STA Travel are good discount operations specialising in student fares and other cheap deals. Both are found across the US and Canada. IACE Travel New York (☎ 212-972 3200, e iace@interport.com) specialises in budget flights between the US and Japan.

Canadian Airlines International, which operates out of Vancouver, often matches or beats the best fares available from the USA. Low-season return fares from Vancouver to Tokyo start as low as C$928. Travel Cuts, the Canadian student travel organisation, offers cheap one-way and return Vancouver-Tokyo flights (they can be as low as C$800/1000 one-way/return) depending on the season.

Travel Cuts' Web site (w www.travelcuts .com) has more information.

The UK

Expect to pay UK£500 to UK£600 for a one-year open return ticket with a good airline via a fast route. Air France is a reliable choice but you'll have to change planes in Paris. KLM is handy for travellers coming from the north of England and Scotland, though again you'll have to change planes, at Schipol. British Airways, ANA and JAL also offer regular flights.

Check STA Travel, Campus Travel, or the weekly listings magazine *Time Out* for the latest details. STA, in particular, can put together round-the-world routes incorporating Tokyo on the itinerary.

You can also fly to Hong Kong and buy an onward ticket from one of Hong Kong's very competitive travel agencies. London–Hong Kong flights are much more competitively priced than London-Tokyo ones. If you don't mind going to Hong Kong en route to Tokyo, a London–Hong Kong–London plus a Hong Kong–Tokyo–Hong Kong ticket may be the cheapest option.

Continental Europe

Most direct flights between Europe and Japan fly into Tokyo. Typical low-season fares from major European cities to Tokyo are as follows: Berlin DM940 (Aeroflot); Rome L1,400,000 (EgyptAir); Paris 4000FF

(KLM). Check the Just Travel site at W www.justtravel.de for flights from Germany. Check W www.anyway.fr for flights from France.

Australia

Two well-known agents for cheap fares are STA Travel and Flight Centre. STA Travel (☎ 131 776 Australia-wide, W www.statravel .com.au) has offices in all major cities and on many university campuses. Flight Centre (☎ 131 600 Australia-wide, W www .flightcentre.com.au) also has dozens of branches.

If your travel plans are flexible some of the cheapest fares are with Garuda and Malaysia Airlines. Return fares start from A$1100 in the low season, and both airline routes include a stopover, but the flights have many restrictions. Other good deals are Korean Air and Asiana Airlines flights, both via Seoul. Returns start from A$1331. Direct flights to Tokyo with Qantas, Japan Airlines and Ansett Australia all start at around A$1738.

Fares to Australia from Tokyo usually start at around ¥65,000 for flights with stops (¥91,000 nonstop).

Direct flights take 9.5 hrs.

New Zealand

STA Travel New Zealand (☎ 0800-100 677) and Flight Centre (☎ 0800-354 4487) are again the cheapest agencies.

From Auckland there are a range of options for getting to Tokyo, including flights with Air Pacific via Nadi, starting at NZ$1505; Malaysian Airlines, via Kuala Lumpur, starting at NZ$1440; and Singapore Airlines, via Singapore for around NZ$1539. Expect to pay around NZ$1860 for a direct flight with Air New Zealand.

Flights to New Zealand from Tokyo usually start at around ¥67,000 with stops (¥100,000 nonstop).

Direct flights are 11 hrs.

Asia

Most Asian nations have air links with Japan. South Korea is particularly popular, because it's often used as a place to take a short holiday from Japan when one's visa is close to expiring. Immigration authorities treat travellers returning to Japan after a short break in South Korea with great suspicion.

South Korea Numerous flights link Seoul and Pusan with Tokyo. A one-way/return Seoul-Tokyo flight purchased in Seoul costs around US$190/350. From Tokyo, flights to Seoul are the cheapest way out of Japan. Low-season return fares start as low as ¥19,000; there are several departures daily. Getting seats is usually not a problem, even during peak flying season.

China Of the Asian air links, Hong Kong has the greatest frequency of daily flights to Japan. There are several daily flights on JAL, ANA and JAS. Hong Kong–Tokyo return costs around US$900. Check with Hong Kong Student Travel Bureau (☎ 2730 3269) or Phoenix Travel (☎ 2722 7378).

There are also flights between Tokyo and Beijing, Shanghai, Guangzhou and Dalian. Beijing-Tokyo costs around US$800 return. Tokyo prices for flights between Tokyo and Beijing start at around ¥40,000 return.

Taiwan Agents handling discounted tickets advertise in the English-language *China News* and *China Post*. The average price for a Taipei to Tokyo return flight is NT$11,000, though cheaper deals are available. Leaving Tokyo, you can find return tickets to Taipei for as low as ¥39,000. If you are stopping off in Taiwan between Hong Kong and Japan, check out China Airlines tickets, which allow a stopover in Taipei before continuing to Tokyo's convenient Haneda airport.

Other Asian Centres There are regular flights between Tokyo and other cities like Manila, Bangkok, Kuala Lumpur, Singapore and Jakarta. Bangkok and Penang offer the cheapest South-East Asian prices for flights to Tokyo. Tokyo prices for low-season return tickets include Manila ¥45,000, Bangkok ¥43,000, Kuala Lumpur ¥55,000, Singapore ¥48,000 and Jakarta ¥57,000.

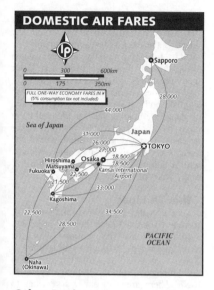

DOMESTIC AIR FARES

FULL ONE-WAY ECONOMY FARES IN ¥
(5% consumption tax not included)

Sea of Japan

PACIFIC OCEAN

Other Regions
There are also scheduled flights between Japan and South America, Africa and the Middle East.

Domestic Air Services
For travel on Honshū, it is often cheaper and quicker to travel by shinkansen than by air. This will depend on your destination. If you're heading quickly off Honshū (eg, to Sapporo, Fukuoka/Hakata or Naha), it is well worth considering flying. Most Tokyo domestic flights use Haneda airport.

The main domestic carriers are ANA, JAS and JAL. Japan's major domestic carrier is JAL, which offers only limited domestic services. Tickets can be purchased at any travel agency or directly through the airlines. There is little discounting of tickets, so it makes no difference how you buy them.

TRAIN
Arriving in Tokyo by train is a simple affair. Most of the major train lines terminate at Tokyo station on the Japan Railways (JR) Yamanote line. For day trips to areas such as Kamakura, Nikkō, Hakone and Yokohama, the most convenient means of transport is

usually one of the private lines. With the exception of the Tōbu Nikkō line, which starts in Asakusa, all of them start from somewhere on the Yamanote line.

Japan Railways is actually several separate private railway systems which provide one linked service. This arrangement makes little difference to the visitor though, as JR gives every impression of being a single operation, which indeed it was for more than a century. To most Japanese, JR is known as *kokutetsu* – *koku* means 'national' and *tetsu* means 'line' (literally, iron, short for 'iron road').

There are basically three types of train transport in or out of Tokyo: shinkansen, JR and private trains. See the Getting Around chapter for the subway, which services central Tokyo.

For JR schedules, fares, routes, lost baggage and discounts on services, hotels and rent-a-cars, call the JR East-Infoline in Tokyo on ☎ 03-3423 0111 (open 10am-6pm weekdays, but not on holidays). The Japan National Tourist Organization (JNTO) also puts out a handy *Railway Timetable* booklet in English. The Green Window (Midori-no-Madoguchi) offices in the larger JR stations handle inquiries and bookings.

JR has an on-line shinkansen schedule in English (W www.asahi-net.or.jp/~ev7a-ootk/time/etime_012.htm), which also indicates seat availability.

Osaka/Kyoto/Kansai International Airport
Train travel between Tokyo and these major destinations takes three forms: shinkansen, regular Tōkaidō trains and night trains. Shinkansen (see the Shinkansen section following) is by far the fastest and most convenient way to go. A one-way, non-reserved shinkansen seat between Tokyo and Kyoto costs ¥13,220 (2¾ hours); and between Tokyo and Osaka costs ¥13,750 (three hours).

You can also take regular JR Tōkaidō express trains to Kyoto (¥7930, about eight hours) to avoid the hefty shinkansen surcharge, but this is going to eat up most of a day and require several annoying changes of train en route. The Kyoto to Osaka leg will cost another ¥550 and add 30 minutes to this journey.

There are also JR night trains between Tokyo and Kyoto (¥8000, about seven hours), usually departing around 11.45pm. While some are reserved-only sleeper trains, most are standard trains with upright seats. Bear in mind that some night departures run straight through, while others stop en route, requiring bleary-eyed train changes. Buy your tickets at Tokyo station, where the staff at the information counter at the main ticket office can explain everything in English.

Travel between Kansai international airport (KIX) and Tokyo is best done via Osaka (there are no direct trains between Tokyo and KIX). The fastest route uses the *Haruka* airport express train between the airport and Shin-Osaka station (¥2470, 45 minutes), and then the shinkansen between Shin-Osaka and Tokyo (¥13,750, three hours). You can go via Osaka station or Kyoto, but this will involve more travel time and, in the case of Osaka, at least one more train change.

Shinkansen

There are three main shinkansen lines that connect Tokyo with the rest of Japan: the Tōkaidō line passes through central Honshū, changing names along the way to the San-yō line before terminating at Fukuoka/Hakata in northern Kyūshū; the Tōhoku line runs north-east via Utsunomiya and Sendai as far as Morioka (with another sub-route which branches off at Fukushima and travels to Yamagata); and the Jōetsu line runs north to Niigata. The line you'd most likely use is the Tōkaidō line, as it passes through Kyoto and Osaka. All three lines start at Tokyo station, though the Tōhoku and Jōetsu lines also stop at Ueno station.

A new service to Nagano is the Asama shinkansen, with frequent departures daily from around 6am to 10pm.

Note that there are different types of shinkansen – the difference being the combination of speed and the number of stops. On the Tōkaidō shinkansen line (for Kyoto, Osaka and KIX), the three types are: *nozomi*, *hikari* and *kodama*. Of these, the nozomi is the fastest and all seats are reserved, the hikari is the next fastest and probably the most useful for the traveller, and the kodama is the slowest (though still infinitely faster than regular Tōkaidō line express trains).

While these trains are clearly labelled in English, both on the trains themselves and on departure boards, you can also tell them apart by appearance: the nozomi is the newest and most streamlined, while the humble kodama looks rather old-fashioned, with a bulbous nose and a patina born of many years of service.

Other JR Lines

As well as the Tōkaidō shinkansen line, there is a Tōkaidō line to the same areas, but stopping at all the stations that the shinkansen zips through. Trains start at Tokyo station and pass through Shimbashi and Shinagawa stations on their way out of town. There are also express services to Yokohama and Izu-hantō Peninsula, via Atami, and from there trains continue to Nagoya, Kyoto and Osaka.

If you are keeping expenses down and travelling long distance on the Tōkaidō line, there are some late-night services that do the Tokyo to Osaka run, arriving early the next morning. Some of them will have sleepers available.

Travelling in the same direction as the beginning of the Tōkaidō line, the Yokosuka line offers a much cheaper service to Yokohama and Kamakura. Like the Tōkaidō line, the Yokosuka line starts at Tokyo station and passes through Shimbashi and Shinagawa stations on its way out of Tokyo.

Branching off to the west from Tokyo, running through the centre of the Yamanote line loop and on through Shinjuku and Tachikawa, is the Chūō line. It eventually takes you into Nagano prefecture, containing the Japan Alps and the historical town of Matsumoto.

Northbound trains start in Ueno. The Takasaki line goes out to Kumagaya and Takasaki, with connections from Takasaki to Niigata. The Keihin-Tōhoku line follows the Takasaki line as far north as Ōmiya,

Trans-Siberian Railway

A little-used but fascinating way to enter or leave Japan is via the Trans-Siberian Railway. It won't be useful if you're leaving Japan in a hurry – visas and bookings take time – but despite some bad press, the train can still be a great means of connecting Europe and Asia.

There are actually three trans-Russia railway routes, one of which is to travel directly across Siberia from Moscow, followed by a flight from either Vladivostok or Khabarovsk – an expensive option. Air connections between Japan and Vladivostok and Khabarovsk are via Niigata in northern Honshū. Since these are not discounted, they tend to be expensive: ¥70,000 one-way. There are also ferry connections between Niigata and Nakhodka (near Vladivostok).

Cheaper are the Chinese Trans-Mongolian and Russian Trans-Manchurian routes, both of which start in Moscow and end in Beijing. Once you're in China, there are ferry connections with Japan via Tianjin (Tanggu) and Shanghai (see the Boat section of this chapter).

For more information outside Japan, you can contact an overseas JNTO office or China International Travel Service (CITS), or check out deals offered by travel outfits detailed in Lonely Planet's *China* or *Russia, Ukraine & Belarus* guides. In Tokyo, call the TIC (☎ 03-3201 3331) or Eurastours (☎ 03-3432 6161).

東京 東京 東京 東京 東京 東京 東京

from where it heads to the far north of Honshū via Sendai and Aomori. Overnight trains also operate, for those intent on saving the expense of a night's accommodation.

Note that the faster express services to any of these destinations require an express surcharge, which is paid on top of the basic local train fare.

Private Lines

Private lines are much shorter than JR lines and generally service Tokyo's sprawling suburbs. Though very few go to places of interest to visitors, private lines are usually cheaper than JR lines. Particularly good bargains are the Tōkyū Tōyoko line, running between Shibuya station and Yokohama; the Odakyū line, from Shinjuku to Odawara and the Hakone region; the Tōbu Nikkō line, running from Asakusa to Nikkō; and the Seibu Shinjuku line from Shinjuku to Kawagoe.

BUS

Generally intercity buses are little or no cheaper than trains, but are sometimes a good alternative for long-distance trips to areas serviced by expressways. The buses will often run direct, so you can relax instead of watching for your stop, as happens on an ordinary train service.

A number of express buses run between Tokyo, Kyoto and Osaka. Overnight buses leave at 10pm and 11pm from Tokyo station, and arrive at Kyoto and Osaka between 6am and 7am the following morning. They cost from ¥8180 one-way, ¥14,480 return. A return ticket must be used within six days of purchase. The buses are a JR service and can be booked at a Green Window office in the larger JR stations. The main JR highway bus office (☎ 03-3215 0498) is on the south end of the Yaesu side of Tokyo station. Buses depart from in front of the office. Direct buses also run from Tokyo station to Nagoya, Nara and Kōbe.

From Shinjuku station, buses run to the Fuji and Hakone regions, including, for Mt Fuji climbers, direct services to the fifth stations. See the Mt Fuji section in the Excursions chapter for more details.

BOAT

Japan has ferry services to South Korea, China and Taiwan, but the South Korea and China services run from the Kansai region, not from Tokyo, while Taiwan services operate from faraway Okinawa.

South Korea

South Korea is the closest country to Japan, and therefore a popular visa-renewal point. The main ferry departure/arrival points for Japan-South Korea travel are Shimonoseki, at Honshū's far western end, and Fukuoka/Hakata, on the southern island of Kyūshū. There is a ferry and high-speed hydrofoil

GETTING THERE & AWAY

service. Both operate from Pusan in South Korea.

Ferries depart daily from Shimonoseki on the Kampu Ferry service's (☎ 0832-24 3000) vessels *Hamayū* or *Pukwan*, both of which leave at 6pm daily and arrive in Pusan at 8.30am the following morning. One-way fares start at ¥6800 for students, rise to ¥8500 for space on the floor of a large, tatami room, ¥12,000 for a four-berth cabin and ¥14,000 for a two-berth cabin. There's a 10% discount for return tickets.

Known as the 'Beetle' (☎ 03-3240 5692 in Tokyo; 092-281 2315 in Fukuoka/Hakata), the hydrofoil costs around ¥13,000 one-way and ¥24,000 return from Fukuoka/Hakata to Pusan. It makes the trip in just three hours and runs daily. The Camellia Line (☎ 092-262 2323) ferry departs in the early evening three times a week, and takes 15 hours. Prices start from ¥9000 one-way and ¥17,100 return.

China

The Japan-China International Ferry (☎ 06-6536 6541, Japanese only) service connects Shanghai and Osaka/Kōbe. The number of departures varies with the seasons. In the off season it's nearly empty, but in summer it can be crowded. A 2nd-class ticket costs around ¥20,000.

Ships from Kōbe to Tanggu (near Tianjin) leave from Kōbe every Thursday at noon and arrive in Tanggu the next day. Economy/1st-class tickets cost ¥22,500/35,000. The food is reportedly dire so bring your own victuals. Tickets can be bought in Tianjin from the shipping office (☎ 22-31 2243) at 89 Munan Dao, Heping District. In Kōbe, the office (☎ 078-321 5791) is at the port.

Taiwan

Arimura Sangyō (☎ 098-869 1320 in Naha, 03-3562 2091 in Tokyo) operates a weekly ferry service between Taiwan and Okinawa, sometimes via Ishigaki and Miyako in Okinawa prefecture. The Taiwan port alternates

between Keelung and Kaohsiung. Departure from Okinawa is on Thursday or Friday; departure from Taiwan is usually on Monday. It takes 16 to 19 hours. Fares from Okinawa start at ¥15,750 (economy). Fares from Taiwan are slightly cheaper.

In Taiwan, contact either the Yeong An Marine Company in Taipei (☎ 02-771 5911), Kaohsiung (☎ 07-551 0281), or Keelung (☎ 02-424 8151).

Domestic Ferries

From Tokyo, there are also long-distance ferries to other islands of Japan: Kushiro on Hokkaidō (¥14,700); Kōchi (¥10,600) and Tokushima (¥8610) on Shikoku; Kokura in northern Kyūshū (¥12,600); and Naha on Okinawa (¥20,050). For information about these services, ring the Ferry Service Center (☎ 03-3501 0889) in Tokyo.

Getting Around

Tokyo has an excellent public transport system. There are very few worthwhile spots around town that aren't conveniently close to a subway or Japan Railways (JR) station. When the rail network lets you down, there are generally bus services, though these are harder to use if you can't read *kanji*.

Useful Kanji

Transport

limited express train	特急列車
express train	急行列車
local train	普通列車
east entrance/exit	東口
west entrance/exit	西口
south entrance/exit	南口
north entrance/exit	北口
central entrance/exit	中央口
ticket office	きっぷうりば
shinkansen ticket office	新幹線きっぷうりば
reserved seats	指定席
this train	この電車
next train	つぎの電車
train after next	次々発
shinkansen	新幹線
nozomi	のぞみ
hikari	ひかり
kodama	こだま
train bound for (Osaka)	行き電車（大阪）

Other Terms

smoking section	喫煙車
nonsmoking	禁煙車
vacant taxi	空車
occupied taxi	満車

東京 東京 東京 東京 東京 東京 東京

Most residents and visitors use the railway system far more than any other means of transport. It is reasonably priced, frequent (generally at most five minutes between trains on major lines in central Tokyo) and stations have conveniences like pay lockers for baggage storage. The only drawback is that the system shuts down at midnight or 1am and doesn't start up again until 5am or 6am.

Subway trains have a tendency to stop halfway along their route when closing time arrives. People who get stranded face an expensive taxi ride home or have to wait for the first morning train. Check time schedules posted on platforms for the last train on the line if you plan to be out late.

Avoiding Tokyo's rush hour is a good idea, but may be impossible if you're on a tight schedule. Commuter congestion tends to ease between 10am and 4pm, when travelling around Tokyo – especially on the Yamanote line – can actually be quite pleasant. Before 9.30am and from about 4.30pm onward, there'll be cheek-to-jowl crowds on all major train and bus lines.

AIRPORTS

Tokyo has two airports: Narita, which handles most international traffic, and Haneda, which is used mostly for domestic flights.

Narita Airport

Narita is 66km outside of Tokyo, but if you can forget its inconvenient location, you'll find Narita is an excellent, modern airport with a host of services.

The airport is divided into Terminal 1 and Terminal 2, which are connected by a free shuttle bus service. From Terminal 1, board this bus at the No 0 bus stop, and from Terminal 2, board at the No 8 and 18 stops. Note that some of the airport's services are only available in the newer Terminal 2.

At both terminals there are post offices, currency exchange counters (generally open daily from 7am to 10pm, though the one in Terminal 2 on the 1st floor is open to 11pm), health clinics (on the underground floor of both terminals) and lots of restaurants and duty-free shops. Both terminals also offer left-luggage services and baggage shipping/ delivery services. ABC is one such company (☎ 3545 1131). ABC can also deliver baggage from Tokyo to the airport if you book in advance.

In Terminal 2, you might be relieved to find showers and day rooms for napping (main building, 3rd floor; showers ¥600/hr, day rooms ¥2000 for four hours) and a children's play room (free), available to passengers who have completed their emigration procedures (Terminal 2 satellite building, 3rd floor).

There are several information counters in both terminals, and the staff speak English; the main counter for foreign visitors is in Terminal 2 on the 1st floor (☎ 0476-34 6251). The counter is open from 9am to 8pm daily.

On the way in or out of Narita airport, you may notice a heavy security/police presence. Narita was built on land rather forcefully appropriated from local farmers, and the airport has a history of demonstrations, and even occasional threats of terrorism. This can slow down road access to the airport, but usually doesn't affect rail transport.

Arriving Customs and immigration procedures are usually straightforward, although they're more time-consuming for *gaijin* than for Japanese. A neat appearance will speed your passage through passport control and customs, while anyone with even a slightly 'hippy' look is asking for a visit to 'the room'.

Everything at Narita is clearly signposted in English, and you can change money in the customs halls of either terminal or in the arrival halls. The rates will be the same as those offered in town.

The airport Tourist Information Center (TIC; ☎ 0476-34 6251) is an important stop in the arrival lobby of Terminal 2. It has a wealth of information – at the very least, pick up a subway map and the *Tourist Map of Tokyo*. The office is open daily from 9am

to 8pm. The TIC is to the far right of the A arrival lobby as you exit the customs hall.

Narita airport also has a Japan Railways (JR) office where you can make bookings and exchange your Japan Rail Pass voucher for a pass, if you're planning to start travelling straight away.

Leaving Check-in procedures are usually very efficient at Narita, but you should arrive at the airport at least two hours before your departure time. Passport control and security procedures are similarly efficient (bring your embarkation card, which you should have received upon arrival; if you don't have one, you can get a blank form before going through passport control).

Haneda Airport

Haneda is the airport all Tokyo expats still wish was Tokyo's main air hub. Unfortunately, all international traffic now goes via Narita airport (with the exception of China Airlines), and only domestic fliers and charter flights can make use of this conveniently located airport.

Haneda doesn't have Narita's services infrastructure, yet there are post offices, banks, left-luggage services and baggage shipping companies. Nor does Haneda have a dedicated English-language information counter, though there is usually someone who can answer your questions in English. Haneda's information number is ☎ 03-5757 8111. Operators usually speak some English.

TO/FROM NARITA AIRPORT

Narita is 66km east of central Tokyo, and getting into town can take anything from 50 minutes to two hours, depending on your mode of transport.

Bear in mind that there are two terminals at Narita – all airport transport has prominently displayed lists of airlines and the terminal they use. For flight information for Narita airport, ring ☎ 0476-34 5000. For general (non-flight) information, phone ☎ 0476-32 2802 or ☎ 0476-32 2105. The Tourist Information Center (TIC) counter at Narita can be reached on ☎ 0476-34 6251.

Train

Trains conveniently depart from stations directly under the airport terminals. There are three rail services between both terminals at Narita airport and Tokyo: the private Keisei line (☎ 0476-32 8505), the JR Narita Express (N'EX; ☎ 3423 0111) and the regular JR 'Airport Narita' *kaisoku* (rapid train service).

The Keisei service runs into Nippori and Ueno; from either place you can change to the Yamanote line, which runs to Ikebukuro, Shinjuku, Tokyo station and other destinations. The N'EX and Airport Narita services run into Tokyo station (Map 8), from where you can change to almost anywhere. N'EX also runs less frequently into Shinjuku, Ikebukuro and Yokohama.

On the private Keisei line, two trains run between Narita airport and Ueno station: the Skyliner, which runs nonstop (¥1920, one hour); and the limited express *(tokkyū)* service (¥1000, one hour 11 minutes). Both the Keisei stations in Terminals 1 and 2 are clearly signposted in English. The final destination, Ueno, is on the Yamanote line and the Hibiya and Ginza subway lines. Those travelling to Ikebukuro or Shinjuku are advised to get off one stop before Ueno at Nippori station, also on the Yamanote line.

Going to the airport from Ueno, the Keisei station is right next to the JR Ueno station. You can buy advance tickets for the Skyliner service at the ticket counter, while express and limited express tickets are available from the ticket dispensing machines. JR Nippori station has a clearly signposted walkway to the Keisei Nippori station.

The JR N'EX is fast, smooth and comfortable, but does not run as frequently as the private Keisei line. N'EX services to/from major train stations are as follows:

destination	time	price
Tokyo station	55 minutes	¥2940
Shinjuku station	1½ hours	¥3100
Ikebukuro station	1¾ hours	¥3110
Yokohama station	1½ hours	¥4180

N'EX runsfrom Narita approximately every half hour between 7am and 10pm to Tokyo, less frequently to other destinations. All seats are reserved but can usually be bought just before departure if the train is not full (if it's full, you can buy a standing ticket for the same price). The JR Airport Narita kaisoku service takes 1½ hours and costs ¥1280 to Tokyo central. All seats on these trains are unreserved, and are a good option if you cannot get a seat on the N'EX.

Limousine Bus

Ticket offices, marked with the sign 'Limousine', can be found in both wings of the arrival building. Don't get excited about the name – they're ordinary buses. They take 1½ to two hours (depending on traffic) to travel between Narita airport and a number of major hotels around Tokyo. Check departure times before buying your ticket, as services aren't frequent. The fare to hotels in eastern Tokyo is ¥2700, while to Ikebukuro, Akasaka, Ginza, Shinagawa or Shinjuku it is ¥3000. You can also go straight to Tokyo station in one hour 20 minutes, or to Shinjuku station (one hour 25 minutes) for ¥3000. Those transferring to domestic flights departing from Haneda airport can take a limousine bus direct for ¥3000. The trip takes about 1¼ hours in light traffic, but leave lots of extra time, as traffic conditions in Tokyo are seldom ideal. For general airport limousine information, ring ☎ 3665 7220.

The Tokyo City Air Terminal (TCAT) in Nihombashi (Map 1) and the Yokohama City Air Terminal (YCAT) at Yokohama station both offer frequent limousine-bus connections to/from Narita airport, as well as check-in services for departing passengers. TCAT buses leave about every 15 minutes and take about one hour, depending on traffic. The fare is ¥2900. The trip from YCAT takes around two hours and costs ¥3000.

If your airline allows you to check your baggage in at TCAT or YCAT, you can take a taxi from your hotel, check in at either terminal and relax. Allow some extra time if you plan to do this.

There is a subway directly under TCAT – it's the Suitengū-mae subway station on the Hanzōmon line. There is also a frequent shuttle bus service between TCAT and Tokyo station (look for the signs on the station's Yaesu side) for ¥200, and to Haneda for ¥700. There are also taxis waiting at TCAT. For further information on TCAT and its services, phone ☎ 3665 7111. For YCAT information, ring ☎ 045-459 4800.

Taxi

A taxi to Narita airport from Tokyo will cost about ¥30,000.

TO/FROM HANEDA AIRPORT

Most domestic flights and China Airlines (Taiwan) flights use the convenient Haneda airport south of the city (officially known as Tokyo international airport).

Getting from Haneda to Tokyo is simple: Take the monorail to Hamamatsuchō station on the JR Yamanote line. The trip takes 20 minutes; trains leave every 10 minutes and cost ¥270. Taxis to places around central Tokyo will cost around ¥7000.

There is also a regular bus service that runs between Haneda and TCAT (¥900 and takes around 30 minutes). Buses also run between Haneda and Ikebukuro (¥1200) and Shinjuku (¥1200).

For information at Haneda, ring ☎ 5757 8111. For China Airlines flights, phone ☎ 3747 4942.

TRAIN

The Tokyo train system can be a bit daunting at first, but you soon get the hang of it. Much initial confusion arises from the fact that Tokyo is serviced by a combination of JR, private inner-city subway lines and private suburban lines. This sometimes means switching between both trains and train systems. It's not as bad as it sounds, however, as the lines are well integrated and can often be traversed with just one purchase of a special combination ticket.

Once you get off the JR Yamanote line and the subway lines, watch for express services. Generally, the longer the route, the more likely you are to find faster train services. The fastest 'regular' trains (ie, slower than a *shinkansen*, or bullet train) are *tokkyū* (limited express services), followed by *kyūkō* (ordinary express), which stop at only a limited number of stations. A variation on kyūkō trains are the kaisoku (rapid service trains). The slowest trains, which stop at all stations, are called *futsū*.

Train designations are usually written in both Japanese and English on the side of the train and on the platform departure board. When no English translation is provided, you're going to have to ask someone or decipher the kanji yourself.

Since the faster trains do not stop at all stations, you must determine if your destination is serviced by an express train before boarding it. There is usually a board on the platform indicating exactly which trains stop where. Trains are colour-coded and you can usually tell what's what even if you don't read Japanese (though smaller destinations are frequently not written in English, so it's a good idea to have your destination written down in kanji before setting out).

Tram

Tokyo has a solitary tram service still in operation. It doesn't really go anywhere special, but it runs from the heart of Shitamachi, passing through a couple of areas that haven't (yet) been claimed by redevelopment.

You can get on the Toden Arakawa tram line from opposite Ōtsuka station, out north of the city on the Yamanote line.

The line passes the Sunshine City building before passing through Zōshigaya. The latter is an interesting area dotted with small temples and shrines. It is perhaps best known for Zōshigaya Cemetery (Map 2), the resting place of Lafcadio Hearn, the remarkable cosmopolitan chronicler of everyday Meiji Japan, and of his contemporary, the immensely popular Edo-born writer Natsume Sōseki.

From Zōshigaya the tram travels south to its terminus in Waseda, not far from Waseda University (where Hearn once taught).

Train Stations

Modern Japanese spend a good part of their lives in train stations, and this fact is reflected

東京 東京 東京 東京 東京 東京 東京

in the wide range of services at most stations. Most importantly, there is the ticket office. In the case of JR stations, there will be signs (sometimes but not always in both English and Japanese) indicating the Green Window (Midori-no-Madoguchi) ticket counter. This is usually posted with a green sign. Here you can buy your tickets and make reservations. In smaller stations this is where you ask for information as well. Stations also have one or more banks of automatic ticket machines (see Buying a Ticket, following).

Most stations also have coin lockers which hold medium-size bags (backpacks won't usually fit). These often come in several sizes, and cost from ¥200 to ¥600. Storage is good for 24 hours, after which your bags will be removed and taken to the station office.

All railway stations have toilets, almost all of which are free of charge (Shinjuku has a few that cost ¥100). Bring toilet paper, as it is not usually provided (this is why advertising in the form of tissue packets handed out on street corners is big business in Japan).

At many stations you can also find several options for food. The smallest of these are kiosks, which sell snacks, drinks, magazines, newspapers (many have copies of Japan's four English dailies), film etc. Next up are stores selling *ekiben* (railway station boxed lunches; see the 'Ekiben – Lunch in Locomotion' boxed text in the Places to Eat chapter). Larger stations also have *tachi-kui* (stand-and-eat) restaurants. Most of these places require that you purchase a food ticket from a vending machine, which you hand to an attendant upon entry (most machines have pictures on the buttons to help you order). Large stations may also have a choice of several sit-down places, most of which will have plastic food models displayed in the front window.

Navigating your way around railway stations in Japan can be confusing, particularly at some of the larger, more complex stations like Tokyo's Shinjuku station. The key is to know where you're going before you get to the station. Most stations have adequate English signposting, and exits are clearly posted with numbers. If possible,

find out which exit to use when you get directions to a destination. Many stations simply have four main exits: north, south, east and west. Since one station may have several different *kaisatsu-guchi* (automated turnstiles), each near a different exit, you should get your bearings and decide where to exit while still on the platform. As a last resort, you can always just exit the station and get your bearings on the ground.

Buying a Ticket

For all local journeys, tickets are sold by vending machines called *kippu jidō hanbaiki*. Above the vending machines is a rail map with fares indicated next to the station names. Unfortunately for visitors, the names are often in kanji only. The best way around this problem is to put your money in the machine and push the lowest fare button (usually ¥130). This will get you on the railway; when you get to your destination, you can correct the fare at an attended ticket gate, or with an automatic fare adjustment machine (see Fare Adjustment, following). On many JR ticket machines, only the stops closest to the station are written on the price chart, not fare amounts. Thus, you may not find a figure saying ¥130. In this case, push the button all the way to the left (with kanji written on it) and this will be the cheapest fare.

If you want to use a combination of JR and private lines, there are ticket-vending machines that enable you to do this; the problem is that there is generally insufficient English labelling to make sense of them. Don't stress yourself trying to figure it out. Buy the cheapest ticket and let the station attendants at the other end of your trip figure out how much you owe – as long as you are polite, no-one will mind. If you find yourself without change, there are vending machines for all lines that accept ¥1000 notes and some that accept ¥10,000 (there are pictures of the bills accepted on the machines).

There are two buttons on the machine that may come in handy if you completely bungle the operation. First is the *tori-keshi* (cancel) button, which is usually marked in English. The second is the *yobidashi* (call) button, which will alert a staff member that you need assistance (they usually pop out from a hidden door between the machines – it can be surprising).

See Orange Cards under Japan Railways (JR) for an easy option of paying for JR trains.

Fare Adjustment Many travellers and even long-term residents never bother to figure out the appropriate fare when buying tickets (particularly for short inner-city hops). They just grab the cheapest ticket and are on their way. If you choose to do this, you have two choices upon arrival at your destination: An attended ticket gate or the fare-adjustment machine.

At an attended gate, simply hand over your ticket and the attendant will inform you of the additional fare. A fare-adjustment machine is almost as simple and saves time if the gate is congested. There's a slot near the top of the machine into which you insert your ticket. The screen will tell you how much to pay, then spit out your change (if any) and a new ticket. You can use this ticket in the ordinary automated turnstiles. Fare-adjustment machines usually have some English instructions. Fare-adjustment machines usually sit slightly apart from the ticket machines to void congestion.

Tokyo Combination Ticket A Tokyo Combination Ticket is a day pass that can be used on all JR, subway and bus lines within the Tokyo metropolitan area. It costs ¥1580. It is available at Pass offices, which can be found in major subway stations. Stations with Pass offices are marked with a triangle on local subway maps.

Japan Railways (JR)

Yamanote Line The most useful line in Tokyo is the JR Yamanote line, which does a loop around the city, taking in most of the important areas (see Map 1). The trains are silver with a green stripe. You can do the whole circuit in an hour for the ¥130 minimum fare – a great introduction to the city.

When you ride the Yamanote, it can be hard to determine where to get off. The signs indicating the name of the station are sometimes hard to see from inside the train (the stop announcements, if they're audible at all, are usually in a language that resembles neither English nor Japanese). Before boarding, look at the board on the platform which shows the stops of the Yamanote and the time to each stop. Count the number of stops: This way you won't have to frantically crane your neck to see where you are each time the train stops.

Chūō Line The JR Chūō line cuts through the centre of the Yamanote line between Shinjuku (Map 3) and Tokyo (Map 8) stations. Trains on this line are orange. This line is continuous with the Sōbu line until Ochanomizu station. At Ochanomizu the lines split – the Chūō heading down to Tokyo station and the Sōbu heading out to the eastern suburbs. Trains on the Sōbu line are yellow, so telling them apart is easy. The Chūō line is about the fastest route between Shinjuku and Tokyo stations (rivalled by the Marunouchi subway line).

Other Lines The Yokosuka line runs south to Kamakura from Tokyo station (Map 8) via Shimbashi (Map 7) and Shinagawa (Map 1) stations. The Tōkaidō line travels in the same direction from Tokyo station, providing access to Izu-hantō Peninsula.

Some other main lines are the north-bound lines (Takasaki, Keihin-Tōhoku, Saikyō) to Saitama Prefecture and beyond, the Jōban and Narita lines to the north-eastern satellite towns in Saitama and Chiba prefectures, and the Sōbu and Keiyō lines (see Map 1) heading east towards Chiba city (and Tokyo Disneyland) and the convention city at Makuhari Messe.

Orange Cards If you get tired of fumbling for change, the JR system offers the option of 'orange cards'. These are available in denominations of ¥1000, ¥3000, ¥5000 and ¥10,000. With a ¥5000 card you get an extra credit of ¥300; a ¥10,000 card gives you a bonus of ¥700. Fares are automatically deducted from the cards when you use them in the orange-card vending machines. For longer-term visitors, passes called *teiki-ken* are available between two stops over a fixed period of time, but you really have to use the ticket at least once a day for it to pay off.

Tokyo Rinkai Shin-Kōtsū Line (Yurikamome)

Also known as the Tokyo Waterfront New Transit Line – or just the Rinkai Line – this new line (see Map 1) services the Tokyo Bay area's Odaiba, Daiba and Ariake developments (Map 6). It's a monorail that leaves from Shimbashi, just south of Ginza, crosses the Rainbow Bridge and terminates in Ariake, on an artificial island in Tokyo Bay. The Shimbashi station is above ground on the east side of JR Shimbashi station (Map 7). Ticket machines provide ample English explanation. The fare from Shimbashi to Aomi and Ariake is ¥370.

Private Lines

Most of the private lines service suburban areas outside Tokyo, but some of them also connect with popular sightseeing areas. The private lines almost always represent better value for money than the JR lines. The ones you are most likely to use are Shibuya's Tōkyū Tōyoko line, which runs south to Yokohama; Shinjuku's Odakyū line, which runs south-west out to Hakone; and Asakusa's Tōbu Nikkō line, which goes north to Nikkō.

SUBWAY

There are 13 subway lines, of which eight are TRTA lines and four are TOEI lines. This is not particularly important to remember, as the services are essentially the same and have good connections from one to the other, although they do operate under separate ticketing systems. The colour-coding and regular English signposting make the system easy to use – you soon learn that the Ginza line is orange and that the Marunouchi line is red. Perhaps the most confusing part is figuring out where to surface when you have reached your destination – there is almost always a large number of subway exits. Fortunately, the exits are numbered and maps are posted, usually close to the ticket turnstiles.

Generally, the subway system is indispensable for getting to areas that lie inside the loop traced by the Yamanote JR line. The central Tokyo area is served by a large number of lines that intersect at Nihombashi (Map 8), Ōtemachi (also Map 8) and Ginza (Map 7), making it possible to get to this part of town from almost anywhere. Most fares within the Yamanote loop are either ¥160 or ¥190.

All TRTA information counters (found near the automatic turnstiles) have a very useful English map and brochure called *Subways in Tokyo* explaining the system in detail.

Buying a Subway Ticket

This is essentially the same as buying a regular train ticket. You need different tickets for the two subway systems, but many of the automated ticket machines sell 'combination tickets', which allow you to transfer from one system to another without buying a new ticket. The bad news is that the button is usually marked only in Japanese (it can be found in the top row of buttons on the newer machines). The best advice is to buy a SF Metro Card (see the following section), which can be used on all subway lines.

SF Metro Card This card is almost indispensable. SF Metro Cards are prepaid magnetic cards good for all the subway lines in Tokyo. You purchase them from ordinary automatic ticket machines labelled (in English too) with 'SF Metro Card', in denominations of ¥1000, ¥3000 and ¥5000. Insert the amount, push the 'Metro Card' button, then the cash amount button and the card will appear.

Insert the card into the automatic turnstiles as you would a normal ticket – don't forget to grab it as you exit the turnstile! The turnstiles will automatically deduct ¥160 from the card as you enter the subway system, and then any amount above that figure, if necessary, when you leave. If you have less than ¥160 left on the card, you will not be able to enter the system. Take the card to a ticket machine, insert it and whatever change is necessary to bring the figure to

GETTING AROUND

¥160. The machine will spit out a new ticket and the now worthless Metro Card.

Other Ticket Deals The TRTA subway system (the more extensive of the two) has some money-saving ticket offers. An 11-ride ticket can be bought at vending machines and offers 11 rides for the price of 10. The One-Day Open ticket can also be bought at vending machines for ¥710, and offers unlimited use of the TRTA system for the day of purchase. Also see Tokyo Combination Ticket under Buying a Ticket.

BUS

Many Tokyo residents and visitors have never set foot on a bus. Train services are great; buses are much more difficult to use and they are at the mercy of Tokyo's sluggish traffic. Services also tend to finish fairly early in the evening.

At some bus stops there are signs indicating in English the destinations of the buses that stop there. But most of the time, if you do not read Japanese, you'll have to ask someone at the stop, or you can use a bus map.

Bus fares are a flat ¥200 for adults and ¥100 for children (primary school age and younger) and are paid into the fare box next to the driver as you enter the bus. Change for ¥1000 notes and coins will be given. A tape recording announces the name of each stop as it is reached, so listen carefully and press the button next to your seat when yours is announced. If you are planning to make use of the bus system, pick up a copy of the city government's excellent *Toei Bus Route Guide* at the Tokyo Metropolitan Government Offices (Map 3) in west Shinjuku (ask at the information counter). The Tourist Information Center (TIC; at Narita airport, or in the Tokyo International Forum at Yurakucho, near Tokyo station) also has a good English bus route map.

CAR & MOTORCYCLE

Driving yourself around Tokyo is by no means impossible but is likely to bring unnecessary frustrations. Parking space is limited and expensive, the traffic moves very slowly, traffic lights are posted on virtually every street corner (every 50m or so) and unless you are very familiar with the city, getting lost will be a common occurrence. Overall, you are much better off using public transport. If you do intend to drive in Japan, note that driving is on the left side. If you're going a long distance and intend to use Japan's expressways, the tolls are very expensive, averaging ¥27 a kilometre.

Still interested? Get a copy of *Rules of the Road*, available from the Japan Automobile Federation (JAF; ☎ 3436 2454) for ¥2000. The JAF office is close to Kamiyachō subway station on the Hibiya line.

Car Rental

For those who enjoy a challenge, there are car rental agencies in Tokyo that will hire you one of their vehicles upon presentation of an international drivers' licence.

Nippon Rent-a-Car (☎ 3485 7196) is the largest agency in Tokyo, with some 150 branches. Three other car rental agencies which usually have English speakers on hand are Dollar Rent-a-Car (☎ 3567 2818), Hertz (☎ 0120-489 882) and Toyota Rent-a-Lease (☎ 3264 0100).

Typical rates for small cars are ¥8000 or ¥9000 for the first day, and ¥5500 to ¥7000 a day thereafter. On top of this there is a ¥1000 per day insurance fee. Mileage is usually unlimited.

Motorcycle

Many foreigners living in Tokyo end up getting themselves a motorbike. It can be a good way to get around town, especially after the trains have stopped running. The best place to take a look at what's available and get some information in English is the area of motorbike shops on Korinchō Rd, near Ueno station (Map 9). Some of the shops there have foreign staff. If you have a motorbike licence, you could also try hiring a motorbike. SCS (☎ 3827 5432) hires out scooters for around ¥7000 per day, and 250cc bikes from around ¥13,000 and up.

If you buy a motorbike, you will need a motorbike licence (for up to 400cc, your foreign licence is transferable) and your

Bicycle basket-baby

Bicycle rack against wall

Sumō wrestlers heading home after the match

Family picnic in the park

Sunday among the *sasa* leaves

Daruma dolls – icons of business success

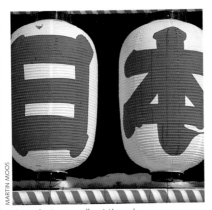

Paper lanterns spell out 'Japan'

One of Japan's 20 million vending machines

Thirsty flower salesman outside Nippori station

bike will need to be registered. Bikes up to 125cc are registered at your ward office; bikes over 125cc are registered with the Bureau of Traffic.

TAXI

Taxis are so expensive that you should only use them when there is no alternative. Rates start at ¥660, which buys you 2km (after 11pm it's 1.5km), then the meter rises by ¥80 every 274m (every 220m or so after 11pm). You also click up about ¥80 every two minutes while you relax in a typical Tokyo traffic jam. Taxi vacancy is indicated by a red light; a green light means there's a night-time surcharge and a yellow light means that the cab is on call.

If you have to get a taxi late on a Friday or Saturday night, be prepared for delays and higher prices. The same applies any day of the week for the first hour or so after the last trains run. At these times, *gaijin* (foreigners) may find themselves shunned like lepers because their ride is likely to be a short one, whereas the drunken worker holding up two fingers (to indicate his willingness to pay twice the meter fare) is probably bound for a distant suburb. There is no point getting annoyed. With only around 50,000 taxis operating in Tokyo, complaints of a taxi shortage are rife – even the locals have problems flagging one down once the trains have shut down for the night.

Tokyo taxi drivers rarely speak any English, so, if you don't speak Japanese, it's a good idea to have your destination written down in Japanese. Even if your destination has an English name, it is unlikely the driver will understand your pronunciation. Watch out for the automatic doors on taxis. Don't slam the door shut when you get in or leave – the door will magically shut itself.

BICYCLE

One look at Tokyo will convince even the most ardent cyclist that this is not the place for pedal-powered transport – the roads are crowded, exhaust fumes can get pretty thick, the shoulders of roads are full of parked cars and there are no bike paths.

That said, a surprising number of Tokyo residents brave the perils and do get around by bicycle.

Don't try picking up a used bike from the piles of discarded bikes found around railway stations – the police are in the habit of pulling over riders and checking the bike's serial numbers. If the one you're riding turns out to have been stolen, you'll have a bit of explaining to do.

WALKING

The only way to explore areas like Shinjuku, Shibuya and Ueno is on foot. Walking between areas, however, is another story. It is possible, for example, to walk from Shibuya to Roppongi in around an hour, but it is not an appealing stroll. Once you leave the commercial areas clustered around train stations, you can quickly find yourself in a wasteland of grey buildings and noisy overhead expressways.

For keen walkers, there are extensive walks in the Imperial Palace area, around Ueno and in Asakusa. For some ideas, pick up a copy of the TIC's *Walking Tour Courses in Tokyo* and *One Day Hiking Courses from Central Tokyo* pamphlets. Alternatively take off to Nikkō, Kamakura or Hakone, where there are splendid countryside walks with interesting cultural attractions. Also see the walking tours in the Things to See & Do chapter.

BOAT

Vingt-et-un (☎ 3436 2121) offers daytime cruises out of Tokyo Bay; a straight cruise costs ¥2040 (or from ¥5100 with a meal). Evening cruises cost ¥2550 (from ¥10,200 with a meal).

See the Asakusa section of the Things to See & Do chapter for information on cruises down the Sumida-gawa river.

ORGANISED TOURS

There are tours available for both the Tokyo metropolitan area and for areas further afield. Tours are also given by several factories and commercial institutions (see the Japan Inc Tours boxed text in the Things to See & Do chapter).

For tours of Tokyo, one of the most reliable operators is Hato Bus Tours (☎ 3435 6081). Its Panoramic Tour takes in most of Tokyo's major sights and costs ¥9800, this includes lunch. Probably the widest range of Tokyo tours is available from the Japan Travel Bureau's (JTB) Sunrise Tours office (☎ 5260 9500). Sunrise offers general sightseeing tours, such as morning and afternoon tours (¥5000). Both Hato and Sunrise offer English-speaking guides and/or taped explanations and headsets.

Night tours of the city are also offered by Sunrise Tours and by Gray Line (☎ 3433 5745). Sunrise Tours offers a Kabuki Night tour which includes a *sukiyaki* dinner and *kabuki* at Ginza's Kabuki-za Theatre for ¥9,800.

All of these tours pick up their guests at various major hotels around town. The main Hato bus pick-up is on the Marunouchi side of Tokyo station. Both Sunrise and Gray Line also offer tours to sightseeing spots around Tokyo.

Things to See & Do

It is perhaps best not to think of Tokyo as one city at all, but a ring of cities connected by the JR Yamanote loop line. Those areas not on the Yamanote line, like Roppongi, Tsukiji and Asakusa, are nonetheless within easy reach, as the whole area is crisscrossed by Tokyo's excellent subway system.

This chapter and the remaining Tokyo chapters roughly follow a counterclockwise circuit of the Yamanote line, beginning with the areas around Tokyo station and ending in Akasaka. You'll soon see that each of these subcities has a distinctive character.

Here is an introduction to the main hubs on the Yamanote loop.

Imperial Palace, Ginza, Marunouchi & Nihombashi (Maps 8 & 7)

These areas around Tokyo station are usually considered the true centre of Tokyo, as they contain the main railway station, the imperial residence, the financial district and some of the main shopping areas. With relatively wide streets, lots of open space and (mostly) dignified architecture, this is one of the more pleasant parts of the city.

Kanda (Map 8)

A few stops north-east of Tokyo station, Kanda is the academic centre of Tokyo, with several major universities and a whole neighbourhood devoted to bookshops. Nearby Akihabara holds perhaps the world's thickest concentration of electronics shops.

Ueno & Asakusa (Map 9)

A few stops to the north of Kanda is Ueno, the cultural centre of Tokyo, with an abundance of museums and performance halls. Ueno and its neighbour Asakusa, two stops away on the Ginza subway line, retain some Shitamachi flavour, and those in search of traditional Japan will find a bit of it here.

Ikebukuro (Map 2)

The next main stop on the Yamanote line west of Ueno is Ikebukuro, trapped in time between high-tech Tokyo and the tumble-down suburbs of old Edo. One of Tokyo's main shopping and nightlife areas, Ikebukuro is awash with gaudy advertising, strolling shoppers and an army of touts beckoning passers-by into a variety of nightspots.

Shinjuku (Map 3)

Four stops south of Ikebukuro, Shinjuku is the heart of modern Tokyo, with the city government offices on one side of the station and a bustling nightlife district on the other. The east side features the futuristic *Blade Runner* atmosphere of flashing neon associated with Tokyo. If you have the energy, it's great; if you don't, well, keep moving.

Shibuya (Map 4)

A few stops further is Shibuya, the main stomping ground of Tokyo's youth, where it seems as if everyone over 30 has been banished. What draws youth here are trendy shops, game halls, karaoke boxes and cheap international food.

Words & Sights

Finding sights is easier if you familiarise yourself with these common nouns:

kōen	park	公園
teien/en	garden	庭園／園
tera/dera/ji	temple	寺
jinja/jingū	shrine	神社／神宮
hakubutsukan	museum	博物館
bijutsukan	art museum	美術館
biru/kan/kaikan		
	building/hall	ビル／館／会館
sen	railway line	線
eki	railway station	駅
depāto/hyakkaten		
	department store	デパート／百貨店
tōri/dōri	avenue	通り
hashi/bashi	bridge	橋
mon	gate	門

東京 東京 東京 東京 東京 東京 東京

Ōdaiba (Map 6)

This development on reclaimed land in Tokyo Bay has hardly proved the huge commercial success envisaged by planners, but it still offers plenty to see and do. Japan's largest ferris wheel is here, alongside Toyota's flagship showroom-cum-amusement-park Mega-web where you can take virtual car (of course, Toyota) rides into the Futureworld. In this same development, mysteriously named Palette Town, is the eye-boggling futuristic-retro Venus Fort shopping mall.

Other Hubs

In Akasaka, Roppongi, Ebisu, Harajuku, Aoyama and Nishi-Azabu, things are a little less crowded and intense, and some of the better restaurants and nightspots can be found in these districts.

With all these areas to choose from, you're bound to find at least one that suits you. The best part is, if you get tired of one place, you can hop on a train and find an entirely new 'city' waiting just a stop or two away.

HIGHLIGHTS

Tokyo offers a glimpse into both the future – as the modern metropolis *par excellence* – and Japan's fascinating past. A well-rounded visit should discover both.

For high tech, visit some of the showrooms in Ginza, or some of the towering multifunction buildings that have sprung up in west Shinjuku. Japanese consumer culture is at its best (or worst) in the fashionable areas of Ginza, Shibuya, Harajuku, Aoyama and Akasaka, not to mention Akihabara, the garish discount 'Electric Town'.

Tokyo often looks its best by night, and an evening stroll through the east side of Shinjuku is not to be missed. Ginza and Shibuya are also worth a twilight excursion. For real late-night action, head for the bright lights of Roppongi, an area that parties until the first morning train on weekends.

A taste of traditional Japan can be had by a visit to Meiji-jingū in Harajuku, Asakusa's famed temple Sensō-ji, or any of the many other temples and gardens tucked away throughout the city. If there's time, visit one of the museum re-creations of old Edo. The Edo-Tokyo Museum is the best; the Fukugawa Edo Museum is also very good.

Tokyo has some splendid gardens, such as the Hama Rikyū Onshi-teien in Tsukiji (near Ginza), Koishikawa Kōraku-en near Kanda and Rikugi-en between Ikebukuro and Ueno. The Higashi Gyoyen (Imperial East Palace Garden) is a popular place for a stroll.

Tokyo is the best place in Japan to visit museums and galleries. Many are concentrated in Ueno-kōen, making the park well worth a day's outing. If nothing else, see Tokyo Kokuritsu Kindai Bijutsukan (the Tokyo National Museum), which holds the world's largest collection of Japanese art.

IMPERIAL PALACE AREA (MAP 8) 皇居

The area around the Imperial Palace is one of the best places in Tokyo for leisurely exploration, with lots of open areas and parks. You can catch glimpses of the normally closed palace from the surrounding areas, and the moats are picturesque, especially when the cherry blossoms are out. Just north of the Imperial Palace East Garden and close to Kudanshita subway station are Kitanomaru-kōen Park, with its museums, and Yasukuni-jinja.

Imperial Palace

This is the home of Japan's emperor and the imperial family. Unfortunately, the **palace** *(open 2 Jan and 23 Dec only)* itself is closed to the public for all but two days a year. But it is possible to wander around its outskirts and visit the gardens, from where you can at least get a partial view of the palace with the bridge **Nijū-bashi** in the foreground. The palace is a reconstruction, completed in 1968, of the Meiji Imperial Palace, destroyed during the aerial bombing of WWII.

On the Imperial Palace grounds once stood **Edo-jō**, in its time the largest castle in the world. Edo-jō was first home to a feudal lord who was assassinated in 1486. The castle fell into disuse until 1590, when Tokugawa Ieyasu chose it as the site for an impregnable castle from which the *shōgunate* was to rule all Japan until the Meiji Restoration.

Edo-jō was fortified by a complex system of moats, and the grounds included numerous watch towers and armouries. By the time the Meiji emperor moved to Edo in 1868, large sections of the old castle had been destroyed in the upheavals leading to the transfer of power. Much that remained was torn down to make way for the new Imperial Palace.

It is an easy walk from Tokyo station, or from Hibiya and Nijū-bashi-mae subway stations, to Nijū-bashi. The walk involves crossing **Babasaki Moat** and the expansive **Imperial Palace Plaza**. This vantage point gives you a picture-postcard view of the palace peeking over its fortifications, with Nijū-bashi in the foreground.

Higashi Gyoen

Also known as the Imperial Palace East Garden, this garden *(admission free; open 9am-4pm, closed Mon and Fri, and 15 Dec-3 Jan)* is the only corner of the Imperial Palace proper that is open to the public. It makes for a pleasant retreat after wandering the outskirts of the Imperial Palace or sightseeing in Ginza. Entry is through one of three gates, Ōte-mon, Hirakawa-mon and Kitanahebashi-mon, which were entrances to Edo-jō. Most people enter through Ōte-mon, a 10-minute walk north of Nijū-bashi. This was once the principal gate of Edo-jō, and the garden is at the centre of the old castle site. The garden includes a tea pavilion, a Japanese garden and expansive lawns. It is worth buying a map at the rest house, which is on your right shortly after you enter through Ōte-mon. Check out the list of prohibited behaviour on the back of the map, including the stricture against making 'hideous noises'.

When you enter, you'll be given a numbered plastic chip which you must carry with you and return upon exiting the garden. Presumably, this security measure reflects jitters about the garden's proximity to the imperial quarters. Last entry is at 3pm.

Kitanomaru-kōen

This park *(admission free)* is quite pleasant, and is home to a few museums and **Nihon Budōkan Hall** *(☎ 3216 5123; admission and opening times vary by event)*. It's also,

oddly enough, the final resting place of recently deceased ex-prime minister Keizō Obuchi. The park is best reached from Kudanshita or Takebashi subway stations. If you're walking from the Imperial Palace East Garden, take Kitahanebashi-mon, turn left and look for Kitanomaru-kōen on the other side of the road.

South-east of the Budōkan is the science museum **Kagaku Gijitsukan** *(☎ 3212 2440; admission ¥600; open 9.30am-4.50pm)*, which has good exhibits. There's little in the way of English explanations, but the museum provides a useful booklet in English.

At the south of the park, facing the Imperial Palace East Garden, is the contemporary art museum **Tokyo Kokuritsu Kindai Bijutsukan** *(☎ 3561 1400; admission ¥420; open 10am-5pm Tues-Sun)*, which is scheduled to reopen after renovation in late 2001. The Kindai Bijutsukan has a collection of Japanese art from the Meiji period onwards. With over 3000 exhibits, it is arguably the best collection in the country.

Nearby, the **Kōgeikan** *(☎ 3211 7781; admission ¥420; open 10am-5pm Tues-Sun)* is a craft museum that houses ceramics, lacquerware and dolls.

Yasukuni-jinja

If you take the Tayasu-mon gate exit (just past the Budōkan) from Kitanomaru-kōen and turn left you'll find **Yasukuni-jinja** *(☎ 3261 8326; admission free; open 9.30am-4.30pm daily)*, literally 'Peaceful Country Shrine'. Given that it is a memorial to Japan's war dead, enshrining some 2.5 million souls who died in combat, by its very name the shrine invites controversy.

In the years leading up to and during WWII, Yasukuni-jinja became Tokyo's chief shrine of State Shintō. Despite a constitutional commitment to the separation of religion and politics, and a renunciation of militarism, in 1979 a group of class-A war criminals was enshrined here. The shrine has also been visited by leading Liberal Democratic Party (LDP) politicians on the anniversary of Japan's defeat in WWII (15 August).

Whatever your feelings about honouring Japanese war dead, Yasukuni-jinja is

Tokyo for Free

There's no getting around it – Tokyo is an expensive city. But those on a tight budget need not despair; if you're willing to use your imagination and do a little walking, Tokyo offers a host of things to do for free. These suggestions will cost no more than the train ticket to get there.

Parks Unlike Tokyo's gardens, Tokyo's parks are free, and provide a welcome escape from the urban sprawl. Just grab a *bentō* and or some baked bread and you've got a picnic. Good spots are Kitanomaru-kōen (Map 8), Yoyogi-kōen near Harajuku (Map 4), Ueno-kōen in Ueno (Map 9) and Hibiya-kōen near Ginza (Map 7).

Galleries Most private galleries don't charge admission. Indeed, these galleries are often rented by individual artists who are delighted by a foreigner's interest in their work. Ginza (Map 7) is the best place to hunt for them. Department store galleries (on upper floors) are another good bet; if these are not free, admission is often cheaper than a museum entry fee.

Temples & Shrines Shrines are almost always free in Tokyo and most temples only charge to enter their *honden* (main hall). Sensō-ji in Asakusa and Meiji-jingū in Harajuku are two good places to start. See the boxed text 'Nippori to Nishi-Nippori Walking Tour' in this chapter for some lesser known temples and shrines.

Company Showrooms OK, they're really just another form of advertising, but some showrooms in Tokyo are like small museums and they're all free. The Toyota Mega-web showroom in Odaiba (Map 6) is great for auto enthusiasts and Sony Building in Ginza (Map 7) is great for just about anyone. Kids especially love the free video games. Other showrooms can be found in Ginza, Shinjuku and Harajuku/Aoyama. See Other Attractions in this chapter for details.

Tsukiji Central Fish Market You can wander the world's biggest fish market and its great External Market for hours at no cost; Map 7.

Skyscrapers Several skyscrapers have free observation floors, eg, Tokyo Metropolitan Government Offices building No 1 in west Shinjuku (Map 3), Shinjuku Sumitomo building (also Map 3) and Tokyo Big Sight (Map 6; see Convention & Exhibition Centres under Other Attractions in this chapter). Avoid the pricey observation decks like the one in Ikebukuro's Sunshine Tower.

Free Food Samples It may be a little embarrassing, but you can put together a free and often delicious lunch from the food samples laid out in the larger department stores' food sections. Takashimaya in Ginza (Map 8) and Seibu Loft and Tōbu in Ikebukuro (Map 2) usually have good selections. If you're going to make a daily practice of this, we suggest varying your appearance a little.

Bookshops Unlike some other countries, in Japan no-one will object to you spending hours reading books and magazines on display in bookshops. There's even a word for the practice: *tachiyomi* (a standing read).

Information For an idea of current goings-on, and more freebies, check out the JNTO list at W www.japantravelinfo.com/press/press_free_things.html.

interesting to visit. The enormous *torii* (gates) at the entrance are, unusually, made of steel; and the second set are made of bronze. The inner shrine area is quite beautiful and is laid out in the style of Japan's most important Shintō edifice, Ise Shrine, 100km south-east of Kyoto.

In stark contrast to the sinister black *uyoku* vans patrolling the area (uyoku is a right-wing youth movement; see the boxed text 'The Uyoku' in the Facts about Tokyo chapter), the shrine grounds are home to a flock of doves whose presence seems calculated, as these birds are rarely seen in other parts of Tokyo.

Next to the shrine is **Yasukuni Yūshūkan Museum** (☎ 3261 0998; admission ¥500; *open 9am-4.30pm*), with treasures from Yasukuni-jinja and other items commemorating Japanese war dead. An English-language pamphlet is available. The museum's exhibits include a *kaiten*, or human torpedo, which is a submarine version of the *kamikaze* airplane. There are displays of military uniforms, *samurai* armour and a panorama of 'the Divine Thunderbolt Corps in final attack mode at Okinawa'.

There are two exhibits you should see. The first deals with Japan's attack on Pearl Harbor. Lengthy excerpts from books, many written in English by foreign scholars, are on display. Highlighted sections argue that Japan was forced into launching the attack by American and British foreign policy of the time.

The second is the 'miracle coconut' set afloat by a Japanese soldier in the Philippines shortly before his death in 1944. The coconut floated round the Pacific for 31 years before washing up in Japan's Taishimachi harbour, very near his widow's home town. You can still make out the Japanese characters which the doomed man wrote on the coconut before tossing it into the ocean.

You can also walk down the path that leads behind the main hall to a pleasant pond featuring some gargantuan carp. You can feed them with food from a nearby dispenser for ¥100 a handful.

TOKYO STATION AREA (MAP 8)
東京駅付近

This includes **Tokyo station** (*information* ☎ 3212 6470; *open 10am-6.30pm daily*), its west side a replica of Amsterdam's central station; Nihombashi to the east; and Marunouchi, Tokyo's most prestigious office district, to the west. Though it is not rich in sights, the station area is home to **Nihombashi Bridge** (the iron pole on its north end indicates the old geographical centre of Tokyo); the prestigious **Mitsukoshi department store** (☎ 3241 3311; *open 10am-7pm*); **Yaesu underground arcade** (*open 10am-9pm*), with its hundreds of small shops and restaurants; a couple of art museums; the Tokyo International Forum; and the Tourist Information Center (TIC).

The **Tokyo Stock Exchange** (☎ 3666 0141; admission free; *open 9am-11am and 1pm-4pm Mon-Fri*) is a 10-minute walk east from Nihombashi subway station. You can also take the No 10 or 11 exit of Kayabachō subway station and walk north for around five minutes on the side street to the left of the Yamatane Bijitsukan art museum. The exchange has a gallery on the 2nd floor from which to observe all the frenzied activity. There are explanatory videos and stock trading simulation games that add to the excitement. For information on English tours, see the boxed text 'Japan Inc Tours', later in this chapter.

Three blocks north of the Takashimaya department store is the **Kite Museum** (☎ 3275 2704; admission ¥200; *open 11am-5pm, closed Sun and public holidays*), which boasts some 4000 kites from all over the world, exhibited on a rotating basis. Although there are some stunning kites, particularly the Japanese ones, the museum is very cramped and lacks explanatory material. Take the lift to the 5th floor from Taimeiken restaurant.

A little east, on the corner of Eitai-dōri, is the **Yamatane Bijitsukan** (☎ 3239 5911; *admission ¥500 or ¥1000 for special exhibits; open 10am-4.30pm Tues-Sun*) on the 8th and 9th floors of the Yamatane Securities building. This art museum includes an interior garden and a collection of Japanese paintings.

If you walk back west to Chūō-dōri and make a left turn, on the far left side of the intersection with Yaesu-dōri is the **Bridge-stone Bijitsukan (Map 7)** (☎ 3563 0241; admission ¥700; open 10am-5.30pm Tues-Sun). There is a glut of French impressionist art in Tokyo, but this private collection of the Bridgestone Tyre Company's founder rates highly. Impressionist paintings by Japanese artists are also featured.

Tokyo International Forum (Map 7)

In Yūrakuchō, midway between Tokyo station and Ginza, this is a wonderful building (☎ 3201 3331; admission free; open 8am-11pm). The prominent glass wing looks like a fantastic ship plying the urban waters of central Tokyo – perhaps the maritime touch is intentional, as the building represents a traditionally isolated island nation's efforts toward internationalism.

The west wing is a phantasma of cantilevered, overhanging spaces and cavernous atriums. Together, the two wings hold a variety of meeting halls and convention centres. On the basement floor on the north side of the building is the main Tokyo **Tourist Information Center** (TIC; ☎ 3201 3331; open 9am-5pm Mon-Fri, 9am-noon Sat, closed Sun), the foyer of which is home to an excellent photographic gallery.

There's a variety of restaurants and cafes throughout the building, a small library with mostly Japanese material on floor B1, and an ATM corner (accepting internationally issued cards) and a self-service fax/photocopy centre on the 4th floor of the glass wing. Free internet access is available in the **Cultural Information Lobby** (open 10am-8pm)

It's well worth a side trip to see the Forum, truly one of Tokyo's architectural marvels. At night, the glass hall takes on the appearance of a purple-and-orange-hued giant space colony.

GINZA (MAP 7) 銀座

This is the Tokyo shopping district that everyone has heard of. In the 1870s, Ginza was one of the first areas to modernise, featuring novel (for Tokyoites of the time) Western-style brick buildings. Ginza saw Tokyo's first department stores, sidewalks and other Western emblems of modernity like the gas lamp. Today, other shopping districts rival Ginza in opulence, vitality and popularity, but Ginza retains a distinct snob value. Check out the topnotch department stores like **Wakō** (☎ 3562 2111), **Mitsukoshi** (☎ 3562 1111) and **Matsuya** (☎ 3567 1211), all open from 10am to 7pm. The window displays are always a creative treat.

Ginza overflows with small galleries, craft shops and showrooms – and you should at least be able to afford a cup of coffee at one of the discount coffee shops huddled among the exclusive boutiques.

The best starting point for a wander is **Sukiyabashi crossing**, a 10-minute walk east of the Imperial Palace, or out the Sukiyabashi crossing exit at Ginza subway station. The streets of Ginza are closed to traffic on weekends and holidays, making these times especially pleasant for a stroll.

Sony Building

Right on Sukiyabashi crossing is the Sony building (☎ 3573 2371; admission free; open 11am-7pm), which has fascinating hands-on displays of Sony's many products, including some which have yet to be released. Although there's often a wait, kids love the free video and virtual reality games on the 6th floor. If nothing else, you can put your feet up and relax for a while in one of the building's two Hi-Vision theatres. The building also has a Toyota showroom, an Internet cafe and two of Tokyo's finest restaurants: Sabatini di Firenze and Maxim's de Paris.

Galleries

Galleries, many so tiny they only take a couple of minutes to see, are scattered throughout Ginza, but are concentrated in the area south of Harumi-dōri, between Ginza-dōri and Chūō-dōri.

Idemitsu Art Museum (☎ 3213 9402; admission ¥500; open 10am-4.30pm Tues-Sun) holds an eclectic selection of Japanese, Chinese and Western art collected by a petroleum magnate. The museum also provides an excellent view over the Imperial Palace. It is a five-minute walk from Hibiya or Yūrakuchō stations, on the 9th floor of the Kokusai building, next to Teikoku Gekijō Theatre (Imperial Theatre).

The best photographic galleries around here are probably **Nikon Salon** (☎ 3248 3783; admission free; open 10am-7pm, closed Sun) and the **Contax Gallery** (☎ 3572 1921; admission free; open 10.30am-6.30pm Tues-Sun). Both have free, changing exhibits. Nikon Salon is in the Matsushima Gankyōten building (3rd floor), opposite Matsuya department store on Chūō-dōri. The Contax Gallery is on the 5th floor of the building next door to the San-ai building on Chūō-dōri; there is no English sign at ground level.

A friendly private art gallery worth a look is **Art Museum Ginza** (☎ 3571 2285; admission free; hours vary according to the exhibition.), west down the street from the Sony building on Sotobori-dōri. This gallery shows some very experimental art, including video and sculptural installations.

Kabuki-za

To the east, along Harumi-dōri, is this famed *kabuki* theatre (☎ 3541 3131). Even if you don't plan to attend a performance, take a look at the building, an interesting fusion of Western and Japanese architecture.

World Magazine Gallery

Just around the corner from Kabuki-za is the World Magazine Gallery (☎ 3545 7227; admission free; open 11am-7pm Mon-Fri). It stocks about 1200 magazines from around the world, and although loans cannot be made, you are free to sit down and read anything you please. Twice a year the gallery sells off its magazines for the previous six months – look for announcements in the *Japan Times* or the tourist literature. It also has a coffee shop where you can enjoy a drink while you read.

Hachikan-jinja

Hachikan-jinja (admission free) is so small that you might stroll past and not notice it

is there – which is what makes it worth pausing for. Real-estate values in Ginza have generally forced places of worship elsewhere (or relocated them to the rooftops of Ginza's temples of commerce). Located near Shimbashi station, this is one shrine that remains at street level, a feat that was achieved by building over the top of it.

Hibiya-kōen

If Ginza has left you yearning for greenery, retrace your steps along Harumi-dōri, back through Sukiyabashi crossing to Hibiya-kōen (admission free). The park is actually just west of Ginza in Hibiya, an area notable for the Imperial Theatre and its cinema complexes, but it's only a brief walk west of Sukiyabashi crossing. It was Tokyo's first Western-style park, and it makes for a pleasant break.

If you are then in need of refreshment head for the **Nihonshu Jōhōkan** (☎ 3519 2091; admission free; open 10am-6.30pm Tues-Sun, closed Sat, Sun and public holidays), grandly translated as the Japan Sake Information Pavilion, in nearby Nishi-shimbashi. Don't let the name fool you – it's an office block, not a pavilion. Some of the very finest *sake* is available here for a flat rate of ¥500.

TSUKIJI (MAP 7) 築地

Tsukiji is famous for its fish market, the world's largest, but there are several other sights here, including the temple **Tsukiji Hongan-ji** (admission free; open 6am-4pm), just south of the Tsukiji subway station, which looks as if it had been magically transported from New Delhi. The Indian touch is a tribute to the birthplace of Buddhism.

Just before the entrance to the market, have a look at the shrine **Namiyoke-jinja** (admission free), where wholesalers and middlemen come to pray before entering the market. Its highlights are the giant gold parade mask in the main hall and the dragon-shaped water spigots over the purification basins. Next to the fish market on the Shimbashi side is one of Tokyo's most beautiful gardens, the Hama Rikyū Onshi-teien.

While most people get to Tsukiji by taking the Hibiya subway line to Tsukiji station, you can also walk from central Ginza in about 15 minutes. If you make the early-morning trip to the fish market, you could return to Ginza on foot, taking in Kabuki-za theatre and some department stores on the way.

Tsukiji Central Fish Market

This is one of Tokyo's top attractions and definitely worth a visit. If it lives in the sea, it's probably for sale here – acres and acres of fish and fish products passing hands in a lively, almost chaotic atmosphere. Everything is allotted its own area: mountains of octopus, rows of giant tuna, endless varieties of shellfish, tanks of live unnamable fish.

To get an idea of the size of the fish market (Tsukiji Ichiba; admission free; open 24 hours, closed 2nd & 4th Wed of the month, Sun and public holidays), consider this: 2500 tonnes of fish are sold here daily, worth over US$23 million; that's 670,000 tonnes of fish worth over US$6 billion a year. On our last visit someone had just purchased a single tuna for a meagre ¥20,000,000.

The wholesale market is not open to the general public, which is probably a blessing, given that you'd have to be there well before 5am to see the auctions. You are free to visit the middlemen's market, though, and wander around the stalls set up to sell directly to restaurants, retail stores and other buyers. It's fun, and you don't have to arrive *that* early; as long as you're there before 8am, there will be something going on. Wear old shoes – there's a lot of muck and water on the floor – and don't get run down by the electric carts that prowl the narrow aisles.

Also, take a stroll through the **Tsukiji External Market** (*Tsukijijō-gaishijō;* ☎ *3541 9466; admission free; open 5am-1pm, closed Sun*), which you pass through on the way to the main market. This is a good option if you've arrived too late for the action in the main market. Here, you'll find all kinds of seafood, cooking supplies and produce for sale, in addition to durables like baskets and pottery – good, low-cost souvenir alternatives. The **produce market** is

also worth a look. It's north-west of the main fish market. Tsukiji External Market is closed on the second and fourth Wednesday of every month and on public holidays.

The done thing is to top off your visit with a *sushi* breakfast in one of the nearby sushi shops. There are plenty of small, cheap places in the narrow alleys of Tsukiji External Market, and larger, more upscale ones off Harumi-dōri and Shin-Ōhashi-dōri.

Hama Rikyū Onshi-teien

This garden (☎ *3541 0200; admission ¥300; open 9am-4.30pm*) is one of Tokyo's finest, featuring a large pond with an island and a pavilion. It was a *shōgunal* palace, and extended into the area now occupied by the fish market. Besides visiting the park as a side trip from Ginza or Tsukiji Market, consider setting out from Asakusa via the Sumida-gawa cruise (see Asakusa later in this chapter).

KANDA (MAP 8) 神田

Kanda was a bustling commercial and residential district back in the days of old Edo, and it is another area where something of Edo's spirit lingers. It can be found in the specialised commercial districts and in the old-style restaurants that lurk in the side streets. Kanda is not one of Tokyo's main attractions, but for the visitor with time to spare, it is worth a look.

Akihabara

Akihabara, once Tokyo's only stop for discounted electronics and computers, has recently seen increased competition from elsewhere, especially Shinjuku. Its response has been to slowly turn to the boom market in animation and cartoon manga. That said, it's still the place to shell out on the latest DVD that you couldn't possibly live without. See the Shopping chapter for details.

Yushima Seidō A Confucian school during the Tokugawa regime, Yushima Seidō (☎ *3251 4606; admission free; open 9.30am-4pm*) is one of Tokyo's few Confucian shrines. There is a bronze statue of Confucius in the main hall. Turn up at weekends and holidays to see the building's interior. It's near Ochanomizu station.

Transportation Museum Just south of Akihabara station (Electric Town is to the north) on the far side of Kanda-gawa, is the Transportation Museum (☎ 3251 8481; adult/child ¥310/150; open 9.30am-5pm Tues-Sun), a great place for kids and adults alike. This is trainspotter heaven – you can pretend to drive a virtual JR Yamanote train around Tokyo and no-one will call you a nerd.

Russian Orthodox Nikolai Cathedral This is for building junkies only, as you can only view the onion dome from outside. From the Transportation Museum, walk straight ahead, turn right and follow the road along the river to the second bridge. Turn left here onto Hongo-dōri; the cathedral is on the right. Don't mistake it for a love hotel.

Jimbōchō

This is a neighbourhood of booksellers, close to some of Tokyo's more prestigious private universities and schools (see the boxed text 'Tokyo's Bookshops' in the Facts for the Visitor chapter).

Jimbōchō can be reached in a 15-minute walk from Akihabara by heading south down Chūō-dōri then turning right into Yasukuni-dōri. You can also walk down Yasukuni-dōri from Yasukuni-jinja or catch the subway to Jimbōchō station.

UENO (MAP 9) 上野

Ueno Hill was the site of a last-ditch defence of the Tokugawa shōgunate by about 2000 Tokugawa loyalists in 1868. They were duly dispatched by the imperial army, and the new Meiji government decreed that Ueno Hill would become one of Tokyo's first parks.

Today, Ueno-kōen is Ueno's foremost attraction. The park has a number of museums, galleries and a zoo that, by Asian standards at least, is pretty good.

Ueno is interesting for a stroll. Opposite Ueno station is Ameyoko arcade (see later

---

Fireworks

The Japanese call them *hanabi* (fire-flowers), and when the heat of summer is at its worst, the skies over Tokyo suddenly burst into bloom with these incandescent flowers. If you're in Tokyo in late July or early August, when the biggest displays take place, make every effort to see one.

Huge sums of money are spent on hanabi by corporations keen on public exposure, and Japanese fireworks displays are among the best in the world. They usually start at sunset and continue for up to two hours. The crowds really turn out for hanabi, and public transport is packed both coming and going – arrive early, bring a picnic and linger for a long time after the show. The following are some of Tokyo's best shows; inquire at the TIC for exact dates.

Sumida-gawa Hanabi Taikai Last Saturday of July; the biggest fireworks display of its kind in Tokyo is held on the Sumida-gawa in Asakusa; best viewed from between Sakura-bashi and Komagata-bashi, walk from Asakusa station.

Edogawa-ku Hanabi Taikai Early August; east of the city, almost out to Chiba – best viewed from Shinozaki-kōen; walk 15 minutes from Koiwa station, on the JR Sōbu line.

Tokyo Bay Big Hanabi Taikai Mid-August; fireworks are launched from Harumi Wharf in Chūō-ku; take the bus from Tokyo station or walk 20 minutes from Tsukiji.

Tamagawa Hanabi Taikai Late July; fireworks take off from Futako-tamagawa-kōen in Setagaya-ku, a short walk from Futako-tamagawa station on the Tōkyū Shin-tamagawa line.

東京 東京 東京 東京 東京 東京 東京

---

in this section), a market area selling everything from dried fish to fake Rolexes. Two stops from Ueno on the Ginza subway line is Kappabashi-dōri, a great place for real versions of all those plastic food displays.

Shitamachi History Museum

Just around the corner from McDonald's, south of Ueno station, is the Shitamachi History Museum (☎ 3823 7451; admission ¥300; open 9.30am-4pm Tues-Sun), which re-creates life in the plebeian quarters of old Tokyo through an exhibition of typical Shitamachi buildings. These include a merchant's shop, a sweet shop, the home and business of a copper-boiler maker, and a tenement house (take off your shoes and look around inside).

Ueno-kōen

This park (☎ 3828 5644; admission free; open 5am-11pm daily) has several names: its Sunday name, which no-one ever uses, is Ueno Onshi Kōen; the locals dub it Ueno no Oyama; and Westerners call it Ueno Park. Whichever you prefer, there are two entrances. The main one takes you straight into the museum and art gallery area, a course that might leave you worn out before you get to Ueno's temples. It's better to start at the southern entrance between Ueno's JR station and Keisei station, and do a little temple viewing on the way to the museums. From the JR station, take the Keisei station exit and turn right. Just around the corner is a flight of stairs leading up into the park.

Slightly to your right at the top of the stairs is the mother-of-all-meeting-places the Saigō Takamori statue. This image of a samurai walking his dog proves that between hacking each other to pieces, samurai had the time for more domestic pleasures.

Bear to the far left and follow a wide tree-lined path until you reach Kiyōmizu Kannon-dō (admission free). The temple's model is Kiyōmizu-dera in Kyoto, not that there is any real comparison – the Tokyo version might have seen better days. Nevertheless, it's definitely worth a browse. Women who wish to conceive a child leave a doll here for the senjū Kannon (the 1000-armed goddess of mercy), and the accumulated dolls are burnt ceremoniously on 25 September.

From the temple, continue down to the narrow road that follows the pond Shinobazu-ike. Through a red torii (gate) is Benten-dō (admission free), on an island in the pond. Benten-dō is a memorial to Benten, a patron goddess of the arts. Behind the temple you can hire a peddle boat for 30 minutes (¥500) or a row boat for an hour (same price).

Make your way back to the road that follows Shinobazu-ike and turn left. Where the road begins to curve and leaves the pond behind, there is a stair pathway to the right. Follow the path and take the second turn to the left. This takes you into the grounds of Tōshō-gū jinja (☎ 3822 3455; admission ¥200; open 9am-5.30pm, to 4pm in winter). Established in 1627 (the present building dates from 1651), this is a shrine which, like its counterpart in Nikkō, was founded in memory of Tokugawa Ieyasu, declared a divinity after his death. Miraculously, it has survived Tokyo's many disasters, making it one of the few early Edo structures extant. There is a good view of Five-storey (Kanei-ji) Pagoda to your right as you take the pathway into the shrine. The pathway itself is fronted by a stone torii and lined with 200 stone lanterns rendered as gifts by daimyō (feudal lords) in the Edo period.

Tokyo Metropolitan Museum of Art

Not far from Tōshō-gū jinja, the Tokyo Metropolitan Museum of Art (☎ 3823 6921; admission free, or ¥900-1100 for special exhibits; open 9am-5pm daily) has a number of galleries showing contemporary Japanese art, Western art and Japanese arts such as ink brush and ikebana (flower arranging). The museum also has an excellent, free art library. (The museum is closed on the third Monday of each month.)

Ueno Zoo The zoo (☎ 3828 5171; adult/ child/young child ¥600/300/free; open 9.30am-4.30pm Tues-Sun) is not worth slotting into a tight itinerary, but in good weather it can be pleasant. Among the Japanese, the zoo is very popular for its pandas. The best time to see them is during feeding time at 3.30pm (they're not on view on Friday). There are also snow leopards, lowland gorillas and Bengal tigers.

The zoo is divided into two areas, linked by a monorail. The southern half of the zoo contains the children's petting zoo. The outdoor exhibits here are much nicer than the indoor ones, which tend to be a little dark and depressing.

Tokyo Kokuritsu Hakubutsukan The National Museum (☎ 3822 1111; admission ¥420; open 9am-4.30pm Tues-Sun) is worth going out of your way to visit. It holds the world's largest collection of Japanese art, although only a portion of its vast collection is displayed at any one time.

The museum has four galleries, the most important of which is the Main Gallery – straight ahead as you enter – which houses a very impressive collection of Japanese art, from sculpture and swords to lacquerware and calligraphy. The Gallery of Eastern Antiquities, to the right of the ticket booth, has a collection of art and archaeological finds from all over Asia. Hyōkeikan Hall, to the left of the ticket booth, houses Japanese archaeological finds. There is also a room devoted to Ainu artefacts.

Finally, there is the Gallery of Hōryū-ji Treasures, which is only open on Thursday, and then only 'weather permitting'. The exhibits (masks, scrolls etc) are from Hōryū-ji in Nara. Because these are more than 1000 years old, the building often remains closed if it is raining or humid.

Kokuritsu Kagaku Hakubutsukan This science museum (☎ 3822 0111; admission ¥420; open 9am-4.30pm Tues-Sun) is usually nothing special: displays are limited in scope and quality, and can be covered in less than an hour. Excellent special exhibitions are often held, but these cost extra (usually an extra ¥500 or so). Ask at the park information centre. Most regular exhibits aren't labelled in English, though you can buy a pamphlet (¥300). At least stop by to see the life-sized model of the blue whale outside.

Kokuritsu Seiyō Bijitsukan This museum (☎ 3828 5131; admission ¥420; open 9.30am-7pm Tues-Sun) holds an impressive collection of Western art (probably the most extensive in Asia). The main building was designed by Le Corbusier, and the garden contains originals by Rodin. The emphasis is on French impressionists. Entry to temporary exhibitions usually costs extra.

Other Attractions Back toward the south entrance of Ueno-kōen you will find the **Tokyo Metropolitan Festival Hall** (☎ 3828 2111; admission varies), a venue for classical music, and **Ueno-no-Mori Art Museum** (☎ 3272 8600; admission free; open 10am-5pm daily), which has a variety of exhibition spaces for changing exhibits, particularly calligraphy.

Ameyoko Arcade
Directly opposite the southern exit to JR Ueno station is Ameyoko arcade (open 10am-7pm). Cross the road and enter beneath the big romaji sign. This fascinating jumble of market-style shops, game parlours and restaurants huddled together in the shadow of the overhead Yamanote line is worth a wander.

The Ameya-yokocho (its full name) was famous as a black-market district in the early years following WWII, and is still a lively bargain shopping area. Many of the same tourist items on sale at inflated prices in Ginza sell here at more reasonable rates. Shopkeepers are also much less restrained than those in other shopping areas in Tokyo, brazenly hawking their goods with guttural cries to the passing crowds. It is one of the few areas in which some of the rough and readiness of old Shitamachi lingers.

Check out the basement of the Ameyoko Center building, where Chinese and Korean merchants have set up their own shopping arcade. If you're looking for Chinese cooking ingredients, this is the place.

Korinchō Rd
Just north of Ueno station is the Korinchō Rd motorcycle centre, and the interesting motorcycle museum on the 3rd and 4th floors of the Corin Motors clothing shop. This is a good area to pick up new and second-hand motorbikes. Several shops have native-English speakers on staff.

ASAKUSA (MAP 9)

浅草

The most famous sight in Asakusa is the temple Sensō-ji, also known as Asakusa Kannon-dō. The temple was founded in the 7th century, according to tradition. Asakusa itself emerged as an important commercial and entertainment area during the Edo period. Asakusa and the nearby red-light area of Yoshiwara (now divested of its former glory, lingering only in a few bath houses and shabby love hotels) lie at the very heart of Edo's Shitamachi.

Like Ueno, Asakusa is well worth a directionless stroll – here the spirit of old Edo hasn't been banished by the razzle-dazzle of modern Tokyo. In early Edo times, Asakusa may have been a halfway stop between the city and Yoshiwara, but in time the area emerged as a pleasure quarter in its own right, eventually becoming the hub of that most beloved of Edo entertainments, kabuki. In the very shadow of Sensō-ji, a fairground atmosphere harboured a wealth of decidedly secular entertainment – from kabuki to brothels.

When Japan ended its isolation with the Meiji Restoration, it was in Asakusa that the first cinemas and music halls appeared; Western opera first graced the Japanese stage at Asakusa's long-gone Teikoku Gekijō Theatre (Imperial Theatre). It was also in Asakusa that another Western export – the striptease – first found a Japanese audience. It almost failed to catch on, such was the popularity of a rival form of risque entertainment – female sword fighting. The inspired introduction of a bubble-bath show saved the day. Famed movie-maker and comedian Kitano Takeshi (Beat Takeshi) got his start in showbiz here, telling gags between acts.

Asakusa never quite recovered from aerial bombing in the closing months of WWII. Although Sensō-ji was rebuilt, the bright lights have shifted elsewhere.

The Tourist Information Centre (TIC), located across the street from Kaminari-mon gate, has English speakers on hand who can give you handy maps and tips on events and activities.

If you're around at the end of August – call the TIC for exact dates – don't miss the Asakusa Samba Carnival. This, the most un-Japanese of all Tokyo festivals, is put on by Brazilian-born Japanese, and it comes as close as anything to restoring Asakusa to its pre-WWII bawdy glory.

Sensō-ji

Sensō-ji (☎ 3844 1575; admission free; open 24 hours) enshrines a golden statue, an image of the goddess Kannon, which was miraculously fished out of nearby Sumida-gawa by two fishermen in AD 628. In time, a temple was built to house the image, which has remained on the spot through successive rebuildings of the temple.

If you approach Sensō-ji from Asakusa subway station, you will enter through **Kaminari-mon** (Thunder Gate). The gate houses a pair of scowling protective deities: Fūjin, the god of wind, on the right; and Raijin, the god of thunder, on the left.

Straight on through the gate is **Nakamise-dōri**, a shopping street set within the actual temple precinct. Everything from tourist trinkets to genuine Edo-style crafts is sold here. There's even a shop selling wigs to be worn with a *kimono*. Be sure to try the *sembei* (savoury rice crackers) that a few shops specialise in – you'll have to queue though, as they are very popular with Japanese tourists as well.

Nakamise-dōri leads north to the main temple compound, but it is hard to say if the Kannon image really is inside, as you cannot see it – not that this stops a steady stream of worshippers making their way up the stairs to the temple, where they cast coins, clap ceremoniously and bow in a gesture of respect. In front of the temple is a large incense cauldron where people go to rub smoke against their bodies to ensure good health. If any part of your body (as far as modesty permits) is giving you trouble, you should give it particular attention when applying the smoke.

The temple itself is a post-1945 concrete reproduction of the original, but the building is not the sole reason to visit. The atmospheric energy is the real attraction.

Shitamachi Walking Tour (Asakusa)

Map 9
Time: About two hours
Distance: About 3km
Highlights: Kappabashi-dōri, old stores, Chingo-dō-ji

If you've spent a few days in Tokyo, you'll notice the difference between Asakusa and other parts of the city as soon as you pass into Nakamise-dōri. For the most part, the Japanese vision of the future has swallowed up Tokyo, and for this reason it is worth taking a stroll outside the precincts of Sensō-ji. What you get is not so much an abundance of sights as an alternative to Japan Inc.

To start, exit Sensō-ji the way you entered it – through Hōzō-mon at the temple end of Nakamise-dōri. Turn right here and follow the road around the perimeter of the temple grounds. Look for **Chingo-dō-ji** on your right, next door to the back entrance to Dempō-in. This temple is an interesting oddity: founded in 1883, it was constructed for the 'raccoon dogs' living in the Sensō-ji precincts. This stretch of road also has a flea market feel about it – there are often stalls set up along the outside of the temple precincts. You can pick up some interesting festival accessories here.

If you follow the road round to the right, you pass an arcade with shops selling traditional items at reasonable prices. Look for shops selling *yukata* (cotton robes) and *kimono*. Farther along is the **Hanayashiki Amusement Park** (☎ 3842 8780; open 10am-6pm, closed Tues; admission adults/ children ¥900/400, rides average ¥300-400). The amusement park dates back to 1853, and so, it would seem, do some of the fairly rickety-looking rides.

From Hanayashiki take a left and another left and you will enter what is left of **Rokku**, Asakusa's old cinema district. It is all a little down-at-heel nowadays, and the few remaining cinemas seem to restrict their screenings to Japanese pornography – at least they all carry the familiar lurid posters depicting naked women trussed up like hams, their meek eyes casting plaintive looks at the tattooed torturers standing over them. As you wander through, consider that this was once the most lively of Tokyo's entertainment districts – how times change. Presiding over the area today, just next door to the Big Boy restaurant, is the **Rox building**, a shopping centre notable primarily for its failure to endow Asakusa with an air of cosmopolitan modernity. Near the Rox building is **Asakusa Engei Hall**, where performances of *rakugo* (story telling) are held.

Ahead is another arcade. Mostly it is taken up by Japanese restaurants specialising in tempura and so on. However, worth a look are the traditional *sembei*-making shops. These savoury crackers are very popular, and in the open-fronted shops in the arcade you can watch them being produced.

The arcade takes you back onto Kamanarimon-dōri, which is lined with excellent Japanese restaurants. Turn right here and cross over Kokusai-dōri. Following the small road that runs to Kappabashi-dōri, to your left is a block that is dotted with temples, most of them quite small. The largest is **Tokyo Hongan-ji**, which is on your left just before you get to Kappabashi-dōri.

Kappabashi-dōri is Tokyo's wholesale restaurant supplies area. It's chock-a-block with shops selling wax food models, bamboo cooking utensils, customised cushions and even the red lanterns (*aka-chōchin*) that light the back alleys of Tokyo by night. Turn right into Kappabashi-dōri and walk up the road a few blocks, before crossing over the road and walking back in the other direction.

The landmark that tells you you've reached the end of your Shitamachi tour and done the rounds of the plastic food shops is the **Niimi building**, crowned with an enormous chef's head – you can't miss it. It's on the corner of Asakusa-dōri, and a few minutes down the road to your left is Tawara-machi subway station on the Ginza line.

On your left, just before you reach the temple, is the garden **Dempō-in**. Unfortunately it is not open to the public – but this does not stop you from peering over the fence and taking a look at one of Tokyo's most beautiful gardens. The garden contains a pond and a replica of a famous Kyoto teahouse.

Behind Sensō-ji, to the right, is **Asakusa-jinja**. Unlike its Buddhist neighbour, Asakusa-jinja is a Shintō shrine, a tribute to the comfortable coexistence of Japan's religions. It was built in honour of the brothers who discovered the Kannon statue. The shrine dates back to 1649, and is the site of one of Tokyo's most important festivals, the Sanja matsuri, a three-day extravaganza of costumed parades, lurching *mikoshi* (portable shrines) and stripped-to-the-waist *yakuza* sporting remarkable tattoos.

Taikokan Drum Museum (☎ *3842 5622; admission adults/children ¥300; open 10am-5pm Wed-Sun)* is well worth checking out for its splendidly interactive exhibit – bash away on anything unless it's marked with a red dot. It's on the second floor of the Miyamoto festival goods store on Kokusai-dōri, opposite the police box.

Kappabashi-dōri

One stop west of Asakusa on the Ginza line (get off at Tawaramachi) or a 10-minute walk from Sensō-ji is Kappabashi-dōri, a restaurateur's heaven. Gourmet accessories include colourful, patterned *noren* (split doorway curtains), crockery and oodles of wax food models. Whether you want steak and chips, a lurid pizza, a bowl of *rāmen* or a plate of bolognese complete with an upright fork, it is all on this street. Most items aren't particularly cheap, but the majority of them are very convincing and certainly make unusual souvenirs.

Sumida-gawa Cruise

'Cruise' is a slight overstatement, but in its time Sumida-gawa was a picturesque river punctuated by delicate arched bridges. It's no longer so, but a cruise is a good way to get to or from Asakusa and look at some of Tokyo's new bay area developments. It's

also a good option when the summer heat takes the fun out of walking.

The *Suijō Bus* departs from a pier below Asakusa's Azuma-bashi and goes to the garden Hama Rikyū Onshi-teien (Map 7; ¥620), Hinode Pier (Map 1; ¥660) and on to Ōdaiba Seaside Park (Map 6; ¥400) and the Museum of Maritime Science (¥520). The best option is to buy a ticket to Hama Rikyū Onshi-teien (you'll still have to pay the ¥300 entry fee for the garden). From the garden it's a 15-minute walk into Ginza. Boats leave daily between 9.50am and 7.35pm. Take an English leaflet when you buy your ticket; it describes the 11 bridges you'll pass under between Asakusa and Hama Rikyū Onshi-teien.

IKEBUKURO (MAP 2)
池袋

Ikebukuro has been creeping upmarket, giving the area a cosmopolitan sheen. Today, provincial old Ikebukuro is home to some of the world's biggest department stores, one of the tallest buildings in Asia, the world's largest automobile showroom, the escalator from hell and the second-busiest station in Tokyo. The obligatory fashionable shopping plazas have started to spring up, and the CD superstore invasion has bestowed branches of HMV and Virgin Records.

For the time being, Ikebukuro lags behind other areas of Tokyo in terms of vibrancy and attractions, but it can be worth spending an afternoon or morning in the area. Most sights are on the eastern side of Ikebukuro station; the west side is mainly notable for the Tokyo Metropolitan Art Space.

Tokyo Metropolitan Art Space

Part of the 'Tokyo Renaissance' plan, the Art Space (☎ *5391 2111; admission varies by event; open 9am-10pm)* has that I.M.Pei-greenhouse thing going on. The plaza-like area in front of the building is a popular place to hang out, munch on Big Macs and practise the latest dance moves. The building is designed mainly for performance art, featuring four halls: one large, one medium and two small. If you're not there for a

Goth girls gather on Sundays at Harajuku station

Kari-chata blossoms

A Sōbu JR train crossing the Sumida-gawa river

Get behind your favourite *sumō* wrestler

MICHAEL TAYLOR

Catching up outside Shimbashi station

JOHN ASHBURNE

An art gallery in Harajuku

JOHN McINNES

Outside the Tokyo Metropolitan Museum of Art

MICHAEL TAYLOR

Pop culture at Harajuku station

JOHN HAY

Reflections of Tokyo

show, the building is memorable mainly for its soaring escalator ride.

Metropolitan Plaza

Just across the road from the Metropolitan Art Space, the Metropolitan Plaza (☎ 5954 1111; open 11am-8.30pm daily) is a multi-floor collection of designer boutiques and restaurants. On the ground floor is **Tōbu Art Museum** (☎ 5391 3220; admission ¥1000; open 10am-6.30pm, closed Wed), which houses exhibits of contemporary Japanese art. The 6th floor has a huge HMV store.

Tōbu Department Store

With 29 floors, it's possible to spend all day in this place (☎ 3981 2211; open 10am-8pm, closed Wed) – but try not to, won't you? On floors 10 to 17 of the main building, you'll find most of the store's restaurants, while the two basement floors house the 'groceteria' (food section).

Seibu Loft

On the western side of the station, this is Seibu's (☎ 3981 0111; open 10am-8pm, closed Tues) biggest branch. The 12th floor has an art museum.

Sunshine City Alba

Billed as a city in a building (☎ 3989 3331), this is basically another opportunity to partake of that quintessential Japanese pastime – shopping.

With 60 floors (mostly office space), there are some diversions. For ¥620, you can take the world's second-fastest lift to the 60th-floor observatory and gaze out at Tokyo's murky skyline. **Sunshine International Aquarium** (☎ 3989 3466; adult/child ¥1600/800; open 10am-6pm) is one of the best in Tokyo. **Sunshine Planetarium** (☎ 3989 3475; adult/child ¥800/500; open noon-5.30pm Mon-Fri, Sat & Sun 11am-6.30pm) is an option, though shows are in Japanese.

Not in the Sunshine City building itself, but in the World Import Mart building (7th floor) of Sunshine City, is the **Ancient Orient Museum** (☎ 3989 3491; admission ¥500; open 10am-4.30pm daily), which is

strictly for those with a special interest in ancient odds and ends such as coins and beads.

Toyota Amlux

Toyota Amlux (☎ 5391 5900; admission free; open 11am-8pm Tues-Sat, 10am-7.30pm Sun and public holidays) is touted as the world's largest automobile showroom. It is five floors of blatant Toyota self-promotion, but with neat ambient sound effects and a majestic escalator ride, it is worth a brief detour. Toyota Amlux is next to Sunshine City, 10 minutes from the eastern exit of Ikebukuro station.

SHINJUKU (MAP 3)
新宿

Shinjuku is a city in itself and without doubt the most vigorous part of Tokyo. If you have only a day in Tokyo, Shinjuku is the place to go. Two million people a day pass through Shinjuku station and its crowded, sprawling underground tunnels and caverns can reduce newcomers to gibbering wrecks – avoid the shakes by knowing where you are going beforehand and keeping a close lookout for the English signposting.

Shinjuku effectively divides into two areas demarcated by the station. On the west side are the skyscrapers, several of which are worth visiting, including the latest addition to the skyline, the imposing Tokyo Metropolitan Government Offices. The eastern side of the station is far and away the liveliest part of Shinjuku.

West Side

As the city's high-rise centre, this is supposed to be one of the few stable areas in earthquake-prone Tokyo – hopefully, that's true.

Tokyo Metropolitan Government Offices

Known as Tokyo Tochō (☎ 5321 1111; admission free; open from 9.30am), these two adjoining buildings have stunning architecture and great views from the twin observation floors of the 202m-tall No 1 building. Despite the critics, most visitors are won over by the buildings' complex symmetries and computer-chip appearance.

Particularly impressive is the spacious Citizen's Plaza in front of the No 1 building – more reminiscent of a Roman amphitheatre than anything Japanese.

The No 2 building is also appealing, with its three-tiered asymmetrical design. Connecting the two buildings is an open plaza called Fureai-Mall. With several modern

West Shinjuku Walking Tour

Map 3
Time: About three hours
Distance: About 3km
Highlights: Tokyo Metropolitan Government Offices, Shinjuku NS building, Shinjuku Sumitomo building

The west exit of Shinjuku station leads into an underground mall lined with shops and restaurants. There are some good lunch-time specials to be had here. Follow the mall to the Shinjuku post office exit and take the stairs to the right. Ahead of you is the **Shinjuku Center building,** which offers the Toto Super Space, a bathroom and kitchen display venue complete with a 'Toilet Zone' and a free observation port on the 53rd floor. Next door is the Yasuda Kaisai-Kaijo building. On the 42nd floor is **Tōgō Seiji Art Museum** (☎ 3349 3081; entry ¥500; open 9.30am-4.30pm Tues-Fri). The museum is notable mainly for its purchase, at more than ¥5 billion, of Van Gogh's *Sunflowers*. The museum is, however, mainly a forum for the work of the Japanese artist Tōgō Seiji.

The **Shinjuku Mitsui building** is only worth a detour if you are a photography buff. On the 1st floor is the **Pentax Forum** (☎ 3348 2941, admission free; open 10.30am-6pm daily). The exhibition space has changing exhibits by photographers sponsored by Pentax. The best part, however, is the vast array of Pentax cameras, lenses and other optical equipment on display. It is completely hands-on – you can snap away with the cameras and use the huge 1000mm lenses to peer through the windows of neighbouring buildings.

On the opposite corner of the intersection is the **Shinjuku Sumitomo building**, which bills itself as 'a building that's actually a city', a concept the Japanese seem to find particularly appealing (Sunshine City in Ikebukuro, and Shibuya's Mark City are two others). The Sumitomo building has a hollow core. The ground floor and basement feature a 'jewel palace' (a jewellery shopping mall) and a general shopping centre. There is a free observation platform on the 51st floor – a good deal when you consider the inflated prices being charged by Tokyo Tower and Sunshine City for entry to their observatories.

By now you must have noticed the towering **Tokyo Metropolitan Government Offices**. Some 13,000 government workers sweat over the administrative paperwork of running Tokyo in these buildings. The Citizen's Plaza features shops, restaurants, a passport section and, curiously, a blood donation room.

If you are in the mood for a bit of eccentric high tech, the interior of the **Shinjuku NS building**, just down the road, is hollow, like the Sumitomo building, featuring a 1600 sq metre area from which you can gaze upward at the transparent roof. Overhead, at 110m, is a 'sky bridge'. The square itself features a 29m pendulum clock, listed by the *Guinness Book of Records* as the largest in the world. The 29th and 30th floors have a large number of restaurants, including a branch of the Spaghetti Factory. On the 5th floor, you can browse through the showrooms of Japanese computer companies in the OA Centre.

At this point you have basically exhausted west Shinjuku's walking possibilities, unless you opt for a stroll in the rather drab **Shinjuku Chūō-kōen** park. The best option is probably to walk back to Shinjuku station via the underground arcade and grab a coffee or a bite to eat along the way.

sculptures scattered about, this is a good spot for a picnic lunch.

To reach the No 1 building's observation floors, take one of the two 1st-floor lifts.

The north observatory is open from 9.30am to 10pm, and is closed Monday. The south observatory is open 9.30am to 5.30pm; weekends and holidays it closes at 7pm (closed Tuesday).

East Side

Shinjuku's east side is an area to wander through and wonder. While the west side is showy, administrative and planned, Shinjuku's east side is spontaneous chaos. The chief east-side attractions include the shrine **Hanazono-jinja** (☎ 3200 3093), scene of a great weekly Sunday morning flea-market, many department stores, and the colourful, if sleazy, **Kabukichō** and **Golden Gai** areas.

From Shinjuku station's eastern exit, your first sight is the **Studio Alta** building, with its huge video screen showing ads and video clips day and night. The sheltered area beneath the screen is Shinjuku's most popular meeting place, though like the Almond coffee shop in Roppongi, it has become so popular that finding the person you're meeting is something of an ordeal. Opposite Studio Alta, close to the My City exit of Shinjuku station, is a small concrete plaza that has become a popular spot for bands to perform in the evenings.

To the right of Studio Alta, about 100m up Shinjuku-dōri, on your left, is the old branch of the **Kinokuniya bookshop** (☎ 3354 0131; open 10am-8pm, irregular holidays). The sheltered area here is also a popular meeting place. Around Kinokuniya are shops selling discounted clothes and shoes, and some cheap second-hand camera shops thrive in the backstreets. The area abounds in fast-food joints, cheap noodle shops, reasonably priced Western food and some of the best Chinese food in Japan.

Of all the department store art museums in Tokyo, **Isetan Museum** (☎ 3352 1111; admission ¥500-1000; open 10am-7.30pm, closed Wed) in Isetan department store is considered the best. Exhibitions change frequently and they never disappoint. Admission changes with exhibitions.

Takashimaya Times Square (☎ 5661 1122) contains a Takashimaya department store, HMV records, an IMAX theatre, two food courts, a Joypolis virtual reality game centre, a Tōkyū Hands department store and countless smaller stores. Check out what Japanese mall-rats look like here. The new branch of Kinokuniya bookshop in the annex of the complex (connected by an aerial walkway) houses perhaps the largest collection of English-language books in the city.

HARAJUKU & AOYAMA (MAP 4)
原宿／青山

Harajuku and Aoyama melt into each other, yet they are trashy-trendy ying-yang incarnate. Harajuku teems with teenagers swapping pocket money for Mickey Mouse caps and string vests (Takeshita-dōri is the place to see them in action), while Aoyama is the domain of chic boutiques and ersatz Parisian cafes. A stroll down Harajuku's tree-lined Omote-sandō into Aoyama comes as a welcome relief from the push-and-shove chaos of other consumer villages like Shinjuku.

The chief attractions are Meiji-jingū – one of Japan's finest shrines – the bustling action of Takeshita-dōri and Aoyama's Nezu Fine Art Museum and Watari Museum. Try and fit in a cup of coffee on Omote-sandō along the way.

East of Harajuku and Aoyama, Nishi-Azabu is a buffer zone between Tokyo chic and the let-it-all-hang-out approach of Roppongi. There aren't many attractions by day in Nishi-Azabu, but it's home to some of Tokyo's best restaurants and clubs.

Harajuku

One of the best (and trendiest) attractions in Harajuku is Omote-sandō. This tree-lined avenue sports al fresco coffee shops, trendy boutiques and a good cross section of restaurants. Omote-sandō is at its best on a Sunday, when the street is closed to traffic and Tokyo's beautiful people come to strut their stuff. (See the boxed text 'Tokyo Cafe Society' in the Places to Eat chapter.)

THINGS TO SEE & DO

East Shinjuku Walking Tour

Map 3
Time: About two hours
Distance: About 2km
Highlights: Kabukichō, Golden Gai, department stores

Shinjuku Station   Takashimaya B1

From inside Shinjuku station, follow the east exit or Kabukichō exit signs. Once you have passed through the ticket gates, take the 'My City' exit. As you surface, directly ahead of you is the **Studio Alta building**. You can't miss its enormous video screen.

Continue walking east down Shinjuku-dōri. This area is good for bargain men's clothing and shoes. A little farther on is **Kinokuniya bookshop**, with its superb collection of English books (especially books on Japan and Japanese text books) on the 7th floor. Continue walking and you pass **Mitsukoshi department store** on the right and **Isetan** (arts and crafts, fashionable boutiques and **Isetan Museum**) on the left.

Turn left at Isetan and walk down to Yasukuni-dōri. Down a lane on the opposite side of the road is **Hanazono-jinja** – not one of Tokyo's major shrines, but it's nestled so close to Tokyo's most infamous red-light district that its clientele can make for some interesting people-watching. The shrine has a reputation for bringing success to business ventures – both legitimate and otherwise.

Exit Hanazono-jinja onto **Golden Gai**, a tiny warren of alleyways devoted entirely to small, stand-up watering holes. Traditionally the haunt of bohemian Tokyoites (writers and the like), it is a safe area to take a walk through, even by night. You may not, however, be welcome in some of the bars, where it's regulars only. By day it is usually deserted. It is also an area that is said to be gradually being bought up by Seibu – in which case it will probably not be long before we see another department store going up here. However, for the time being Golden Gai hangs on.

Continue in the same direction along the alleyways that run parallel to Yasukuni-dōri and you reach **Kabukichō**, Tokyo's most notorious red-light district. Despite its reputation, it's a relatively safe area to stroll around. Most of what goes on in these environs is pretty much off limits to foreigners, though single *gaijin* males are likely to be approached by touts offering to take them to an overpriced strip club.

Kabukichō must be one of the more imaginative red-light areas in the world, with 'soaplands' (massage parlours), love hotels, 'no-pants' coffee shops (it's the waitresses who doff their briefs, not the customers), peep shows, so-called pink cabarets ('pink' is the Japanese equivalent of 'blue' in English), porno-video booths and strip shows that involve audience participation. As you walk through streets lined with neon signs and crowded with drunken salarymen, high-pitched female voices wail out invitations to their establishments through distorting sound systems, and Japanese punks earn a few extra yen passing out advertisements for telephone clubs. *Tere kura*, as these clubs are known, have become particularly popular. Japanese men pay an hourly fee for a room, a telephone and a list of girls' telephone numbers – if the two like the sound of each other, they can make a date to meet.

Continue along the perimeter of Kabukichō and look for the enormous **Koma Theatre**, which started off as a movie theatre, but quickly switched to stage performances. It still hosts performances of a more mainstream variety than those elsewhere in Kabukichō. The square facing the Koma is ringed by cinemas and is also a popular busking spot at night, though *yakuza* are usually quick about moving anyone too popular along. Look for the **Virtual Theatre** – a high-tech, full-sensory impact cinema – which is also located in this square. Take any of the lanes radiating off the square to see Kabukichō at its best.

From this point wander back to Yasukuni-dōri and take one of the lanes that connect it with Shinjuku-dōri. Like much of Shinjuku, these lanes are lined with restaurants, shot bars and shops. It's another area popular with buskers and good to linger (look for the revolving *sushi* bars) if the crowds aren't too overwhelming.

東京 東京 東京 東京 東京 東京 東京 東京 東京 東京 東京 東京 東京 東京 東京

Further down Omote-sandō at the intersection with Meiji-dōri is a Harajuku landmark, **Laforet** (☎ *3475 0411; opening hours vary from boutique to boutique*). A large space on the front of the building is used for cryptic advertising. At LP's last visit the winter sales were advertised by a giant neon-yellow bog roll. You'll see a fascinating spectrum of trendy types passing in and out – it's a popular spot with talent-spotting Japanese photographers. Inside are fashionable boutiques; downstairs is a HMV, where you can check out the latest CDs on the headphones provided.

Turning right onto Meiji-dōri (look for the Condomania shop on the corner), you could walk into Shibuya in around 15 minutes.

Further down Omote-sandō, look for the **Oriental Bazaar** (see the Shopping chapter) and a host of boutiques with names like 'Gallerie de Pop' and 'Coccoon'. The best known of Harajuku's boutiques is the **Hanae Mori building** (☎ *3406 1021; open 10.30am-7pm daily*), designed by Tange Kenzō and featuring the work of Hanae Mori, perhaps Japan's most famous fashion designer. There is also an antiques bazaar in the basement.

Meiji-jingū Next door to Yoyogi-kōen, this is without a doubt Tokyo's, if not Japan's, most splendid Shintō shrine (*admission free; open dawn till dusk*). Completed in 1920, Meiji-jingū was constructed in honour of Emperor Meiji and Empress Shōken. Unfortunately, the shrine was destroyed by WWII bombing. Rebuilding was completed in 1958.

It might be a reconstruction, but unlike many others, Meiji-jingū was rebuilt with all the features of a Shintō shrine preserved. The shrine itself was built with Japanese cypress, while the cypress for the huge torii came from Ali Shan in Taiwan.

In the grounds of the shrine (on the left, before the second set of torii) is the park **Meiji-jingū-gyoen** (☎ *3379 5511; admission ¥500; open 9am-4.30pm*). This park, formerly an imperial garden, has some very peaceful walks and is almost deserted on weekdays. It is particularly beautiful in June, when the irises are in bloom.

Cos-play-zoku

When Tokyo's forces of Law and Order donned their riot gear to oust the Takenoko-zoku – the dancers clad in bright pastel clothes, with fifties rockabilly haircuts – from Yoyogi-kōen park, no-one imagined that the Takenokozoku would be replaced by an even odder, younger crowd.

Enter the Cos-play-zoku, the Costume Play Gang. Mainly teenage girls from the dormitory towns and cities around Tokyo's fringe, the Cos-play-zoku assemble at Harajuku's Jingu-bashi each weekend, bedecked in Gothic make-up, a mixture of SM queen arch-vamp, black taffeta, blue lipstick and cartoon nurse exaggeration.

Cos-play-zoku are united in their fondness for Japanese *visual-kei* (visual type) bands, such as L'Arc En Ciel and Zard, and a sense of pride in their alienation. Many of the girls are *ijime-ko*, kids bullied in school, who find release and expression in their temporary weekend identities.

The end result is Tokyo's most fun circus, as each weekend hordes of excited photographers, bewildered tourists and plain voyeurs gather to catch the show. The girls revel and primp and pose for the cameras until dusk, when they hop back on the trains for the slow return to 'normal' life in the faceless housing blocks of Chiba and Kawasaki.

東京 東京 東京 東京 東京 東京 東京

As you approach Meiji-jingū, there are so many signs indicating the way to the **Meiji-jingū Treasure Museum** (☎ 3379 9222; admission ¥200; open 9am-4.30pm) that you tend to feel obliged to pay it a visit. In fact, the collection of items from the lives of the emperor and empress is not very exciting. It includes official garments, portraits and other imperial odds and ends. (The museum is closed on the third Friday of each month.)

If you visit the shrine on a weekend, check out the Cos-play-zoku – see the boxed text earlier in this chapter.

Yoyogi-kōen Sunday in Yoyogi-kōen (admission free; open dawn till dusk) used to be one of Tokyo's prime attractions, when local bands gathered to give free concerts on the pathways into the park. Sadly, the police have put a stop to this, and now Yoyogi-kōen is just another park. That said, with lots of wide open spaces and some flowering trees, it's not a bad place for a picnic or some sports on the grass.

You can still catch glimpses of the former musical spectacle if you go on a Sunday, because a few die-hard performers haven't heard that the show is over. In particular, the city's rockabilly fans can still be seen doing highly stylised 1950s dance routines to taped music. One wonders how long this cult will survive.

If you cross the pedestrian overpass from the park that leads down toward Shibuya, you may find a flea market in the open space on the other side. There is a bandstand here as well, and on some weekends, Tokyo's hip-hop community gets together and revives another ancient dance style, in this case, break dancing.

Ota Memorial Art Museum This museum (☎ 3403 0880; admission ¥500, extra for special exhibitions; open 10.30am-5.30pm Tues-Sun) has an excellent collection of ukiyo-e (wood-block) prints and offers a good opportunity to see works by Japanese masters of the art, including Hiroshige. The museum is closed from the 26th to the end of each month.

Takeshita-dōri This teeming alley veers somewhere between teenage kitsch and subcultural fetish. Look for outrageously gaudy jewellery, punk accessories, trendy hair boutiques, fast-food joints and cuddly toys.

Aoyama

Aoyama is not rich in sights, but it's only a 15-minute walk from Harajuku. The area is worthwhile mainly for the fashionable Killerdōri, and for several museums and galleries.

If you arrive in Aoyama from Harajuku along Aoyama-dōri, keep walking until you reach Gaien-nishi-dōri. This is better known as **Killer-dōri**, so named for its fashionable boutiques. On the right-hand corner of the intersection is the **Japan Traditional Craft Center** (see Arts, Crafts & Antiques in the Shopping chapter for details). On the corner diagonally opposite the craft centre is another boutique building, regarded highly by Tokyoites, **Bell Commons** (☎ 3475 8123; open 11am-8pm daily).

Up Killer-dōri, on the left-hand side, is the progressive, often provocative **Watari Museum of Contemporary Art** (☎ 3402 3001; admission ¥1000; open 11am-7pm Tues-Sun). The building houses an excellent art bookshop **On Sundays** (☎ 3470 1424; open 11am-7pm) with its small coffee shop in the basement, and exhibition space for young nonmainstream artists. Browse its enormous collection of obscure postcards (around ¥150 each).

Back down the other end of Aoyama-dōri, south of Omote-sandō, are some minor attractions. The boutique-laden **Spiral building** (☎ 3498 1171; opening hours vary) will interest architecture fans. There is a coffee shop in the front of the building, and modern art exhibitions are sometimes held in the atrium. Kottō-dōri, which runs south-east off Aoyama-dōri, close to the Spiral building, has a number of pricey antique stores.

Nezu Fine Art Museum This museum (☎ 3400 2536; admission ¥1000; open 9.30am-4pm Tues-Sun) in Minami-Aoyama is a highly rated exhibition space with a well-established collection of Japanese art – paintings, calligraphy and sculpture – as well as

Chinese and Korean art exhibits and a tea-house where tea ceremonies are performed (however, these are not open to the public). There are around 7000 exhibits here, including some 'Important Cultural Properties'. As well as some notable Japanese art, Sinophiles will find the collection of Shang dynasty bronzes particularly interesting.

The museum is nestled amid delightful gardens (21,000 sq m) with seven traditional teahouses. From Omote-sandō subway station, walk down Omote-sandō away from Harajuku. Turn right at the end of the road and look for the museum on the left.

Honda Welcome Plaza On Aoyama-dōri, beside the Aoyama-itchōme subway station, is the Honda Welcome Plaza (☎ 3423 4118; admission free; open 10am-6pm daily), a showroom in which classic Honda Grand Prix motorcycles and Formula One cars are displayed. Displays also include the latest Honda products and a projection room with a 'sonic floor', where you can watch races with the sensation that you are actually in the thick of it all.

Aoyama Rei-en Cemetery (open 24 hours) This cemetery is a prestigious spot from which to retire into the great unknown. Lafcadio Hearn, John Manjiro and Natsume Soseki are all pushing up the daisies here. It is can also be a pleasant, shady retreat from Aoyama chic, except during the karaoke-and-vomit-fest that is cherry blossom viewing.

SHIBUYA (MAP 4) 渋谷

While it may look like Shinjuku, Shibuya goes about its business with an air of diligently acquired elegance. The area is studded with department stores that vie for the patronage of cash-loaded young Japanese. Shibuya is not rich in sights, but it is a good place for department store browsing, shopping and dining out.

If you leave JR Shibuya station by the north-west (Hachiko) exit, you'll see one of Shibuya's main sights and the exit's namesake: a statue of the dog Hachiko. The story of this dog is rather touching: in the 1920s,

a professor who lived near Shibuya station kept a small Akita dog, who would come to the station every day to await his master's return. The master died in 1925, but the dog continued to show up and wait at the station until his own death 11 years later. The poor dog's faithfulness was not lost on the Japanese, and they built a statue to honour his memory. The statue itself is nothing special; it's usually surrounded by a pack of young Tokyo cool dudes.

Mark City Shibuya
This brand spanking new shopping megacomplex (☎ 3780 6103; opening hours vary) promises, rather optimistically, to 'Make Shibuya adult'. It's a great rainy-day, people-watching, window-shopping venue. Shibuya Excel Hotel Tokyu is here.

Tepco Electric Energy Museum
Called Denryoku-kan, the Tepco Electric Energy Museum (☎ 3477 1191; admission free; open 10.30am-6pm, closed Wed) is the building on Jingū-dōri with the R2D2-shaped silver-domed building (visible from the Hachiko statue). It is one of Tokyo's better science museums, offering seven floors of dynamic exhibitions on every conceivable aspect of electricity. There are innumerable hands-on exhibits. Get the excellent, free English handout at the reception desk.

NHK Studio Plaza
This is a broadcasting museum (☎ 5400 6900; admission ¥200; open 10am-6pm), with sets from Japanese drama serials and exhibitions demonstrating the behind-the-scenes activity on a broadcasting set. It's a reasonably entertaining rainy day activity. The plaza is closer to Harajuku station than it is to Shibuya station. NHK is closed one Monday of every month.

Tobacco & Salt Museum
Not to be confused with the National Car Wax and Yogurt Museum, this small museum (☎ 3476 2041; admission ¥100; open 10am-6pm Tues-Sun) has some fairly interesting exhibits detailing the history of tobacco and the methods of salt production

practised in premodern Japan (Japan has no salt mines and until recently harvested salt from the sea). As usual, there's little in the way of English explanations, but a lot of the material is self-explanatory. There are no warnings about the risks of smoking and areas are set aside for those who crave a good smoke after touring the museum.

Love Hotel Hill

Take the road up Dogen-zaka to the left of the 109 building, and at the top of the hill, on the side streets that run off the main road, is a concentration of love hotels catering to all tastes. The buildings alone are interesting, representing a range of architectural pastiche, from miniature Gothic castles to kitsch *Arabian Nights*. It's okay to wander in and take a look.

Beam Building

The Beam building *(admission free; open 10am-8pm)* is usually cited as one of Tokyo's more startling examples of vulgar architecture. Maybe, but in Shibuya it hardly stands out. The building houses several karaoke parlours and hundreds of the latest electronic games. Though admission is free, the games eat through those ¥100 coins at an alarming rate.

▷ROPPONGI (MAP 4)
六本木

There's no reason to come here by day, but by night it's the capital of Tokyo. See the Entertainment chapter for more.

EBISU (MAP 5) 恵比寿

Ebisu cannot compete with big hubs on the Yamanote line, but its small size and comfortable atmosphere make for enjoyable strolling. Ebisu is probably best considered a nightspot, as it houses some good restaurants and bars. If you come during the day, most sights worth seeing are in the new Ebisu Garden Place, which is easily reached from JR Ebisu station by an aerial walkway.

Ebisu Garden Place

This is a complex of shops, restaurants and a 39-floor tower surrounded by an open

mall area, perfect for hanging out on warmer days. Ebisu Garden Place *(☎ 5423 7111)* also features the headquarters of **Sapporo Breweries**, which contains the **Beer Museum Yebisu** *(☎ 5423 7255; admission free; open 10am-6pm Tues-Sun)*. There are lots of good exhibits, the best of which is the 'Tasting Lounge', where you can sample Sapporo's various brews in a pleasant space decorated with, er, rare European beer steins.

There are lots of outdoor cafes scattered around the complex. If you're hungry, most serve light meals as well. The restaurants on the 38th and 39th floors of **Ebisu Garden Place Tower** offer excellent views.

Ebisu Garden Place houses the **Tokyo Metropolitan Museum of Photography** *(☎ 3280 0031; admission ¥500, ¥600 for special exhibits or ¥1000 for a ticket to all exhibits; open 10am-6pm Tues-Sun)*, the city's largest photography exhibition space. Most exhibits are highly respected, not least in the wing devoted to computer-generated graphics.

AKASAKA (MAP 7)
赤坂

Akasaka is the area with the greatest concentration of top-notch hotels, including the ANA, New Ōtani and Akasaka Prince. These effectively form a ring around the centre of Akasaka, a huddle of narrow streets lined largely with restaurants. There may not be much in the way of sights besides Hie-jinja and the occasional museum, but Akasaka is the place to indulge in some of Tokyo's best food.

Hie-jinja

The shrine itself is by no means one of Tokyo's major attractions; it's modern, drab and largely cement. The highlight is the walk up to the shrine through a 'tunnel' of orange torii. On a sunny day, the play of the light on the torii is pretty, but Hie-jinja is only worth going out of your way for when the cherry blossoms are out. If you're wondering about the carved monkey clutching one of her young, she is emblematic of the shrine's ability to offer protection against the threat of a miscarriage.

Akasaka Detached Palace

This is known officially as Geihinkan, or State Guesthouse *(closed to public)*. It was built in 1909, with an eye to Versailles and the Louvre, as the residence of the crown prince (later Emperor Hirohito), and aimed to bestow the imperial family with a residence matching their royal counterparts in Europe. Today the palace is used as a guesthouse for visiting dignitaries.

The palace (set in its own grounds 15 minutes' north-west of Akasaka) can be viewed from the outside at its west entry gate. Don't trudge up here unless you have an abiding interest in neo-baroque architecture.

National Diet Building

Gaining admission to this austere building is more trouble than it is worth. You will need to organise it with your embassy or via an introduction from a Diet member – fat chance of the latter for the average visitor. Rest assured, however, that you are not missing much. Proceedings within are notoriously dull.

Suntory Museum of Art

The Suntory Museum of Art *(☎ 3470 1073; admission ¥700-1000; open 10am-5pm Tues-Sun)* is on the 11th floor of Suntory Hall, and offers a pleasant area in which to view its collection of over 2000 traditional artefacts, including lacquerware and pottery. The premises also have a library and a tea room where you can indulge in that most celebrated of Japanese leisure pursuits, the tea ceremony (an extra charge of ¥500).

Hotel Sights

Even the luxury hotels in Akasaka deserve a mention. Notable is the **New Ōtani (Map 4)** *(☎ 3265 1111)*, which has managed to preserve part of a 400-year-old garden that once belonged to a Tokugawa regent. On the 6th floor of the New Ōtani Garden Court building (the north building), the **New Ōtani Art Museum** *(☎ 3221 4111; admission free for hotel guests, ¥500 or higher for nonguests; open 10am-6pm Tues-Sun)* has a decent collection of modern Japanese and French paintings. If you're still in Akasaka at night,

try a hotel sky-bar and check out the night view of Tokyo.

Ark Hills

Ark stands for 'Akasaka-Roppongi knot' – pinioned between Akasaka and Roppongi is a much-touted 'subcity' featuring display rooms, banks, restaurants, entertainment and even housing. It's worth a browse, as much for an insight into how the Japanese see the future as anything else.

Aoyama-dōri

Down Aoyama-dōri, in the direction of Aoyama-itchōme subway station (Map 4), are a couple of sights. About halfway to the station, on the left side, is **Sogetsu Kaikan** *(☎ 3408 1126; admission free, ¥4850 for a lesson; open 10am-5pm)*, a centre for the Sogetsu school of avant-garde ikebana. On the 6th floor is **Sogetsu Art Museum** *(☎ 3408 9112; admission ¥500; open 9.30am-5pm, closed Sun)*, with its bewilderingly eclectic collection of art from across the centuries and the four corners of the world – from Indian Buddhas to works by Matisse. Aoyama-dōri is closed on the second and fourth Saturday of each month.

OTHER ATTRACTIONS

Many of the attractions listed here are off the main colour maps. Where no map reference is given, see Map 1 for the general location; individual listings give details on transportation and directions.

Tokyo Tower

As a tourist attraction, Tokyo Tower (Map 7) *(☎ 3433 5111; admission ¥820; observation platforms open 9am-8pm, to 9pm in Aug)* is an anachronism. Built in 1958 for broadcasting through the Kantō region, it was modelled on the Eiffel Tower – it is just over 30m higher than its Parisian counterpart. The ¥820 price gets you to the 'Grand Observation Platform' (150m) – getting up to the Special Observation Platform (250m) costs another ¥600.

As a tourist trap, the tower is probably not worth seeing but if you're there, the Tokyo Tower also features an overpriced aquarium (¥800), a wax museum (¥870), the uninspired Holographic Mystery Zone (¥410) and showrooms.

The tower is a fair trudge east from Roppongi. If you must go, take the Hibiya subway line one stop to Kamiyachō station.

Parks & Gardens

Many of Tokyo's parks and gardens are described earlier in this chapter. Those listed here are all inside the loop of the Yamanote line and can be easily reached.

Koishikawa Kōraku-en Right next to the Kōraku-en Amusement Park (see Amusement Parks, later in this chapter) is one of the most beautiful and least-visited (by foreigners at least) gardens *(admission ¥300; open 9am-5pm)* in Tokyo. Established in the mid-17th century, it incorporates elements of Chinese and Japanese landscaping. Any visitor to Tokyo with even the slightest interest in gardens should make a point of visiting this one.

Rikugi-en North of the city near JR Komagome station on the Yamanote line, Rikugi-en *(admission ¥300; open 9am-4.30pm)* is a fine garden with landscaped views unfolding at every turn of the pathways that crisscross the grounds. The garden is rich in literary associations: its name is taken from the six principles of *waka* poetry, while the garden invokes famous scenes from Chinese and Japanese literature.

Shizen Kyoiku-an Unique in Tokyo, the Nature Study Garden (Map 5) *(☎ 3441 7176; admission ¥210; open 9am-4.30pm Tues-Sun, to 5pm in summer)* tries to preserve the original flora of Tokyo in undisciplined profusion. There are some wonderful stress-relieving walks through wild woods and swamps, making this one of Tokyo's least known and most appealing getaways.

To get there, take the east exit of Meguro station on the Yamanote line and walk straight ahead for around 15 minutes; look for the garden on the left. You can also take any of the buses that leave from in front of the east exit of Meguro station and get off at the first stop (Shirogane-dai).

Shinjuku-gyoen On Shinjuku-dōri, right in front of Shinjuku-gyoen-mae subway station, Shinjuku-gyoen (Map 3) *(admission ¥200; open 9am-4.30pm Tues-Sun)* has a Japanese garden, a French garden, a hothouse containing exotic tropical plants and, near the hothouse, a pond with giant carp.

Museums & Galleries

As well as the museums and galleries described earlier in this chapter, Tokyo has the following mainstream places. Those with more arcane interests should turn to the TIC's *Museums & Art Galleries* pamphlet or to *Tokyo Museums – A Complete Guide* by Thomas & Ellen Flannigan, which has everything from the Parasitological Museum to the Fisherman's Culture Museum.

Edo-Tokyo Museum Undoubtedly the best recent addition to Tokyo's profusion of museums is Edo-Tokyo Museum (Map 1) *(☎ 3626 8000; admission ¥600; open 10am-6pm Tues-Sun, until 8pm on Fri)*. This massive, futuristic building houses a re-creation of old Edo and post-Meiji Tokyo. The six floors of exhibits and display areas are presented with praiseworthy attention to detail, and you're free to wander and have a hands-on experience of Tokyo's past. The main exhibit is life-size, but there are smaller models, including one of old Edo-jō. It is well worth the entry charge. Edo-Tokyo Museum is east of the city, close to Ryōgoku station on the JR Sōbu line.

Sumō Museum Also close to Ryōgoku station is Kokugikan Sumō Hall and the adjoining Sumō Museum *(☎ 3622 0366; admission free; open 10am-4.30pm Mon-Fri)*. Note that when sumō tournaments are on at the stadium, only those holding tickets to the matches can enter the museum.

Kantō Earthquake Memorial Museum Ten minutes' walk from the Sumō Stadium is the Kantō Earthquake Memorial Museum *(☎ 3623 1200; admission free;*

open 9am-5pm Tues-Sun), with sobering exhibits about the 1923 earthquake.

Tokyo Metropolitan Teien Art Museum

This museum *(☎ 3443 0201; admission varies with exhibits; open 10am-6pm)* hosts art exhibitions, but its appeal lies principally in the building itself, an Art Deco structure built in 1933 and designed by French architect Henri Rapin. It was originally the home of Prince Asaka-no-miya (1887–1981), Hirohito's uncle, who was pardoned for his part in the 'Rape of Nanjing' because of his aristocratic status. It became a museum in 1983. To get there, take the east exit of Meguro station on the Yamanote line and walk straight ahead for around 15 minutes; the museum is on the left. Or, take any of the buses that leave from in front of the east exit of Meguro station and get off at the first stop (Shiroganedai). Entry to the attached garden costs ¥100. The museum is closed on the second and fourth Wednesday of each month.

Meguro Museum of Art

This museum *(☎ 3714 1201; admission ¥900; open 10am-6pm Tues-Sun)* is usually worth a visit, but you can check the *Tokyo Journal* to see what's currently on display. The building is a delight – it's airy and well-lit compared with many other Tokyo art museums, and there is a coffee shop with pleasant views of the grounds on the 1st floor. Take the west exit of Meguro station, walk straight ahead down Meguro-dōri and turn right onto Yamanote-dōri. The museum is on the right.

Fukagawa Edo Museum

A rather long way from anywhere else, east of the city near Monzen-nakachō subway station on the Tōzai line, is the Fukagawa Edo Museum (Map 1) *(☎ 3630 8625; admission ¥300; open 9.30am-4.30pm)*. This museum is a real treat, and well worth the effort of getting out to see it. In a cavernous room, the museum re-creates a 17th-century Edo neighbourhood. You can slip off your shoes, explore the homes, and handle the daily utensils and children's toys. The museum is

closed on the second and fourth Monday of each month.

Japanese Sword Museum

Fans of Japanese swords highly recommend this collection *(☎ 3379 1386; admission ¥525; open 9am-4pm Tues-Sun)* of more than 6000 swords. The nearest station is Sangubashi station near Yoyogi-kōen park on the Odakyū line.

Hatakeyama Memorial Hall

For anyone with an interest in tea ceremony, check out Hatakeyama Memorial Hall *(☎ 3447 5787; admission ¥500; open 10am-4.30pm Tues-Sun; best to ring beforehand)*, east of Shinagawa station. The extensive collection includes many 'Important Cultural Properties' and is complemented by a tea-ceremony garden.

Hara Museum of Contemporary Art

Also south of the city, in Shinagawa, this art museum (Map 1) *(☎ 3445 0651; admission ¥1000; open 11am-5pm Tues-Sun)* is one of Tokyo's more adventurous art spaces. Given that exhibitions change frequently, it is a good idea to check what's on before making your way out here. The Bauhaus design and the cafe, which overflows into a delightful garden, are attractions in themselves. The museum is around 15 minutes' walk from Shinagawa station on the JR Yamanote line.

Asakura Chōso Museum

In Nippori, this is worth a visit for the building and grounds. The museum (Map 9) *(☎ 3821 4549; admission ¥300; open 9.30am-4.30pm, closed Mon and Fri)* commemorates sculptor Asakura Fumio (1883–1964), whose primary work consisted of realistic sculptures of people and cats. But the real attraction is the traditional Japanese house and garden at the back of the museum, designed by the artist. You're free to wander the lovely house, sit on the *tatami* (mats) and enjoy the peaceful view over the garden. Upstairs in the Morning Sun Room and the Poised Mind Room are some excellent ink scrolls and beautiful old *tansu* (wooden chests). For directions, see the boxed text

'Nippori to Nishi-Nippori Walk' further in this section.

Museum of Maritime Science Down in the Ōdaiba/Tokyo Bay area, this large, ship-shaped museum (Map 6) (☎ 5500 1111; adult/child ¥700/400; open 10am-5pm, to 6pm weekends and holidays) looks like a classic tourist trap, but is actually one of Tokyo's better museums. There are four floors of excellent displays dealing with every aspect of ships and shipping, with loads of highly detailed models, including a 4m-long version of the largest battleship ever built, the Yamato, stunning in detail and craftsmanship. There are lots of hands-on exhibits which kids will love, and a pool on the museum's roof where, for ¥100, they can pilot radio-controlled boats and submarines.

Alongside the main building, two boats are moored: a floating tourist trap (the Floating Pavilion) and a retired Antarctic survey vessel (the Soya).

To get there, take the Yurikamome New Transit line from Shimbashi station and get off at the Fune-no-kagakukan stop (the museum's name in Japanese). Alternatively, take the Rinkai Fukutoshin line; the museum is a short walk south-west of the Tokyo Teleport station.

Temples
Sengaku-ji This temple (Map 1) (☎ 3441 5560; admission ¥200; open 9am-4pm) is included in Tokyo's sights for the story that surrounds it, that of the '47 Rōnin'. A rōnin is a masterless samurai, and these ones plotted for two years to have vengeance on the man who caused the death of their master, Lord Asano. Vengeance was undertaken knowing that they too would have to forfeit their lives. After having brought the head of his enemy to their master's grave, 46 of them were condemned to commit seppuku (ritual self-disembowelment) in the samurai fashion – the 47th apparently got off on a technicality. The story, with its theme of paying the supreme sacrifice in the name of loyalty, has captured the Japanese imagination like no other story, having been adapted into countless films and plays. The

temple is close to Sengaku-ji subway station on the Toei Asakusa line.

Zōjō-ji Behind Tokyo Tower is this former funerary temple (Map 7) (☎ 3432 1431; admission free; open dawn till dusk) of the Tokugawa regime. Like many sights in Tokyo, it has been rebuilt several times in recent history; the last time was in 1974.

Nevertheless, Zōjō-ji remains an interesting temple to visit if you're in the vicinity. The main torii date from 1605, and are among the nation's 'Important Cultural Properties'. On the temple grounds there is a large collection of statues of the bodhisattva Jizō.

Zōjō-ji is a 10-minute walk north of the Shiba-kōen stop on the Toei Mita subway line (walk towards Tokyo Tower).

Gokoku-ji This temple (☎ 3941 0764; admission free; open dawn till dusk) is easily reached from Ikebukuro, but gets surprisingly few visitors. One of the few surviving Edo temples, it dates from 1680. The beautiful main hall is labelled an 'Important Cultural Property'. You can get there from Gokokuji subway station (look for the English signposting inside the station), two stops south-east from Ikebukuro on the Yūrakuchō line. The temple is approached via a steep flight of stairs.

Cemeteries
Strolling through a cemetery may seem like a grim form of entertainment, but cemeteries in Tokyo are usually quite pleasant and make a nice change from the concrete monotony of streets and skyscrapers.

Yanaka Cemetery North of Ueno-kōen and just south of Nippori station is Yanaka Cemetery (Map 9) (open dawn till dusk), one of Tokyo's oldest. It is worth taking a stroll through the cemetery and continuing to Ueno on foot. The quiet Yanaka area has many old Buddhist temples and speciality shops. (See the boxed text 'Nippori to Nishi-Nippori Walk'.)

Zōshigaya Not far south of Sunshine City and Ikebukuro's commercial activity is the

Nippori to Nishi-Nippori Walk

Map 9
Time: About three hours with stops
Distance: About 2km
Highlights: Yanaka Cemetery, Asakura Chōso Museum, temples
Best Season: Cherry blossom/autumn foliage seasons

cc

Spared aerial bombing during WWII, the area around Nippori and Nishi-Nippori stations retains some of the flavour of Edo. It is an area of small temples, atmospheric old cemeteries and pleasant little shops. The following walk is a suggested route from Nippori to Nishi-Nippori stations on the Yamanote line, but you should take the time to deviate from the path as your whim suggests. Note that there are no admission fees to enter the grounds of the temples listed here, but some charge fees to enter their inner precincts.

To start, take the south exit from Nippori station. Taking a right out of the exit will lead you across the railway tracks to a stairway leading up to **Yanaka Cemetery** (Yanaka Rei-en). You can orient yourself here using the large area map at the base of the stairs. At the top of the stairs, walk on about 60m until you see a temple on your left, **Tenno-ji**, which belongs to the Tendai Buddhist sect. In the main courtyard there is a large Buddha image cast in 1690, reminiscent of the Great Buddha in Kamakura.

Leaving Tenno-ji, you enter Yanaka Cemetery proper. You can either stick to the route on the accompanying map and continue straight down the main road which leads past a police box, or take small detours to explore the cemetery. Either way, make your way to the public toilet about 100m past the police box and turn right (west) through the graves toward a residential/mercantile area. After a quick dogleg, this will bring you out in front of a quaint shop selling Buddhist religious goods. Turn right here.

Right after the shop, you will pass **Jōzai-ji**, a temple which is worth a quick look. The next temple on the left is **Chōan-ji**. This Rinzai sect temple was established in 1669. About 30m past Chōan-ji, on the left you will see **Matsujuan** soba restaurant. This makes a good lunch stop.

Next on the left is **Kannon-ji**, a Shingon sect temple consecrated to Kannon. The grounds contain another small cemetery, which is pleasant for poking around in. Continuing on, you will pass **Kaizō-in**, which is more of an administrative centre than a temple and can safely be missed.

Diagonally across from Kaizō-in, the **Sandara Kōgei** basket store has a good collection of Japanese crafts The quality is fairly high and prices are reasonable. Past this, on the left you will see **Ryūsen-ji**, another small Nichiren temple with a cemetery on its grounds. This is worth a quick look. Soon after Ryūsen-ji, on the right, you will see **Asakura Chōso Museum**. The perfectly preserved Japanese house at the back of the main building is accessed via a door on the 1st floor. See Other Attractions in this chapter for details. After leaving the museum continue another 100m or so to the next main intersection. Here, in front of you on the right is the entrance to **Keiō-ji**. This is a pleasant little Nichiren temple with an old wooden *honden* (main hall).

After leaving Keiō-ji, if you're hungry you can walk to nearby *Darjeeling restaurant* for a curry lunch (¥850) or a tea set (¥750); otherwise, take the narrow Suwadai-dōri, which runs along the left side of the temple, heading north toward Nishi-Nippori station.

As you continue north, you will pass several small temples. The most notable of these is **Yōfuku-ji**, the gate of which houses two fierce-looking *nio* guardian figures. Not far beyond this the road leads you straight into **Suwa-jinja**, a shrine, established in 1205, with good views from the grounds.

After the shrine, the road leads straight on to **Nishi-Nippori-kōen**. Turn right and then left and you'll find yourself at Nishi-Nippori station, where you can catch a Yamanote line train or the Chiyoda subway.

東京 東京 東京 東京 東京 東京 東京 東京 東京 東京 東京 東京 東京 東京 東京

old residential district of Zōshigaya. Its **cemetery** (Map 2) *(open dawn till dusk)*, around 10 minutes' walk south of Sunshine City, is the final resting place of author Lafcadio Hearn. It can also be reached from Higashi-Ikebukuro station on the Yūrakuchō line. Take exit No 5, turn right and right again to reach the cemetery.

Just south of the cemetery is the **Zōshigaya Missionary Museum** *(admission free; open 9am-4.30pm Tues-Sun)*, a fine wooden structure that was the home of one John Moody McCaleb, who devoted 50 years of his life to good works in Japan. It is well worth a visit.

Convention & Exhibition Centres
In the Rinkai-town section of Tokyo Bay, the **Tokyo International Exhibition Center (Map 6)** *(☎ 5530 1111; admission varies with different exhibits; open 8am-6pm daily)* is perhaps the most spacious venue of its kind in the Tokyo region. Better known as 'Tokyo Big Sight', this is one building that's worth a trip just to see it. It's reached by the Yurikamone line, which leaves from Shimbashi station, or the Rinkai-Fukutoshin line from Tennōsu.

Makuhari Messe *(☎ 043-296 0001; admission varies; opening time varies)*, east of Tokyo in the Tokyo Bay area of Chiba, attracts more than 10 million people annually to the events held in its exhibition halls.

Hotels and department stores are another often-used forum for major conferences and displays. English-language newspapers and the *Tokyo Journal* regularly list conventions and exhibitions. The Japan External Trade Organization (JETRO; ☎ 3582 5522) publishes a comprehensive listing of Japan's annual trade fairs. Other large sites include:

Harumi Tokyo International Fair Ground
(☎ 3533 5311) 5-3-53 Harumi, Chūō-ku, Tokyo
Pacifico Yokohama (☎ 045-221 2121) 1-1-1 Minato Mirai, Nishi-ku, Yokohama
Sunshine Convention Center (☎ 3989 3486) 3-1 Higashi-Ikebukuro, Toshima-ku, Tokyo; Map 2
Tokyo Ryūtsū Center (TRC) (☎ 3767 2190), 6-1-1 Heiwajima, Ōta-ku, Tokyo
Tokyo Trade Center (☎ 3434 4241) Tokyo Trade Center Building, 1-7-8 Kaigan, Minato-ku, Tokyo

Concert Halls & Event Venues
Tokyo plays host to an impressive line-up of events, from concerts to lectures to sporting events. The best way to learn what's going on is by getting a copy of the *Tokyo Journal*. You can also pick up the *Tokyo Weekender* from the TIC or ask the staff directly about things of particular interest to you. These are some of Tokyo's larger concert halls and event venues:

Ariake Colosseum (☎ 3529 3301) Tokyo Bay area, near Kokusai Tenjijō station; tennis, volleyball, pro-wrestling, sumo; 10,000 seats; Map 6
Kokugikan Sumō Hall (☎ 3623 5111) Sumida-ku, near Ryōgoku station; sumō, boxing, pro-wrestling, concerts; 11,000 seats; Map 1
Kōrakuen Hall (☎ 5800 9999) Bunkyō-ku, near Kōrakuen station; boxing, pro-wrestling, concerts; 2500 seats
Nihon Budōkan Hall (☎ 3216 5100) Chiyoda-ku, near Kudanshita station; martial arts tournaments, concerts; 14,000 seats; Map 8
Orchard Hall (☎ 3477 3244) Shibuya, near Shibuya station's Hachiko exit; opera, classical music, some sports; 2150 seats
Shibuya Kōkaidō (☎ 3463 1211) Shibuya, near Shibuya station's Hachiko exit; rock/pop concerts, traditional Japanese music concerts; 2318 seats
Tokyo Dome (Big Egg) (☎ 5800 9999) Bunkyō-ku, near Kōrakuen station, three minutes from Suidōbashi station; Yomiuri Giants and Nippon Ham Fighters baseball games, concerts (but the acoustics are crap), other sports; 15,000 seats

Showrooms
The headquarters of most of Japan's big companies are located in Tokyo, and there are ample opportunities to check out their latest products displayed in company showrooms.

Since these are all forms of advertising, it goes without saying that they are free. See the relevant area entries for details.

Honda Welcome Plaza Aoyama; classic Honda Grand Prix motorcycles and Formula One cars; Map 4
Pentax Forum West Shinjuku; Japan's best photographers and Pentax' best gear; see the boxed text 'West Shinjuku Walking Tour' in this chapter; Map 3

Ōdaiba/Tokyo Bay Walking Tour

Map 6
Time: About four hours with stops
Distance: About 2.5km
Highlights: Harbour views, Museum of Maritime Science, Tokyo Big Sight

Tokyo is rediscovering the fact that it's a waterfront city, and recent years have seen a spate of development in and around the Tokyo Bay area. Perhaps the most popular Tokyo Bay spot is the Ōdaiba/Ariake area. Ōdaiba and Ariake are serviced by the Tokyo Rinkai Shinkōtsū Sen ('Tokyo Waterfront New Transit Line' or 'Yurikamome line'). There's also the extension of the Rinkai Fukutoshin line.

Tokyo Bay makes a nice change from the congestion of central Tokyo. The following day walk takes in a few of the parks, and some of the museums and attractions which have sprung up over recent years. More than a scenic walk, it should be considered a good chance to breathe the sea air and escape the city for a while.

To start, take the Yurikamome line from Shimbashi station near Ginza to Daiba station. The ride itself is interesting, as it crosses **Rainbow Bridge** and affords good views of bay area developments. Upon arrival at Daiba, you have several choices: head to the futuristic Fuji Television Japan Broadcast Center, which offers a studio tour and observation platform; head to Shiokaze-kōen park to relax by the sea; or walk over to the Decks Tokyo Beach complex for a bite to eat. Whatever you do, don't miss Tokyo's very own **Statue of Liberty**, studiously turning its back to the Rainbow Bridge.

The **Fuji Television Japan Broadcast Center observatory** *(¥500; open 10am-9pm Tues-Sun)* is inside the ball-shaped structure on its upper floors. On clear days, it affords good views of the bay and Rainbow Bridge. A ticket to the observatory also gets you into the Fuji Studio Tour, although this is probably of little interest to foreign visitors as it is all in Japanese.

The **Decks Tokyo Beach complex** houses dozens of trendy restaurants and shops. Since most of the restaurants offer good views to go with the food, the prices tend to be a bit steep.

Shiokaze-kōen park is a good spot for a waterside picnic on warmer days.

The next stop is the **Museum of Maritime Science** (Fune-no-kagakukan). This can be reached by following the shoreline south or by following the map walkways. The ship-shaped museum is one of the better museums in Tokyo. You'll find scores of excellent ship models and displays.

From the Museum of Maritime Science you have the option of taking the train or walking to **Palette Town** complete with its humongous Ferris-wheel, Italian Renaissance shopping mall, Venus Fort and state-of-the-art Toyota showroom **Mega Web**. If you walk, en route check out the **Flame of Liberty** statue. You can't miss it – it's like a V2 rocket stuck in a pile of cat-litter.

Once more you can walk or take the train to the next stop: **Tokyo International Exhibition Center**, better known as 'Tokyo Big Sight'. If you walk (about 20 minutes), follow the 'Center Promenade' walkway. This leads across the flat middle of the island, with the monolithic towers of the bay area rising on all sides. After crossing **Dream Bridge**, Tokyo Big Sight comes into view.

The Big Sight's main hall looks like an Egyptian pyramid which fell to earth upside-down – certainly one of Tokyo's architectural wonders. On the 8th floor of the main hall there is a restaurant and bar, *JW's California Grill* (☎ 5530 1221), which serves American-style food at mid-budget prices. For a good view of the bay, you can take the lifts or escalators to the roof of the hall, which is open to visitors any time a conference is not in session.

From Tokyo Big Sight there are two ways to return to central Tokyo: either take the Yurikamome line back to Shimbashi, or walk over to the Rinkai Fukutoshin line and go two stops to Shin-Kiba station. There, transfer to the JR Keiyō line, which will take you to Tokyo station in less than 10 minutes.

Sony Building Ginza; Tokyo's first and best showroom; Map 7

Toyota Amlux Ikebukuro; Toyota's product line on display; Map 2

Toyota Mega-web Ōdaiba; all the Toyota range, and great simulation rides; Map 6

Amusement Parks

Number one on any list of Tokyo amusement parks has to be **Tokyo Disneyland (Map 1)** (☎ 047-354 001; adult price from ¥5500; open 9am-7pm). Only the Japanese signs reveal that you're a long way from Orange County – Tokyo Disneyland is a near-perfect replica of the famous Californian original. A few rides may be in slightly different locations, but basically you turn left from the entrance to the African Jungle, head straight on to Fantasyland or turn right to Tomorrowland.

The all-inclusive 'passport' costs ¥5500/4800/3700 for adults/children/children under 11 and gives you unlimited access to all the rides. Tokyo Disneyland is closed for about a dozen days a year (most of them in January).

There are often long queues at popular rides – you can wait for 30 minutes to an hour. Donald Duck-hunting crowds are usually lighter in the morning and heavier on weekends and holidays.

To get to Tokyo Disneyland, take the Tōzai subway line east to Urayasu station. Follow the 'direct bus to Disneyland 340m' sign out of the station. A shop-lined lane leads to the Disneyland bus station, where a ticket will cost ¥200.

Alternatively, take the Yūrakuchō subway line to Shin-Kiba station and then the JR Keiyō line to Maihama station, right in front of Disneyland's main gate. The Keiyō line runs all the way to Maihama from Tokyo station (there's a Disneyland information counter at the Yaesu exit).

Shuttle buses to Tokyo Disneyland also run from Tokyo (¥600), Ueno (¥600) and Yokohama (¥1000) stations, from Narita (¥2000) and Haneda (¥700) airports and from the nearby Disneyland hotels.

Next to Kōrakuen station on the Marunouchi subway line, 3km north of the Imperial Palace, is **Kōraku-en Amusement Park** (☎ 5800 9999; admission for adults/children ¥1200/800, ticket for all rides ¥3300; open 10am-8pm). Some rides here are not for the faint-hearted. Try the Spinning Coaster Maihime or the Thrill Ride. A ticket for all rides costs ¥3300. The park shuts at 6pm in winter, and 10pm in summer.

Similar to Kōraku-en Park is **Toshimaen Amusement Park** (☎ 3990 8800; admission ¥1000, rides around ¥400; open 9am-5pm). It has thrill rides with names like Hydropolis and Cork-Screw. To get to the park, take the Seibu-Ikebukuro line east to Toshimaen station. The park closes later in the height of summer.

Game Rooms

Tokyo is chock-a-block with game rooms, ranging from tiny local joints to huge complexes. The big places are concentrated in Shibuya (Map 4) and Shinjuku (Map 3). If you don't read Japanese, some of the games may be utterly incomprehensible, although kids seem to find Nintendo an international language.

In Shibuya, the **Beam building** is a huge complex that offers something electronic for everybody.

Joypolis is a chain of game rooms which specialises in virtual reality and sports simulation games. The two main locations are in Shinjuku's Takashimaya Times Square complex, on the 10th and 11th floors (☎ 5361 3040; admission ¥300, multi-game ticket ¥2900; open 10am-11.15pm) and down in the Tokyo Bay area in the **Deck's Tokyo Beach building (Map 6)** (☎ 5500 1801; admission ¥500; multi-game ticket ¥2900; open 10am-10.45pm) – see the 'Ōdaiba/Tokyo Bay Walking Tour' boxed text in this chapter. A book of five tickets to the bigger rides and games is ¥2600.

If you're tired of shelling out wads of cash for games that end in a matter of minutes, head to the **Sony building (Map 7)** (☎ 3573 2371; admission free; open 11am-7pm) in Ginza, which has several Play Stations with the latest game software that you can play for free. The downside is that you have to queue with a lot of young Tokyoites for the privilege.

Sumō wrestlers depicted in iron

Two women in traditional Japanese *kimono*

Painting *kanji* on temple roofing tiles

Wooden wish batons at a temple

A woman in *kimono* at Meiji-jingū shrine

Tsukiji – the world's largest fish market

Have a ball at the Fuji observatory in Ōdaiba

Horseback archery – culture day at Meiji-jingū

Japan Inc Tours

Japan is one of the world's mightiest industrial powers, but few people have ever seen how this economic giant operates up close. Guided tours will give you some insight into the day-to-day workings of 'Japan Inc'. The tours listed here are free, regularly scheduled and conducted in English, provided you give advance warning. At most of the contact numbers, someone will be present who speaks English. If this is not the case, or you would like more information, call the TIC (☎ 3201 3331). For additional tours, pick up the TIC's *Industrial Japan* handout. For all of these tours, reserve as early as possible.

Nissan Motors Nissan offers tours of its Oppama automobile plant (one hour by train from Tokyo), it has two tours starting at 10am and 2pm. Both tours run only on the second and fourth Tuesday of each month, and last two hours; contact the Nissan Communications Department (☎ 6867 5013).

Honda Motors Honda has tours of three of its automobile plants, Sayama, Suzuka and Hamamatsu, but only the Hamamatsu tour is offered in English. To join the Hamamatsu English tour, you must apply in writing two months in advance to Honda Motor Company, Hamamatsu Factory, 1-13-1, Aoi-Higashiyama, Hamamatsu-shi, Shizuoka Prefecture. Hamamatsu is one or two hours (by train) west of Tokyo.

Asahi Beer Asahi (☎ 3762 9384) offers tours (one hour 20 minutes) of its Sumida Ward brewery three times a day, Monday to Friday. English-speaking guides are available; reservations are necessary for groups of more than five people. The brewery is across the Sumida-gawa from Asakusa.

Suntory Suntory will guide you through its Minato Ward brewery (☎ 3470 1131) on Monday and Friday, eight times a day. Reserve a few days in advance for the English tour. Their main factory in Fuchu (☎ 0423 60 9591) also offers a tour and sampling.

Asahi Newspapers The *Asahi Shimbun* newspaper (Map 7) (☎ 3545 0366) offers tours of its Chūō Ward office and printing plant three times a day. Reserve at least two days in advance for an English guide.

Stock Exchange In central Tokyo, the Tokyo Stock Exchange (☎ 3666 0141) offers free tours in English, by appointment, on weekdays from 1.30pm to 2.30pm.

Bank of Japan The bank offers tours of its operations and international department. Ring for reservations (☎ 3279 1111, ext 4659). It's in Nihombashi, Hongoku-cho.

東京 東京 東京 東京 東京 東京 東京 東京 東京 東京 東京 東京 東京 東京 東京

ACTIVITIES
Cultural

The TIC has a wealth of information on cultural activities and courses, from Zen meditation to ikebana. The following are contact numbers for some of the many schools and associations around Tokyo. It is also worth checking the regular listings in the *Tokyo Journal* and the English-language newspapers.

Acupuncture Known as *hari*, acupuncture is far more commonly practised in Japan than most people realise. Two places that perform acupuncture and are somewhat used to foreigners are:

Baba Kaiseidō Acupuncture Office (☎ 3432 0260) 2-4-5-305 Shiba Daimon, Minato-ku
Chinese Acupuncture Studio (☎ 3464 5819) 2-15-1 Dogenzaka, Shibuya-ku

Tokyo with Children

Tokyo is a very child-friendly city, with lots of attractions designed especially for kids – and a good excuse for adults to visit, too. The following should get you started:

The **National Children's Castle** (Map 4) *(Kodomo no Shiro; adult/child ¥500/400; open 12.30pm-5.30pm Mon-Fri, 10am-5.30pm Sat & Sun)* has playrooms, puppet theatres, a swimming pool and lots of events just for children. There's even a hotel next door built especially for those with young children. Located off Aoyama-dōri, take the Ginza subway line to Omote-sandō station, go out the B2 exit and walk towards Shibuya.

The **Tokyo Metropolitan Children's House** *(Tokyo-to Jido Kaikan)* has several play areas, a hands-on art studio where children can make pottery and origami, a library of *manga* comics, and a monthly schedule of events. It's 300m north-east of Shibuya station, next to Mitake-koen.

Tokyo's **Transportation Museum** (Map 8) *(☎ 3251 8481; adult/child ¥310/150; open 9.30am-5pm Tues-Sun)*, in Akihabara, is a museum both children and adults can enjoy, with great displays on all modes of transport, especially trains.

The ship-shaped **Museum of Maritime Science (Map 6)** *(☎ 5500 1111; adult/child ¥700/400; open 10am-5pm, to 6pm weekends and holidays)* is filled with detailed model ships, hands-on displays and even a pool for piloting remote-control submarines. The museum is in the Ōdaiba/Tokyo Bay area.

Although **Ueno Zoo (Map 9)** *(☎ 3828 5171; adult/child/young child ¥600/300/free; open 9.30am-4.30pm Tues-Sun)* is pretty much like other zoos round the world, it does have a petting zoo, and its proximity to the other attractions of Ueno-kōen is a bonus. See the Ueno section of this chapter for more information.

Your kids will be delighted to try the latest games in some of the world's largest **video game rooms** (see Other Attractions in this chapter). You can find smaller video game centres in almost every neighbourhood.

Colourful ornamental **carp** are fascinating, and your kids can feed them at some gardens and shrines, where a bag of carp food is ¥100. The pond behind Yasukuni-jinja (Map 8) is a good spot; Rikugi-en (north of the city – see Parks & Gardens under Other Attractions) has perhaps the largest and most beautiful carp in Tokyo.

If you've exhausted the options above and want a sure-fire hit with the kids, be prepared to spend a little time and money at **Tokyo Disneyland (Map 1)** *(☎ 047-354 001; adults from ¥5500; open 9am-7pm)*. See Amusement Parks under Other Attractions for more details.

東京 東京 東京 東京 東京 東京 東京 東京 東京 東京 東京 東京 東京 東京 東京

Bonsai Large hotels and department stores often have *bonsai* displays. Devotees should make the 30-minute trip north from Tokyo to visit Bonsai Village at Bonsai-machi, Omiya, Saitama.

Calligraphy Known in Japanese as *shodō*, calligraphy lessons are available at the Koyo Calligraphy Art School (☎ 3941 3809) in Ōtsuka, south-east of Ikebukuro, in Bunkyo-ku.

Cuisine Japanese cooking classes are served up at Egami Cooking School (☎ 3269 0281), very near Ichigaya station in central Tokyo. There's also Akasaka B Cooking School (☎ 3582 9074) in Akasaka (Map 7), as well as Cooking House Kuroda (☎ 045-261 5181) in Yokohama.

Ikebana There are lots of ikebana (flower arranging) schools around Tokyo. To find out about courses, call Ikebana International (☎ 3293 8188, *Ochanomizu Square Building, 1-6 Surugadai, Kanda, Chiyoda-ku*). Some schools provide instruction in English; prices start at around ¥3000 an hour.

Language The TIC's *Japanese & Japanese Studies* leaflet lists government-accredited schools that belong to the Association of International Education (☎ 3485 6827). The association can also be contacted directly, as can the Association for the Promotion of Japanese Language Education (☎ 5386 0080).

Costs at private language schools vary greatly, depending on the school's status and facilities. For part-time or seasonal intensive study, tuition fees average about ¥50,000 per term. For full-time study, there is usually an application fee of ¥5000 to ¥30,000, an administration charge of ¥50,000 to ¥100,000 and annual tuition fees of ¥400,000 to ¥750,000. The benefit of studying full-time is that it entitles you to a student visa, with which you can work up to 20 hours a week, thereby offsetting some of the tuition costs.

Shiatsu Lessons in English are available for *shiatsu*, or finger-pressure massage. Contact Dr Kimura at the Iokai Shiatsu Center (☎ 3832 2983). These places offer shiatsu massage (call first for an appointment):

Kōjimachi Rebirth (☎ 3261 3493) 1-5-7 Hirakawachō, Chiyoda-ku
Namikoshi Shiatsu Center (☎ 3583 9326) 5-5-9 Akasaka, Minato-ku
Shiatsu Nanaka (☎ 045-743 2134) 3-44 Miyamotochō, Yokohama

Tea Ceremony The Kenkyusha Eigo Center (☎ 5261 8940) in Iidabashi has one-off lessons (¥5000) and three-month courses (¥34,000) in English.

Zen Some organisations and temples around Tokyo hold talks and Zen meditation sessions in English, including Dogen Sanga (☎ 3235 0701) in Hongo-sanchōme. The following Tokyo temples offer regular Zen sessions to beginners and have someone on hand who can speak English:

Eihei-ji (Soto sect) (☎ 3400 5232) 2-21-34 Nishi-Azabu, Minato-ku
Soun-in (Rinzai sect) (☎ 3844 3711) 4-1-12 Higashi-Ueno, Taito-ku
Taiso-ji (Soto sect) (☎ 3917 6290) 7-1-1 Komagome, Toshima-ku
Tokyo Hannya Dojo (Rinzai sect) (☎ 5245 7678) 1-6-1 Hirano, Kōtō-ku

---

Tea Ceremony

Combining the arts of cooking, ceramics, *haiku*, calligraphy and flower arrangement with a dash of Zen, tea ceremony (*chanoyu*) is perhaps the most concentrated of all Japanese experiences.

With the right attitude, chanoyu is a wonderful diversion. Just remember: no-one is going to hold it against you if you don't know the exact procedure. The trick is simply to follow the lead of the Japanese in attendance. If there aren't any present, your host will explain what to do. And relax: the point of the ritual is to forget the cares of the world and concentrate on the tea at hand.

The following hotels offer chanoyu to foreign visitors with English explanation.

Imperial Hotel (☎ 3504 1111) Cost ¥1500. Chanoyu from 10am-4pm Mon-Sat. The Imperial is at Toko-an, on the 4th floor; you should call for an appointment.

Hotel Ōkura (☎ 3582 0111) Cost ¥1050. Chanoyu from 11am-noon, 1pm-5pm. Ceremonies are held at their Chosho-an tea-room on the 7th floor; call for an appointment.

Hotel New Ōtani (☎ 3265 1111) Cost ¥1050. Chanoyu at 11am and 1pm Thurs-Sat. Appointments are required for more than five people.

東京 東京 東京 東京 東京 東京 東京 東京

Friends of the Western Buddhist Order also has regular courses on Buddhism and meditation, and can be contacted through Mr Kevin Duffey (☎ 044-754 6189). Similarly, Tibet House (☎ 3353 4094) in Shinjuku offers courses on Tibetan Buddhism.

Some Buddhist temples in Kamakura offer *zazen* meditation sessions on weekends. Hokoku-ji's sessions are aimed at the beginner, while those run by Kenchō-ji and Engaku-ji are more suited to experienced practitioners (see Kamakura in the Excursions chapter).

Public Baths & Hot Springs
For details on *sentō* (public baths) and *onsen* (hot springs), see Public Baths & Hot Springs in the Entertainment chapter.

Traditional Sports

Martial arts such as *aikidō, jūdō, karate* and *kendō* can be studied in Tokyo, as well as the less popular sports such as *kyūdō* (Japanese archery) and sumo. Addresses in Tokyo include:

All-Japan Jūdō Federation (☎ 3812 9580)
c/- Kodokan, 1-16-30 Kasuga, Bunkyō-ku
Amateur Archery Federation of Japan
(☎ 3481 2387) Kishi Memorial Hall, 1-1-1 Jinan, Shibuya-ku
International Aikidō Federation (☎ 3203 9236) 17-18 Wakamatsuchō, Shinjuku-ku
Japan Karate Association (☎ 3462 1415) For information on how to get there, ring Mr Yamamoto, Mr Hashimoto or Mr Yagyu at Wise International (☎ 3436 4567); all three speak English.
Japan Kendō Federation (☎ 3211 58045)
c/- Nihon Budōkan, 2-3 Kitanomaru-kōen, Chiyoda-ku
Nihon Sumō Kyokai (☎ 3623 5111) Kokugikan Sumo Hall, 1-3-28 Yokoami, Sumida-ku

Participatory Sports

Unless you are based in a five-star hotel with its own facilities, most short-term visitors to Tokyo will probably have to do without their favourite sporting activities. High population density and shortage of land mean a high demand for recreational space. This pushes up prices and creates long waiting lists.

Cycling Long-distance cycling in Tokyo isn't much fun. Keen cyclists who want information on bicycle rental, purchase or cycling courses can contact the following organisations, all in the same building in Akasaka (Map 7): Japan Cycling Association *(☎ 3583 5628)*, the Japan Bicycle Promotion Institute *(☎ 3583 5444)* or the Bicycle Culture Center *(☎ 3586 5930)*.

Golf Tokyo is undoubtedly the most expensive place in the world to play a game of golf. The cheaper option would be a visit to one of the many multistorey golf ranges that dot the landscape.

Skiing & Snowboarding Skiing has been popular for a long time in Japan, and snowboarding is currently all the rage among Japanese youth. There is no lack of places to do either in the Kantō region. The problem is the expense and the difficulty of getting to the ski areas. One place popular with Tokyoites is Akakura. For more information, contact the TIC office, which can give details about prices and transportation.

Surfing Most people don't realise quite how popular surfing is in Japan. Around Tokyo, the most popular surf beaches are those on Miura-hantō Peninsula and around Kamakura, especially between Kamakura and Enoshima. Unless a typhoon hits, don't expect much in the way of waves; the breaks are mostly beach breaks averaging a metre at best.

Swimming Like everything else, taking a swim in a pool in Tokyo can be costly and bound by unaccustomed rules. In the summer months, it's probably better to head to the beaches of Miura-hantō and around Kamakura. Otherwise, the following places have pools which accept visitors:

Big Box Seibu Sports Plaza (☎ 3208 7171) ¥1545 for the whole day; open noon to 10pm Sunday; Map 2 next to Takadanobaba station
Yoyogi National Stadium (☎ 3468 1171) ¥460 for the day; open noon to 4pm; Map 4 close to Harajuku station

Tennis Court reservations are sometimes needed up to a month in advance. If you are just in Tokyo on a short stay, it's probably better not to bother. You might try the following places if you're really set on a game.

Hibiya-kōen (☎ 3501 6428) ¥1300 per hour; 9am to 9pm; Map 7
National Stadium Tennis Court (☎ 3408 4495) ¥700 per person per hour in the morning, ¥900 in the afternoon; 9am to 4.30pm; close to Gaien-mae subway station

Windsurfing The sport of windsurfing is growing in popularity, but as with other equipment-intensive sports in Japan, it is not cheap. The most popular spots in the Tokyo area for windsurfing are the beaches of Kanagawa and Chiba. For details on places that rent boards, call the Tokyo TIC.

Places to Stay

Tokyo offers a diversity of accommodation options. At the upper end of the market are luxury hotels with facilities to rival the best hotels anywhere. At the other end of the scale are youth hostels, capsule hotels and *minshuku* (the Japanese version of B&B). Between these extremes are mid-range business hotels, so-called love hotels (cheap hotels used for trysts by Japanese, but fine for a regular stay) and *ryokan* (traditional Japanese inns).

Youth Hostels

Tokyo's youth hostels are much like youth hostels elsewhere: not much atmosphere, a mixture of dorms and private rooms, and strict rules concerning curfew and check-out time. They can also be noisy. On the plus side, they are used to foreigners and are cleaner than many of their overseas counterparts. A room in a typical youth hostel is about ¥3200, cash only. Membership may not be necessary.

Capsule Hotels

More private, claustrophobic, and coffin-sized, the capsule hotel comes with bed, reading light, TV, and alarm clock. Despite their size, prices still range from ¥3500 to ¥4800, depending on the area and the facilities (also cash only). Capsule hotels are rarely familiar with foreign guests; most of their business comes from drunken office workers who have missed the last train home. Many have a well-appointed bath area similar to a good local *sentō* (public bath).

Useful Japanese

hotel	ホテル
ryokan	旅館
minshuku	民宿
youth hostel	ユースホステル
capsule	カプセルホテル

東京 東京 東京 東京 東京 東京 東京

Love Hotels

Similarly quirky is the love hotel. Rooms here are generally rented out for one or two hours at a time, but late in the evening there will usually be fairly reasonable all-night rates (around ¥7500, no credit cards accepted). Of course, prices can soar if you request the all-leather S&M deluxe suite with the African-safari-meets-Elvis decor…

Love hotels are distinguished by their discreet entrances – high bushes, large stones out front, underground parking and so on – installed so that patrons can duck in and out in complete anonymity. Once inside, the anonymity continues: you choose a room from a bank of illuminated pictures on the wall. If the picture is not illuminated, the room's already taken. Once you've decided, either push a button or say the number to a hidden clerk. Payment is through a slot in the wall. Once you've paid, you'll be handed a key and must make your own way to the room.

Posted outside love hotels are signs indicating the rates for a one- or two-hour stay, discreetly referred to as a *kyūkei* (rest), or for an overnight stay, *tomari*. Note that most places will not allow you to check in for an overnight stay until 10pm or 11pm. Furthermore, some of these places are not used to dealing with foreigners. However, if you act like you know what you're doing and can muster a little Japanese (saying 'kyūkei' or 'tomari' will suffice), there should be no problems. Same-sex guests may be refused at some love hotels. If this happens, insist that you are travelling as friends (*tomodachi*) and you may get in.

Ryokan

For those who crave a really traditional Japanese experience with *tatami* (mat-floor) rooms and *futon* (mattresses) instead of beds, nothing beats a night in a ryokan. Although the more exclusive establishments can charge ¥25,000 (and often much more),

PLACES TO STAY

Staying at a Ryokan

The Japanese tendency is to make the procedure at a *ryokan* seem rather rarefied for foreign comprehension, and some ryokan are wary of accepting foreign guests. However, many are used to catering for foreigners, and once you've grasped the basics, it really isn't that hard to fit in.

On arrival at the ryokan, you leave your shoes at the entrance steps, don a pair of slippers, and are shown by a maid to your room, which has a *tatami* floor. Slippers are taken off before entering tatami rooms. Instead of using numbers, rooms are often named after auspicious flowers, plants or trees.

The room usually contains an alcove *(tokonoma)*, probably decorated with a flower display or a calligraphy scroll. One side of the room will contain a cupboard with sliding doors for the bedding; the other side will have sliding screens covered with rice paper and may open onto a veranda with a garden view.

The room maid usually serves tea with a sweet on the low table surrounded by cushions *(zabuton)* in the centre of the room. At this time you'll be asked to sign the register. A tray is provided with a towel, cotton robe *(yukata)* and belt *(obi)*, which you put on before taking your bath *(o-furo)*. Remember to close the left side of the yukata over the right – the reverse order is used for dressing the dead. In colder weather, there will also be an outer jacket *(tanzen)*. Your clothes can be put away in a closet or left on a hanger.

At some ryokan, there are rooms with private baths, but the communal ones are often designed with 'natural' pools or a window looking onto a garden. Bathing is communal, but sexes are segregated. Make sure you can differentiate between the bathroom signs for men and women (see the Toilets & Public Baths section in the Facts for the Visitor chapter) – although ryokan will often have signs in English. Many inns will have family bathrooms for couples or families.

Dressed in your yukata after your bath, you return to your room where the maid will have laid out dinner – in some ryokan, dinner is provided in a separate room but you can still wear your yukata for dining. Dinner usually includes standard dishes such as miso soup, pickles *(tsukemono)*, vegetables in vinegar *(sunomono)*, hors d'oeuvres *(zensai)*, fish either grilled or raw *(sashimi)*, and perhaps *tempura* and a stew. There will also be plenty of bowls for rice, dips and sauces. Depending on the standard of the accommodation, meals at a ryokan can become flamboyant displays of local cuisine or refined arrangements of *kaiseki* (a cuisine that obeys strict rules of form and etiquette for every detail of the meal and setting).

After dinner, while you are pottering around or strolling in the garden – or in the o-furo again – the maid will clear the dishes and prepare your bedding. A mattress *(futon)* is placed on the tatami floor and a quilt put on top.

In the morning, the maid will knock to make sure you are awake, then come in to put away the bedding before serving breakfast – sometimes this is served in a separate room. Breakfast usually consists of pickles, dried seaweed *(nori)*, raw egg, dried fish, miso soup and rice. (Foreign stomachs may need some time to digest this new experience.) After breakfast, the day is yours, fresh in the afterglow of Japanese hospitality.

東京 東京 東京 東京 東京 東京 東京 東京 東京 東京 東京 東京 東京 東京 東京

there are a number of relatively inexpensive ryokan in Tokyo. These places are generally more accustomed to foreigners than their counterparts in more remote parts of Japan, and the rules tend to be a bit more relaxed as a result.

While some ryokan will allow you to pay by credit card, you should always ask at check-in if you hope to do so. The ryokan listed in this chapter are generally budget; those wishing to stay in mid-range and top-end ryokan should inquire at the Tourist Information Center (TIC – see Tourist Offices in the Facts for the Visitor chapter), which has listings and will handle reservations.

Minshuku

Similar to ryokan, but generally simpler in decor and cheaper, are minshuku. These are private homes that accept visitors and offer food, usually both breakfast and dinner. They are friendly places, and you can often get to know other travellers, both Japanese and foreign, especially in places where meals are taken communally in a dining room.

Minshuku in Tokyo generally cost about ¥6000 to ¥8000 per person (cash only), including two meals, making minshuku one of your better travel bargains. You will find that few minshuku owners speak English. The best way to secure lodging is through the Japan Minshuku Center (☎ 3216 6556, English spoken) in the basement of the Kōtsū Kaikan building (Map 7) in Ginza. It will handle all reservations and payments, and will give you a map to your minshuku. It's closed on Sunday and national holidays.

Business Hotels

A very common form of mid-range accommodation is the so-called 'business hotel'. Generally these are economical and functional places – a step up from the capsule hotel – geared to the lone traveller on business, though many in Tokyo also take couples. In Tokyo, a room in a business hotel will have a pay TV and a tiny bathroom, and cost between ¥6000 and ¥12,000. Like ryokan, some business hotels accept credit cards, but you should always ask when you check in. There is no room service, and you will usually be required to check out at 10am or 11am and check in after 3pm or 4pm. At some of the nicer business hotels, there are large shared baths and saunas in addition to the private ones in the guest rooms.

Business hotels are identifiable by their small size (usually three to five floors); their simple, often concrete, exteriors; and a sign, usually in both English and Japanese, out the front. While you can't expect much English from the front desk clerk, if you smile and speak slowly you should be okay.

Hotels

Once you leave the budget and mid-range category and enter the top-end bracket, you can expect to find all the amenities of top hotels anywhere in the world. The staff speak English, the rooms are spotless and the service impeccable. In addition, most hotels in Tokyo have several good restaurants and bars on their premises, many of which offer outstanding views over the city.

Gaijin Houses

Those on a low budget who plan on setting up shop in Tokyo may want to consider a 'gaijin house'. Many of these are private houses or apartments that have been partitioned into rooms and rented out to *gaijin* (foreigners). In general, gaijin houses are not an option for the short-term visitor, but for those planning an extended stay, they may initially be the only affordable option.

Other Options

The TIC can give you information about several other lodging options in and around Tokyo, including *shukubō* (staying on the grounds of a temple), *onsen* (hot-spring resorts) and converted farmhouses. It also has information for travellers with special needs, eg, seniors, those with children and disabled visitors.

Tax

Keep in mind that a 5% consumption tax applies to room rates across all accommodation categories, with the exception of gaijin houses and some of the other budget options. For the more expensive styles of accommodation (generally rooms that cost over ¥15,000), a 3% local tax is also added to the 10% to 15% service charge.

Reservations & Information

If you need more information before you leave home, contact your nearest Japan National Tourist Organization (JNTO) office. Or, if you are in Japan, visit the Tokyo or Narita offices of the TIC. These offices can supply useful publications listing ryokan, hotels and business hotels such as *Hotels in Japan*, *Japan Ryokan Guide*, *Japanese Inn Group* and the *Directory of Welcome Inns*. Also at the main JNTO office in Tokyo

(Map 7) is a free booking service, provided that you stay at a member of the Japan Welcome Inn hotel group. For those who'd like an authentic hot-spring resort experience, get JNTO's *Japanese Hot Springs*, which details some of the more popular onsen areas within easy reach of Tokyo.

Where to Stay

If you are not on a budget, areas such as Akasaka and Ginza are ideal places to be based. There are even some mid-range hotels in this part of town, though you won't find anything under ¥7500 for a single room. From this point prices spiral ever upward – anything from ¥20,000 for a single to ¥30,000 for a double – as you move into the giddy heights of opulent indulgence offered by hotels of international renown, such as the Hotel Ōkura and the Imperial Hotel. If your budget doesn't reach five-star levels, you can find cheaper accommodation with easy access of central Tokyo by staying somewhere on the Yamanote line.

Around the Yamanote line, business and entertainment districts like Shinjuku or Ikebukuro will have capsule hotels from around ¥4000 per night or business-hotel singles from ¥7000 to ¥9000. For the same price, a couple could even find a room in a love hotel from 10pm or 11pm. Shinjuku, a very convenient area in which to be based, has some international-class hotels, mainly concentrated on the west side of the station. Ikebukuro, Kanda and Ueno have some particularly good deals in the business-hotel category.

Most of the more reasonably priced accommodation, such as ryokan, are less conveniently situated. Nevertheless, areas like Ueno and Ikebukuro have a number of budget accommodation options. Asakusa is another area with a number of ryokan popular with foreigners.

PLACES TO STAY – BUDGET

Tokyo is an expensive city. Budget travellers arriving from other parts of Asia are likely to be shocked at the cost of accommodation. Even travellers who come well supplied with funds often find that too large a chunk of their daily expenses go into a place to sleep, and some end up cutting their trip short as a result.

There is really no way around this problem, as there are no true accommodation bargains in the city. Even dormitory lodging (care of Tokyo's two youth hostels) is up around ¥3200. Once you leave the youth hostel bracket, the next option to consider is Kimi Ryokan in Ikebukuro – probably the best entry in the budget category.

A step up in price are the economy hotels banded together as the Welcome Inn Group. The majority of these fall into the budget ryokan category, but some business hotels are also included. Prices average ¥6000 for a single and ¥8000 for a double/twin. The advantage of hotels in this group is that they are accustomed to dealing with foreigners (an important consideration, even in Tokyo), and they can be booked before you leave home.

If you wish to book from overseas, you will have to get a Welcome Inn Group reservation form from your nearest JNTO office (see Tourist Offices in the Facts for the Visitor chapter). Bookings need to be made at least two weeks before departure, and you will need a confirmed air ticket. If you book for your day of arrival, you will need to be scheduled to land before 3pm. Bookings can also be made in Tokyo at the Narita and Tokyo TIC offices.

Youth Hostels

The cheapest short-term options in Tokyo are the youth hostels in Iidabashi and Yoyogi. The drawbacks are the usual youth hostel restrictions – you have to be out of the building between 10am and 3pm (10am and 5pm at Yoyogi) and you have to be home by 10pm in the evening – a real drag in a city like Tokyo. Finally, there's a three-night limit to your stay, and the hostels can often be booked out during peak holiday periods. The consensus is that the Yoyogi Youth Hostel is the better option of the two.

Tokyo International Youth Hostel (☎ 3235 1107, fax 3267 4000) **Map 8** Dorm bed ¥3250, ¥4300 with two meals, sleeping sheet ¥150 for three nights. Just south of Iidabashi station, this place might be a showcase for Japan's youth hostels (it's on the 18th floor of a towering office block, providing great views), but a business-like atmosphere prevails. You aren't required to be a member, but you are asked to book ahead and provide some identification (a passport will do) when you arrive. To get there, exit from Iidabashi station (either JR or subway) and look for the tallest building in sight (it's long, slender and glass fronted). The Narita TIC has an instruction sheet on the cheapest means to get to the hostel from the airport.

Yoyogi Youth Hostel (☎ 3467 9163, fax 3467 9417) **Map 4** Dorm bed ¥3000 per person per night. You're supposed to be a youth hostel member to stay here, but non-members can pay ¥600 for a 'one welcome stamp'. No meals are available, but there are cooking facilities. Take the Odakyū line to Sangūbashi station and walk toward the Meiji-jingū Shrine gardens. The hostel is in a fenced compound – not a former prison camp, but the National Olympics Memorial Youth Center – in building No 14. Staff may let you exceed the three-night limit if it is not crowded.

Ryokan & Other Accommodation

Suzuki Ryokan (☎ 3821 4944) **Map 9** Singles without bathroom ¥4000, doubles with bath ¥8000. In Nippori, an easy reach from Narita airport. Some rooms have private bathroom and all have TV. Take the Keisei line from Narita and get off at Nippori, the last stop before Ueno. Turn right at the Ueno end of the platform and look for the ryokan to the right as you exit the station. There is an English sign. It's near one of Tokyo's most pleasant neighbourhoods for a stroll.

Kimi Ryokan (☎ 3971 3766, fax 3987 1326) **Map 2** Singles/doubles/twins ¥4500/6500/7500. Deserving a special mention, the Kimi is in Ikebukuro, not a bad location from which to see Tokyo; it's 10 minutes from Shinjuku and 20 minutes from Ginza. The rooms are relatively inexpensive by Tokyo standards, nicely designed in Japanese style, and the place is friendly, clean and relaxed about the hours you keep – just remember to inform the staff if you're going

to be out late. One nice touch is the constantly changing *ikebana* in the common areas. The Kimi lounge is a good meeting place, with a useful notice board which has recently expanded into the nearby Kimi Information Center. Kimi Ryokan is justifiably popular – book a room as early as possible. The staff speak English. To get there, go out the west exit of Ikebukuro station, or go to the police box on the west side, just past Marui department store, and say 'Kimi Ryokan' to the policeman on duty. He'll give you a map.

In Ueno (Map 9) are several budget ryokan, all members of the Welcome Inn Group.

Sawanoya Ryokan (☎ 3822 2251, fax 3822 2252) **Map 9** Singles/doubles/triples from ¥4700/8800/12,000. Closed 29 Dec-4 Jan. This ryokan is close to Nezu subway station on the Chiyoda line. Take the Nezu crossing exit and turn right onto Kototoi-dōri. Turn left at the fourth street on your left – Sawanoya Ryokan is a couple of minutes down the road on your right. If you're coming from Narita, it would probably be easier and just as cheap to share a taxi from Ueno station.

Ryokan Katsutaro (☎ 3821 9808, fax 3821 4789) **Map 9** Singles/doubles/triples ¥4500/8400/12,300 without bath. With bath, rooms are slightly more. A popular choice with travellers, this place is a bit closer to Ueno station. If you follow the road that runs alongside Shinobaza-ike pond for about 10 minutes, you'll see the ryokan on the right, just past the police box (don't turn right at the police box; go straight across the intersection). You can also get to the ryokan from Nezu subway station.

Asia Center of Japan ryokan (☎ 3402 6111, fax 3002 0738) **Map 4** Singles without bath ¥5100, twins and doubles from ¥6800. This is a popular place near Aoyama-ichōme subway station on the Ginza line. Like Kimi Ryokan, it attracts many long-term guests, and even though it's a lot bigger than the Kimi, it's still often fully booked. The station is under the easily recognisable Aoyama Twin Tower building on Aoyama-dōri. Walk north-east past the Tower building then turn right (toward Roppongi); the Asia Center is a short walk up the third street on the left. Rooms have pay TV.

Sakura Ryokan *(☎ 3876 8118, fax 3873 9456)* Singles/doubles ¥5300/9600. This place is just one stop from Ueno on the Yamanote line (Uguisudani station). Take the southern exit and turn left. Pass the Iriya subway station exits on the left – Sakura Ryokan is on the right-hand side of the second street on your left. If you're exiting from Iriya subway station on the Hibiya line, take the No 1 exit and turn left.

Hotel New Koyo *(☎ 3873 0343, fax 3873 1358,* **e** *new-koyo@tctv.ne.jp* **w** *www .newkoyo.com)*. Tokyo's cheapest rooms are to be found at this flophouse-turned-guesthouse. Basic but clean Western and Japanese singles (Japanese are slightly larger) are ¥2700. There are also two doubles priced at ¥4800. Reserve well in advance. It's two stops north of Ueno on the Hibiya line. Take a left out of Minowa station's exit 3, and walk to the next set of lights. Take a left, walk past three sets of lights and turn right just before the Lawson's convenience store. It's on the right in the second block.

Ryokan Sansuisō *(☎ 3441 7475, fax 3449 1944)* Singles/doubles/triples ¥5500/8600/ 12,000. Close to Gotanda station on the Yamanote line, this is not the greatest of locations, but it's only a few stops south of Shibuya. Take the exit furthest from Shibuya and go out on the left-hand side. Turn right, take the first right after the big Tōkyū department store and then the first left. Turn left and then right, continue past the bowling centre and look for the sign on the right directing you down the side road to the ryokan.

Asakusa also has a few reasonably priced ryokan.

Taito Ryokan *(☎/fax 3843 2822,* **e** *jptaito@ libertyhouse.gr.jp,* **w** *www.libertyhouse .gr.jp)* **Map 9** Singles/doubles ¥3000/6000. Great value, English-speaking managers, and a funky Shitamachi (downtown) location make this a winner. It can be noisy, and palatial it ain't, but who cares at this price.

Take exit 3 from Tawaramachi station (Ginza line), and walk north towards the Asakusa View Hotel, turn left at the police box into Kikusui-dōri, and the ryokan is on the right-hand corner. The Web site has a map.

Ryokan Mikawaya *(☎ 3843 2345, fax 3843 2348)* **Map 9** Singles/doubles without bath ¥6000/11,000. In an interesting area, just around the corner from Sensō-ji. It is on a side street off the shop-lined street leading into the temple. From Kaminarimon, the street is a few streets up on the left – there is a toy shop and a shoe shop on the corner. The ryokan is on the left-hand side of the road.

YMCA Asia Youth Center *(☎ 3233 0611, fax 3233 0633)* **Map 8** Singles/doubles/ triples ¥7000/13,000/16,800. The centre takes both men and women. It's halfway between Suidōbashi and Jimbōchō subway stations. Don't be fooled by the name: it's actually quite close to a business hotel in cost and no different in service.

Ryokan Shigetsu *(☎ 3843 2345, fax 3843 2348)* **Map 9** Japanese-style singles/ doubles ¥9000/15,000, larger Japanese-style suites ¥25,000 and Western-style singles/ doubles ¥7300/14,000. New, clean and friendly, Ryokan Shigetsu is just around the corner from Ryokan Mikawaya. Try the Japanese bath, which has a view of Sensō-ji's five-storey pagoda.

Capsule Hotels

Capsule hotels are generally a male domain, and you find them in large hubs and nightlife districts. Most are open from 5pm to 10am.

Green Plaza Shinjuku *(☎ 3207 5411)* **Map 3** ¥4100 per night. Just down the road from the Prince Hotel, this hotel is on Shinjuku's east side. The front desk is on the 3rd floor; take the lift from the basement.

Shinjuku Kuyakusho-Mae Capsule Hotel *(☎ 3232 1110)* **Map 3** ¥4300 per night. This place is right in Shinjuku's sleazy Kabukichō.

Capsule Inn Akasaka *(☎ 3588 1811)* ¥4000 per night. In Akasaka, not far from Akasaka station, follow Akasaka-dōri south-west from the TBS broadcasting station to find the hotel on the left.

Capsule Hotel Fontaine Akasaka (☎ 3583 6554) **Map 7** ¥4800 per night. Closer to Akasaka-mitsuke station on Hitotsuji-dōri this upmarket capsule hotel is one of the few that accepts women, but it does so only on Friday, Saturday and Sunday. According to the English-language brochure however 'Dead drunks are requested to keep out.' Right!

Capsule Hotel Riverside (☎ 3844 1155) **Map 9** ¥3300 per night. Rooms here are a bargain, and they accept women too. The entrance is hidden behind the building, just west of Azuma-bashi.

Gaijin Houses

Although a few gaijin houses quote daily or weekly rates, they are generally not an option for short-term visitors. If you are planning a long stay, however, a gaijin house may be the only affordable option. The slowdown in the Japanese economy has led to less foreigners heading to Tokyo in search of work; consequently, it is easier than it used to be to find a room in a gaijin house. Typically prices range from ¥40,000 per month for a bed in a shared room to ¥70,000 for a private room, with no deposits or key money required.

Conditions in gaijin houses vary enormously, and you should definitely check out several places before deciding. The best ways to find a gaijin house are by word of mouth from other foreigners, looking in the *Tokyo Journal* or the *Tokyo Classifieds*, or going through an agency. Agencies are generally the fastest and easiest way to go, as they have extensive listings and will handle all the arrangements with the landlord. Some agencies are:

Fontana (☎ 3382 0151) Tokyo's largest listing and best rates
Friendship House (☎ 3765 2288, e welcome@ gaijinhouse.com) Above average standard places in Nippori, Itabashi, Oimachi and Kichijoji
Kettle House (☎ 3645 4028, fax 3645 4303, w www.bamboo-house.com) Accommodation across the city

PLACES TO STAY – MID-RANGE

The mid-range bracket mainly comprises business hotels. There's very little to distinguish one from another, and their main attraction is convenience. Every area has at least one with singles/doubles from about ¥7500/12,000. Generally, each room will have a built-in bathroom with shower, bath and toilet, a telephone, and pay TV. A few savvy ones have Internet access.

Few mid-range hotels have English-speaking staff. The lower the price in a business hotel, the less likely it is that the staff are accustomed to dealing with foreigners. It is highly unlikely you'll be turned away, however. Listed room prices rarely include consumption tax – expect 5% to be added.

There are plenty of love hotels in any of Tokyo's entertainment districts, but particularly in Shinjuku, Shibuya, Roppongi and Ikebukuro. All-night rooms range in price from about ¥6000 to ¥9000, but 'all night' doesn't start until 10pm or 11pm, when the regular hour-by-hour customers have run out of energy.

Tokyo Station Area (Maps 7 & 8)

Hotels here offer mid-range standards at top-end prices, simply because real estate values are so high. You are paying for the location.

Yaesu-Ryūmeikan (☎ 3271 0971) **Map 8** Singles/doubles ¥8,600/15,400. The Yaesu-Ryūmeikan's Japanese-style rooms are the best deal in this locale.

Yaesu Terminal Hotel (☎ 3281 3771, fax 3281 3771) **Map 8** Singles/doubles or twins ¥10,800/15,800. Between Tokyo station and Takashimaya department store, this fairly economical option has a business-hotel feel. The rooms are quite small, but the prices are a bargain for this area.

Yaesu Fujiya Hotel (☎ 3273 2111, fax 3273 2180) **Map 7** Singles/doubles/twins from ¥12,500/17,000/22,000. A little south of the station, this hotel is very convenient for business at the Tokyo International Forum. The rooms are a bit more spacious than some of the other mid-range hotels in the area. Given its location, it's good value.

Tokyo Station Hotel (☎ 3231 2511, fax 3231 3513) **Map 8** Singles/doubles or twins from ¥10,000/19,000. If you can't face any more travel upon arriving at Tokyo station, this is a good, long-standing option. The rooms are pretty basic, but you can't beat the location on the Marunouchi (west) side of the station. Light sleepers should request rooms on the west side, furthest from the trains.

Hotel Kokusai Kankō (☎ 3215 3281, fax 3215 1140, **W** *www.kokusai-kanko.co .jp/e-index.html*) **Map 8** Singles/doubles/ twins start at ¥14,000/23,000/23,500. Almost directly on top of Tokyo station, on the Yaesu (east) side, this hotel is fairly characterless, but quieter than the Tokyo Station Hotel.

Tokyo Marunouchi Hotel (☎ 3215 2151, fax 3215 8036) **Map 8** Singles/doubles/twins start at ¥13,000/23,000/21,000. Ordinary 209-room hotel within walking distance of Tokyo station near the city's financial epicentre. It's north of the station, above the Tōzai subway line's Ōtemachi station.

Ginza (Map 7)
Ginza is not the best place to look for midrange accommodation, as prices reflect the posh surroundings, but it's certainly a good area in which to be based.

Hotel Ginza Dai-ei (☎ 3545 1111, fax 3545 1177) Singles/doubles/twins start at ¥11,400/ 15,600/17,500. Just north of Kabuki-za Theatre, this is a standard business hotel. The less than pristine condition of the hotel reflects the prices but it's still a bargain for this part of town.

Hotel Alcyone (☎ 3541 3621, fax 3541 3263) Singles ¥11000 per person. A souped-up business hotel handy to Tsukiji market and Ginza, it has 74 Western and Japanese rooms, the latter more comfortable. Soak in the large communal bath. To get there, take exit A5 from Higashi Ginza station on the Hibiya and Toei Asakusa lines. Turn left at the Junanaju bank and it's on your left after100m.

Ginza Nikkō Hotel (☎ 3571 4911, fax 3571 8379, **W** *www.nikkohotels.com/japan/ ginza.html*) Singles/doubles/twins start at ¥10,000/20,000/24,000. A step up in terms of quality and price, Ginza Nikkō is a quality hotel in a prime location – right on Sotobori-dōri between Ginza and Shimbashi.

Ginza International Hotel (☎ 3574 1121, fax 3289 0478) Singles/doubles/twins start at ¥13,000/18,000/20,000. This hotel is near the Ginza Nikkō and in a similar class.

Kanda (Map 8)
The Kanda area, comprising Jimbōchō and Akihabara, is neglected by many travellers looking for mid-range accommodation. It's actually a fine place to be based, close to central Tokyo, but still quiet. Add good bookshops, a great variety of restaurants, and rates a few thousand yen cheaper than more fashionable parts of town and it becomes more attractive.

Central Hotel (☎ 3256 6251, fax 3256 6250) Singles/doubles/twins start at ¥6500/ 9800/9800. This is about the cheapest business hotel in Kanda and the rooms are small and simple. There's a sauna and large bath, although these are a little seedy.

New Central Hotel (☎ 3256 2171, **W** *www.inn-info.co.jp/english/hotels_kanto/ hotel025.html*) Singles/doubles/twins start at ¥8900/12,200/14,200. Part of the same chain as the Central Hotel, the New Central is plusher and pricier. The large bath and sauna are great for aching travellers' bones.

Tokyo Green Hotel Ochanomizu (☎ 3255 4161, fax 3255 4962) Singles/ twins start at ¥8400/14,200. Perhaps the nicest business hotel in Kanda, this is a clean, new place. The common areas here have a nice woody/bamboo theme, and the staff are friendly. Simple, reasonably priced meals are available.

Grand Central Hotel (☎ 3256 3211, fax 3256 3210) Singles/doubles/twins start at ¥8600/12,200/13,200. The third link in the 'Central' hotel chain is a standard-issue business hotel with rooms slightly larger than the other two Centrals.

Tokyo Ochanomizu Hotel Juraku (☎ 3251 7222, fax 3251 7447) Singles/ doubles/twins start at ¥9500/12,500/14,500. Not far from Ochanomizu station, this is somewhere between a regular hotel and a business hotel. The rooms are quite simple and on the small side. On the whole, it's probably better to save the money and go to one of the above business hotels.

Hotel New Kanda (☎ 3258 3911, fax 3258 3909) Singles/doubles/twins start at ¥9,500/ 14,000/15,000. Right around the corner from Akihabara, this is one of Kanda's only real hotels (as opposed to business hotels). It's basic with an attached Italian restaurant.

Ueno (Map 9)

With the Keisei Airport Express only minutes away and with some of Tokyo's most famous cultural attractions, Ueno is not a bad place in which to be based. Very convenient. Mid-range accommodation consists primarily of standard business hotels and a few simple hotels. There are also a few ryokan nearby.

Kinuya Hotel (☎ 3833 1911) Singles/ doubles or twins ¥6700/11,200. The location is good but we found the staff are rather cool – perhaps they are unused to foreign guests. You may not care about the reception given the prices.

Hotel Green Capital (☎ 3842 2411) Singles/doubles/twins 7500/11,000/11,500. This is a typical business hotel quite close to Ueno station. The rooms are clean and new, and the staff are polite. Prices are also competitive. It's a little tricky to find; look for a black marble front and a metal sign with green lettering at street level.

Hotel New Ueno (☎ 3841 3221, fax 3842 7806) Singles/doubles/twins from ¥8500/ 16,000/14,000. Directly across from Ueno station, this is a good choice in terms of location. The rooms are standard business-hotel style but prices are a little higher than at other Ueno business hotels.

Ueno Terminal Hotel (☎ 3831 1110) Singles/doubles/twins start at ¥8200/14,000/ 16,500. The place is clean, and the staff are used to foreign guests. Look for a white building with a white-on-brown sign in Japanese.

Hotel Pine Hill Ueno (☎ 3836 5111) Singles/doubles or twins ¥7800/14,500. One of a number of good places on the south side of Ueno-kōen park, this large, clean hotel has pleasant, English-speaking staff. Considering its location and quality, the rooms here are a bargain.

Hotel Parkside (☎ 3836 5711, fax 3831 6641) Singles/doubles or twins start at ¥9200/16,100. Japanese-style rooms are ¥16,600 for two. 'Imagine that you are breathing deeply in a forest in fresh green. Imagine that you are listening to birds singing away in the forest. Imagine that you are singing and dancing with your friends under the sunlight shining through the leaves of trees. We would like to provide all such atmospheres and services in our hotel.' The Parkside sets itself a tough target, but actually, it *is* rather pleasant, especially the rooms at the front.

Suigetsu Hotel Ogai-so (☎ 3822 4611, fax 3823 4340) Japanese-style rooms, including Japanese breakfast, start at ¥16,000 for two people (breakfast and dinner service is also available). Western-style rooms start at ¥9300 for a single, with breakfast. On the west side of the park, the Suigetsu is for those who want a change from the typical Western-style hotel. This hotel has mostly Japanese-style tatami rooms, and there are several large Japanese-style baths. Though the hotel is built around a Japanese garden, its structure is largely Western. There is no English sign; look for a white-on-blue Japanese sign and a grey granite building.

Asakusa (Map 9)

Asakusa is an interesting place to stay, if you don't mind sacrificing central location for a funky Shitamachi atmosphere. Options here are similar to those in Ueno: mostly business hotels and a few simple hotels. If you're going to stay in old Asakusa, you may want to try a ryokan.

As for the business hotels, most are down on Kaminarimon-dōri.

Asakusa Plaza Hotel (☎ 3845 2621) Singles/doubles/twins start at ¥7000/ 10,500/11,000. This standard-issue business hotel is conveniently located near some of the city sights. The front desk is upstairs, above Dunkin' Donuts.

Hotel Top Asakusa (☎ 3847 2222) Singles/doubles/twins start at ¥8200/13,500/

15,000. This is a slightly nicer hotel; the front desk is on the 3rd floor.

Asakusa View Hotel (☎ 3842 2117, fax 3845 0530) Singles/doubles/twins start at ¥13,000/21,000/25,000. In a different class altogether is this luxurious 28-storey hotel boasting an assortment of restaurants, a swimming pool, a Japanese-style floor and a shopping area. A drink in the 28th-floor St Cristina bar is a good way to enjoy the night lights of Asakusa.

Ikebukuro (Map 2)

Ikebukuro has lots of mid-range accommodation – most of it business hotels. This being one of Tokyo's nightlife areas, there are also lots of love hotels and a few capsule hotels scattered about. Be warned that the capsule hotels in this neighbourhood are not nearly as accustomed to foreign guests as their cousins in Akasaka or Shinjuku.

Hotel Castle (☎ 3988 6711) ¥6300 for one or two people overnight. Perhaps the cheapest mid-range option is the love hotel near the Kimi Ryokan (see the Budget section). This is a real love hotel, and the owners aren't that used to foreign guests.

Business Hotel Ikebukuro Park (☎ 3982 8989, fax 5396 1789) Singles/doubles or twins start at ¥7000/10,000. Room rates are about the cheapest in its class, however the management appears unaccustomed to dealing with foreigners.

Hotel Star Plaza Ikebukuro (☎ 3590 0005, fax 5992 0005) Singles/doubles start at ¥7000/10,000. Japanese-style rooms are ¥10,000 for two. This is a friendly place in the same price range.

Hotel Grand City (☎ 3984 5121, fax 3984 5127) Singles/twins start at ¥7300/11,800. On the east side of Ikebukuro station, the Grand City is a standard business hotel with relatively inexpensive rates.

Ikebukuro Royal Hotel (☎ 5396 0333, fax 5396 2226) Singles/doubles start at ¥7500/11,500. Not too far from the station, this is another basic business hotel with lots of good restaurants nearby. The rooms are nothing special.

Hotel Sun City Ikebukuro (☎ 3986 1101, fax 3984 8657) Singles/doubles or twins start at ¥7800/12,600. Expect basic rooms with a few on-premises drinking and dining options.

Ark Hotel (☎ 3590 0111, fax 3590 0224) Singles/doubles/twins start at ¥8800/16,000/17,000. Japanese-style rooms are ¥17,000 for two people. Near the Hotel Grand City, the Ark has clean, newish rooms and polite staff.

Hotel Sunroute Ikebukuro (☎ 3980 1911, fax 3980 5286) Singles/doubles or twins start at ¥9000/15,600. This hotel is recommended for those who want a break from spartan business hotels. Just up the street from Bic Camera, it has pleasant, clean rooms and a friendly staff, some of whom speak English.

Shinjuku (Map 3)

Shinjuku is a good hunting ground for business hotels accustomed to foreign guests. Moreover, the intense competition in the area helps keep prices down. Along with Kanda, this is one of the best places for mid-range accommodation.

City Hotel Lornstar (☎ 3356 6511, fax 3350 9505) Singles/twins/doubles start at ¥7000/10,000/13,000. This oddly named place is about as cheap a business hotel as you'll find in these parts. It's small, clean and new, but little English is spoken. The Lornstar is in east Shinjuku, in Nichōme.

Hotel Sunlite Shinjuku (☎ 3356 0391, fax 3356 1223) Singles/doubles/twins ¥8300/14,000/13,500. This place in east Shinjuku is clean and relatively new, and the staff are quite polite. Rooms are small, as are the windows, but the place is well maintained. If the main building is full, ask about the annex.

Park Hotel (☎ 3355 3768) Singles/twins start at ¥7700/13,400. While it gets no raves for warm, friendly service, the rooms are a little larger than at most business hotels and the prices competitive. It's just south of the Takashimaya Times Square complex, next to the Kinokuniya annex.

Central Hotel (☎ 3354 6611, fax 3355 4245) Singles/doubles or twins start at ¥10,000/16,000. Once you negotiate the smoke-filled lounge, you'll find the decidedly tatty rooms. Worth considering only if the other options listed are full (which is unlikely).

Star Hotel Tokyo (☎ *3361 1111, fax 3369 4216*) Singles/doubles/twins from ¥9000/ 17,000/18,000. Just a short stagger from Kabukichō across the railway tracks in west Shinjuku, the hotel's rooms and service are pleasantly dull.

Shinjuku New City Hotel (☎ *3375 6511, fax 3375 6535*) Singles/doubles/triples start at ¥9400/16,200/20,100. On the far side of Shinjuku Chūō kōen park, the New City is very convenient for anyone with business in the Tokyo Metropolitan Government Offices. The rooms here are slightly larger than usual for a business hotel, while the prices are average.

Shinjuku Washington Hotel (☎ *3343 3111, fax 3342 2575*) Singles/doubles/twins start at ¥11,300/17,000/17,500. This place offers business-hotel accommodation with regular hotel-style restaurants and amenities. Rooms are average, but the views from the upper floors are excellent.

Hotel Sunroute Tokyo (☎ *3375 3211, fax 3379 3040*) Singles/doubles/twins start at ¥12,500/17,000/18,000. South-west of Shinjuku station, the Sunroute offers rather plain rooms and a convenient location for business in west Shinjuku.

Hotel Century Southern Tower (☎ *5354 0111, fax 5321 8025*) Singles/twins start at ¥17,000/22,000. Equally well-placed, and quite a bit posher, the recently built Century Southern boasts great views and, wonder of wonders, Nintendo in every room. Especially good value if two share.

Shibuya (Map 4)

Shibuya is not as rich in accommodation as some of Tokyo's other built-up neighbourhoods. There are very few business hotels, and the regular hotels have little to recommend them over similar options in more interesting parts of Tokyo.

Shibuya Excel Hotel Tokyu (☎ *5457 0309, fax 5457 0309*) Singles/doubles/twins start at ¥15,000/20,000/22,000. Priciest, but pick of the bunch, is this new hotel towering over the Mark City shopping complex. Rooms are spacious, and come with satellite

TV and data-port connections. It has great views at night.

Shibuya Business Hotel (☎ *3409 9300, fax 3409 9378*) Singles/doubles/twins start at ¥8400/11,200/11,900. This startlingly unimaginatively named establishment is the cheapest choice in the area. It is located on a backstreet behind Shibuya post office. The reception appears rather unfamiliar with dealing with foreigners, but should be able to cope. Rooms are small but sufficient. There is no English sign; it's in a white building, and the entrance is down a small alley.

Shanpia Hotel Aoyama (☎ *3407 2111, fax 3407 2879*) Singles/doubles/twins start at ¥8700/16,600/17,000. This is a better choice, with decent rooms and a few restaurants in the building. It's also quite close to Shibuya sights and shopping.

Hotel Sunroute Shibuya (☎ *3464 6411, fax 3464 1678*) Singles ¥6700 with shared bath. Singles/doubles/twins from ¥10,000/ 13,000/17,500 with private bath.

Shibuya Tōbu Hotel (☎ *3476 0111, fax 3476 0903*) Singles/doubles/twins start at ¥11,800/14,400/17,000. Probably the nicest place to stay in Shibuya, the rooms are clean, the common areas are pleasant, there are loads of in-house restaurants and the staff speak English.

Shibuya Tōkyū Inn (☎ *3462 0109, fax 3498 0189*) Singles/doubles/twins from ¥14,600/21,200/22,600. Although it's closer to Shibuya station, it's probably not worth paying this much for rooms similar to those at the Shibuya Tōbu.

Children's Castle Hotel (☎ *3797 5677*). Singles/twins/family-size rooms ¥6400/ ¥14,000/20,400 (very young children free). The main advantage of staying here is that guests are entitled to use the facilities of the adjoining Children's Castle at discounted rates. Facilities include a pool, a gym, and theatres and playrooms designed to keep the hyperactive ones entertained. That said, neither the hotel nor the Children's Castle are designed for foreign travellers, though it's likely your kids won't mind. Look for the unusual many-headed statue out front.

Roppongi (Map 4)

Roppongi is not the place to look for accommodation. There are few hotels of any class in this primarily entertainment district. You do have one decent mid-range choice, right near the famous Roppongi crossing:

Hotel Ibis (☎ 3403 4411, fax 3479 0609) Singles/doubles/twins start at ¥11,500/ 14,100/19,000. This is a clean, modern hotel with a few restaurants and bars in the building (if you just can't face the insanity on the streets below). This being Roppongi, you can count on the staff being used to foreign guests.

Other than Hotel Ibis, if you're intent on staying near Roppongi's bright lights, look a little to the north in Akasaka.

Akasaka (Map 7)

Akasaka is a good base if you want access to central Tokyo and a lively nightlife. In addition to all the top-end hotels, there are a few mid-range options, many of which are located on Akasaka-dōri, past the TBS broadcasting station on the way to Roppongi. You can also try one of Akasaka's capsule hotels.

Akasaka Yōkō Hotel (☎ 3586 4050, fax 3586 5944) Singles/twins start at ¥8900/ 14,000. This is a reasonably priced business hotel about midway between Akasaka and Roppongi. Although it's quite simple, the rooms are clean and the staff are friendly.

Marroad Inn Akasaka (☎ 3585 7611, fax 3585 7191) Singles/doubles/twins here start at ¥9400/15,000/13,500. On the same street as the Akasaka Yōkō, 100m closer to Roppongi, this is another standard business hotel with similar features.

PLACES TO STAY – TOP END

Tokyo's many top-end hotels are usually no more expensive than similar hotels elsewhere in the world, *and* you get Japan's legendary high standard of service.

Ginza, Akasaka and Shinjuku (mainly the west side) have the highest concentration of top-end hotels. Any of these areas would make a convenient base.

Tokyo Station Area (Map 8)

Palace Hotel (☎ 3211 5211, fax 3211 6987, W *www.palacehotel.co.jp/index_e.html)* Singles/doubles/twins from ¥24,000/29,000/ 28,000; business suites ¥56,000; larger suites from ¥100,000. This hotel is directly alongside the Imperial Palace putting it in the running for the best location in Tokyo. Many rooms command impressive views, the service is wonderful and the restaurants are among the best in Tokyo. If you aren't lucky enough to get a good view from your room, you can always have dinner in the 10th-floor Crown Restaurant – a great place to admire the lights of central Tokyo.

Ginza (Map 7)

Along with Akasaka, Ginza is home to the thickest concentration of elite hotels anywhere in Tokyo. Prices here reflect the glamorous surroundings and proximity to Tokyo station, great shopping, good restaurants and the political/financial districts. Ginza is a lot more pleasant for strolling than some of the louder and gaudier areas of Shinjuku and Ikebukuro.

Mitsui Urban Hotel (☎ 3527 4131) Singles/doubles start at ¥14,000/21,000, twins at ¥21,000. This is a stylish hotel, with a retro 70s touch, near Shimbashi station.

Ginza Tōkyū Hotel (☎ 3541 2411) Singles/doubles/twins from ¥16,000/26,000/ 24,000. This is a spacious hotel not far from Tsukiji market.

Ginza Dai-Ichi Hotel (☎ 3542 5311, fax 3542 3030) Singles/doubles/twins start at ¥16,000/26,000/25,000. Similar to the Ginza Tōkyū, the advantage here is the array of good restaurants and bars that grace its upper and lower floors. English is spoken too.

Ginza Tōbu Hotel (☎ 3546 0111, fax 3546 8990) Singles/doubles or twins start at ¥17,000/23,000. There are spacious rooms, good restaurants and bars, in this clean, new hotel just south of Kabuki-za theatre.

Dai-Ichi Hotel (☎ 3501 5161) Singles/ doubles/twins start at ¥27,000/34,000/ 30,000; suites from ¥80,000. Up a level in elegance and price, this fine hotel combines a modern skyscraper with classical interior design. The upper floors afford excellent views over the city. It's not far from Hibiya-kōen park.

Dai-Ichi Hotel Annex (☎ *3501 5161*) Singles/doubles/twins from ¥22,000/26,000/42,000. Those who want the luxury of the Dai-Ichi Hotel in a somewhat pared-down and more economical package can stay at the nearby Annex.

Imperial Hotel (☎ *3504 1111, fax 3581 9146*) Singles/doubles from ¥30,000/35,000; tower rooms from ¥110,000. Within walking distance of the sights of Ginza and Hibiya-kōen park, this is one of Tokyo's grand old hotels. Rooms are large and tastefully appointed, in a very elegant setting. Your chance to try Japanese hospitality at its best.

Hotel Seiyō Ginza (☎ *3535 1111, fax 3535 1110,* e *hsgmktng@tkf.att.ne.jp,* w *www.seiyo-ginza.com*) Guest rooms ¥48,000-72,000; suites from ¥85,000. The Seiyō Ginza is like no other hotel in Tokyo; indeed, it doesn't even feel like a hotel – it's more like a very wealthy friend's impossibly dignified chateau. There's no front desk as such, just a very discreet room with a very discreet staffer who takes care of the details of your stay. Most rooms come with a personal secretary, and this is only the start.

Kanda (Map 8)

Yama no Ue Hilltop Hotel (☎ *3293 2311, fax 3233 4567*) Singles/doubles/twins start at ¥15,000/22,000/24,000. The only worthy top-end hotel in Kanda is the Hilltop. On a hill next to Meiji University, one gets the impression that this is where the parents of some of the wealthier students stay when they're in town. The place is an anachronism, like something out of 1930s Hollywood. It also bills itself as a 'hotel to maintain health' (as opposed to the all-too-common 'inn to destroy health'). What this means is clearly and calmly explained by the brochure: 'Oxygen and negative ions are circulated into the rooms and its refreshing atmosphere is accepted by many, including prominent individuals, as most adequate for work and rest.' Yes indeed, and it is a nice, dignified hotel.

Ueno (Map 9)

Hotel Sofitel Tokyo (☎ *5685 7111, fax 5685 6171*) Singles/doubles or twins start at ¥17,000/22,000. You can't miss this weird Lego-land structure looming over Ueno-kōen's boating pond. It's described as a 'boutique hotel' – the rooms and common areas are hung with fine art, and the whole hotel has a fashionable air to it. Its unique construction affords good views from every room, particularly those facing Ueno-kōen.

Ikebukuro (Map 2)

Unless you have a good reason to be based here, there seems little point in paying top-end prices to stay in bawdy Ikebukuro. For the same money, you can get good accommodation *and* pleasant surroundings in places like Akasaka, west Shinjuku and even Ginza. However, if you need to be based in Ikebukuro, there are two choices in this class.

Sunshine City Prince Hotel (☎ *3988 1111, fax 3988 7878*) Singles/doubles/twins start at ¥15,000/24,000/22,000. In the Sunshine City complex, the hotel has rather chaotic common areas and the whole place feels slightly tatty. It's east of Ikebukuro station.

Hotel Metropolitan (☎ *3980 1111, fax 3980 5600*) Singles/doubles or twins start at ¥16,500/22,000. This hotel, on Ikebukuro's west side, is the better option. The hotel has all the amenities you'd expect, including ample dining and entertainment options, some of which are located on the 25th floor, affording good views over Tokyo and beyond.

Shinjuku (Map 3)

Shinjuku Prince Hotel (☎ *3205 1111, fax 3205 1952*) Singles/doubles/twins start at ¥15,000/17,000/26,000. In east Shinjuku, next to Seibu Shinjuku station, the Prince is a rather drab choice in this price bracket. The rooms are plain, and the lobby area is rather chaotic and dimly lit.

Keiō Plaza Inter-Continental (☎ *3344 0111, fax 3345 8269*) Singles/doubles or twins start at ¥16/000/24,000. Located in west Shinjuku, this 47-storey hotel provides excellent views of the area and quick access to the station.

Hilton Tokyo (☎ 3344 5111, fax 3342 6094) Singles/doubles start at ¥22,000/ 26,000; suites from ¥60,000. Expect great service, sports facilities, a convenient location and a variety of good restaurants. The hotel also has a 'hotel within a hotel' on its upper five floors catering specially to the business traveller, with a fully staffed business centre and a 'guest relations officer' to help organise your affairs.

Hotel Century Hyatt (☎ 3348 1234, fax 3344 5575) Singles/doubles or twins from ¥31,000/34,000. Not far from Hilton Tokyo, Hotel Century Hyatt offers a similar level of service and very spacious rooms, both Western and Japanese style, and a 26th-floor penthouse pool. If you happen to be in the neighbourhood, pop into the lobby and see the mother of all chandeliers.

Park Hyatt Tokyo (☎ 5322 1234, fax 5322 1288, W tokyo.hyatt.com/tyoph/) Singles/doubles ¥41,000/46,000; suites from ¥100,000. For a hotel experience unlike any other, check out this breathtaking top-ender on the upper floors of the new 53-storey Shinjuku Park Tower – it's a veritable island of luxury in the sky. The rooms are new, clean, very stylish and complemented by some of the most impressive bars and restaurants in Tokyo. Add to this the rooftop pool, the exercise studio overlooking the city and a great spa bath/sauna room, and you've got one of the city's best hotels. Even if you don't stay, at least stop by for a drink in the Sky Bar; you'll understand why when you get there.

Roppongi (Map 7)

Sadly, Roppongi is not rich in hotel accommodation of any class; it's better to look just a little to the north in hotel-rich Akasaka. If you're intent on staying in Roppongi, there is one fine choice:

Roppongi Prince Hotel (☎ 3587 1111, fax 3587 0770) Singles/doubles/twins start at ¥19,500/24,500/23,000. High standards prevail at this fashionable, high-tech hotel built around a huge atrium with an outdoor heated swimming pool at its centre. After a

swim, you can head to one of the hotel's excellent restaurants or bars. The nightlife of Roppongi is only 10 minutes' walk away.

Ebisu (Map 5)

Ebisu is a pleasant place to stay if you want a break from larger areas like Shinjuku or Ginza. In this class, there is only one real option:

Westin Hotel Tokyo (☎ 5423 7000, fax 5423 7600, W www.westin.co.jp/english/) Singles/doubles/suites from ¥30,000/36,000/ 80,000. This is modelled in the tradition of the grand European hotels, with elegant common areas and classically designed rooms. There are also six good restaurants and three bars, plus Ebisu Garden Place right on the doorstep.

Akasaka (Map 7)

Akasaka probably has such a high concentration of luxury hotels because it is a great area in which to be based: there are loads of good restaurants nearby, the political and business centres are within walking distance and Roppongi's nightlife is just down the road.

Akasaka Tōkyū Hotel (☎ 3580 2311) Singles/doubles/twins start at ¥16,000/ 28,000/23,000 – good value for the heart of Akasaka. Just above Akasaka-mitsuke subway station, this place boasts lots of good bars and restaurants scattered throughout the building – several of them on the 14th floor, giving good views over central Tokyo.

ANA Hotel Tokyo (☎ 3505 1111, fax 3505 1155) Singles/doubles/twins start at ¥24,000/ 31,000/28,000. Midway between Akasaka and Roppongi in the fashionable Ark Hills area, this modern 37-storey hotel is an excellent choice. It has all the amenities – fitness clubs, an outdoor pool, saunas, salons, shopping, and lots of good bars and restaurants. The Astral Sky Bar affords a view over Tokyo as far as Mt Fuji on clear days.

Capitol Tōkyū Hotel (☎ 3581 4511, fax 3581 5822) Singles/doubles or twins from ¥23,000/35,500. This hotel is an elegant place on the same hill as Hie-jinja shrine. It's built around a fine Japanese garden, with good restaurants and bars to take in the view. In warmer months, you can make use of the outdoor swimming pool.

Akasaka Prince Hotel (☎ *3234 1111, fax 3262 5163,* ⓦ *www.srs-worldhotels.com/japan/tokyo/hotel_nrtaka.html)* Western-style singles/doubles/twins start at ¥24,000/36,000/32,000; Japanese-style suites start at ¥95,000. Something of a landmark, rooms at this skyscraper hotel provide excellent views and spaciousness, a commodity in short supply in Tokyo.

Hotel New Ōtani (☎ *3265 1111, fax 3221 2619)* **Map 4** Singles/doubles/twins start at ¥27,500/32,500/40,000. Not far from the Akasaka Prince, the New Ōtani is renowned for the Japanese garden around which it is constructed. This massive hotel has all the amenities you'd expect, including extensive shopping areas, restaurants and private meeting rooms, yet it is somewhat impersonal. Thirty rooms on the 21st floor are reserved for women only.

Hotel Ōkura (☎ *3582 0111, fax 3582 3707)* Singles/doubles/twins start at ¥28,500/37,000/40,000. Near the US embassy, this hotel is at the top of a very exclusive bunch. It's home to visiting dignitaries and businesspeople. With a fine Japanese garden, elegant common areas and some of Tokyo's best restaurants, there's little reason to leave the hotel. Business travellers will also appreciate the executive salon service, offering all the staff and equipment necessary to run your business on the road.

Other Areas

The following is a brief list of recommended hotels on the periphery of the Tokyo area:

Hotel Pacific Meridian (☎ 3445 6711, fax 3445 5733) Singles/doubles from ¥22,000/25,000; Map 1 near Shinagawa station

New Takanawa Prince Hotel (☎ 3442 1111, fax 3444 1234) Singles/doubles/twins from ¥22,000/30,000/30,500; Map 1 close to Shinagawa station

Takanawa Prince Hotel (☎ 3447 1111, fax 3446 0849) Singles/doubles/twins from ¥17,500/30,000/24,000; near Shinagawa station

Tokyo Prince Hotel (☎ 3432 1111, fax 3434 5551) Singles/doubles or twins from ¥24,000/25,000; Map 7 near Onarimon subway station

If you need easy access to Narita airport, the following hotels are recommended:

Holiday Inn Tōbu Narita (☎ 0476-32 1234, fax 32 0617) Singles/doubles from ¥12,000/19,000; five minutes by taxi to airport

Hotel Narita Tōkyū (☎ 0476-33 0109, fax 33 0148) Singles/twins/doubles from ¥11,800/19,000/19,200; 10 minutes by taxi to airport; ⓦ www.panpac.com/japan/narita/hotels/hotel.html

Narita ANA Hotel (☎ 0476-33 1311, fax 33 0244) Singles/doubles from ¥14,000/21,000; 10 minutes by taxi to airport

LONG-TERM
Rental Options

Anyone renting an apartment in Tokyo will have to fork out a lot of money up front. You will often have to go through a real estate agency, whose fee is a month's rent. Then there's the landlord's 'key money' *(reikin)* – two to three months' rent, usually required again after two years. You never see it again. After this, there is the deposit (one or two months' rent) and an up-front payment of one or two months' rent. Imagine getting an apartment for a very reasonable ¥85,000 per month, then add up all these costs and you'll see why people stay so long in gaijin houses.

If you *do* decide to rent, you're lucky at least that, nowadays, there are lots of real-estate agents in Tokyo who speak English and are familiar with helping foreigners find rental places. The following places are worth a try.

Kimi Information Center (☎ *3986 1604)* **Map 2** This centre in Ikebukuro has comprehensive listings of apartments at very reasonable prices.

Ogura Real Estate (☎ *3586 8017)* This agency in Roppongi is open from 9.30am to 6pm, closed Sunday.

Also check *The Japan Times, Tokyo Classifieds* and *Tokyo Journal* for current listings.

Finally, almost every apartment for rent in Tokyo requires a Japanese guarantor. If you have a full-time job, your boss will generally do this for you. Understandably, however, Japanese are generally not eager to sign on as guarantors, especially to foreigners they have only known briefly. It's best not to embarrass newly acquired friends by asking.

Serviced Apartments

If you are based in Tokyo for a couple of months or longer, serviced apartments are an option. Look in *The Japan Times* or *Tokyo Journal*. Prices vary dramatically depending on size, location and services provided. No key money is required, but you generally pay a one-month deposit. For anything halfway decent, be prepared to spend between ¥100,000 and ¥180,000 per month.

Some helpful agencies that deal in serviced apartments are listed below (English is spoken on all these numbers):

Nihon MKD (☎ 3780 2611) Tokyo
Fontana (☎ 3382 0151) Tokyo
House Builder (☎ 3405 0130) Tokyo
Arai Housing (☎ 0473-98 3370) Yokohama

Places to Eat

No city in Asia can match Tokyo for the sheer variety and quality of its restaurants. As well as refined Japanese cuisine, Tokyo is filled with great international restaurants – everything from cous-cous to Cambodian curries. Really serious gourmands can seek out the *Tokyo Restaurant Guide* by John Kennerdell and the excellent Tokyo Food Page at W www.bento .com/tokyofood.html.

But Tokyo can be as much greasy spoon as gourmet chic. All commercial and residential areas harbour multitudes of cheap eateries where you can grab a quick, cheap bite. At lunch, when workers pour out of offices, most restaurants also provide cheap *teishoku* (set-menu meals).

During the day, the best eating areas are the big shopping districts: Akasaka, Shibuya, Shinjuku, Harajuku and Ginza. Shinjuku may be the best daytime option, with department store *resutoran-gai* (restaurant floors) providing an endless selection of reasonably priced restaurants and the best affordable Chinese food in town. There are a vast number of restaurants around and under Shinjuku station and in the busy entertainment area.

Good Japanese and international cuisine is more expensive, but if you're happy to spend ¥3000 for a meal and a drink, there is no shortage of excellent choices. If you want gourmet, Tokyo delivers.

For information on Japanese cuisine and eating establishments see the Food special section, later in this chapter.

Vegetarian

Vegetarian food is less common than you might expect in Tokyo. Luckily, many places which aren't strictly vegetarian serve a good variety of non-meat/non-fish dishes, eg, Japanese noodle and tofu shops. Pick up the Tourist Information Center's (TIC's) *Vegetarian & Macrobiotic Restaurants in Tokyo* hand-out. This lists strictly vegetarian restaurants, whole food shops, *shōjin-ryōri*

(Buddhist temple fare) restaurants and Indian restaurants that offer a good selection of vegetarian dishes.

Food Etiquette

When eating in Japan there are some implicit rules, but they're fairly easy to remember. If you're worried about putting your foot in it, relax – the Japanese don't expect you to know everything and are unlikely to be offended as long as you follow the standards of politeness of your own country. For many rules (lifting soup bowls, slurping noodles and so on) just follow the locals.

Among the more important eating 'rules' are those regarding chopsticks. Don't stick them upright in your rice – that's how rice is offered to the dead! Passing food from your chopsticks to someone else's is a similar no-no. When taking food from shared plates, avoid using the business end of your chopsticks – invert them before reaching for that tasty morsel.

Before digging in, it's polite to say 'Itadaki-masu', literally 'I will receive'. At the end of the meal you should say 'Gochisō-sama deshita', a respectful way of saying that the meal was good.

If you're out for a few drinks, remember that you're expected to keep the drinks of your companions topped up. Don't fill your own glass: wait for someone to do this for you. It's polite to hold the glass with both hands while it is being filled. The Japanese equivalent of cheers is 'Kampai!'.

If someone invites you to eat or drink with them, they will be paying. In any case, it's unusual for bills to be split. Generally at the end of the meal, something of a struggle ensues to see who gets the privilege of paying. If this happens, it is polite to at least make an effort to pay the bill – it is extremely unlikely that your Japanese 'hosts' will acquiesce. Exceptions to this are likely among younger Japanese.

東京 東京 東京 東京 東京 東京 東京

PLACES TO EAT – BUDGET

You can easily eat cheap in Tokyo. Probably the most common budget filler is the *rāmen* shop. The cheapest dish is always plain *rāmen nami*, a hearty bowl of noodles (¥450 to ¥900). Noodle shops serving *udon* (thick white noodles) and *soba* (thick brown noodles) can be equally budget-friendly.

Japanese Cuisine

Check out Shinjuku, Asakusa, Ueno and Ikebukuro for inexpensive grub. However there are always cheap places in and around railway stations, on the restaurant floors of department stores and in shopping arcades. Look for simple, relatively unadorned places. You can also watch where office workers go to eat.

For serious yen-pinching, look for a *tachi-kui* (stand-and-eat) place, where you get simple dishes for as low as ¥200. The established ones often have great food (for the price). Find them in and around the busier railway stations. At modern tachi-kui, you choose the dish you'd like from a vending machine outside the store, which, if you're lucky, has pictures of the dishes above the buttons. The machine will issue a plastic token that you hand to one of the workers inside.

Tokyo Station Area (Map 8) Below the station there is an underground shopping mall with all manner of inexpensive Japanese and Western-style restaurants. Japanese dishes include noodles, *tonkatsu* (deep-fried breaded pork cutlet), *teishoku* and extensive coffee shop fare.

Out of the station you'll find some bargains on the restaurant floors of nearby department stores.

Takashimaya (☎ 3211 4111) **Map 8** seems to have the best selection of the department stores. Stroll through its wonderful B1 food floor (and try a few free samples). In the sub-basement (B2), there's a cafeteria-style eatery with standard lunch items, many offered as set meals, ranging from ¥800 to ¥2000. Choose what you'd like from the display case (they're identified by number), buy a ticket and give it to your waiter.

There's much tastier, slightly pricier food in the *restaurants* on the 6th floor of Takashimaya's annex Konomi Shokudō. Here, for remarkably reasonable prices you can choose from *tempura* (fish and vegetables cooked in batter), *unagi* (eel with a sweet sauce), *sushi*, noodles and Kyoto cuisine. Prices range from ¥700 to ¥3000.

Ginza (Map 7) Despite its reputation as Tokyo's ritziest area, Ginza is home to some very reasonably priced restaurants. Indeed, if you're put off by the gaudy lights and in-your-face advertising of Shinjuku or Ikebukuro, Ginza can be a great place to look for good restaurants in pleasant surroundings.

For inexpensive lunch and dinner sets, try Ginza's department stores, in particular the 8th floor of *Matsuya*, the 2nd basement floor of *Matsuzakaya* and the 1st and 2nd basement floors of *Hankyū*. On the 2nd basement floor of Hankyū is *Naokyū Rāmen*, one of the cheapest and most popular rāmen places in town – at ¥400 for rāmen and ¥300 for *gyōza* (Chinese dumplings) it's understandably packed for lunch and dinner – try off-peak. There's no English sign, but it's right next to the Spud coffee shop.

For inexpensive noodles try *Dondon*, on the other side of the tracks from Ginza in the direction of Hibiya. Lunch sets start at ¥800. Try the tempura udon for ¥900.

Tendon Tenya (☎ 5565 6903) Tempura ¥490. This chain offers fast-food tempura and has a branch in Ginza.

Don-don Tei Lunch sets start at ¥980. This standard-issue lunch place usually displays its daily special out front.

Tsukiji Sushikō Tsukiji 4-Chome-ten (☎ 3547 0505) Nothing over ¥350. Excellent value, super clean, spacious. Budget sushi, on the corner next to the Kyōbashi post-office.

Ōdaiba (Map 6) *Soup Stock Tokyo* (☎ 3599 2333) Soup at ¥800. 'Soup for all!' proclaims this friendly, inexpensive fast-soup restaurant in the Venus Fort shopping complex. Try the garlic soup with *onsen tamago* (hot-spring boiled eggs).

Shinjuku (Map 3) *Negishi* (☎ *3232 8020*) Mains ¥1050. Tasty beef tongue is the speciality of this restaurant, advertised as health food and served with vegetables, a clear soup and a bowl of *tororo* rice (rice served with ground sticky potato). Order the *negishi* teishoku (double teishoku) if you're really hungry. There's a picture menu but no sign. It's easy to spot, though – look for the glass front and polished-wood interior. Don't forget to pour the tororo over your rice!

Kanda & Akihabara (Map 8) Kanda teems with students and Akihabara with electronic bargain hunters, so cheap eats – especially at lunch – are easy to find.

Hisago (☎ *3294 0141*) Meals less than ¥1000. A step up from the cafeterias, this hip place run by a 'croquette master' (Hisago is in the sporting goods section of town) has been feeding Meiji University students for years. Look for the rustic wooden facade.

Tokyo's 'big three' buckwheat noodle restaurants are all in this neighbourhood, and the only effective way to find out which you prefer is to try them all.

Kanda Yabu Soba (☎ *3251 0287*) Meals from ¥800. A Kanda institution, this celebrated buckwheat noodle shop is indeed rather special. The authentic surroundings add to the atmosphere, but it's the noodles that carry the day. To really fill up you'll need two or three dishes. Look for queues of eager customers in front of a traditional building surrounded by a wooden fence.

Matsuya (☎ *3251 1556*) Meals from ¥700. Just around the corner from Yabu Soba, Matsuya is less crowded though still hugely popular. Try plain *zaru* soba (cold noodles with seaweed), then follow it up with the *Kamo nanban*. The waitresses here are friendly-but-tough dames of the old Edo school.

Muromachi Sunaba (☎ *3241 4038*) From ¥700. Third in the soba triumvirate, 'the Sand Pit' is less cocky than Yabu Soba and even more laid-back than Matsuya. Try the excellent *Tenzaru* soba with a side order of *yakitori* (skewers of grilled chicken). Turn right from the east exit of Kanda station, and walk south down Chūō-dōri towards Mitsukoshi department store. Turn right at Muromachi 4-chome crossing and the shop is 50m on your left.

Jangara Rāmen Honten (☎ *3251 4059*) Rāmen from ¥960. Open 11am-11pm Mon-Sat, 11am-9.30pm Sun. Original shop in a hugely popular chain, specialising in Kyushu style noodles in that notoriously stinky pork broth. Handily placed for post-Akihabara shopping (expect to queue for up to half an hour though). Try the *Zenbuiri rāmen* – it has something of everything in it.

Ueno (Map 9) The Ueno area is a happy hunting ground for cheap food. You'll find a good variety of cheap Japanese places in and around *Ameyoko arcade*. Many shops display food models in the window, and lunch specials and teishoku are likely to cost around ¥800. There's lots of rāmen and 'automatic sushi' (see Food special section, later in this chapter) on the station end of the arcade. You can also pick up take-away foods – such as yakitori, rice balls and fruit – from vendors in the arcade.

Ueno Yabu Soba (☎ *3831 4728*) Meals from ¥1000. Near the arcade, just south of Marui department store. Ueno Yabu Soba is famous, but the atmosphere is too much like a chain restaurant. To really fill up get the *tenseiro* set, which includes tempura, for ¥1800.

Maguroyāsan (☎ *3844 2732*) Lunch ¥1000, dinner ¥2500. 'Maguro' means tuna, and if it can be made from tuna, it's probably on the menu, including exotic and tasty *maguro gyōza* (tuna-filled dumplings) for ¥400. The lunch sets are especially good value. This friendly restaurant is non-smoking during lunch hours. It's 50m north of Kinko's.

Asakusa (Map 9) Not surprisingly, the old Shitamachi area of Asakusa is teeming with Japanese restaurants. The best place to look is Kaminarimon-dōri and the small streets surrounding Nakamise-dōri. If you just want a snack, the authentic *sembei* (cracker) stores of Nakamise-dōri and the food tents in front of Sensō-ji Temple are a good bet.

PLACES TO EAT

Rāmen-tei Hanayashiki (☎ *3842 8781*) Rāmen from ¥500. Look for the pictures of rāmen in the window to find this eatery, opposite Dempō-in. It serves about the cheapest plain rāmen in town. A nicer option is its spicy *Shisen* (Szechuan) rāmen.

Edokko (☎ *3841 0150)* From ¥1300. Nearby Edokko serves that great Asakusa speciality, tempura, in a very authentic atmosphere. Try its *tendon* (bowl of rice topped with tempura shrimp and vegetables) at lunch. The place has a traditional wooden facade and white *noren* (restaurant door curtains, usually bearing the name of the establishment) curtains outside.

Tenya (☎ *5828 5918)* From ¥490. On Kaminarimon-dōri, this place serves roughly the same fare as Edokko but in a fast-food atmosphere at fast-food prices. It's only recommended if you are in a real hurry or on a very tight budget.

Tonkyu (☎ *3841 8718)* From ¥1000. Closed Thurs. Also on Kaminarimon-dōri, just to the right of Kaminari-mon Gate, is a small family-run restaurant that serves good tonkatsu at reasonable prices. Its *rōsu katsu* teishoku is recommended. Look for the food models in the window as there is no English sign.

Raishūken (☎ *3844 7409)* From ¥700. Open noon-7pm, closed Tues. Step back in time in this 40-year-old rāmen shop. The Japanese describe this as *natsukashii no aji,* 'the taste of nostalgia'. Order an *ōmori* – a large bowl of Taiwan-style noodles in a soy-based soup.

Ikebukuro (Map 2) If you can't find a budget meal in Ikebukuro you aren't trying. All you have to do is walk a few a minutes from the station and look for the plastic food displays conveniently labelled with prices.

Komazushi (☎ *3590 0581)* Plates from ¥120. One of a number of revolving sushi restaurants on the station's east side, popular Komazushi is worth recommending for its friendly atmosphere. It's near a giant pachinko parlour.

Tonbo (☎ *3986 1686)* From ¥1200. Come for good tonkatsu, fried shrimp and related fare. The Tonbo *tonkatsu* teishoku

(pork cutlet set meal) and *ebi furai* teishoku (fried-shrimp set meal) are good. Tonbo is on the station's west side.

Seibu, Tōbu and Marui department stores all have **restaurant floors** in their upper reaches – Seibu alone has around 50 restaurants, many specialising in Japanese regional cuisines. The dishes are all on display in plastic outside. Enjoy.

Takadanobaba (Map 2) *Ichiban Dori* (☎ *3204 2648)* Meals from ¥700. In the basement of the F1 building, across from the station, you'll find this simple restaurant specialising in chicken dishes. Lunch sets are a good deal – try the chicken *teriyaki donburi* (rice bowl). No English sign. It's in front of you as you descend the stairs to the basement.

Shinjuku (Map 3) Speed-loving Shinjuku is a good place to hunt for bargains. However, the intense competition has resulted in a lot of *bad* cheap food. Beware of the *tabehōdai* (all-you-can-eat) specials offered by many places – the quality is usually as low as the price. The automatic sushi places are pretty grim as well; it may be only ¥120 per plate, but what you're likely to get is leathery sushi of unknown origin. It's probably safer to pay more at a good place. But if you look carefully, Shinjuku probably still has Tokyo's best selection of bargain eats. Look on the streets on the east side of Shinjuku station.

There's a lot of rāmen in Shinjuku (goes with the drinking) but much is dismal stuff.

Tenkaippin (☎ *3232 7454)* Sets from ¥600. This place is a cut above the rest; sets include fried rice and dumplings. Specify 'kotteri' for thick soup or 'asari' for thin. Look for the red lanterns and red-and-white decor.

Keika Kumamoto Rāmen (☎ *3354 4591)* From ¥650. Out toward Shinjuku Sanchōme. Authentic rāmen is served here; try the *chashūmen*. There's no English sign but it's the only rāmen place in the neighbourhood.

Shinjuku Negishi (☎ *3232 8020)* Sets around ¥1000. The beef tongue and beef stew sets are tasty stuff at this cosy, Japanese country fare specialist in Kabukichō.

Ekiben – Lunch in Locomotion

Ekiben are one of those delightful Japanese institutions. A contraction of the words *eki* (railway station) and *bentō* (lunch box), every railway station worth its salt has an ek-iben stand, and some stations are famous for their ekiben.

Legend has it that the first ekiben were served in 1885 at Utsunomiya station, not far from Tokyo. Back in those days, pickles and rice balls were standard fare. How times change. There are close to 3000 varieties nowadays, and stations contend to produce ever more exotic ones – a station might fea-ture mushroom, marinated boar or trout eki-ben. Prices are reasonable, if you consider that you're not buying a hastily flung-together take-out. Famous ekiben tend to go from ¥1000 upward, although cheaper ones are often available on trains.

東京東京東京東京東京東京東京

It's not far from the Prince Hotel, sand-wiched between Peking Rāmen and Tainan Taami Taiwanese restaurant. Look for the wood carvings over the door.

Harajuku, Aoyama & Nishi-Azabu (Map 4) These areas are more cosmopoli-tan than most others; as a result of the culi-nary colonisation there is little in the way of inexpensive Japanese food. There are, how-ever, a few exceptions.

Hiroba (☎ 3406 6409) Lunch buffet from ¥1260. In the Crayon House building, one block behind the Hanae Mori building. A vegetarian's delight, this small place offers an excellent organic lunch buffet.

Home (☎ 3406 6409) From ¥1800. Hi-roba's sister store, located in the same build-ing. More of a sit-down-and-order place.

Shibuya (Map 4) Japanese restaurants in Shibuya are slowly succumbing to a tide of foreign invaders, but you can still find some budget places. The *food floors* of large de-partment stores will yield lots of noodle, fried cutlet and set-meal restaurants.

Shizenkan (☎ 3476 2591) Lunch and dinner about ¥1500. On the east side of the station, this 'natural food' restaurant serves a variety of set meals, all displayed outside with prices and caloric contents. Look for the English sign: 'Healthy Boutique' (and we thought it was a restaurant ...).

Ebisu (Map 5) You can find lots of cheap, standard-issue lunch places in the Ebisu JR station's Atre building, but for more inter-esting fare check out the following.

Shunsenbo (☎ 5469 9761) Lunch ¥1000, dinner ¥3800. Great value for money at this place specialising in tofu dishes and *shabu-shabu* (see Food special section later in this chapter). There's an English menu. It's on the ground floor of the Ebisu Prime Square Plaza.

Kazuki (☎ 3496 6885) Rāmen from ¥1000. Famed 24-hour rāmen shop just up the hill from Wendy's. Their *miso chaarshu-men* (soy-bean paste soup with extra pork) is a good post-clubbing calorie-fest. There is table service upstairs.

Ippu-do (☎ 5420 2225) From ¥700. An-other nationally famous rāmen shop, spe-cialising in *tonkotsu* pork-broth noodles. The *Akamaru Shinmi* rāmen is tailored to-wards the Tokyo palate, the *Shiromaru* is pure Kyushu. It's just east of the Shibuya-bashi post office.

Santoka (☎ 5421 0336) From ¥1200. The third contender in the Great Ebisu Rāmen battle. Small, often packed. Try their 'limited edition' *Gentei* rāmen. It's one block south of Ebisu -higashi-kōen.

Roppongi (Map 4) Although it's re-garded as Tokyo's foreign playground, you can still grab a cheap bite of Japanese food in Roppongi.

Tsukiji Sushikō Roppongi-ten (☎ 3408 0505) Nothing above ¥350. Open to 5am. Good value, tasty, clean, budget sushi on the 1st floor of the building that houses Citibank at Roppongi crossing. Always busy.

Shōjikiya (☎ 3401 8333) Unagi sets ¥1950, simpler sets ¥1000. Visit this place for teishoku. The name means 'honest

PLACES TO EAT

store', and that's what you'll get: honest Japanese cooking. It's very close to the Roppongi crossing. There is no English sign and the place is set back a little from the street; look for the plants near the door.

Akasaka (Map 7) There is not much bargain Japanese food in upper-crust Akasaka. However a few of the mid-range Japanese places offer lunch specials for around ¥1000.

Ōdaiba (Map 6) As it's a popular 'de-to supoto' (date spot) there's not much budget Japanese cuisine down in Ōdaiba.

Wakō (☎ 3599 6555) Dishes from ¥780. Standard-fare teishoku at reasonable prices at this place in Deck's Tokyo Beach. Try the tonkatsu.

Hina Zushi (☎ 5531 0017) From ¥1800, all-you-can-eat ¥4300. Good sushi at this place on Restaurant Row. Its all-you-can-eat special is the real bargain (if at ¥4300 'bargain' is the right word).

International Cuisine

Tokyo has some fine international restaurants, but few are cheap. However the ones listed in this section all serve lunch sets for less than ¥1000. At dinner some prices rise.

Ginza (Map 7) *Potohar (☎ 3496 1177)* Business lunch ¥890. Billed as a Malaysian and Pakistani restaurant, this place covers a lot of ground. Its multi-ethnic business lunch is a great deal: a choice of four curries, tea or lassi, and all the naan and rice you can eat. It's just north of Matsuzaka department store on the 8th floor of the Star building.

Volks (☎ 3501 7979) Steaks and salads ¥1000-2000. A steakhouse around the corner from Matsuya department store. There is a picture menu to help you order.

Kanda (Map 8) Though Kanda has some cheap international restaurants, the mid-range places are where the action is. If you're on a budget you might want to try some of these places for lunch.

Ueno (Map 9) This is not the place to look for bargain international cuisine, unless you

consider McDonald's 'cuisine'. But there are two decent Indian restaurants near Ameyoko arcade with lunch specials for around ¥1000.

Maharaja (☎ 3572 7196) All-you-can-eat specials ¥890-1300. The lunch-time 'viking' (all-you-can-eat special) includes four curries, rice and naan.

Samrat (☎ 5688 3226) All-you-can-eat lunch starts at ¥890. This is not the city's most exciting Indian.

Asakusa (Map 9) Not too much nouvelle cuisine in old Shitamachi. You're pretty much limited to fast-food chains, all of which are represented in the small streets around the Nakamise-dōri arcade.

Capricciosa (☎ 3843 7721) Lunch ¥830, dinner around ¥2000. Happily, this Italian place serves enough-for-two portions at budget prices. For dessert, you can try the *Real Italian Gelato* down the street.

Ikebukuro (Map 2) There are lots of cheap international places to eat in Ikebukuro.

Joidar (☎ 3981 5546) Meals start at about ¥2000. Right around the corner from the Kimi Ryokan, this Thai place is authentic, if a bit grubby. Menus are in Thai and Japanese.

Oriental Kitchen (☎ 3982 7828) Lunch ¥980, two-hour dinner ¥1980. Really hungry? Considering the price, these vast all-you-can-eat buffets of just about every major Asian food you'd care to name are pretty good. There's also an all-you-can-drink special (¥1280) for those who don't care where they drink. It's on the 2nd floor of its building.

Mekong (☎ 3988 5688) All-you-can-eat lunch buffet ¥1000, dinner from ¥2000. Good soups, dull atmosphere. It's just down from Marui department store.

Capricciosa (☎ 5396 0773) Lunch ¥830, dinner around ¥2000. Head here for large portions of cheap Italian food. The atmosphere is a little classier than this chain restaurant's average.

You can also head for the excellent *restaurant floors* of Tōbu, Seibu or Mitsukoshi department stores.

Takadanobaba (Map 2) In addition to all the standard fast-food outlets, those in search of economical international food in 'Baba may want to sample the filling Italian fare at *Capricciosa (☎ 3205 2881)*.

Shinjuku (Map 3) This is the place to look for good deals on international food. However, as with Japanese cuisine, there's a lot of real junk mixed in with the bargains in Shinjuku. Beware of all-you-can-eat specials and other such deals – there's a reason why the food is so cheap.

Peking (☎ 3200 3560) Meals around ¥1100. This restaurant in Kabukichō gets no awards for warm and friendly service, but the Chinese-style rāmen is authentic – and so are the Chinese staff. Rāmen starts at ¥800 and six gyōza go for ¥300. Look for the Japanese sign, red awning and pictures of rāmen in the window.

Istanbul (☎ 3225 4080) Lunch sets from ¥780. Out by Sanchōme, this pleasant restaurant offers very good Turkish food at bottom-end prices. At dinner the prices rise, but the quality does not change.

Court Lodge (☎ 3376 7733) Lunch ¥800, dinner ¥1500. Try the godamba roti at this Sri Lankan place in west Shinjuku. The very good Sri Lankan lunch set has two curries.

For a more adventurous eating experience, walk through down-market Kabukichō to the Asian neighbourhoods of **Shokuan-dōri** or **Shin-Ōkubo-dōri**. You'll know you've arrived when you stop hearing Japanese; it's a foreign language here.

For authentic Korean food in this area, head to **Korea Town** (just off the northern end of **Map 3**) on Shokuan-dōri, east of the JR tracks. Here all the Korean specialities are available, like yaki-niku (Korean barbecue; 'galbi' or 'bulgogi' in Korean) and industrial-strength gimchi (spicy fermented vegetables).

Kankoku-fu (☎ 5273 3887) Mains from ¥2000. With the food as good as the atmosphere is bad, this is a winner. Order any dish and they'll serve you a table full of side dishes to accompany it. The bibimbap (a rice dish with vegetables) is a good, filling choice. Don't even try speaking Japanese – it's Korean or sign language. It's diagonally across from the 24-hour convenience store.

Harajuku, Aoyama & Nishi-Azabu (Map 4) If you want international cuisine this is the place, with more bistros, cafes and trattorias than most small European cities. Atmosphere may take precedence over cuisine, but there's always a pleasant place to sit and watch the world go by.

The heart of it all is the famous promenade of Tokyo's young and beautiful, Omote-sandō. The street is lined with outdoor cafes, most of which are slavish reproductions of the French ones – some are so realistic that courteous Japanese service seems distinctly out of place (see the Tokyo Cafe Society boxed text later in this chapter). Other options exist along Aoyama-dōri and on the pleasant streets of Nishi-Azabu. Be warned that this is one of Tokyo's more glamorous areas and you're paying for the location. There are some bargains, however, so read on.

Rat Ngon Store (☎ 3478 9467) Meals from ¥1000. No rodents at this friendly spot offering reasonably priced, Asian-ish sets ('rat ngon' means very tasty in Vietnamese). It's near the west end of Takeshita-dōri, behind Pop-land, tucked in on the 3rd floor of an apartment building, next to a barber specialising in Afros.

Apetito (☎ 3497 0170) Lunch or dinner around ¥700 (including a drink). A popular little shop that sells sandwiches far superior to the limp versions you find in convenience stores. It also sells a variety of coffee shop drinks – and there's a patio. This is about the best budget option in these parts. Apetito is right next to Royal Host family restaurant.

Bengawan Solo (☎ 3408 5698) From ¥3000. Miss the islands? For a taste of the South Seas head to this long-established Indonesian restaurant out on Roppongi-dōri. The gado gado lunch and the beef in coconut cream are favourites.

Ghee (☎ 3401 4023) Curry sets ¥1000. For good curries in a casual atmosphere Ghee, a little off the main Harajuku drag, is a great offbeat choice. Look for the white plaster facade and a small English sign.

Shibuya (Map 4) There are lots of cheap international restaurants catering to the youthful masses who descend on Shibuya each day. Many are on the food floors of the huge department stores that crowd the area.

New York Kitchen (☎ 5457 7755) From ¥600. A good lunch stop with real bagels, a good choice of salads and cheap coffee. Eat in or take out.

Fungo (☎ 3477 8795) Meals around ¥800. This sandwich shop and cafe is most likely to appeal to foreign tastes. In addition to good sandwiches, Fungo serves burgers, espresso, cappuccino and American micro-brewed beers. It's on the 3rd floor of the Parco III department store.

For other foreign fare look along the smaller streets surrounding the station.

Charlie House (☎ 3464 5552) Less than ¥1000. This Cantonese noodle restaurant on Kōen-dōri serves authentic Chinese noodles. The good food is complemented by a rustic wood interior. Turn at the tobacco machines down the small side street and look for the English sign.

Siam (☎ 3770 0550) Lunch ¥1000, dinner ¥2000. Good value all-you-can-eat lunch and inexpensive dinners at this restaurant run by Thai chefs. It closes early though.

Samrat (☎ 3770 7275) Curries less than ¥1000. Samrat serves the usual Indian curries and curry sets. Closer to the station, it's just around the corner from the popular foreigner's bar Hub. There's usually a tout outside beckoning people in.

Court Lodge (☎ 3376 7733) Lunch around ¥1000, dinner ¥2000. For more imaginative Indian and Sri Lankan food, head south to this place. Look for the large yellow English sign.

Ebisu (Map 5) The requisite fast-food chains are scattered around Ebisu JR station, but that's about it for budget international food.

Festbrau (☎ 3442 5111) Mains around ¥2500. Pseudo-German fare perhaps, but the sausages, steak and seafood here are reasonably priced, as is the draft beer. This 'grand beer hall' seats 500 and it's often full. It's in the basement of Ebisu Garden Place's 'beer station'.

Roppongi (Map 4) It only makes sense that in Roppongi, Tokyo's foreign nightlife playground, there would be a lot of international restaurants. The problem is this is a pretty ritzy playground. There are a few cheap restaurants in the area, however, where you can bulk up before wading into all those bars.

Havana Cafe (☎ 3423 3500) Mains less than ¥1000. One of the best places to start a Roppongi evening is at this casual cafe. In addition to great happy hour drink specials it serves reliable stuff like burritos and sandwiches. The place opens onto a quiet backstreet and, as you sip that first drink, it's difficult to imagine that Roppongi lurks just round the corner.

Bourbon Street (☎ 3478 8473) Meals ¥4500, with drinks. Open 6pm-11pm, closed Mon. Go for the shrimp at this classy, intimate cajun specialist. One order of the spicy gumbo will feed two. In the basement of the Core building.

Hamburger Inn (☎ 3405 8980) Mains around ¥1000. A Roppongi institution of the most dubious culinary kind. The main draw is that it's open all night. *Caveat emptor* (buyer beware).

Johnny Rockets (☎ 3423 1955) Mains at least ¥1500. Less chance of salmonella here than at some of the opposition joints. Right at the Roppongi intersection.

Akasaka (Map 7) Along with nearby Roppongi, Akasaka is one of Tokyo's most cosmopolitan neighbourhoods. While most of the action is in the mid-range bracket, a stroll around the narrow streets just west of Akasaka-mitsuke subway station will turn up a number of good lunch-time deals.

Moti (TBS branch ☎ 3584 6640, main branch 3582 3620) Lunch starts at around ¥800. Dinner prices a lot higher. Perhaps Tokyo's best Indian chain, Moto has two branches in Akasaka. The pick of the litter is the northern TBS branch.

Ōdaiba (Map 6) *Khazana* (☎ *3599 6551*) Buffet lunch ¥1000. If you're hungry and on a tight budget, the all-you-can-eat lunch at this Indian spot on the 5th floor of Deck's Tokyo Beach hits the spot. Get there early to score a coveted table out on the deck.

Sam Choy's (☎ *5531 5036*) Lunch ¥1200, dinner ¥2500. Whopping portions of fairly decent Hawaiian-Asian seafood.

There are also a number of Western-style restaurants, at up-market prices, in the Palette Town complex.

Fast Food

You very rarely have to walk far to find a McDonald's or a KFC in Tokyo. A slightly healthier option is a sandwich at Subway or a Western-style bakery.

On the whole, fast-food joints are more expensive than eating in rāmen shops, eg, two pieces of chicken and fries at KFC costs ¥650. Still, many newcomers end up eating at these places simply because of familiarity with the food and ease of ordering.

Japanese versions of burgers can be found in chains like *Mos Burger*, *Lotteria* and *Love Burger*, featuring teriyaki burgers and so on. Those in the know rate Mos Burger as the best of the bunch.

Bakeries & Ice Cream

Often overlooked, bakeries are the budget traveller's best friend. Tokyoites are waking up to the joys of well-made bread, and even simple local bakeries have a good selection. Most places also sell sandwiches and a whole range of sweets and cakes. While bakeries are in just about every neighbourhood, the best bakeries are on the food floors of large department stores.

Those in search of ice cream can choose from local Japanese offerings, which are usually small places selling *sofuto-kuriimu* (soft ice cream in cones, with green tea a popular flavour) and imports like Häagen Dazs, which have proliferated in the more popular central areas.

Self-Catering

Of course, it is always possible to put your own meal together. While convenience stores are the most frequently raided suppliers of do-it-yourself meals, department store food floors are another favourite option. Apart from all the handout samples, there are often specials available – especially at closing time. Department store bakeries make it fairly easy to put together a decent lunch for around ¥500.

Another favourite of Tokyo travellers on a budget is the local *bentō* (boxed lunch) store. These provide take-away meals at very reasonable rates (starting at around ¥400). The meals come in packs and usually include rice, some vegetables and meat or fish.

There are also a couple of Western-style supermarkets in Tokyo that, while often exorbitantly expensive, allow the homesick foreigner to indulge in hard-to-find items from home. Two of the more established supermarkets are *Kinokuniya International* **(Map 4)** (☎ *3400 0022*) in Kita-Aoyama, and *Meijiya* (☎ *3271 1111*) in Kyōbashi **(Map 7)**, Ginza **(Map 7)** and Roppongi **(Map 4)**.

PLACES TO EAT – MID-RANGE

Mid-range dining is where Tokyo really comes into its own. Along with all the wonderful Japanese cuisine, it's also well worth checking out some of the international restaurants for which Tokyo is justly famous.

Japanese Cuisine

Tokyo Station Area (Map 8) If you're looking for delicious food around here, the best advice is to walk south 15 minutes to Ginza (one stop on the Marunouchi subway line). But if you're intent on eating near the station there are some options.

Banya (☎ *3281 5581, fax 3281 5581*) Mains about ¥3000. Come for standard *izakaya* (Japanese-style pub) fare in a rustic farmhouse atmosphere. Unlike most izakaya, it also serves lunch on weekdays. There's no English sign, but it's directly next to a Doutor coffee shop. Look for the faux traditional facade.

Around the corner from Banya, in the direction of Takashimaya department store, you'll find several cosy yakitori places.

Nanban-tei (☎ *275 3473*) Meals about ¥3000. Fill up here on yakitori and a few beers. There's no English sign but you can identify the place by the picture of a chicken on the sign.

Ginza (Map 7) Ginza mysteriously seems to be the yakitori capital of Tokyo. Under the JR tracks just south of Harumi-dōri is a warren of yakitori restaurants known as *Yūrakuchō Yakitori Alley*. It's simple and atmospheric. Most of the restaurants here are outside but if the weather's cold they put up heaters and tents.

Tonton Honten (☎ 3508 9454) Yakitori about ¥3000. While most places around here serve the same fare for the same price, Tonton is the most friendly and has an English menu. It's in the east-west tunnel beneath the tracks. If Tonton is full, walk out the east side of the tunnel and turn left, where you'll be welcomed by the next-friendliest place.

New Torigin (☎ 3571 3334) Meals around ¥3500, including beers. Good yakitori in slightly more up-market surroundings. Walk east into the heart of Ginza. This authentic, popular little place is hidden down a back alley. However it is signposted in English. There's also an English menu. Good for a little *sake* sampling.

Robata (☎ 3591 1905) Mains ¥3000. This is Tokyo's most celebrated izakaya, and one place where if you don't speak Japanese you're going to have to bring a friend who does. Otherwise point at what your neighbour is eating, or throw yourself at the mercy of the staff and say 'omakase shimasu' (you decide). The restaurant is back near the railway tracks but it's hard to spot the sign, even if you can read Japanese; it's better just to look for the rustic weathered facade.

Chichibu Nishiki (☎ 3541 4777) Mains ¥2000. Atmospheric and traditional, this *nomiya* (pub) has good, cheap food in a very authentic setting. It's tucked away behind the Kabuki-za Theatre, north of the Ginza Dai-Ichi Hotel.

Funachū (☎ 3572 0712) Mains ¥3000. Slightly more prestigious fare, back toward Yūrakuchō. Try the mini-*kaiseki* (traditional feast) meal. There is also yakitori, and large beers are inexpensive.

Ichi-zushi (☎ 3596 7758) Lunch ¥2300, dinner ¥7000. While most sushi restaurants in Ginza are wildly expensive, this one on the 1st floor of the Ginza Dai-Ichi Hotel is very reasonable – and you don't need an interpreter. Try the elegant sushi kaiseki.

Shin-hi-no-moto (☎ 3214 8021) Mains ¥2500. This lively izakaya under the tracks in Yūraku-chō is run by an expat manager, Andy, who makes the daily trip to Tsukiji to get the freshest ingredients. A great chance to enjoy the izakaya experience without the language hassles. It's opposite the JAL plaza.

Tsukiji (Map 7) If you make that early-morning trip to Tsukiji's fish market, you have to do it properly – a sushi breakfast or lunch is *de rigueur*. There are quite a few sushi shops close to the market, particularly in the narrow alleys of the Tsukiji External Market, which serve sushi breakfasts of varying quality. For excellent sushi in pleasant surroundings it's better to visit some of the larger, more established places near Harumi-dōri and Shin-Ōhashi-dōri. These are open for lunch and dinner only, usually from 11am.

Edogin Sushi (☎ 3543 4401) Lunch ¥1000-1600, dinner from ¥2000. Famous for fresh, oversized sushi toppings, Edogin offers the three standard grades – *take*, *ume* and *matsu* – of sushi sets. Tempura teishoku is ¥1300 and sashimi teishoku is ¥1000. At dinnertime it's worth paying a little extra to get the *tokujō nigiri* sushi set for ¥2500. There is no English sign on the restaurant, but it's easily identified by the plastic sushi in the window.

Sushi Iwa (☎ 3254 6460) Sushi sets from ¥1000. This Tsukiji institution is on Harumi-dōri. The ¥2000 *ume* sushi set is recommended. Look for the large Japanese sign written in gold on green.

Sushidai (☎ 3541 3738) Sushi from ¥2000. Also on Harumi-dōri, this smallish place serves good sushi. The *ranchi* (lunch) is a good chance to try the catch of the day. There's a small English sign out the front.

Kanda (Map 8) This area has some very famous, long-running Japanese restaurants.

Botan (☎ 3251 0577) Meals from ¥6000. Open noon to 9pm, closed Sun and holidays. One of the few Tokyo restaurants to have survived WWII bombing, Botan is a speciality restaurant serving just one dish: chicken *nabe* (stew), a traditional Edo pot-stew also called *torisuki*. This is a good chance to sample Japanese nabe cooking, where everyone sits round one boiling pot plucking out what looks good with their chopsticks.

Ichi-no-chaya (☎ 3251 8517) Mains around ¥7000. This excellent, authentic izakaya is a sake connoisseur's heaven. The food is also good, with sashimi and nabe heading the list. This is one place where a little Japanese language ability, or a Japanese friend, will go a long way.

Ueno (Map 9) There is plenty of mid-range Japanese food in Ueno.

Ganko-zushi (☎ 5688 8845) Lunch ¥1300, à la carte dinner with drinks ¥4000. Approachable, economical, tasty Ganko-zushi is on the 6th floor of the Nagafuji building, opposite McDonald's. Good sushi and other fare, including several reasonable set meals. It has a picture menu and seems fairly accustomed to foreign customers. On the cheaper side, try the sushi *mori-awase* (assortment) or the tempura bentō.

Kameya Issui-tei (☎ 3831 0912) Lunch around ¥3000, dinner around ¥6000. Just around the corner from McDonald's, elegant Kameya serves high-class food. You aren't going to get far with English here but the daily lunch set is displayed outside. Look for noren curtains over the doorway.

Izu-ei honten (☎ 3831 0954) Meals from ¥2000-4000. Another elegant choice for authentic Japanese food, the speciality here is unagi and it's done well. The Izu-ei unagi bentō is ¥2500 and includes tempura. There is a limited picture menu. Look for the black building with a small pine tree and waterfall out the front.

Echikatsu (☎ 3811 5293) Meals from ¥7000-11,000. Open 5pm-9.30pm, closed Sun. *Sukiyaki* (see the Food special section, later in this chapter) and shabu-shabu in exquisite surroundings in a grand old Japanese house. Many rooms overlook small gardens.

Old Tokyo Restaurants

Although tall buildings, flashing neon lights and vast shopping complexes are exciting, there's no doubt that visitors to Tokyo often feel that they are missing out on a 'real Japanese experience'. A great way to make up for this is to sit down for a meal in a traditional Japanese restaurant. The following are a few select old Tokyo restaurants – for details, see their respective sections in this chapter.

Botan	Kanda
Kanda Yabu Soba	Kanda
Matsuya	Kanda
Echikatsu	Ueno
Chichibu Nishiki	Ginza
Komagata Dōjō	Asakusa
Inakaya	Roppongi
Yūrakuchō Yakitori Alley	Ginza

The staff don't speak English, but will make an honest effort to communicate. Reservations are, however, necessary. Echikatsu is off Kasuga-dōri, 70m past Hotel Yushima on the left side; look for the wooden gate.

Sasa-no-yuki (☎ 3873 1145) Mains from ¥2000. Open 11am-9pm, closed Mon. This is the oldest tofu restaurant in Tokyo, and the food is delicious. Again, little English is spoken, but there's a small English menu. Take the Yamanote line to Uguisudani station, go out the north exit, walk under the elevated highway, and it's about 200m on the left.

Asakusa (Map 9) A good selection of Japanese restaurants can be explored here.

Daikokuya (☎ 3844 1111) Lunch about ¥1800, dinner at least ¥3000. A speciality in Asakusa is tempura, and Daikokuya, just outside Nakamise arcade, is the place to get it. It's authentic and the tempura is excellent. Try the tempura donburi.

Owariya (☎ 3845 4500) Meals from ¥1300. In a similar vein to Daikokuya, but not nearly as atmospheric, this place on Kaminarimon-dōri serves tempura and a variety of noodle dishes.

Akiyoshi Yakitori (☎ 3841 3370) About ¥3500 per head. Good, inexpensive yakitori with a picture menu near the Asakusa View Hotel. The *kushi-katsu* (deep-fried pork and vegetables on skewers) and rice dishes are good too.

Asakusa Imahan (☎ 3842 1800) Mains from ¥7000. Just down the street, this is a great place to try sukiyaki or shabu-shabu. The meat is high quality, the preparation is excellent and the atmosphere is dignified. You're going to have to pay for it, however. Look for the white building on the corner.

Komagata Dojō (☎ 3842 4001) From ¥3000. Open 11am-9pm, daily. A few blocks south of Asakusa station near the river, you'll find a very traditional-looking building next to a small park. This is an elegant old Shitamachi restaurant which serves a fish called *dojō* (something like an eel). This place is highly recommended.

Ikebukuro (Map 2) The best dining in Ikebukuro is international. If you are on the lookout for good Japanese food, the best advice is to head to **Seibu** or **Tōbu** department stores, or try the 7th and 8th floors of the **Metropolitan Plaza**.

Tonerian (☎ 3985 0254) Meals from ¥3000. Ikebukuro has plenty of izakaya. This is one busy place with friendly staff who are used to the occasional gaijin calling in. Prices are reasonable, but they add up quickly – especially if you include a few drinks. Look for all the empty sake bottles piled up outside.

Yōrōnotaki (☎ 3982 5811) Meals from ¥2500. A huge izakaya – generic but cheap and usually cheery. Try the *agedashi dōfu* (deep-fried tofu in a fish stock soup), the yakitori or the sushi – or even fried potatoes. Look for the red and black neon sign (no English). You can't miss it – it's six storeys tall.

Sasashu (☎ 3971 9363) Meals from ¥5000. Open 5pm-10.30pm, closed Sun. High quality sake specialist, serving *kamon-abe* – duck stew. A little Japanese language ability would come in handy here. Across the street from a liquor store, its dignified

old Japanese facade stands out from its seedy neighbours.

Sushi Kazu (☎ 3980 5225) Sushi ¥3000-5000. This good, standard-issue sushi bar is definitely a step up from all those revolving sushi bars in the neighbourhood.

Akiyoshi (☎ 3982 0644) Around ¥2500-4000. Open 5pm-11pm, daily. Tasty yakitori in noisy, unpretentious surroundings. Watch out, though, for the spicy dipping mustard sauce. There's a large picture menu. There's no English sign but you can easily spot the long counters and flaming grills from the street.

Shinjuku (Map 3) Mid-range Japanese food is abundant in Shinjuku. While most of it is in the built-up area on the east side of the station, you can also find some good lunch deals in any of the hotels on the west side.

Suzuya (☎ 3209 4480) From ¥1500. For excellent tonkatsu head to this place on Yasukuni-dōri. The katsu here are high quality (not greasy) and come with filling sets which include rice and miso soup. Recommended are the *hire* katsu teishoku and the *meibutsu chazuke* set. It's on the 2nd floor, with signs at street level.

For an experience of Occupation-era Tokyo – tiny restaurants packed willy-nilly into a wonderfully atmospheric old alley – try *Omoide-yokochō* street beside the JR tracks just north-west of Shinjuku station. Here local workers stop off for yakitori, *oden*, noodles and beer before braving the trains back home. It's pointless to make recommendations: most of the places serve the same thing and few have names. What they serve will be piled high on the counters – just point and eat. Expect to pay about ¥2500 per person for a memorable time.

Tsunahachi (☎ 3358 2788) Meals from ¥2500. Behind Mitsukoshi department store, good tempura at amazingly reasonable prices. Highly recommended is the tempura teishoku. You can choose a table in a *tatami* (woven floor matting) room or at the counter, which offers good views of the cooking action. There's an English menu, and the staff seem accustomed to foreign customers. Look for the brown building with blue noren curtain.

Ibuki (☎ *3342 4787*) From ¥4000. When we first recommended this excellent sukiyaki and shabu-shabu restaurant some five years ago, there was no English sign and it looked dangerously temporary. It's still going strong, has an English menu and sign, and gets a lot of foreign visitors. Sake is ¥500 for a small bottle.

Daikokuya (☎ *3202 7272*) Basic meal from ¥2000 plus ¥1300 for all-you-can-drink. All-you-can-eat yaki-niku, shabu-shabu and sukiyaki courses bring in the students, making this a good place to get wrecked with young Japanese.

Irohanihoheto (☎ *3359 1682*) About ¥3000 per head. Over on Yasukuni-dōri, on the 6th floor of the Piccadilly movie house just east of Wendy's, is this big, lively izakaya with affordable prices. If you can still say the name of the place, keep drinking.

Kurumaya (☎ *3232 0301*) Lunch around ¥2000, dinner ¥4000-6000. The *teppanyaki* is tasty and the surroundings are elegant for east Shinjuku. Kurumaya does seafood and steak sets for around ¥4000. For a splurge, try the *ise ebi* (Japanese lobster) and steak set for ¥5800. There's no English sign, but it's directly across from Kirin City beer hall.

Sasagin (☎ *5454 3715*) **Map 1** Dinner about ¥3000. Classy but relaxed ambience, excellent food and top-notch sake make the trek out to the semi-wilds of Yoyogi-Uehara (four stops on JR's Odakyū line from Shinjuku) well worthwhile. This is possibly Tokyo's best value mid-range restaurant. Take South exit 1, turn right, and it's several minutes' walk on your left. A little Japanese ability would come in handy here.

Harajuku, Aoyama & Nishi-Azabu (Map 4)
This is a cosmopolitan part of town – for good mid-range Japanese choices head to nearby Shinjuku, Roppongi, Akasaka or Ginza.

Shibuya (Map 4)
There are relatively few good options in Shibuya, but there are some.

Akiyoshi (☎ *3464 1518*) Dinner about ¥3000. This pleasant, approachable yakitori restaurant with a large picture menu is also a good place to knock back a few beers. When you've eaten your fill, you can always move on to the Kirin City beer hall across the street.

Sakana-tei (☎ *3780 1313*) Meals around ¥4000, including a few flasks of sake. The concrete decor may not fit everyone's image of an izakaya, but the excellent food and drink more than make up for it. The emphasis at this casual izakaya is on good-quality sake and simple but tasty food. A little Japanese language ability would be useful.

Ebisu (Map 5)
There are two good spots for a meal in Ebisu.

Fujii (☎ *3486 1939*) Noodles from ¥1500. Fresh, handmade udon noodles five minutes' walk from the station. The master here searched all over Japan for the perfect noodle recipe before finding one that satisfied him in Kansai. We recommend the tempura udon. There is no English sign, but you'll see food models in the window just up the street from KFC.

An An (☎ *3498 6863*) From ¥3000. An offbeat izakaya with modern versions of traditional favourites and a generous sprinkling of international choices thrown in. Seating is communal, and if you don't speak Japanese just point at whatever looks good. Look for the very subdued wooden front and the portable sign on the sidewalk.

Denki Kurage (☎ *5420 5901*) From ¥3000. It means 'Electric Jellyfish' but the menu consists of eclectic modern izakaya fare in trendy, relaxed surroundings. It's between Good Day books and Kinko's.

Roppongi (Map 4)
Much of the Japanese fare in Roppongi goes for top-end prices, but there are a few mid-range choices to consider.

Panic Cafe (☎ *3583 4129*) **Map 7** Meals ¥3500-5000. It's a fair walk from the Roppongi crossing, but this is a good place to try teppanyaki with imaginative side dishes and salads. It's a little tricky to find. Once you've passed the Porsche dealer keep an eye peeled on the left. You'll see it after about 60m; it's in a basement.

PLACES TO EAT

Gokoku (☎ *3796 3356*) From ¥6000. Close to the top-end category, but if you're conservative with your drink orders, you can eat for mid-budget prices (for Roppongi). The menu changes daily but it is always hearty Edo-style fare. Unless you speak Japanese, or have a friend who does, you're just going to have to say 'Omakase' ('Please decide for me') to the waiter.

Akasaka (Map 7) In spite of the proliferation of foreign restaurants in the area, Akasaka is still home to some great domestic food. Most of the restaurants are on the narrow streets just west of Akasaka-mitsuke subway station.

Sushi-sei (☎ *3582 9503*) Dinner around ¥5000 with drinks. This is the real deal: great sushi in a great sushi-bar atmosphere. Everyone sits at long counters, the chefs are in constant motion and the customers often stand in line to partake. If you can't be bothered to choose, try the *jō-nigiri* set for lunch (¥1300). At dinner, prices go up and the best thing to do, if you don't speak Japanese, is just to point at whatever looks good; all the fish is laid out for you to see. There's no English sign – look for the noren curtains in the doorway. The place is set back a little off the street.

Tōfuya (☎ *3582 1028*) Lunch ¥800, dinner ¥4000. Another reliable spot for real Japanese cuisine and the atmosphere is authentic too. In addition to its speciality, tofu, there's grilled fish and rice dishes. Lunch is a great deal: there are usually four sets. It's a little tricky to find, on a small side street, one street west of Sotobori-dōri. Look for a traditional exterior across from an electronics shop.

Yakitori Louis (☎ *3585 4197*) Skewer ¥180, main course from ¥2000. Head down Akasaka-dōri west toward Roppongi to find the good Yakitori Louis. It's in a basement, but there's a display at street level. It's about 10 minutes west of the TBS building.

International Cuisine

If you're willing to pay for it, Tokyo has a fantastic array of good international restaurants – its international cuisine rivals that of

any city in the world. Expect to pay a lot more for dinner than for lunch.

Ginza (Map 7) Since Ginza was the first part of Tokyo to 'go international' it's only natural that it's still home to some great international restaurants. One of Tokyo's great ethnic favourites is Indian food.

Ashoka (☎ *3572 2377*) Lunch ¥850, dinner ¥2500. Down Chūō-dōri, just south of Matsuzakaya department store, is this old Tokyo standby. While lunch sets start at ¥850, you'll find that ordering à la carte quickly pushes up the bill. Don't worry, in this case it's worth it. Vegetarians take note: there are several good meatless dishes here.

Maharaja (☎ *3572 7196*) Sets around ¥1500. The tandoori delight is a good choice. It's on Harumi-dōri, diagonally opposite Mitsukoshi department store, downstairs.

Nair's (☎ *3541 8246*) Lunch ¥1500, dinner ¥4000. There always seems to be a queue at lunch for this popular Indian restaurant in east Ginza (toward Tsukiji). The reason is that Nair's small scale allows the proper attention to be paid to the food.

Buono Buono (☎ *3566 4031*) From ¥4000. For Italian food, head to the 2nd floor of the Nishi Ginza department store (in front of the Mullion building) for great food at upper mid-range prices. It stays open until 11.30pm.

Tokyo Station Area (Map 8) *Beck's Coffee* (☎ *3548 0907*) From ¥500. Cheapest white-chocolate cappuccino in town. You can get online free in the adjoining foyer of the Berlitz building before heading next door to Maruzen.

Kanda (Map 8) Mostly due to the fine efforts of three related restaurants in Jimbōchō, Kanda is one of our favourite destinations for good international food at reasonable prices.

Muang Thai Nabe (☎ *3239 6939*) Lunch set ¥1100, dinner about ¥3000. This is a must for Thai-food lovers. At dinner, it serves a Thai version of shabu-shabu called Thai nabe. At lunch, however, the restaurant really comes into its own with one of the best Thai lunch sets in town, including an authentic Thai curry, soup and a spicy salad. It's on the B1 floor of the Iwanami Hall building.

Menam no Hotori (☎ 3238 9597) From ¥4000. Muang Thai Nabe has a more formal branch on the 2nd floor of Iwanami Hall that serves up-market Thai fare of similar quality.

Muito Bom (☎ 3238 7946) From ¥1000. Fans of Brazilian food will want to try the food here. It's of the same high standard as at Muito Bom's sister restaurants. This is also the cheapest of the lot. It's upstairs from Muang Thai Nabe.

Mandala (☎ 3265 0498) Lunch ¥1000, mini-course ¥2200, dinner ¥4000. Across the street and downstairs, this Indian restaurant has obviously spent more time on its food than it has on its faux-Indian decor – good prioritising! The best deal is the curry lunch. Choose from five grades of spiciness and several kinds of curry. Between 2pm and 5pm you can sample its more generous mini-course (there's nothing mini about it). The full dinner course is for special occasions when you can really stretch out and take your time.

Taiwan Yatai (☎ 3254 9229) From ¥2500. If you're in the mood for an outdoor Taiwanese feast (or at least a Japanese version thereof) head to the other side of Kanda.

Asakusa (Map 9) The only decent choices in Asakusa are just across Azumabashi in the *Asahi Beer Flamme d'Or* complex (you can't miss it – it's got the giant 'golden turd' on top).

La Ranarata. (☎ 5608 5277) Lunch ¥2500, dinner around ¥6000. Good Milanese cuisine on the 22nd floor of the Asahi Beer building. Great pizza capricciosa. Not for sufferers of vertigo.

Sumida River Brewing Company (☎ 5608 3831) From ¥600. Next door you can get average pub grub and knock it back with one of three types of fresh beer, which start at ¥530 for a small glass.

Ikebukuro (Map 2) There's no lack of mid-range choices here. Look behind Marui department store – just stroll around and see what the nightly specials are (meals are often prepared and displayed out the front to lure you inside).

Taiwan Hsiao Tiao (☎ 3980 7822) Lunch sets less than ¥1000, dinner around ¥3000. Very near Kimi Ryokan, this self-styled 'Taiwanese gourmet mecca' serves good Taiwanese fare in casual, slightly rustic surroundings. Try the steamed gyōza, the 'healthy' Chinese sake and the crispy duck dishes. There's an extensive picture menu, and the friendly owners are used to foreign diners. Look for the pictures of food in the window.

Pekin-tei (☎ 3986 3131) Mains ¥3000. Near Ikebukuro station, Pekin-tei serves the standard Chinese specialities at somewhat inflated prices. Check what specials are displayed in the window before going in.

Malaychan (☎ 5391 7638) Lunch sets from ¥700. On a corner across from Nishi-Ikebukuro-kōen is one of Tokyo's few Malaysian restaurants. The food is so-so, but it's easy to order from the big picture menu and the drinks are good. *Nasi lemak* is a filling introduction to Malaysian food at ¥1070.

Chez Kibeau (☎ 3987 6666) Around ¥5000. Come to enjoy fine continental cuisine in a pleasant, relaxing basement which feels far removed from the chaos on the streets above. If you can't decide what to drink, English-speaking owner Kibo-san will gladly make a recommendation. In fact, the best thing to do here is simply let Kibo-san make all the decisions, and sit back and enjoy.

Takadanobaba (Map 2) Here are four suggestions for worthwhile international food in 'Baba.

Kao Thai (☎ 3204 5806) Lunch around ¥1000, dinner from ¥2000. Kao Thai is among the cheaper of Tokyo's many Thai restaurants, and serves remarkably authentic food, spicy enough even for the most seasoned Thai traveller.

Yeti (☎ 3208 1766) Lunch around ¥1000, dinner from ¥2000. Yeti serves good Nepali and Indian cuisine in a casual restaurant that feels almost like someone's living room.

Mingalaba (☎ 3200 6961) From ¥1000. Lots of Burmese customers testify to the

PLACES TO EAT

authenticity of this place. Pick up one of the many drums that dot the place as you chow down on coconut-milk curry. On the same floor as Yeti.

Cambodia (☎ 3209 9320) Lunch around ¥1000, dinner from ¥3000. Cambodia is the most expensive of 'Baba's Asian restaurants, but has a mellow atmosphere and tasty, authentic food. Shrimp balls seem to be the most popular items.

Shinjuku (Map 3) Though mid-range Japanese food and street-level offerings are Shinjuku's strong points, all of the big hotels in west Shinjuku have high-quality international restaurants on their upper and lower floors. Some offer affordable lunch specials.

El Borracho (☎ 3354 7046) From ¥1500. For inexpensive Mexican food in a real hole-in-the-wall atmosphere, check it out. As with most Japanese versions of Mexican food, this place is not too authentic, but it isn't bad. El Borracho is next to Mos Burger; look for the Aztec motif.

Raobian Gyozakan (☎ 3348 5810) From ¥3000. For authentic thick-skinned Beijing-style gyōza and other Chinese fare, come and eat here, across the street from Keiō department store. The gyōza here are so good that you don't need sauce for dipping. The atmosphere is pure retro Tokyo, especially the back, with waiters materialising from secret passageways. Note, however, that portions are small. It's best to go with a group and order one of the courses. It has an English menu.

Tainan Taami (☎ 3232 8839) Mains from ¥2500. Great Taiwanese cuisine in a rowdy izakaya atmosphere. There are other branches in Suidōbashi (☎ 3263 4530), Ginza (☎ 3571 3624) and Shibuya (☎ 3464 7544), but the best is the Shinjuku branch. The menu has photographs of the dishes.

Tokyo Dai Hanten (☎ 3202 0121) From ¥4000. On the 3rd floor of the unfortunately named Oriental Wave building. Much of the food is overpriced, but the yum cha service is not bad. This is one of the few places in Tokyo where correct yum cha form is observed by bringing the snacks around on trolleys. Go on a Sunday, take your time and sit near the main aisles.

Rose de Sahara (☎ 3379 6427) Courses from ¥3500. Guinea fowl in orange sauce is not exactly thick on the ground in Tokyo. Rose de Sahara has cornered the market and charges accordingly. Nevertheless, with its African decor and sounds this place creates a good atmosphere.

Harajuku, Aoyama & Nishi-Azabu (Map 4) This is the least Japanese of all Tokyo areas – you may even feel as though you've been transported to Europe (or, rather oddly, Mexico) – and the area is chock-a-block with good international cuisine. A lot of the offerings are scattered along the Omote-sandō promenade, but you'll also find some good restaurants in Nishi-Azabu and along Aoyama-dōri. And don't forget the cafes for some great people-watching.

Tacos del Amigo (☎ 3405 9996) Mains from ¥3000. A good place to combine drinking and dinner, this Mexican restaurant near Harajuku station has a pleasant indoor/outdoor atmosphere. A little pricey, but fun. Average nosh.

Casa Monnon (☎ 3499 2559) From ¥3000. For tastier Mexican, head to Nishi-Azabu, where the good stuff is served in cosy, casual surroundings.

Fonda de la Madrugada (☎ 5410 6288) From ¥6000. For the best Mexican in Tokyo, head up past the Turkish embassy to this favourite with expats and the business community. Complete with open courtyards and strolling musicians, everything from the rooftiles to the chefs has been imported from Mexico. It's not cheap, but it's worth the expenditure. Hope you like marriachi though.

El Mocambo (☎ 3405 9996) From ¥2000. For more generalised Latin fare, such as Cuban, Brazilian and Peruvian, try El Mocambo. This is a casual place to hang out and drink after you've filled up on food. It's near Aoyama cemetery. Look for the small English sign; the restaurant is in the basement.

Topkapi (☎ 3498 3510) Around ¥2000 per head. In this tiny little basement joint everyone squeezes round the same table for

Tokyo Cafe Society

Lately there's been a boom in open-air restaurants and cafes in Tokyo. Granted it will never be Paris, but Tokyo now has its own cafe society, and people-watching over a cappuccino has become an economical alternative to shopping as a leisure-time activity.

If the sun is shining and the leaves are on the trees, Harajuku's Omote-sandō is the place to be. The street is dotted with slavish reproductions of French cafes and the constant parade of Tokyo characters makes for superb people-watching. Harajuku's rival in the cafe stakes is trendy Daikanyama.

These are recommended cafes where you can get coffee for around ¥500 a cup, light meals for about ¥1000 and a variety of alcoholic drinks.

Cafe de Rope A popular central spot in Aoyama; the prices are a little high but the people-watching is great.

Bamboo A little off the main drag, but the great patio more than compensates for its less-than-central location; the sandwiches are cheap as well.

Studio V This place can't make up its mind: is it a flower shop or a coffee shop? Actually it's both – a pleasant, mellow place, but not a top spot for people-watching.

Stage Y2 Another popular cafe right near Harajuku station, perfectly situated for the Sunday afternoon fashion parade.

Spiral Cafe All right, it's not outdoors at all, but for a slice of chic Aoyama life and a cool artistic interior, check out this cafe inside the famous Spiral building.

Cafe Michelangelo Full of beautiful people, in Daikanyama.

Cafe Artifagose Great cheeses and breads, and al fresco seating. The locals pronounce it Arto-Fagos. Another Daikanyama hot-spot.

Gazebo Cafe Cheaper than the Arti with good sandwiches, half-way between Ebisu and Daikanyama.

Cafe Juliet Nice outdoor seating area, good grub, in Daikanyama.

some of Tokyo's best Turkish food. It's tricky to find – look for the pink stairwell and the odd Turkish posters hanging above the doorway.

Son of the Dragon (☎ 3402 9419) Around ¥2500 per head. 'Ryunoko' (in Japanese) serves pretty good Sichuan cuisine in a smoky basement off Meiji-dōri. Try the *banbanji* (cold chicken and sesame sauce) and any of the noodle dishes.

Tony Roma's (☎ 3479 5214) Meals from ¥3000. Open 5pm-10.30pm Sun-Thurs, until 12.30am Fri & Sat. Calorie-crazy American-style ribs and onion rings, and salads for the non-ravenous. It's on Aoyama-dōri.

Trattoria La Pecora (☎ 5772 6876) From ¥3000. Closed Mon. Cosy little bistro just off Killer-dōri near the Watari-um, serving Italian 'home cooking'.

Bistro de la Cite (☎ 3406 5475) Lunch sets around ¥2500, dinners border on top-end. Out in Nishi-Azabu, this French restaurant has cosy, wooden decor and provides a nice escape from the madness outside – close your eyes and imagine you're in Provence.

Las Chicas (☎ 3407 6865) From ¥2500. Pleasant, spacey – this is where cool and wannabe-cool expats come to pose and peer. The yuppie-style food is pretty good – from pizzas to salads to sandwiches – and the wine list is solid. There's also a bar to repair to and a computer with free Internet access (you may have to wait in line).

Fujimama's (☎ 5485 2262, fax 5485 2261) Meals from ¥3500. A very pleasant, and hugely popular 'fusion' restaurant mixing and matching European and Asian ingredients under the auspices of chef/co-owner Mark Vann. Good California wines, and especially nice rooms upstairs in what was once a tatami maker's workshop. It's directly behind the Penny Black store. Reservations at least a week in advance are recommended.

Nishi-Azabu is a prime hunting ground for Thai food, and most of the places are above average in quality.

Rice Terrace (☎ 3498 6271) Lunch sets from ¥1000, dinner around ¥3000. Everyone's favourite for tasty Thai food in cool surroundings. It's down a small street off of Gaien-nishi-dōri.

東京 東京 東京 東京 東京 東京 東京

Monsoon Cafe (☎ *3400 7200)* From ¥2500. Nearby Monsoon serves decent Thai fare in semi-outdoor cafe-style surrounds. This is a good option for tropical drinks and just hanging out, though there's an annoying two-hour limit at busy times.

Maenam (☎ *3404 4745)* Dinner about ¥2000. It looks like a big miss, with it's tacky decor and garish neon, but the food is actually decent. All the Thai favourites are available. This is also a good spot for a few drinks with some spicy snacks.

Bindi (☎ *3409 7114)* From ¥2000. Surprisingly, Indian food is rather rare in these parts. The friendly couple who run this place turn out reliable Indian food for reasonable prices. It's in the basement of the building next to the Lawson convenience store, off Roppongi-dōri.

Shibuya (Map 4) There's no shortage of good international cuisine here. The best places to look are the small streets around the station and the built-up shopping areas around the giant department stores.

Tainan Taami (☎ *3464 7544)* Meals from ¥3000. This is a great choice for good Taiwanese fare in raucous, if slightly smoky, surroundings.

Reikyō (☎ *3461 4220)* From ¥3000. For similar Taiwanese fare and surroundings to Tainan Taami, check out Reikyō. It's in a triangular red-brick building. There is no English sign.

Bougainvillea (☎ *3496 0659)* From ¥3000. Across from Bunkamura, this restaurant serves Vietnamese food. It's no great shakes, but if you've got a hankering for South-East Asian this will probably do the trick.

Kantipur (☎ *3770 5358)* From ¥3000. This Nepali restaurant seems to borrow a lot from India (perhaps dal bhat is a limited menu for a restaurant). It's a little bit back from the street not easy to spot. Head south from the Kirin City beer hall and you'll see it on your right after about 10 minutes.

Ebisu & Daikanyama (Map 5) Daikanyama rivals Harajuku and Aoyama as the centre of Tokyo cafe society. It's a good

place to grab a cappuccino and do some people-watching. You'll also find plenty of trendy foreign restaurants, some good, some merely fashionable.

Cafe Michelangelo (☎ *3770 9517)* From ¥1500. Tokyo's best imitation of a Parisian cafe. The beautiful people flock here at weekends, more for the ambience than the food.

Cafe Artifagose (☎ *5489 1133)* From ¥1300. A great selection of cheeses and breads and nice al fresco seating make this a popular spot.

Gazebo Cafe (☎ *3461 4348)* From ¥1000. Even cheaper than the Arti, this place has good sandwiches, though the view is less than prepossesing. It's half-way between Ebisu and Daikanyama.

Cafe Juliet (☎ *3770 5656)* From ¥1200. Reasonably priced pasta and sandwiches here, and good but rather pricey coffee. Nice outdoor seating area too.

KM Fils (☎ *5457 1435)* Lunch ¥2500, dinner ¥5000. A bit pricey but worth it at this French place (pronounced in Gallic fashion 'Kar-em') downstairs from Cafe Juliet.

Monsoon Cafe (☎ *5489 3789)* From ¥2500. This hugely popular place on Kyūyamate-dōri is a multi-level affair of outdoor terraces and spacious dining rooms. It's especially pleasant in summer. The food, though none too special, is an interesting mix of South-East Asian classics such as Vietnamese spring rolls and Malaysian satay.

Mai-Thai (☎ *3280 8751)* Lunch sets about ¥1000, dinner about ¥3500. A new spin on Thai cuisine, the yam salads and spicy shrimp dishes are especially recommended. Look for the real Bangkok tuk-tuk parked outside.

Roppongi (Map 4) Clustered within 10 minutes' walk from the Roppongi crossing are dozens of fine foreign restaurants, many of which double as drinking spots for post-dinner relaxation.

Cerveza (☎ *3478 0077)* Drinks around ¥1000. This sounds Mexican – it's not. It's a beer specialist where you can try to work your way through the 100-beer menu while putting away good international food, from

Chinese to American. As at other Tokyo beer specialists, you're going to have to pay for it.

Moti Darbar *(☎ 3479 1939)* Lunch sets around ¥1000, dinner averages ¥3000. This branch of the hugely popular Indian restaurant is on Roppongi-dōri right above the subway station. Another branch is on Gaien-higashi-dōri. Both Motis serve up some of Tokyo's best Indian food, but the nod goes to the former for the whole package of food, ambience and attentive service.

Bellini's Trattoria *(☎ 3470 5650)* Lunch around ¥1500, dinner ¥3000. The place to go for good Italian food and excellent street-side people-watching. In addition to a wide selection of Italian favourites, there are lots of drink choices, including cappuccino and espresso.

Hard Rock Cafe *(☎ 3408 7018)* Meals from ¥3000. We figure you know what to expect here – loud music, oversized portions of passable American food and plenty of reasonably priced drinks.

Tony Roma's *(☎ 3408 2748)* From ¥3000. In the same building as the Hard Rock Cafe, Tony Roma's has been doing pretty good business in Tokyo as a purveyor of American-style barbecued spare ribs with all the fixings.

Bernd's Bar *(☎ 5563 9232)* **Map 7** Meals from ¥3500 with a few beers. Something of a toss-up between a bar and a good German restaurant, German favourites are served with some excellent German beer to wash them down.

Akasaka (Map 7) Akasaka has lots of mid-range international choices. Most of the good places are on the small streets just west of Akasaka-mitsuke subway station, with a few scattered along Akasaka-dōri on the way to Roppongi.

Trattoria Marumo *(☎ 3585 5371)* Lunch about ¥1500, dinner about ¥3000. Pleasant atmosphere and pretty good food at this pizzeria. There are loads of food models in the window. There's a more formal Marumo out on Akasaka-dōri.

Mugyodon *(☎ 3586 6478)* Meals from ¥3000. Popular, extremely friendly Korean place, open for dinner only. This is a great place to sample the real Korean stuff, not the Japanese version.

Chez Prisi *(☎ 3224 9877)* Lunch specials from ¥1700, dinner around ¥5000 with drinks. The daily lunch specials are advertised on a blackboard in the window of this small Swiss place. It serves reliable food in pleasant surroundings. Chez Prisi is just past the police box; look for the English sign.

Tokyo Joe's *(☎ 3508 0325)* Lunch ¥3000, dinner from ¥5000. Tokyo Joe's doesn't overdo the decor, and its speciality is stone crab, imported daily from Florida. It's tasty stuff.

Fisherman's Wharf *(☎ 3583 0659)* Lunch starts at ¥3000, dinner ¥6000. Fisherman's Wharf is heavy on the nautical theme and the food is just what you'd expect: crab, shrimp, oysters and so on, prepared American style.

PLACES TO EAT – TOP END

Business travellers beware: Tokyo has been rated the most expensive city in the world for dining out. Luckily, now that the heady days of the bubble economy are behind us, even the most elegant establishments have lowered their prices. It's still possible to drop ¥100,000 on a sumptuous sushi feast in Ginza, but it's now also possible to enjoy food almost as good for a tenth of that price.

Top-end dining in Tokyo is generally going to cost a minimum of ¥10,000 per head. If this doesn't faze you, there is no shortage of elegant establishments in which to indulge a passion for haute cuisine. The following is a very selective list; guests at Tokyo's five-star hotels will also find top-end dining options just an elevator ride away.

Japanese Cuisine

Ginza (Map 7) If you're looking for restaurants to bust your budget wide open in Tokyo, dine in Ginza. Fortunately, the really outrageous places don't really cater to foreigners and are hardly identifiable as restaurants anyway – you'll need a wealthy Japanese friend to get you through their discreet doors. That said, there are several more down-to-earth places in Ginza where you can sample first-rate food.

Kyubei (☎ *3571 6523*) Sushi dinners around ¥10,000. With Tsukiji just down the street, it's not surprising that Ginza boasts some of Tokyo's best sushi restaurants. Kyubei, in southern Ginza near Shimbashi, is an elegant place. It's not just the sushi you're paying for, it's the wonderful surroundings. You'll have a tough time finding the place if you look for the Japanese sign. Instead, look for the very elegant Japanese facade set back a little from the street.

Jiro Sushi (☎ *3535 7053*) About ¥30,000 per person. Considered by some to be the best sushi in Tokyo, this place serves sublime sushi. Expect to be put off lesser sushi for the rest of your days. Jiro Sushi is in the basement of the building opposite the Sony building.

Munakata (☎ *3574 9356*) Set course ¥5000, dinner around ¥10,000. If you've been looking for a place to try kaiseki, drop in here. This is a relatively cheap and approachable kaiseki restaurant, in the basement of the Mitsui Urban Hotel.

Ten-Ichi (☎ *3571 1949*) Lunch from ¥7000, dinner ¥8500. One of Tokyo's oldest and best tempura restaurants is about five minutes from Sukibayashi crossing. This is the place to try tempura the way it's meant to be: light and crispy, without any greasiness. If this branch is full there's another branch in the basement of the Sony building.

Roppongi (Map 4) For thoroughly approachable top-end Japanese restaurants, Roppongi is the place. People here are so used to foreigners wandering in off the street that they hardly blink.

Kisso (☎ *3582 4191*) **Map 7** Lunch from ¥1300-5000, dinner about ¥10,000. On the B1 floor of the Axis building, this is a good place to sample Japan's gourmet cuisine: kaiseki ryōri. Here, you can comfortably walk in and sit down to an unforgettable feast. It's best to order a course and leave everything up to the chef.

Fukuzushi (☎ *3402 4116*) Around ¥10,000 each. Decidedly more relaxed than at some of the more traditional places in Ginza and Tsukiji and you'll be served some of the best sushi in town. The fish

here is fresh, the portions large and there's even a cocktail bar.

Seryna (☎ *3402 1051*) Mains without drinks ¥10,000-15,000. There are three restaurants under the Seryna roof: the *Seryna Honten* (main store), which serves shabu-shabu and sukiyaki; *Mon Cher Ton Ton*, which serves Kōbe beef; and *Kani Seryna*, serving crab. Seryna has some of Japan's best luxury food in elegant, if musty, foreigner-friendly surroundings. A longtime favourite of splurging Tokyo expats.

Inakaya (☎ *3405 9866*) Meals from ¥10,000. Open daily 5pm-11pm At the Nogizaka end of Gaien-higashi-dōri in Roppongi, Inakaya has achieved fame and favour as a top-end *robatayaki* (drinking restaurant serving grilled foods). It does raucous, bustling, 'don't stand on ceremony' robatayaki with gusto. It's possible to spend lots of money *and* have fun. There's another *Inakaya* (☎ *3586 3054*) in Akasaka.

Akasaka (Map 7) Luxury hotels are the best place to look for approachable top-end Japanese cuisine in Akasaka. Try the *restaurant floors* of the New Ōtani, the Ōkura or the Akasaka Prince.

Ten-Ichi (☎ *3583 0107*) Lunch from ¥7000, dinner ¥8500. Akasaka branch of Ginza's famous tempura restaurant.

International Cuisine

Ginza (Map 7) *Maxim's de Paris* (☎ *3572 3621*) Lunch sets from ¥6000, dinner courses from ¥20,000. Open 11.30am-2pm, 5.30pm-9pm, closed Sun. Superior French cuisine in the basement of Ginza's Sony building. The interior and the menu are dead ringers for the original in Paris.

Sabatine di Firenze (☎ *3573 0013*) Lunch from ¥3800, dinner from ¥10,000. Open noon-3pm, 5.30pm-11pm daily. In the Sony building, this restaurant serves excellent northern Italian fare in a faithful reproduction of its twin in Florence. Everything is over-the-top Italian, but the prices are not excessive considering the location.

Shinjuku (Map 3) *New York Grill* (☎ *5323 3458*) Meals up to ¥10,000. Among all the fine restaurants in the hotels of west Shinjuku, it's worth going out of your way for this place on the 52nd floor of the Park Hyatt Tower. This is power dining at its best – hearty portions of steak and seafood and a drop-dead view. One bargain worth mentioning is the ¥3800 Sunday brunch. Warm up with a few drinks at the adjoining New York Bar.

Harajuku, Aoyama & Nishi-Azabu (Map 4)

Trendy Harajuku is the closest thing Tokyo comes to having a 'Little Paris', and the many French restaurants are proof.

L'Amphore (☎ 3402 6486) Lunch for two with wine about ¥12,000, dinner for two with wine about ¥25,000. One of the best French restaurants in the city, the atmosphere is spot-on and it avoids the overly formal feeling which is the bane of so many top-end French places in Tokyo. It's easy to spot: look for the French sign.

L'Orangerie de Paris (☎ 3407 7461) Lunch set ¥4000. In the Hanae Mori building on Omote-sandō, this is another elegant choice. The lunch set is good value and dinners are reliable. Especially recommended is the Sunday brunch.

Aux Sept Bonheurs (☎ 3498 8144) At least ¥10,000. Boutique Chinese cuisine served in the style of a fine French restaurant. This is one of Tokyo's most highly regarded restaurants. The courses are a fabulous succession of small but wonderfully prepared delicacies.

Ebisu (Map 5) *Taillevent-Robuchon* (☎ 5424 1338) Lunch with wine around ¥8000, dinner with wine around ¥16,000. Open noon-2.30 pm, 6pm-9.30pm, closed Sun. Top-notch French fare in a faithful reproduction of a Louis Quinze chateau. Very posh. On the grounds of the Ebisu Garden Place complex.

Roppongi (Map 4) *Spago* (☎ 3423 4025) Lunch around ¥3000, dinners around ¥6000 with drinks. Californian cuisine. Even this bastion of Beverly Hills excess has had to come to terms with economic realities, and cut prices. Nice sunny lunch area.

Akasaka (Map 7) The best place to look in Akasaka is in the main luxury hotels: the Hotel Ōkura, the New Ōtani, the Akasaka Prince and the Capital Tōkyū.

Tohkalin (☎ 3505 6068) Lunch from ¥4000, dinner from ¥8000. On the 6th floor of the Hotel Ōkura, Tohkalin is reported to have the best Chinese food in Tokyo, and that's saying a lot. It is possible to eat here for mid-range prices if you stick to the simpler dishes, but you'll be under serious pressure to splurge when you see what's available. Then there's, er, access to the Ōkura's wine cellar.

Keyaki Grill (☎ 3581 8514) Lunch from ¥3000, dinner from ¥5000. Excellent continental cuisine in the B1 floor of the Capital Tōkyū hotel. Those in the know report that this is the best of its kind in Tokyo.

PLACES TO EAT

FOOD

Japanese food is one of the world's most diverse cuisines. While you may have tried only *sushi*, *tempura* and *sukiyaki* in your home country, there are actually over 20 main types of Japanese cooking, each as different as pizza is from hamburger.

These days, the influence of foreign cuisines and availability of imported ingredients have considerably enriched the Japanese diet, but most meals are still based on the traditional mainstays of rice, miso soup and *tsukemono* (Japanese pickles). Of these three, rice is very much the central element, so much so that the Japanese words for 'rice' and 'meal' are the same: *gohan*. Everything else is just *okazu* (food to be eaten with rice), from humble pickles to the finest cut of Kōbe beef.

Those in search of a truly Japanese experience will probably want to avoid the ubiquitous fast-food emporiums. However, some may baulk at charging into an unfamiliar restaurant where both the language and the menu are likely to be incomprehensible. The best way to get over this fear is to familiarise yourself with the main types of Japanese restaurants so that you have some idea of what's on offer and how to order it. Those timid of heart should take solace in the fact that the Japanese will go to extraordinary lengths to understand what you want and will help you to order.

With the exception of *shokudō* (all around eateries) and *izakaya* (drinking restaurants), most Japanese restaurants are speciality restaurants serving only one type of cuisine. This naturally makes for delicious eating, but does limit your choice. The following sections introduce the main types of Japanese restaurants, along with the most common dishes served. With a little courage and effort you will soon discover that Japan is a gourmet paradise where good food is taken very seriously.

Shokudō 食堂

A shokudō, or 'eating place', is the most common type of restaurant in Japan, found near railway stations, tourist spots and just about any other place where people congregate. Easily distinguished by plastic displays in the window, these inexpensive places usually serve a variety of Japanese *(washoku)* and Western *(yoshoku)* foods.

At lunch, and sometimes dinner, the easiest way to order at a shokudō is to order a *teishoku*, or set-course meal (sometimes also called *ranchi setto*, lunch set, or *kōsu*). This usually includes a main dish of meat or fish, a bowl of rice, miso (soy-bean paste) soup, shredded cabbage and a few tsukemono.

Most shokudō also serve a fairly standard selection of *donburi-mono* (rice dishes) and *menrui* (noodle dishes).

When you order noodles, you can choose between *soba* (thin brown) and *udon* (thick white) noodles, both of which are served with a variety of toppings. If you're at a loss as to what to order, simply tell the waiter 'kyō-no-ranchi' (today's lunch) and they'll do the rest.

You can expect to spend about ¥800 to ¥1000 for a meal at a shokudō. Some of the more common dishes you'll be able to choose from at a shokudō are:

Rice Dishes

katsu-don	カツ丼	a bowl of rice topped with a fried pork cutlet
oyako-don	親子丼	a bowl of rice topped with egg and chicken
niku-don	肉丼	a bowl of rice topped with thin slices of cooked beef
tendon	天丼	a bowl of rice topped with tempura shrimp and vegetables

Noodle Dishes

(Add 'soba' or 'udon' to the following when ordering)

kake	かけ	plain noodles in broth
kitsune	きつね	noodles with fried tofu
tempura	天ぷら	noodles with tempura shrimp
tsukimi	月見	noodles with raw egg on top
zaru	ざる	cold noodles with a dipping sauce, popular in summer

Izakaya 居酒屋

An izakaya (drinking restaurant) is the Japanese equivalent of a pub, but with a wider selection of food. It's a good place to visit when you want a casual meal, plenty of food choices, a hearty atmosphere and, of course, lots of beer and *sake*.

When you enter an izakaya, you are given the choice of sitting around the counter, at a table or on a *tatami* floor. You usually order a bit at a time, eg, *yakitori*, *sashimi* and grilled fish, as well as Japanese versions of foods like French fries and beef stew.

Izakaya can be identified by their rustic facades, red lanterns bearing the Chinese characters for izakaya, and crates of sake and beer bottles outside their doors. Since izakaya food is casual drinking fare, it is usually fairly inexpensive. Depending on how much you drink, you can expect to pay ¥2500 to ¥5000 per person.

Some of Tokyo's best izakaya can be found in Tokyo's big shopping districts, Ginza and Ikebukuro.

In addition to the following dishes, refer to the Yakitori and Sushi & Sashimi sections later on for other choices.

agedashi-dōfu	揚げだし豆腐	deep-fried tofu in a fish stock soup
jaga-batā	ジャガバター	baked potatoes with butter
niku-jaga	肉じゃが	beef and potato stew
shio-yaki-zakana	塩焼魚	a whole fish grilled with salt
yaki-onigiri	焼きおにぎり	a triangle of grilled rice with yakitori sauce
poteto furai	ポテトフライ	French fries
chiizu-age	チーズ揚げ	deep-fried cheese

hiya-yakko	冷奴	a cold block of tofu with soy sauce and scallions
tsuna sarada	ツナサラダ	tuna salad over cabbage
yaki-soba	焼きそば	fried noodles with meat and vegetables
kata yaki-soba	固焼きそば	hard fried noodles with meat and vegetables
sashimi mori-awase	刺身盛り合わせ	a selection of sliced sashimi

Robatayaki 炉端焼き

Similar to an izakaya; *robatayaki* means 'hearthside cooking' and every effort is made in these restaurants to re-create the atmosphere of an old country house – which was always centred on a large hearth or *irori*.

Eating at a robatayaki is a feast for the eyes as well as the taste buds: You sit around a counter with the food spread out in front of you on a layer of ice, behind which is a large charcoal grill. You don't need a word of Japanese to order; there are menus, but no-one uses them – just point and eat. The chef will grill your selection and pass it to you on a long wooden paddle – grab your food quickly before he snatches it back. The drink of choice is beer or sake. Expect to spend about ¥5000 per head.

Not as common as izakaya, robatayaki usually have rustic wooden facades modelled on traditional Japanese farmhouses. For a classic, albeit pricey, robotayaki experience, you can't beat Roppongi's Inakaya (Map 4).

Okonomiyaki お好み焼き

The name means 'cook what you like', and an *okonomiyaki* restaurant provides you with an inexpensive opportunity to do just that. At an okonomiyaki, you sit around a *teppan* (iron hotplate) armed with a spatula and chopsticks to cook your choice of meat, seafood and vegetables in a cabbage and vegetable batter.

Some places will do most of the cooking; you season the result with bonito flakes *(katsuo bushi)*, soy sauce *(shōyu)*, parsley, Japanese Worcestershire-style sauce and mayonnaise. Cheaper places will simply hand you a bowl filled with the ingredients. If this happens, don't panic. First, mix the batter and filling thoroughly, then place it on the hot grill, flattening it into a pancake shape. After five minutes or so, use the spatulas to flip it and cook for another five minutes. Then dig in and enjoy.

Don't worry too much about preparation of the food – as a foreigner you'll be expected to be inept and the waiter will keep a sharp eye on you to make sure no real disasters occur.

Most okonomiyaki places also serve *yaki-soba* (fried noodles) and *yasai-itame* (stir-fried vegetables). The food is usually washed down with mugs of draught beer.

You can expect to spend about ¥1500 per person for a full meal and a beer at an average okonomiyaki. Finding an okonomiyaki restaurant is fairly easy, since most have glass fronts so you can see inside. If not, you'll have to look for the *kanji* somewhere on the sign.

mikkusu okonomiyaki	ミックス焼き	mixed fillings of seafood, meat and vegetables
modan-yaki	モダン焼き	okonomiyaki with fried egg
gyū okonomiyaki	牛お好み焼き	beef okonomiyaki
yasai okonomiyaki	野菜お好み焼き	vegetable okonomiyaki
negi okonomiyaki	ネギお好み焼き	thin okonomiyaki with scallions

Yakitori 焼き鳥

Yakitori means 'skewers of grilled chicken', a popular after-work accompaniment to beer and sake. At a yakitori restaurant you sit around a counter with the other patrons and watch the chef grill your selections over charcoal. It's best to order a few skewers of several varieties and then order seconds of the ones you really like. Remember that one serving often means two or three skewers (be careful – the price listed on the menu is usually that of a single skewer).

In summer, the beverage of choice at a yakitori restaurant is beer or cold sake (hot in winter). A few drinks and enough skewers to fill you up should cost from ¥3000 to ¥4000 per person. Yakitori joints are usually small places, often near railway stations, and are best identified by a red lantern outside and the smell of grilling chicken.

There are two wonderful places with a classic yakitori atmosphere, reminiscent of Occupation-era Japan: Yūrakuchō Yakitori Alley (Map 7) and a street called Omoide-yokochō (Map 3).

yakitori	焼き鳥	plain, grilled chicken
hasami/negima	はさみ/ねぎま	pieces of white meat alternating with leek
sasami	ささみ	skinless chicken breast pieces
kawa	かわ	chicken skin
tsukune	つくね	chicken meat balls
gyū-niku	牛肉	pieces of beef
rebā	レバ	chicken livers
tebasaki	手羽先	chicken wings
shiitake	しいたけ	Japanese mushrooms
piiman	ピーマン	small green peppers
tama-negi	たまねぎ	round, white onions
yaki-onigiri	焼きおにぎり	a triangle of rice grilled with yakitori sauce

Sushi & Sashimi 寿司/刺身

Like yakitori, sushi is considered a side dish for beer and sake. Nonetheless, people often make a meal of it and it's one of the healthiest meals around. Although sushi is now popular in the West, few foreigners are prepared for the delicacy and taste of the real thing. Without a doubt, this is one dish that the visitor to Japan should sample at least once.

There are two main types of sushi: *nigiri-zushi* (served on a small bed of rice – the most common variety) and *maki-zushi* (served in a seaweed roll). Lesser known varieties include *chirashi-zushi* (a layer of rice covered in egg and fish toppings), *oshi-zushi* (fish pressed in a mould over rice) and *inari-zushi* (rice in a pocket of sweet, fried tofu). Whatever kind of sushi you try, it will be served with lightly vinegared rice. In the case of nigiri-zushi and maki-zushi, it will contain a bit of *wasabi* (hot, green horseradish).

Sushi is not difficult to order. If you sit at the counter of a sushi restaurant you can simply point at what you want. You can also order à la carte from the menu. When ordering, you usually order *ichi-nin mae* (one portion), which usually means two pieces of sushi (though the price on the menu will be that of only one piece). The easiest order is an assorted plate of nigiri-zushi called *mori-awase*. These usually come in three grades: *futsū nigiri* (regular nigiri), *jō nigiri* (special nigiri) and *toku-jō nigiri* (extra-special nigiri). The difference is in the type of fish used. Most mori-awase contain six or seven pieces of sushi. Of course, you can order fish without the rice, in which case it is called sashimi.

Dip the sushi in shōyu, which you pour from a small decanter into a low dish. If you're not good at using chopsticks, don't worry, sushi is one of the few foods in Japan that is perfectly okay to eat with your hands. Slices of pickled ginger *(gari)* help refresh the palate.

Be warned that a good sushi restaurant can cost upward of ¥10,000, while an average place can cost from ¥3000 to ¥5000 per person. One way to sample the joy of sushi on the cheap is to try an automatic sushi place, usually called *kaiten-zushi*, where the sushi is served on a conveyor belt which runs along a counter. Here you simply reach up and grab whatever looks good. You're charged according to how many plates of sushi you've eaten. Plates are colour-coded according to price, and the cost is written somewhere on the plate itself or on a sign on the wall. You can usually fill yourself up for ¥1000 to ¥2000 per person.

Automatic sushi places often have miniature conveyor belts in the window, while regular sushi restaurants often sport fish tanks in the window or a white lantern with the characters for sushi written in black letters. For the freshest sushi on the planet, head down to Tsukiji, where you can see the raw materials on sale in the giant fish market before sitting down to a fabulous sushi breakfast or brunch.

Some common sushi and sashimi dishes are:

ama-ebi	甘海老	sweet shrimp
awabi	あわび	abalone
ebi	海老	prawn or shrimp
hamachi	はまち	yellowtail

ika	いか	squid
ikura	イクラ	salmon roe
kai-bashira	貝柱	scallop
kani	かに	crab
katsuo	かつお	bonito
maguro	まぐろ	tuna
tai	鯛	sea bream
tamago	たまご	sweetened egg
toro	とろ	the choicest cut of fatty tuna belly, very expensive
unagi	うなぎ	eel with a sweet sauce
uni	うに	sea urchin roe

Sukiyaki & Shabu-Shabu
すき焼き／しゃぶしゃぶ

Restaurants usually specialise in these dishes. Sukiyaki is a favourite of most foreign visitors to Japan. When made with high-quality beef, like Kōbe beef, it is a sublime experience. Sukiyaki consists of thin slices of beef cooked in a broth of soy sauce, sugar and sake, and is accompanied by a variety of vegetables and tofu. After cooking, all the ingredients are dipped in raw egg (the heat of the ingredients tends to lightly cook the egg) before being eaten.

Shabu-shabu consists of thin slices of beef and vegetables cooked by swirling the ingredients in a light broth and then dipping them in a variety of special sesame seed and citrus-based sauces. Both of these dishes are prepared in a pot over a fire at your private table – the waiter or waitress will usually help you get started and then keep a close watch as you proceed. The key is to take your time and add the ingredients a little at a time, savouring the flavours as you go.

Right: *Tempura* may have been borrowed from 16th-century Portuguese seafarers but it has become a quintessentially Japanese food. It was popular as 'fast food' in the old Edo days, but today refined cooking methods are used to subtly unlock the ingredients' essence – making tempura emblematic of Japanese food.

Sukiyaki and shabu-shabu restaurants usually have a traditional Japanese decor and sometimes a picture of a cow to help you recognise them. Ordering is not difficult. Simply say 'sukiyaki' or 'shabu-shabu' and indicate how many people are eating. Expect to pay between ¥3000 and ¥10,000 a head.

One of the best places to try these dishes made with high-quality beef is Asakusa Imahan (Map 9).

Tempura 天ぷら

This famous Japanese food is not actually Japanese, but was borrowed from Portuguese traders in the 16th century. Since then, though, the Japanese have transformed it into something uniquely their own. Good tempura is portions of fish, prawns and vegetables cooked in fluffy, nongreasy batter.

When you sit down at a tempura restaurant, you will be given a small bowl filled with a light brown sauce *(ten-tsuyu)* and a plate of grated *daikon* radish; mix this into the sauce and dip each piece of tempura into it. Tempura is best when it's hot, so don't wait too long – use the sauce to cool each piece and dig in. While it's possible to order à la carte, most diners choose to order a teishoku (full set), which includes rice, miso soup and Japanese pickles.

You should expect to pay between ¥2000 and ¥10,000 for a full tempura meal.

Finding tempura restaurants is tricky, as they have no distinctive facade or decor. If you look through the window, you'll see customers around the counter watching the chefs as they work over large woks filled with oil. Many luxury hotels in Japan have tempura restaurants on their premises.

In Tokyo, you need look no further than the famous Ten-Ichi chain (Map 7) for heavenly tempura. For cheaper tempura, head to the area around the temple Sensō-ji in Asakusa (Map 9).

Rāmen ラーメン

The Japanese adapted this dish from China and produced one of the world's most delicious fast foods. Rāmen dishes are big bowls of noodles in a meat broth served with a variety of toppings, such as sliced pork, bean sprouts and leeks. In some restaurants you may be asked if you'd prefer *kotteri* (thick) or *assari* (thin) soup. Other than this, ordering is simple: Just sidle up to the counter and say 'rāmen nami' (for regular size) or 'rāmen dai' (for a large portion). Expect to pay between ¥500 and ¥900 for a bowl. Since rāmen is originally Chinese food, some rāmen restaurants also serve *chāhan* or *yaki-meshi* (fried rice), *gyōza* (dumplings) and *kara-age* (deep-fried chicken pieces).

Rāmen restaurants are easily distinguished by their long counters lined with customers hunched over steaming bowls. You can also hear a rāmen shop – it is considered polite to slurp the noodles. In fact rāmen aficionados claim that slurping brings out the full flavour of the broth.

Kappabashi-dōri in Shitamachi – the only place to go when you need to buy fake, wax food

A carousel of grilled fish

Anyone for apricot pie?

Takoyaki ingredients

Sushi and *sashimi* for your dining pleasure

An *okonomiyaki* stall – 'cook what you like'

JOHN HAY

Traditional meal of prawn, cuttlefish & seaweed

PAUL DYMOND

Octopus for sale – Tsukiji fish market

MICHAEL TAYLOR

It's polite to slurp your noodles at a *rāmen* bar

PAUL DYMOND

Nabemono communal cooking – each diner places some ingredients in the pot

Tokyo is home to the world capital of rāmen: the streets surrounding the east exit of JR Shinjuku station. In these crowded streets it seems as if there is a rāmen joint for every person in Tokyo.

rāmen	ラーメン	standard issue, the cheapest item on the menu – soup and noodles with a sprinkling of meat and vegetables
chāshū-men	チャーシューメン	rāmen topped with slices of roasted pork
wantan-men	ワンタンメン	rāmen with meat dumplings
miso-rāmen	味噌ラーメン	rāmen with miso-flavoured broth
chānpon-men	ちゃんぽんメン	Nagasaki-style rāmen with assorted vegetables and meat in the broth

Soba & Udon そば／うどん

Soba noodles are thin, brown, buckwheat noodles, while udon noodles are thick, white, wheat noodles. Most Japanese noodle shops serve both soba and udon prepared in a variety of ways. Noodles are usually served in a bowl containing a light, bonito-flavoured broth, but you can also order them served cold and piled on a bamboo screen with a cold broth for dipping. By far the most popular type of cold noodles is *zaru soba*, which is served with bits of *nori* (seaweed) on top. This comes with a small plate of wasabi and sliced scallions – put these into the cup of broth and eat the noodles by dipping them in this mixture. At the end of your meal, the waiter will give you some hot broth to mix with the leftover sauce, which you drink like a kind of tea. As with rāmen, feel free to slurp as loudly as you please.

Soba and udon places are usually quite cheap (about ¥900), but some fancy places can be a lot more expensive (the decor is a good indication of the price).

Being a traditional food, you can usually spot soba and udon places by their rustic wooden facades, which occasionally have food displays in the window. For great soba and udon in atmospheric surroundings, try Kanda Yabu Soba (Map 8).

Add either the word 'soba' or 'udon' to the following four dishes when ordering:

kake	かけ	plain noodles in broth
kitsune	きつね	noodles with slices of fried tofu
tempura	天ぷら	noodles with tempura shrimp
tsukimi	月見	noodles with raw egg on top (literally, moon viewing)
zaru soba	ざるそば	cold noodles with seaweed strips served on a bamboo tray

GLENN BEANLAND

Left: An order of *unajū* is an elegant way to try *unagi* (eel). The eel is grilled until crisp on the outside but the richly flavoured inner is still tender. It's served, as usual, with rice.

Unagi うなぎ

Unagi is Japanese for eel, an expensive and popular delicacy in Japan. Even if you can't stand the creature back home, you owe it to yourself to try unagi at least once while in Japan. It's cooked over hot coals and brushed with a rich sauce made from soy sauce and sake.

Full unagi dinners can be expensive, but many unagi restaurants offer *unagi bentō* (boxed lunches) and lunch sets for around ¥1500.

Unagi restaurants are easy to spot. Most of them display plastic models of their unagi sets in their front windows and have barrels of live eels to entice passers-by. Tempting huh?

For really good unagi in an elegant setting, you should try Ueno's Izu-ei restaurant (Map 9).

unagi teishoku	うなぎ定食	full-set unagi meal with rice, grilled eel, eel-liver soup and pickles
unadon	うな丼	grilled eel over a bowl of rice
unajū	うな重	grilled eel over a flat tray of rice (larger than unadon)
kabayaki	蒲焼	skewers of grilled eel without rice

Nabemono 鍋物

Nabemono refers to any of a variety of dishes cooked in large cast-iron pots. Like sukiyaki and shabu-shabu, nabemono are cooked at your table on a small gas burner or a clay *habachi*. Eating nabemono is a participatory experience, with each diner putting in ingredients from trays of prepared, raw food.

The most famous nabemono is called *chanko-nabe*, the high-calorie stew eaten by sumō wrestlers during training. Chanko-nabe restaurants are often run by retired wrestlers and the walls are usually festooned with sumō arcana.

Since nabemono are filling and hot, they are usually eaten in winter. They are also popular as banquet and party dishes, since the eating of a nabe dish is a very communal experience. It is difficult to pick out a nabe restaurant – probably the best way is to ask a

Japanese friend for a recommendation. We highly recommend Botan in Kanda (Map 8). This fine old place serves one dish only, chicken nabe, and unless you hate chicken, you'll find it's more than enough.

A few hearty nabemono dishes are:

chanko-nabe	ちゃんこ鍋	sumo wrestler's stew of meat and vegetables
botan-nabe	ぼたん鍋	wild boar stew with vegetables
yose-nabe	寄せ鍋	seafood and chicken stew with vegetables

Fugu ふぐ

The deadly *fugu*, or pufferfish, is eaten more for the thrill than the taste. It's actually rather bland, but acclaimed for its fine texture. Nonetheless, if you have the money to lay out (around ¥10,000), a fugu dinner makes an interesting, if slightly boyish, 'been there, done that' story back home.

Although the danger of fugu poisoning is negligible, some Japanese joke that you should always let the other person try the first piece. If you need a shot of liquid courage to get started, try a glass of *hireza-ke* (toasted fugu tail in hot sake) – the traditional accompaniment to a fugu dinner.

Fugu restaurants usually serve only fugu and can be identified by a picture of a fugu on the sign out the front.

Fugu is a seasonal delicacy best eaten in winter.

fugu teishoku	ふぐ定食	a set course of fugu served several ways, plus rice and soup
fugu chiri	ふぐちり	a stew made from fugu and vegetables
fugu sashimi	ふぐ刺身	thinly sliced raw fugu
yaki fugu	焼きふぐ	fugu grilled on a habachi at your table

Tonkatsu トンカツ

The Japanese have figured out a way to prepare pork that rivals the best steak. *Tonkatsu* is a deep-fried breaded pork cutlet served with a special sauce, usually as part of a set meal *(tonkatsu teishoku)*. Even if you shy away from pork at home, you ought to try this dish once. You'll probably be pleasantly surprised.

Tonkatsu is served both at speciality restaurants and at shokudō. Naturally, the best tonkatsu is at the speciality places, where a full set will run from ¥1500 to ¥2500.

When ordering tonkatsu, you can choose between *rōsu*, a fatter cut of pork, and *hire*, a leaner cut.

Try Shinjuku's Suzuya on Yasukuni-dōri (Map 3) for excellent tonkatsu served with all the trimmings.

Some delicious tonkatsu (pork) dishes are:

tonkatsu teishoku	トンカツ定食	a full set meal of tonkatsu, rice, miso soup and shredded cabbage
minchi katsu	ミンチカツ	minced pork cutlet
kushikatsu	串カツ	deep-fried pork and vegetables on skewers

Kushiage & Kushikatsu 串揚げ/串カツ

Kushiage and *kushikatsu* are deep-fried skewers of meat, seafood and vegetables usually eaten as an accompaniment to beer. Kushi means 'skewer', and if it can be fitted onto a skewer, it's probably on the menu. Cabbage is often eaten with the meal to ease the guilt of eating all that grease.

Order kushiage and kushikatsu by the skewer (one skewer is *ippon*). Like yakitori, this food is popular with salarymen and students, and is therefore fairly inexpensive, though upmarket places exist. Expect to pay from ¥2000 to ¥5000 for a full meal and a couple of beers.

Since they're not particularly distinctive in appearance, the best way to find a kushiage and kushikatsu place is to ask a Japanese friend.

ebi	海老	shrimp
ika	いか	squid
renkon	レンコン	lotus root
tama-negi	たまねぎ	white onion
gyū-niku	牛肉	beef pieces
shiitake	しいたけ	Japanese mushrooms
ginnan	銀杏	ginkgo nuts
imo	いも	potato

Kaiseki 懐石

Kaiseki is the pinnacle of Japanese cuisine, where ingredients, preparation, setting and presentation all come together to create a dining experience quite unlike any other. Born as an adjunct to the Buddhist-inspired tea ceremony, kaiseki is a largely vegetarian affair (though fish is often served, meat never appears on the kaiseki menu). One usually eats kaiseki in the private room of a *ryōtei* (an especially elegant style of traditional restaurant), often overlooking a private, tranquil garden. The meal is served in several small courses, giving one the opportunity to admire the plates and bowls which are carefully chosen to complement the food and seasons. Rice is eaten last (usually with an assortment of pickles) and the drink of choice is sake or beer.

This all comes at a steep price – a good kaiseki dinner costs upward of ¥10,000 per person. Kaiseki lunch is much cheaper – most places offer a bentō containing a sampling of their dinner fare for around ¥2500.

Kaiseki restaurants can be intimidating places to enter, so you may want to bring a Japanese friend or ask them to call ahead and make arrangements. There is usually only one set course, but some places offer a choice of three courses – graded *ume* (regular), *take* (special) and *matsu* (extra-special).

You can give kaiseki a try in surroundings a little more casual than at most ryōtei at Roppongi's Kisso (Map 4).

Teppanyaki 鉄板焼き

Like kaiseki, teppanyaki is a luxury food and is usually reserved for special occasions. The main item is steak, though you can also order chicken, seafood and a variety of vegetables. Like robotayaki, part of teppanyaki's appeal is visual, and the preparation of the food, usually right in front of the diner, takes on the air of a performance. Good wine is the perfect accompaniment to teppanyaki and most places have excellent cellars. Teppanyaki does not come cheap, and you can count on spending over ¥10,000 per person, sometimes two or three times that. Most luxury hotels in Tokyo have teppanyaki restaurants on their premises. Otherwise, Roppongi's Seryna (Map 4) is a very accessible place at which to sample top-end teppanyaki.

Mukokuseki 無国籍

Mukokuseki means 'cuisine without nationality' – meaning international spins put on domestic dishes or new creations by whoever is cooking. Usually you order a succession of small dishes and wash them down with beer or sake. Mukokuseki is often served in restaurants that are similar in atmosphere to izakaya, and prices are comparable. Unfortunately, there is no reliable way of distinguishing a mukokuseki restaurant. Reliably good mukokuseki can be had at An An in Ebisu (Map 5).

Yatai 屋台

Yatai are outdoor restaurants, usually tents erected on city footpaths, but also on temple grounds and at festivals. Like izakaya, yatai are places for both eating, and drinking beer and sake. Yatai menus are quite simple and usually include yakitori, a few stewed items, grilled rice balls and in winter, *oden* (see the Oden section, following). A meal at a yatai is a good way to get to know working-class Japanese, who may be a little surprised to find a foreigner in their midst. Ordering is simple, as everything is laid out for you to see. Since yatai owners pay little in the way of rent and upkeep, they are among the cheapest places to eat in Japan – a full meal's worth of food can be had for around ¥1500, and beers cost about ¥600 a mug. Yatai are easy to spot; just look for a tent with a lantern hanging from it.

Oden おでん

Oden is a simple stew of fish cakes, vegetables and tofu cooked for hours in a broth flavoured with kelp. While this may not sound particularly appealing, it's actually good, filling, inexpensive food. Oden is a winter speciality, eaten to fortify oneself against the cold.

While there are oden speciality shops scattered about, it's easier to find oden at yakitori and yatai restaurants. You can also buy oden from street vendors. In Tokyo, a good place to look for these is around Ueno-kōen Park (Map 9). Oden is easy to order; just point at what you'd like. You can easily fill up on oden for less than ¥1000.

DRINKS
Alcohol

Alcohol is, in some ways, the glue that holds Japanese society together. Alcohol is drunk by almost every adult, male or female, and a good number of teenagers (alcohol is sold from vending machines and underage drinking is not nearly as frowned upon as it is in some countries). Going out for a few rounds after work with co-workers is both the joy and bane of the Japanese salaryman's life. After a few drinks, workers feel secure enough to vent their frustrations and speak their minds, confident that all will be forgiven by the time they arrive at the office in the morning.

Occasionally, drinking crosses the boundary between good-natured fun and ugly inebriation, as anyone who has been in a public park during cherry blossom season can attest. However, drunkenness rarely leads to violence in Japan, so the visitor does not have to be overly concerned.

Beer Introduced at the end of the last century, beer (*biiru*) is now the favourite tipple of the Japanese. The quality is generally excellent and the most popular type is light lager, although recently some breweries have been experimenting with darker brews. The major breweries are Kirin, Asahi, Sapporo and Suntory. Beer is dispensed everywhere, from Tokyo's ubiquitous vending machines to beer halls and even in some temple lodgings.

A standard can of beer from a vending machine is about ¥250, although some of the monstrous cans cost over ¥1000. At bars, a beer starts at ¥500 and climbs depending on the establishment. Draught beer (*nama biiru*) is widely available, as are imported beers.

TONY WHEELER

Left: Casks of *sake* are often left as offerings at Shintō temples. Since ancient times, sake has been offered to the *kami* (gods) who watch over the rice harvest.

Sake Rice wine has been brewed for centuries in Japan. Once restricted to imperial brewers, it was later produced at temples and shrines across the country. In recent years, consumption of beer has overtaken that of sake, but it's still a standard item in homes, restaurants and drinking places. Large casks of sake are often seen piled up as offerings outside temples and shrines, and it plays an important part in most celebrations and festivals.

Most Westerners come to Japan with a bad image of sake; the result of having consumed low-grade brands overseas. Although it won't appeal to all palates, some of the higher grades are actually very good, and a trip to a restaurant specialising in sake is a great way to sample some of the better brews.

There are several major types of sake, including *nigori* (cloudy), *nama* (unrefined) and regular, clear sake. Of these, the clear sake is by far the most common. Clear sake is usually divided into three grades: *tokkyū* (premium), *ikkyū* (first grade) and *nikkyū* (second grade). Nikkyū is the routine choice. These are further divided into *karakuchi* (dry) and *amakuchi* (sweet). Apart from the national brewing giants, there are thousands of provincial brewers producing local brews called *jizake*.

Sake is served *atsukan* (warm) and *reishū* (cold), the former being more popular in the winter. When you order sake, it will usually be served in a small flask called *tokkuri*. Tokkuri come in two sizes, so you should specify whether you want *ichigo* (small) or *nigo* (large). From these flasks you pour the sake into small ceramic cups called *o-choko* or *sakazuki*. Another way to sample sake is to drink it from a small wooden box called *masu*, with a bit of salt at the rim.

However you drink it, with a 17% alcohol content, sake is likely to go right to your head, particularly the warm stuff. After a few bouts with sake you'll come to understand why the Japanese drink it in such small cups.

Particularly memorable is a real 'sake hangover' born of too much cheap sake. The best advice is not to indulge the day before you have to get on a plane.

Shōchū For those looking for a quick and cheap escape route from their sorrows, *shōchū* is the answer. It's a distilled spirit (30% alcohol), which has been resurrected from low esteem (it was used as a disinfectant in the Edo period) to the status of a trendy drink. You can drink it as *oyu-wari* (with hot water) or as *chūhai* (a highball with soda and lemon). A 720ml bottle sells for about ¥600, which makes it a relatively cheap option compared with other spirits.

Wine, Imported Drinks & Whisky Japanese wines are available from areas such as Yamanashi, Nagano, Tōhoku and Hokkaidō. Standard wines are often blended with imports from South America or Eastern Europe. The major producers are Suntory, Mann's and Mercian. Prices are high – expect to pay at least ¥1000 for a bottle of something drinkable.

Imported wines are often stocked by large liquor stores or department stores. Bargains are sometimes available at ¥600, but most of the imports are considerably more expensive.

Prices of imported spirits have been coming down in recent years and bargain liquor stores have been popping up. However, it is probably a good idea to pick up a duty-free bottle or two on your way through the airport.

Whisky is available at most drinking establishments and is usually drunk *mizu-wari* (with water and ice) or *onzarokku* (on the rocks). Local brands, such as Suntory and Nikka, are sensibly priced and most measure up to foreign standards. Expensive foreign labels are popular as gifts.

Most other imported spirits are available. Bars with a large foreign clientele, including hotel bars, can usually mix anything at your request. If not, they will certainly tailor a drink to your specifications.

Drinking Places What you pay for your drink depends on where you drink and, in the case of a hostess bar, with whom you drink. As a rule, hostess bars are the most expensive places to drink (up to ¥10,000 per drink), followed by upmarket traditional Japanese bars, hotel bars, beer halls and casual pubs. If you are not sure about a place, ask about prices and cover charges before sitting down. As a rule, if you are served a small snack with your first round, you'll be paying a cover charge (usually a few hundred yen, but sometimes much more).

Japanese-style places to drink include *izakaya* and *yakitori-ya*. These are cheap places which serve beer, sake and food in a casual atmosphere resembling that of a pub. *Aka-chōchin*, also known as *nomiya*, which display a red lantern outside, are similar pubs for the working class – down-to-earth in price and decor. The cheapest of these places are known as *tachi-nomiya*, where there are no chairs and everyone just stands around and slugs it back.

Nonalcoholic Drinks

Most familiar drinks are available in Japan, with a few colourfully named additions like Pocari Sweat and Calpis Water, and drink machines are on virtually every street corner – for ¥110, refreshment is rarely more than a few steps away.

Coffee & Tea Coffee (*kōhii*) is usually expensive in Japan (¥350 to ¥500 a cup), with some places charging up to ¥1000. Some of the newer chains of coffee restaurants like Doutor or Pronto, or donut shops like Mr Donut (which offers free refills), are cheaper options. Cheaper still is a can of coffee, hot or cold, from a vending machine. Although unpleasantly sweet, at ¥110 the price is hard to beat.

At a coffee shop you'll be asked whether you like your coffee *hotto* (hot) or *aisu* (cold). Black tea also comes hot or cold, with *miruku* (milk) or *remon* (lemon). A good way to start the day is with a *mōningu setto* (morning set) of tea or coffee, and toast and eggs, which costs around ¥350. The following are some of the more common drinks available in *kissaten* (Japanese coffee shops):

kōhii	コーヒー	regular coffee
burendo kōhii	ブレンドコーヒー	blended coffee, fairly strong
American kōhii	アメリカンコーヒー	weak coffee
kōcha	紅茶	black, British-style tea
kafe ōre	カフェオレ	café au lait, hot or cold
orenji jūsu	オレンジジュース	orange juice

Japanese Tea Japanese tea is green and contains a lot of vitamin C and caffeine. The powdered form used in tea ceremony is called *matcha* and is drunk after being whipped into a frothy consistency. More common is leafy green tea (*o-cha*), which is drunk after being steeped in a pot. While *sencha* is one popular variety of green tea, most restaurants will serve a free cup of brownish tea called *bancha*. In summer a cold beverage called *mugicha* (roasted barley tea) is served in private homes.

Japanese tea is very healthy and refreshing, and is said by some to prevent cancer. Most department stores carry a wide selection of Japanese teas.

Entertainment

Tokyo is easily the entertainment capital of Asia – from cinema to *sumō*, there's more than enough to keep you amused.

The best place to find out what's happening is the *Tokyo Journal. Tokyo Classified, Tokyo Weekender, Pia* and the online *Tokyo Q* ([W] www.nokia.co.jp/tokyoq/) are also good resources. See Newspapers & Magazines and Internet Resources in the Facts for the Visitor chapter for more details.

CINEMAS
For the homesick, foreign movies are screened with original soundtracks and Japanese subtitles. American films predominate, but there's also plenty of world cinema. Tokyo has smaller cinemas that regularly screen art-house and cult films.

If you're interested in the local product, revival houses run Japanese film classics. Or you may want to check out some *anime* (animated film). Anime is currently booming, and you can find good first-run films in Tokyo (don't expect any English subtitles or dubbing, though).

The quality of Japanese cinemas has improved drastically in recent years. Cine Amuse in Shibuya deserves special mention for its adventurous programming, and *gaijin*-friendly atmosphere. Most mainstream cinemas in areas like Shinjuku and Shibuya have good sound systems and comfortable seating. Ticket prices, however, are probably the highest in the world, averaging between ¥1700 and ¥2300.

If you can plan ahead, tickets can be bought at certain outlets at discounted prices. A ticket that normally sells for ¥1700 will cost ¥1300 or less this way. There are ticket outlets in Ginza (Map 7) in the basement of the Tokyo Kōtsū Kaikan building; in Shinjuku (Map 3) on the 5th floor of the Studio Alta building and at the lower entrance to Omoide-yokochō; and in Shibuya-ku (Map 4) on the 1st floor of The Harajuku's Laforet building and on the 2nd floor of Shibuya's 109 building.

PERFORMING ARTS
Despite the language barrier many will face, Japanese theatre is a unique and rewarding experience. The Tourist Information Center (TIC; see Tourist Information Centers (TIC) under Tourist Offices in the Facts for the Visitor chapter) can give you performance and booking details, or inquire at the theatres listed in the following sections.

Bunraku
Osaka is the *bunraku* centre of Japan, but performances do take place in Tokyo, in February, May, September and December.

Kokuritsu Geikijō Theatre (☎ 3265 7411) **Map 8** Japan's national theatre is in Nagata-chō, and is the place to go for bunraku.

Butō
Most *butō* troupes are small, underground affairs, making them difficult for the visitor to find. The TIC can help you track down current ones.

Kabuki
Kabuki-za Theatre (☎ 3541 3131, 5565 6000) **Map 7** Tickets ¥2520-16,800. Usually

Making a fashion statement on stage.

two performances daily at 11am and 4pm. The best place to see *kabuki* in Tokyo is in Ginza. Performances and times vary from month to month. For phone bookings, ring at least a day ahead. Earphones providing 'comments and explanations' in English are available at ¥600 (¥1000 deposit) – well worth it.

Performances can last 4½ to five hours. If you're not up to such a long performance, you can get tickets for the gallery on the 4th floor (¥500 to ¥1200) and watch just one act. Unfortunately, earphone guides are not available in these seats. Fourth-floor tickets can be bought on the day of the performance.

Kokuritsu Geikijō Theatre (☎ 3265 7411) **Map 8** Tickets ¥1300-7800. Also has kabuki performances. Again, earphone guides are available.

Nō

Performances are held at various locations around Tokyo. Tickets cost between ¥3000 and ¥10,000, and it's best to get them at the theatre itself. Beware, though, that many viewers – Western and Japanese – find any more than 15 minutes of *nō* excruciatingly boring. It is thus quite acceptable to nod off. Nō in English is about as convincing as Chinese opera in Swahili.

Kanze Nō-gakudō (☎ 3469 6241) **Map 4** This theatre is a 10- to 15-minute walk west of Shibuya station. From the Hachikō exit, turn right and follow the road straight ahead past Tōkyū department store. The theatre is on the right, a couple of minutes down the third street on the left after Tōkyū.

Ginza Nō-gakudō (☎ 3571 0197) **Map 7** Five minutes on south-west of Ginza subway station. Turn right onto Sotobori-dōri in the direction of Shimbashi at the Sukiyabashi crossing; look for the theatre on the left.

Kokuritsu Nō-gakudō (☎ 3423 1331) **Map 3** Also known as National Nō Theatre, this theatre is in Sendagaya on the Chūō/Sōbu line. Exit Sendagaya station in the direction of Shinjuku and follow the road that hugs the railway tracks.

Rakugo

Students of Japanese who want to test their language skills to the hilt can see *rakugo* at the *Asakusa Engei Hall* (Map 9) (☎ 3841 6545) in Asakusa and at the *Suzumoto Engeijō Hall* (Map 9) (☎ 3834 5905) in Ueno. Alternatively, read the hilarious send-up of it in *Dave Barry Does Japan*.

Contemporary Theatre

Tokyo's contemporary theatre scene is effectively off limits to non-Japanese speakers.

There are occasional theatre performances in English given by local and international theatre groups (inquire with the TIC).

CLASSICAL MUSIC

Fans of classical music will not be disappointed in Tokyo; on most nights there are orchestral or chamber music performances. In general, performances by Japanese symphonies are cheaper to attend than those by visiting orchestras.

Four of the main classical performance venues in Tokyo are:

Bunkamura (Map 4; ☎ 3477 9111) in Shibuya
Suntory Hall (Map 7; ☎ 3505 1001) in Akasaka
Tokyo Metropolitan Festival Hall (Map 9; ☎ 3828 2111) in Ueno
Tokyo Metropolitan Art Space (Map 2; ☎ 5391 2111) in Ikebukuro

ROCK

Tokyo has a thriving live music scene, though shows tend to start and finish early (often around 9pm). Tokyo also sees a lot of international acts. Advance ticket prices range from ¥4500 to ¥7000.

Live Houses

The local live music scene, such as it is, can be found in so-called 'live houses'. Most of them are in the outlying student areas such as Shimo-Kitazawa, but there are a few scattered around central Tokyo. There is usually an entry charge (¥2000 to ¥3000).

Loft (☎ 3365 0698) **Map 3** Cover ¥1500-3000. Open 6.30pm-1am Sun-Thur, 6.30pm-2am Fri & Sat. This long-running Tokyo live house is in Kabukichō alongside the Koma Theatre. Often grungy, noisy and smoky, it's got just the right level of sweaty intimacy.

ENTERTAINMENT

Crocodile (☎ *3499 5205*) **Map 4** Entry usually ¥2000 including one or two drinks. In Harajuku, Crocodile has something happening every night. Walk down Omotesandō from Harajuku station, and turn right at Meiji-dōri. Cross the road and continue past an overhead walkway. Crocodile is on your left, in the basement of the New Sekiguchi building.

Shibuya (Map 4) has a few interesting live music venues.

The Cave (☎ *3780 0715*) Entry ¥3000-4000. Come here for high-quality international and local acts.

Club Quattro (☎ *3477 8750*) Entry ¥3000-4000. Dance floors here as well as local and international bands. On the 4th and 5th floors of the Parco building.

Eggman (☎ *3496 1561*) This venue usually features local performers at reasonable entry rates.

La Mama (☎ *3464 0801*) Entry around ¥2000. Just about every Japanese band from Buck-Tick to Melt Banana has passed through here at some time, at various levels of their fame. Take a chance.

Milk (☎ *5458 2826*) **Map 5** Entry ¥2000-3000 including one or two drinks. In Ebisu, this is one of Tokyo's best small live clubs, featuring international punk, hard rock and alternative, along with some of Tokyo's better underground acts. This is a cool space, with three underground levels and a crowd of weirdly wonderful local characters. In the basement below is What the Dickens (see Bars & Small Clubs later in this chapter).

Rock Mother (☎ *3460 1479*) Down in Shimo-Kitazawa, Rock Mother is a good live house. Take the Odakyū line to Shimo-Kitazawa station and exit via the south exit ('minami-guchi'). Turn left, then right, and then left again. Follow the road around to the right and look for the club on your left. The whole area around here is worth a look: It's a kind of downmarket Harajuku or a youth-oriented Shinjuku, with lots of cheap places to eat and drink – very popular with students.

Cover Band Venues

Kento's (☎ *3401 5755*) **Map 4** Cover around ¥1300. If you want 50s covers, Kento's has

Bands

One sure-fire way to have an interesting night out is to scour the local gig listings (*Pia* magazine is a good source) and select a band purely on the absurdity of its name. Aural Russian roulette, but as you'll likely be the only *gaijin* (foreigner) there, you're sure of a warm welcome. Using this technique, this reviewer has seen, amongst others, The Revolting Cocks (revolting), Ingry Mongry (excellent) and The Strange Death of the Soapland Woman (two seriously funky housewives from Osaka). Alas, my favourite, the Ass Baboons of Venus, always seem to be sold out. At the time of writing, Tokyo is hosting Two Hump Camels, Brow Your Horn, Oriental Plug, Jerry Lee Phantom, Drawers Pop Open, and the irresistible Blasstwolicks.

東京 東京 東京 東京 東京 東京 東京

branches all over Japan. The venues attract a young, enthusiastic, bobby-soxed crowd of jivers.

Cavern Club (☎ *3405 5207*) **Map 4** Entry ¥1300. In Roppongi, this is *the* place to hear *Ret It Be*, *She Rubs You*, and the classic *I Am Za Warurusu*. Lots of fun.

JAZZ

Tokyo is a jazz mecca, attracting big names and up-and-coming stars, but attending is an expensive pastime. Even small places charge upwards of ¥5000.

Blue Note (☎ *3407 5781)* **Map 4** Entry ¥7000-15,000. Serious cognoscenti roll up to Tokyo's prime jazz spot, in Aoyama, prepared to shell out much moolah on the likes of Maceo Parker, Sergio Mendes and Chick Corea.

Shinjuku Pit Inn (☎ *3354 2024)* **Map 7** Most shows around ¥3000 but can be ¥10,000-plus if the act is well known. The Pit Inn, on Gyoen-dōri, below Kobe Ranputei restaurant. To get there, take the C5 exit of Sanchōme subway station.

Roppongi Pit Inn (☎ *3585 1063)* **Map 4** Roppongi Pit Inn is reportedly less traditional than its Shinjuku counterpart. Turn right at Almond coffee shop, cross over the road and look for the Pit Inn on your left, about 100m down the road.

Birdland (☎ *3478 3456)* Entry around ¥3000. Roppongi jazz club in the basement of the Square building. Look for all the beautiful people outside waiting to see where the happening spot is tonight.

B-Flat (☎ *5563 2563)* Entry around ¥2500. New, very hip club in Akasaka that often features Latin bands. Follow the street between exits 5a and 5b of Akasaka station, and it's on the right, opposite the Hotel Chanty.

Jazz Swing (☎ *3463 3889)* This dimly lit coffee shop-cum-bar up on the hill is very mellow. It also serves the standard lubricants to good jazz: whiskey and beer.

CLUBS

The Tokyo club scene is at its hottest during the summer, though there is plenty of action year-round. For straight disco action, Roppongi (Map 4) is the place to be. Entry to most Roppongi clubs is around ¥4000 (with some drinks tickets thrown in), which is a risky proposition if you aren't allowed to take a look first. Some clubs will be near dead, even on a Saturday night.

Outside of Roppongi, entry to clubs is usually cheaper (in the ¥2500 range). Clubs are booming in Tokyo: A quick look at the nightlife listings of the English-language monthlies reveals any number of techno, trance, trip-hop, ambient, drum 'n' bass and jungle happenings at clubs around town. Serious clubbers should take a look at the free *Flyer Tokyo, Juice* and its online edition ⓦ *www.tokyojuice.com*, or the Clubs and Bars section of the *Tokyo Journal*, the *Tokyo Classified* or *Tokyo Q*.

Roppongi (Map 4)

Roppongi has something for everyone, though most of the hipper clubs are on the fringes of the area or down near the Nishi-Azabu crossing.

Velfarre (☎ *3402 8000)* Cover ¥5000 for men, ¥4000 for women. Unless you're into mainstream disco, Velfarre has little of interest to the average punter. It's expensive and shuts down at midnight. Still, if you want a disco with all the trimmings, this is it.

Pylon (☎ *3497 1818)* Entry ¥3500 including two drinks. A youth-oriented dance club, playing anything from soul to techno, just a stone's throw from Roppongi crossing. It has four dance floors, but it's still a bit hard to find. Usually open only on the weekends.

Lexington Queen (☎ *3401 1661)* Cover around ¥5500 including drinks and *sushi*. The place to rub shoulders with Naomi, Claudia and Elton, but this Tokyo institution is well past its prime, despite local celebrity Bill Hersey's ability to pull in the stars.

Yellow (☎ *3479 0690)* By the Nishi-Azabu crossing this is one of the most progressive, and hippest, places in town. House, acid jazz, Brazil jazz, techno and foreign DJ nights are all featured.

Luners (☎ *3586 6383)* Entry ¥2500 with two drinks. A palatial new club with the works (including lasers) that hosts a variety of events, including regular gay and lesbian nights. It's in Azabu-jūban 1-chome opposite the Jomo petrol station.

Harajuku, Aoyama & Nishi-Azabu (Map 4)

Aoyama is a hipper, mellower version of Roppongi. The downside is that many of the clubs are maddeningly hard to find. Think of it as the price for being cool.

ENTERTAINMENT

Dinner & Drinks with a View

How about a little perspective on the rat race? Any of Tokyo's many skyscraper bars and restaurants are sure to give you a feeling of being above it all. While many places charge exorbitant rates to go with their views, some are remarkably reasonable, hardly more than you'd pay down at street level. The following are some recommended spots.

Tokyo Park Hyatt In west Shinjuku, this new Park Hyatt Hotel in the Park Tower (Map 3) is *the* place for power drinking in stunning surroundings. If you've got the extra change, you owe it to yourself to knock back a few here – you'll feel like you own the world. On weekday evenings the *Sky Bar* on the 41st floor has a happy-hour special (5pm to 9pm), with all-you-can-eat/drink for ¥4000 for women and ¥5000 for men. At other times, drinks usually go for about ¥1500 each. The Sky Bar is open from 5pm to 11.30pm, Monday to Saturday, and from noon to 10.30pm on Sunday and holidays.

On the next floor, the *New York Bar* offers a similarly stunning view in a cool piano bar atmosphere. On weekdays from 5pm to 7.30pm, an hors d'oeuvre plate and two drinks is ¥2500. Otherwise, the hours and prices are the same as the Sky Bar's. The *New York Grill*, on the same floor, offers great food at top-end prices.

Aurora Lounge Also in west Shinjuku, the *Aurora Lounge*, on the 45th floor of the Keiō Plaza Hotel (Map 3), offers great views and drinks (from ¥1000). It also does a good coffee set during the day. It's open daily from 11.30am to 11.30pm.

On the same floor, the *Polestar* bar is built for gazing out over the city, with each seat facing the windows. Drinks start at ¥1500. It's open daily from 5pm to 11.30pm.

Top of Akasaka Over in Akasaka, on the 40th floor of the Akasaka Prince Hotel (Map 7), this bar offers a great view over central Tokyo in a lounge atmosphere. Drinks start at ¥1300. It's open from 1pm to 2am, Monday to Saturday, and until midnight on Sunday and holidays.

Sunset Lounge For good Bay area views, this lounge, on the 6th floor of the Hotel Intercontinental in Kaigan in Minato-ku, is the place to go. While not all that high, the waterfront location allows unobstructed views of Rainbow Bridge and shipping in the harbour. Drinks start at ¥900. It's open daily from 10am to midnight.

Trianon Up in Ikebukuro, on the 59th floor of the Sunshine 60 building (Map 2), the *Trianon* bar has a good weekend/holiday tart and sandwich buffet for only ¥1600, including drinks, from noon to 4pm. At night, the bar serves drinks from ¥1000. Bar service runs from 6pm to midnight, Monday to Saturday, until 11pm on Sunday and holidays.

東京 東京 東京 東京 東京 東京 東京 東京 東京 東京 東京 東京 東京 東京 東京

Apollo (☎ 3478 6007) Cover ¥2500 including two drinks. Fairly mainstream hip-hop and R&B, but the crowd is usually pretty lively. A good spot for dancing and mingling. Entrance is down an alley to the left of the building (look for the florist).

Blue (☎ 3797 1591) Entry usually ¥1500 including one drink. Popular with mod Tokyo student types, Blue hots up from time to time. The highlight is its cool interior design and cave-like atmosphere. The music is mostly acid jazz. It's quite a walk from central Aoyama, past Blue Note (see Jazz earlier in this chapter). Look for a portable sign at street level. Entrance is down a small walkway, and the club is in the basement.

Maniac Love (☎ 3406 1166) Entry weekdays ¥2000, weekends ¥2500 including one drink. After 5am, ¥1000. Very popular mid-sized club, playing lots of techno. Really comes into its own around 5am, when the serious after-hours crowd come to strut their weird and funky stuff. In best Aoyama tradition, it's a pig to find, behind an unmarked steel door in the basement of the Tera A Omote-sando building on Kottō-dōri.

Shibuya (Map 4)

Club Asia (☎ 5458 1996) Entry ¥2000 including one drink. Music runs towards techno, trance, drum 'n' bass and house. The club plays host to some of Tokyo's bigger DJ events. The place is a little secretive-looking; look for the 1st floor, which has the appearance of a cafe.

Vras (☎ 3770 5457) Entry ¥2000 including one drink. New club, rather sophisticated (for Shibuya), heavy on soul and drum 'n' bass. It's on the ground floor of the Dr Jeekhan's building.

Harlem (☎ 3461 8806) Entry ¥2000 including one drink. Upstairs from Vras, this is Tokyo's prime hip-hop and black music venue.

Two of the larger live venues in Tokyo that regularly host top Japanese bands and international touring artists are On Air, East and West. West is the smaller, less 'mainstream' of the two.

On Air East (☎ 3476 8686) Entry around ¥4500.

On Air West (☎ 5458 4646) Entry around ¥3500.

Sugar High (☎ 3780 3022) Entry ¥1000 for special events. Casual, stylish, small club run by two expat Americans. Watch for their all-you-can-drink specials, when the party really spins out of control.

Shinjuku (Map 3)

Shinjuku is more of a bar and small club scene, but there are a few big dance venues scattered about.

Code (☎ 3209 0702) Cover about ¥2500 including one or two drinks. This cavernous new club in the Shinjuku Koma theatre building has younger Tokyoites dancing and trancing till morning. Resident (often gaijin) DJs spin house, drum 'n' bass and trance. There is a good seating area in

which to take a break. Entrance is on the west side of the theatre.

Liquid Room (☎ 3200 6831) Located in Kabukichō, Shinjuku, it's worth checking out the schedule for this slick club. It usually features live events, but there is a club night at least once a month.

BARS & SMALL CLUBS

A lot of heavy drinking goes on in Tokyo, something you will realise very quickly if you hop on any train from around 10pm onwards. (Fortunately, although there is a lot of falling down and the occasional heaving, very rarely are the Japanese violent drunks.)

All that drinking makes for a lot of bars. As a general rule, avoid places with closed doors. You probably won't get in even if you try, but if you do, the chances are that it is a hostess bar with extortionate drink prices. The best bet is to duck into one of the many

---

Beer Gardens

When summer temperatures soar in July and August, the best way to beat the heat is to head to one of Tokyo's many rooftop beer gardens. Most of these places offer some kind of all-you-can-eat/drink special, and you can fill up for around ¥3000. Most places have a time limit, so if you want to get your money's worth, you're going to have to go early and work fast.

Matsuzakaya Lion Beer Garden (☎ 3572 1111) Ginza; on the roof of Matsuzakaya department store; open daily, 5pm to 9.30pm.

Ikebukuro Parco Tai Tai (☎ 3987 0552) Ikebukuro; on the roof of Parco department store; open daily, 5pm to 10pm.

My City Beer Garden (☎ 5360 7144) Shinjuku, on the roof of the My City store; open Sunday, 4pm to 10pm.

Shibuya Tōkyū Honten (☎ 3477 3478) Shibuya; *yaki-niku* (Korean barbecue) on the roof of the Tōkyū department store's main store; open daily, 5pm to 9.30pm.

Tokyo ANA Hotel Beer Garden (☎ 3505 1111) Akasaka; Akasaka ANA Hotel; open daily, 6pm to 9.30pm.

東京 東京 東京 東京 東京 東京 東京

ENTERTAINMENT

bars with mixed Japanese/foreign crowds: As a rule, they are affordable and friendly.

Roppongi is the gaijin bar capital of Tokyo. There are more small clubs, bars and pubs here than in most medium-sized cities back home. Shinjuku is probably Tokyo's drinking capital, and many bars and pubs here are receptive to foreigners. You can also find lots of good watering holes in Shibuya, Harajuku, Aoyama, Nishi-Azabu, Ginza and Ikebukuro.

Hotel bars often offer calmer surroundings and great views to go with your cocktails.

Roppongi (Map 4)

Roppongi is not part of Japan, not really: It's a multinational twilight zone where gaijin get together with adventurous locals to drink until the first trains at dawn. Because of this, many long-termers avoid it like the plague, leaving it for punters fresh off the plane and gormless riff-raff out trolling for local talent. That said, Roppongi is still the heart of Tokyo's nightlife scene, especially for foreigners. You've got to do it at least once.

On the north side of Roppongi-dōri are a number of interesting choices.

Havana Cafe (☎ 3423 3500) This is a great place to start. Happy-hour specials are good, and there's lots of tasty, inexpensive food to line your stomach for a night of drinking.

People's Bar (☎ 3479 4898) Located in a basement, sometimes this place is hopping, other times it's flat. It attracts an interesting crew and entertains them with good reggae, hip-hop and R&B. The fruit drinks are freshly squeezed and start at ¥600.

Paranoia (☎ 5411 8018) This is a shrine to the horror movie – watch the *Texas Chainsaw Massacre* as you sip your Miller Lite. Interesting choice for a first date. Look for the alien cyclops on the front of the building.

Salsa Sudada (☎ 5474 8806) Entry ¥1500 weekends, free weekdays. North of Gaien-higashi-dōri, this is perhaps the most popular salsa club in salsa-mad Tokyo. If you like salsa, climb the steps and get busy.

Tokyo Sports Cafe (☎ 3404 3675) Before 9pm all drinks ¥500. Heaving, friendly sports bar that offers Kilkenny beer on draft, boasts a huge pool table and, yikes, a talking computerised alcohol tester! Sportswise it's more Rotherham Utd than Chicago Bulls. Early morning it can get quite lively.

Geronimo (☎ 3478 7449) On the 2nd floor of the Yamamuro building, right near the famous Roppongi crossing, Geronimo is described as a shot bar. It gets packed out with all sorts of off-work Tokyo expats and a few of their Japanese associates. At happy hour (6pm to 8pm) all drinks, which usually run around ¥1000, are half-price. Beers are ¥800 no matter what time you go. A serious drinking bar.

The south side of Roppongi-dōri, beyond the landmark Almond coffee shop, is where the largest concentration of hostelries may be found.

Mogambo (☎ 3403 4833) This is the sister club of Geronimo, with a similar clientele and prices. This bar doesn't bother with flashing lights and fancy drinks, just good ol' rock and roll.

Castillo (☎ 3475 1629) Drinks start at ¥600. This small club plays a lot of disco and soul classics. Many people come here to dance, but you can just as easily pull up a chair and sit back for a drink. Castillo has a 30,000-strong LP collection.

Motown House 1&2 (☎ 5474 4605) Drinks from ¥800. The impolite call it 'ho town', but on the pick-up front it's no worse (or better?) than its neighbours, and since it expanded from 1 to 1&2, it can actually be quite relaxed.

Dusk Till Dawn (☎ 5771 2258) The name says it all really. Popular 2nd-floor hangout that fills up with the happy hour (6pm to 9pm), then keeps filling up. Presumably not everyone's there for the Cajun Fish 'n' Chips.

Gas Panic (☎ 3470 7101) One of Roppongi's rowdier cul-de-sacs is full of gas and panic. There's the original *Gas Panic Bar*, plus the *Gas Panic Cafe*, and the *Club 99 Gas Panic*, providing, respectively: cheap drinks and cheaper pick-up lines; cheap drinks, CNN and cheap pizza; and cheap drinks and a dance floor. See a pattern emerging here? The latter's PR is refreshingly honest: 'Always full of people

A beautiful garden of azaleas in bloom

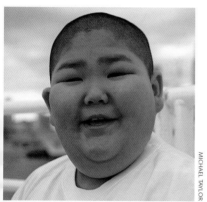

Kai, a young *sumō* wrestler and TV star

Girls leaving Shibuya station

Bridge over Babasaki moat at the Imperial Palace

CHRIS ROWTHORN

Harajuku's Omote-sandō promenade is at its best on a Sunday in Autumn

CHRIS ROWTHORN

Maple foliage in Autumn

CHRIS ROWTHORN

Stone lantern in Koishikawa Kōraku-en gardens

CHRIS ROWTHORN

Ueno-kōen park – a great spot to rest

smashing each other eagerly looking for space to dance'.

Gas Panic Club (☎ 3402 7054) Just off Roppongi-dōri on the 3rd floor of the Marina building, this is a slightly upmarket version of its rowdy progenitor, Gas Panic bar. If you like the Gas Panic chain (and you know who you are), give this shot bar a try.

Bar, Isn't It? (☎ 3746 1598) All drinks ¥500. Up three flights, you'll find this offshoot of a very successful Osaka bar chain. The formula here is simple: a big space, so-so bar food and cheap drinks.

Déjà Vu (☎ 3403 8777) Drinks ¥700. The popularity of this place seems to have slumped, but Saturday night can still find it packed.

Paddy Foley's (☎ 3423 2250) Popular expat pub with friendly Japanese staff, less-friendly American management, and good Irish beer.

Propaganda (☎ 3423 0988) Inexpensive shot bar, famed for its happy-hour specials. Also famed for being one of Roppongi's more popular pick-up joints, if that does anything for you.

Hub 2 (☎ 3478 0803) Plain, pseudo-British-pub, has some bar games, a lot of foreigners hanging about, and Guinness. It's opposite Bellini's Trattoria.

G-Martini's (☎ 3588 6147) **Map 7** Located in the east part of Roppongi, across from the Axis building on the 4th floor of the Five Plaza. Complete with lava lamps, Austin-Powers decor and a menu of more than 30 generously proportioned martinis, the only thing to remind you that you're in Roppongi not Cannes circa 1966 is, naturally, the Shag Room.

Bul-Lets (☎ 3401 4844) Live performances ¥2000 with one drink. Trendy and relaxed 'ambient bar' of the Roppongi crossing, near Nishi-Azabu crossing. This is a pleasant escape from the Roppongi melee.

Shinjuku (Map 3)

Evenings in Shinjuku are underrated by many of Tokyo's residents. There's plenty here, but you have to know where to look. Just promenading under the bright lights of Kabukichō and ducking into a revolving

sushi shop or *yakitori* bar for a bite to eat is a good prelude to a fun night out. Most of the drinking spots are east of the station.

Kirin City (☎ 3350 8935) Beers start at ¥500. Just a few minutes' walk from the station, this popular beer hall has a few outdoor tables from where you can watch the Shinjuku circus.

Clubhouse (☎ 3204 2191) Drinks from ¥800, lunch buffet ¥1000. Ostensibly a sports bar, but really it's a good, friendly place for a drink. Some imported and domestic beers, and a great-value all-you-can-eat international buffet at lunch.

The Dubliners (☎ 3352 6606) If you want to forget that you're even in Japan, try this pub in the Lion building, just a few minutes' walk from the *My City* exit. Good Guinness and loquacious gaijin.

Garam (☎ 3205 8668) Entry free on weekdays, ¥2000 on weekends including two drinks. A cool little reggae club with a friendly owner and no rasta poseurs. It's on the 7th floor of the Pole Star 6 building, above the Circo Parlo game centre.

Club Way (☎ 3203 0294) Entry free weekdays, ¥2000 weekends including two drinks. Above Garam, on the 8th floor, Club Way is another small, popular hip-hop and reggae club.

There are many other small clubs in the same price range doing the hip-hop, house, reggae thing.

Asa (☎ 3232 1892) Opposite the southeast corner of the Koma Theatre, Asa is popular with youthful sunbed addicts.

Club X (☎ 5273 8444) Three blocks east of Asa, opposite the Kani Dōraku restaurant.

Rolling Stone (☎ 3354 7347) Cover ¥500. This club out towards Shinjuku-nichōme is definitely not for the faint-hearted. It's a hang-out for Tokyo's heavy metal kids – lots of leather jackets, outrageous hairdos and cool posing. It really hots up on Friday and Saturday night, when things often get a little out of control. It's ¥800 for a beer. Look for it in the basement next door to a 'soapland'.

Shibuya (Map 4)

Shibuya is one of the more happening places in Tokyo. There are lots of bars and

ENTERTAINMENT

clubs scattered about, mostly on the west side of the station hidden between all those big department stores.

The Cave (☎ 3780 0715) Entry averages ¥2000 including one or two drinks. This was *the* place in the early 90s; now it's just another of Tokyo's many good clubs. There's electronic music and the atmosphere is fittingly cool. Look for the cramped spot hidden down a narrow street near Tōbu department store.

Hub (☎ 3496 0765) If you like faux-English ambience, pub food and a decent selection of beers, this should satisfy. It's part of a chain of English-style pubs with branches all over Tokyo.

Panama Joe's (☎ 3461 9047) Table charge ¥200. For a bar reminiscent of the occupation era, check out Panama Joe's up on Dōgenzaka-dōri. If you just want to sit alone or with a friend and enjoy an honest drink, you'll like Joe's. A small range of food is available. Look for the red-brick building.

Kirin City (☎ 3496 1701) Prices start at ¥500. On the 'other' (south) side of the station, this is your run-of-the-mill Japanese beer hall, serving a variety of inexpensive food and beers.

Harajuku, Aoyama & Nishi-Azabu (Map 4)

These adjoining areas hold some of Tokyo's best nightlife options, and provide a pleasant escape when the Roppongi crush is too much to bear.

Oh God (☎ 3406 3206) It's been going for years and miraculously it is still going. The format seems a little tired, but if your needs run to pool tables and movie screenings, it's just the ticket. From Meiji-jingu-mae station, walk down Omote-sandō and take the first lane on the right after Meiji-dōri. Oh God is in the basement of the building at the end of the lane.

Zest (☎ 3499 0976) This is a popular pub that also serves food.

In Aoyama you'll find several good small club options.

Kiss (☎ 3401 8165) Cover ¥2000. There are four floors to explore. Features include an espresso bar, an Internet cafe which serves light snacks, a disco which plays all kinds of funk, soul, disco and electronic sounds, and a bar (on the top floor). A cool place to build an evening around.

Mix (☎ 3797 1313) Cover charges vary, drinks start at ¥700. You can usually count on this tiny hole in the wall even when others in the neighbourhood are flat. It's small, smoky, crowded and always friendly. Music ranges from reggae to hip-hop. In the vicinity of the Omote-sandō crossing, it's rather hard to find; turn at the SG Dupont Paris store and look for the stairs.

328 (☎ 3401 4968) Also known as San-nippa. Cover ¥2500 Sat. Out in Nishi-Azabu this funky little club-cum-bar attracts a good crowd of international types and locals. It's a refuge from the trendier clubs up in Roppongi. Music is mostly R&B and soul. Roll in at midnight and you're bound to have a good time. It's right near the corner; look for the stairs leading to the basement.

Las Chicas (☎ 3407 6865) This restaurant has a bar and a members' club, both of which are good spots for a drink.

Ginza (Map 7)

Ginza may be ritzy, but there are lots of places where you can have a few drinks for no more than you would pay in Roppongi or Shinjuku. Indeed, if you don't want to deal with the madness of those areas, Ginza is a good place for a relaxing drink.

Henry Africa (☎ 3573 4563) Over by the JR tracks, Henry Africa is a consciously foreigner-oriented Ginza British-style pub. It does a pretty good imitation of merry olde England, with merry olde fish and chips and decent, inexpensive beer.

Pilsen (☎ 3571 3443) Big mugs of beer start at ¥800. True beer-hall ambience and a great selection of foamy ales. The food is widely hailed as some of Ginza's worst.

Lion Beer Hall (☎ 3571 2590) Beers from ¥700, food from ¥600. A bigger, Japanese-style beer hall smack in the middle of Ginza. The food is marginally better than Pilsen's, though the atmosphere leaves plenty to be desired.

Old Imperial Bar (☎ 3504 1111) Drinks start at ¥1000. An impossibly dignified, colonial-style watering hole, this hotel bar is located in the Imperial Hotel over in Hibiya.

Ikebukuro (Map 2)

A lot of nightlife in Ikebukuro consists of sleazy hostess clubs that won't let you in (no matter how politely you try). There are some good *izakaya* (Japanese-style beer halls) around, but for Western-style places, check out the following.

The Dubliners (☎ 5951 3614) Tokyo's *other* Dubliners. In the Spice 2 building near the Tokyo Metropolitan Art Space, this faux-Irish pub offers Kilkenny and Guinness draught for ¥850, and fish and chips for ¥750. The only bummer here is that it shuts down at 11pm.

Bobby's Bar (☎ 3980 8875) Drinks ¥400. Open until 3am weekends, 7pm to 9pm weekdays. If you want to continue drinking, head over to the 3rd floor of the Milano building, where there's darts, table soccer and good music.

The Black Sheep (☎ 3987 2289) Open 6pm till late. Similarly full of late night boozers and musos, it's as fun as the manager is friendly.

Takadanobaba (Map 2)

'Baba, as it is known to locals, is a scaled-down, budget version of Ikebukuro and Shinjuku. There are some good restaurants and a couple of places to have a drink. See Conversation Lounges under Useful Organisations in the Facts for the Visitor chapter for information on *Mickey House*, a conversation club-cum-bar that serves inexpensive drinks and is one of the friendliest places in town for newcomers to drop into.

Billy Barew's Beer Bar (☎ 3209 0952) Beers about ¥800 each. When things wind down at Mickey House (around 11.30pm), the action often moves on to here. Billy's claims to stock 150 brands of beer – see if you can come up with an ungrantable request. It also serves a small selection of (mostly overpriced, diminutive) food.

Ebisu (Map 5)

Ebisu is often passed over by those in search of a nightlife. This is unfortunate,

because a number of good clubs and bars can be found here.

What the Dickens (☎ 3780 2099) One of Tokyo's better English-style pubs. It has a pleasant, spacious feel, and there's usually a band in the corner playing good mellow music. There's nice, hearty food and Guinness on tap. What more do you want?

Shanghai (☎ 3715 2207) Drinks from ¥600. By day it's a coffee shop and at night it still has that feel. This a good place to meet for a light meal and drinks.

Bodeguita (☎ 3715 7721) Very close by, Bodeguita is a centre of Tokyo's booming Latin craze. As soon as everyone's finished eating (there's a good selection of Latin dishes from ¥800) they clear away the tables and it's salsa time – either join in or be crushed. Look for the English sign on the facade; the bar is on the 2nd floor.

Piga Piga (☎ 3715 3431) Entry ¥3000 weekends with a few drink tickets, free weekdays. Just around the corner from Bodeguita is another happening ethnic music enclave, in this case African. Piga Piga is one of the few venues around that hosts live African music. It's filled with Japanese African-wannabes that have to make you wonder. Look for the place in the basement on the corner.

Zona Rosa (☎ 3440 3878) Drinks from ¥800. If Bodeguita hasn't quenched your thirst for things Latin, come here for good margaritas, Mexican beers and a wholesome variety of Latin (mostly Mexican) food. It's underneath the Red Pepper restaurant.

Lazy Cat (☎ 3442 8679) A fun spot run by an expat Liverpudlian, this bar sometimes has acoustic bands. It's tucked down the small alleyway behind Kinko's.

Akasaka (Map 7)

Nightlife options in Akasaka are mostly limited to hotel bars, with one pub-style exception. Fortunately, Akasaka's hotel bars are among the best in town, and travellers on business may find themselves in after-hours negotiations, courtesy of their hosts.

Highlander (☎ 3505 6077) Beers start at ¥850, mixed drinks and whiskies from ¥1400. This bar at the Hotel Ōkura's is classic and dignified, with attentive staff. Low on glitz, high on quality.

Hobgoblin Tokyo (☎ *3585 3681)* Open late. Far better than your average Britpub replica. Run by an Oxfordshire brewery, it has good pub fare and excellent imported microbrews. Try the Black Wych stout. Hobgoblin is in the basement of the building next to the clearly marked Marugen 23 building.

Asakusa (Map 9)

Asakusa is not the place to look for good night spots in Tokyo. Sure, there are a few izakaya scattered about, but generally the area shuts down early.

Kamiya (☎ *3841 5400)* Closed Tues. There is one decent spot for a drink. Opened in 1880, this was the first Western-style bar

The Modern Floating World

During the late Tokugawa period, a colourful world was born in which *kabuki* actors, prostitutes, poets and high-living merchants cavorted in pleasure quarters like Tokyo's Yoshiwara district. This was the so-called 'floating world' (*ukiyo*), an ephemeral world of night pleasures (called *mizu shōbai*, or 'the water trade') centred around *geisha* houses and drinking establishments.

Although prostitution was made illegal during the Allied occupation of Japan following WWII, the water trade is alive and well in Japan, and a new form of floating world exists, one in which gaily painted kimonos have been replaced by gaudy miniskirts and flashing neon lights, particularly in the modern red-light districts of Shinjuku's Kabukichō and the areas around Ikebukuro station.

While it is easy to romanticise the exploits of those otherworldly figures who live on in *ukiyo-e* (woodblock prints), the modern floating world allows for little in the way of sentimentality – today it is primarily a sleazy underworld of illegal South-East Asian sex workers and economically disadvantaged young Japanese women controlled by thoroughly unromantic *yakuza* bosses.

東京 東京 東京 東京 東京 東京 東京

in Japan. The 1st floor is a beer hall, where you pay for drinks as you enter. The 2nd floor is a restaurant.

Ueno (Map 9)

Warrior Celt (☎ *3841 5400)* Until 7pm drinks are ¥500. An outpost of pagan debauchery, on Eki-mae-dōri, where the bartenders crank up the volume. Good selection of Brit and Irish beers.

GAY & LESBIAN VENUES
Bars (Map 3)

Tokyo's gay enclave is Shinjuku-nichōme, east of Gyoen-dōri between Shinjuku-dōri and Yasukuni-dōri. There are lots of little bars here, but some can seem rather daunting to enter.

Arty Farty (☎ *3356 5388)* Table charge ¥500, drinks from ¥800. This is one place that anyone can comfortably walk into. Meeting people is easy here, and it's a good place to learn about the area's other possibilities.

Kinswomyn (☎ *3354 8720)* Drinks ¥700. No cover charge. Friendly, popular lesbian bar run by activist, Tara. On the 3rd floor of the Dai-ichi Tenka building, off Yasukuni-dōri. English spoken.

Check out the *Tokyo Journal*'s Cityscope section, which sometimes has a special insert called Tokyo Out. See also Gay & Lesbian Travellers in the Facts for the Visitor chapter for more resources on current entertainment options.

Clubs

There are not many specifically gay dance clubs in Tokyo, but plenty which are host to a mixed scene. See earlier in this chapter for information on *Yellow*, *Blue* and *Apollo*. Check the *Tokyo Journal*, *Tokyo Q*, and Shinjuku and Shibuya HMV stores (see the Shopping chapter) for information on gay events, including the Ring party, which is held at various clubs around Tokyo.

JAPANESE-STYLE BARS

You've come all this way to Japan only to find yourself drinking in bars that could be in New York, London or Sydney. What to do? No worries: Tokyo has lots of drinking places where you really *do* feel like you're in a foreign country.

The types of places that welcome gaijin are izakaya, *nomiya*, *yakitori* joints and *yatai* (for details on what these places are and how to find them, see the boxed text Food in the Places to Eat chapter). When you go drinking at these, it will help to know a few words of Japanese, but you can usually get by with a smile and some hand signals. Some places will be completely at ease with foreign guests, while others may be a little lost or put out. The trick is to get that first order in, then sit back and enjoy. Chances are one of your Japanese neighbours will cautiously approach, and before you know it, you'll be pouring each other sake and laughing at half-understood jokes.

Ginza (Map 7)

Ginza has two good izakaya to try:

Chichibu Nishiki (☎ 3541 4777) This is a casual, old-style place.

Robata (☎ 3591 1905) Robata is a mid-budget spot famous for its excellent food.

Yūrakuchō Yakitori alley, famous in Tokyo, is under the JR tracks. The yakitori places here aren't drinking spots per se, but you'll soon realise that chicken on a stick is not the only reason people come here – this is drinking food! Beer is as cheap here as anywhere in Ginza and the atmosphere is, well, Japanese. For details, see the Places to Eat chapter.

Ikebukuro (Map 2)

Ikebukuro is a good spot for izakaya. Among the choices are *Sasashu*, *Tonerian* and *Yoronotaki*. Sasashu is a high-class place which serves some of the best sake in town. The other two are cheaper, and serve good, inexpensive food, cheap beer and drinkable sake. For details on all three, see the Places to Eat chapter.

Shinjuku (Map 3)

Yamagoya (☎ 3354 3024) This is a little-known treat in Shinjuku not far east of Isetan department store. Draught beer and sake, plus yakitori and other snacks, are served in a dungeon-like atmosphere, while Japanese

crooners mount a cage-like stage and perform a touch of *karaoke*. Feel free to put in a performance of your own, but don't worry, no-one's going to drag you on to the stage. Enter Yamagoya by a narrow flight of stairs and you'll end up in what seems like the hull of an old wooden ship. Huge, graffiti-covered wooden beams crisscross overhead. Wooden stairs continue down two more levels. The bottom level is the gloomiest, most dungeon-like and definitely the most fun – try not to think about earthquakes. Look for the kanji sign (see map key) outside and the rickety stairs descending into the bar.

Omoide Yokochō arcade offers really cheap yakitori, and plenty of beer and sake to wash it down. Like Yūrakuchō Yakitori alley in Ginza, the places here aren't just for drinking, but that's all a lot of the customers do, and it doesn't hurt to have all those good snacks in arm's reach. Note that some places here are a little wary of foreigners. A good trick is to walk slowly down the alley, peering hopefully into places that look good. When one of the masters invites you in with a hearty 'Irasshaimase!' ('Welcome!'), you'll know you've found a good spot.

Golden Gai (Map 3) For a great area that is hard to categorise, try Golden Gai. The bars here look Western-style, but 10 seconds in any of them will quickly dispel any illusions. For the adventurous traveller, this is one of the city's most interesting night zones. Even if you don't feel like a drink, take a stroll through this warren of tightly packed establishments just to feel the atmosphere – the whole place seems lost in a boozy, rundown time warp.

Most places can hold no more than five or six people at a time, and many keep the dishwashers out on the street to squeeze in one more. Each bar has its own personality, and they run the gamut from gay bars to sports, karaoke and jazz bars, with everything in between.

Being so thoroughly Japanese, it's understandable that some of these places are a little leery of foreigners. You're just going to have to feel them out as you go.

ENTERTAINMENT

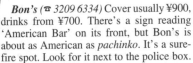

Bon's (☎ *3209 6334*) Cover usually ¥900, drinks from ¥700. There's a sign reading 'American Bar' on its front, but Bon's is about as American as *pachinko*. It's a sure-fire spot. Look for it next to the police box.

Once you leave the security of Bon's, you're on your own, but that's part of the fun. Before long, one of those 'Irasshai!' will be directed at you. Most places charge about ¥900 entry and ¥1000 per beer – over-priced, but you're paying for an institution.

Shibuya (Map 4)

Fujiya Honten (☎ *3461 2128*) It's a bold soul who ventures into this legendary old, *tachi-nomi* (stand-up-and-drink place) on the south-west side of Shibuya station. The Fujiya Honten is as rough as the proverbial rear ends, and filled with post-race punters from the nags at Ōi. Wash down the Oden with beer and sake at rock-bottom prices, and prepare to be engaged in friendly, slurred conversation. Be warned: we've never seen a woman in the place.

Other Areas

You can find Japanese-style drinking spots wherever you look in Tokyo. Shibuya, Kanda and Asakusa have more than their share, and you can even find a few in pricier areas such as around Tokyo station and in Akasaka. Basically, if you keep an eye out for the telltale red lantern and crates of empty sake and beer bottles, you'll find one.

Sentō

Until quite recently, most private homes in Japan did not have baths, so every evening, people gathered their toiletries into a bowl and headed off to the local neighbourhood *sentō*, or public bath. More than just a place to wash oneself, the sentō served as a kind of community meeting hall, where news and gossip were traded and social ties strengthened.

Unfortunately, the number of sentō in Japan is rapidly declining, but there are still enough sentō left in Tokyo and Yokohama for you to sample this most traditional aspect of Japanese life. More than just a cultural experience, however, a soak in a sentō is the ideal way to cure the sore muscles born of a day of sightseeing.

Sentō can be identified by their distinctive *noren* (half-length curtains over the doorway). Sentō noren usually bear the *hiragana* for hot water (occasionally, it may be written in *kanji*). At the bottom of the noren, look for the kanji for men and for women (for these kanji characters, see Toilets & Public Baths entry in the Facts for the Visitor chapter).

Once you've located a sentō, determine the men's or women's side, take off your shoes, place them in a locker in the entryway and slide open the door to the changing room. As you enter, you'll see the attendant, who sits midway between the men's and women's changing rooms, collecting the entry fee. Sentō usually cost between ¥300 and ¥400. Most are open from around 3pm to midnight.

In the changing room, you'll see a bank of lockers and stacks of wicker or plastic baskets. Grab a basket and drop your clothes into it. Find one of the common washbowls *(senmenki)* and place your toiletries in it, then place your basket in a locker (these have keys on elastic bands). Now you're ready for your bath.

Do not step into the bath until you have thoroughly washed your body. This is done at the banks of low showers and water spigots that line the walls of the place. Grab a low stool and plant yourself at an open spot.

Once you've washed thoroughly and removed all the soap, you are ready for a soak in the tubs. At a good sentō, you'll have a choice of hot tub, scalding tub, cold tub, whirlpool bath, sauna and, believe it or not, electric bath (which is meant to simulate swimming with electric eels!).

After soaking away the strains of the day, if you've done everything correctly, you will have achieved a state called *yude-dako*, or 'boiled octopus'. Now stagger home and collapse onto your futon.

東京 東京 東京 東京 東京 東京 東京 東京 東京 東京 東京 東京 東京 東京 東京

PUBLIC BATHS & HOT SPRINGS

Taking a bath may not sound like your idea of entertainment, but a good *sentō* (public bath) or *onsen* (hot spring) is more than just a place to wash: it's a place to relax, socialise and forget about the world outside.

The public bath is a vanishing institution in Tokyo, and it's worth visiting one while it's still possible. The following are a few of Tokyo's more accessible sentō and onsen.

Rokuryu (☎ 3821 3826) **Map 9** Admission ¥380. Open 3.30pm-11pm Tues-Sun. It may feel like a good neighbourhood sentō, but it's actually an onsen. The bubbling amber water contains minerals claimed to cure a number of ailments. Take the Ikenohata Keisei exit of Ueno station, turn right and walk down Dōbutsuen-dōri past the pond Shinobazu-ike. Turn left down the second street after the Suigetsu Hotel. It's on the right; look for the traditional Japanese facade.

Yutopia (☎ 3398 4126) **Off Map** Entry ¥2200 (ask at reception about special discounts). Open 24 hours (baths closed 2am-5am) daily except national holidays. With five floors of baths and saunas, this is closer to a 'bathland' than a humble sentō. Towels, pyjamas and whatever else you might need – including 40-minute massages on the 5th floor for ¥3000 – are provided. To get to Yutopia, take the Marunouchi subway line to Ogikubo station, exit the west side, turn left and walk about 50m; you'll see it on the left.

Two places worth checking out are a short walk west of Azabu-jūban station.

Azabu-juban Onsen (☎ 3403 2610) **Map 4** Entry ¥385. Open 11am-9pm, closed Tues. This simple place, popular with locals, is one of the few true onsen within Tokyo city limits.

Koshino-yu (☎ 3401 8324) **Map 4** Entry ¥1260. Open 3pm-11pm, closed Tues. Downstairs, this is an upmarket bath popular with visitors.

SPECTATOR SPORTS
Sumō

Sumō is the only traditional Japanese sport that pulls big crowds and dominates prime-time TV. Sumō is a fascinating, highly ritualised activity steeped in Shintō tradition.

It's also accessible: unlike say, kabuki, the proceedings are readily comprehensible to the visitor, and sumō is as much spectacle as sport. A visit to a sumō match is a memorable experience of Japanese culture.

Ryōgoku Kokugikan Stadium (☎ 3623 5111) **Map 1** Tickets ¥500-7000. Sumō tournaments at Ryōgoku take place in January, May and September, and last for 15 days. The best seats are bought up by those with the right connections, but upstairs seats are usually available from ¥2300 to ¥7000. Non-reserved seats at the back sell for ¥1500. If you don't mind standing, you can get in for around ¥500. Tickets can be purchased up to a month prior to the tournament, or you can simply turn up on the day. The ticket office opens at 9am, and it's advisable to get there early – keen punters start queuing the night before. Note that only one ticket is sold per person, a device used to foil scalpers. The stadium is adjacent to Ryōgoku station on the Sōbu line, on the north side of the railway tracks.

Baseball

Baseball is Japan's most popular sport, and six of Japan's 12 pro-baseball teams are based in Tokyo.

Tokyo Dome (☎ 5800 9999) **Map 8** The 'Big Egg', as it's affectionately known, is the best place to catch a baseball game. It's close to Kōrakuen and Suidōbashi subway stations. The Big Egg is the home ground of Japan's most popular baseball team, the Yomiuri Giants.

A trip to a Japanese ballpark is truly a cultural experience – the crowd behaviour is completely unlike what you're probably used to at home. The home team's fans often turn up in matching *happi* (half-length coats) and perform intricate cheering rituals in perfect unison led by special cheerleaders, one for each section, who seem to make a job out of whipping fans into a well-ordered frenzy.

ENTERTAINMENT

Soccer World

If soccer's your religion, Tokyo is definitely the *only* place to be based for the FIFA World Cup taking place from 31 May to 30 June 2002 in Japan and neighbouring South Korea.

Eight of the ten venues (Miyagi, Niigata, Ibaraki, Saitama, Yokohama, Shizuoka, Osaka, and Kobe) are all not more than a couple of hours or so commuting distance from the capital by train. Sapporo, Oita and the venues in Korea can all be conveniently reached by plane from Narita or Haneda airports. The three nearest stadia to Tokyo are Ibaraki, Saitama and Yokohama, which between them will host 11 of the 32 games held in Japan.

Ibaraki Stadium (seating 42,000) is the home of one of the J-League's top teams, Kashima Antlers. To get there take the JR Sōbu Line from downtown Tokyo to Kashima-jingū Station (about an hour).

Saitama Super Stadium is the home of the Urawa Red Diamonds, who claim the largest and most fanatic support in the country and seem to model themselves on global powerhouse, Manchester United. The stadium is accessible in just over an hour from central Tokyo using the Namboku Subway Line and train to Urawa-Misano Station on the newly constructed Saitama Line. Alternatively use the JR Keihin Tohoku, Utsunomiya or Takasaki lines to Saitama Shintoshin.

The final itself will take place on 30 June at Yokohama International Stadium, the home ground of the J-League's Yokohama F Marinos, a mere 40-minute journey from downtown Tokyo. The imposing stadium, complete with giant video screens for instant replays and close-ups of the action, is a short 10-minute walk from Shin-Yokohama or Kozukue stations.

If you can't get a ticket to the matches themselves Tokyo has a number of well-established and lively sports bars where you can catch all the action on TV and shout for your team over a few drinks. All of the following places will be heaving soccer madhouses come June.

FootNik (☎ 5330 5301) *Marujo Bldg B1, 3-12-8 Takadanobaba, Shinjuku-ku*
Clubhouse Sports Bar (☎ 3359 7785) *Marunaka Bldg 3F, 3-7-3 Shinjuku-ku*
Half Time (☎ 3209 7114) *1-19-4 Kabuki-cho, Shinjuku-ku*
The Rising Sun (☎ 3352-8842) *Shinsei Bldg 2F, 1-9-3 Yotsuya, Shinjuku-ku*
Tokyo Sports Caf (☎ 3404 3675) *7-15-31 Roppongi, Minato-ku*
Prime Time Caf (☎ 045-477 1121) *Tenko Bldg B1, 3-15-5 Shin-Yokohama, Kohoku-ku Yokohama*

For soccer and up-to-date travel and ticket information keep an eye on the following websites:

FIFA W www.fifa.com and W www.fifaworldcup.com
Japan Organizing Committee W www.jawoc.or.jp/index_e.htm
Japan National Tourist Organization W www.jnto.go.jp
Soccerphile.com (World Cup Webzine) W www.soccerphile.com

Philip Beech

東京 東京 東京 東京 東京 東京 東京 東京 東京 東京 東京 東京 東京 東京

J-League Soccer

Soccer is booming in Japan. Since the country was awarded (jointly with Korea) the 2002 World Cup there's been an increase in popularity of the game, and of the domestic J-league. Japanese soccer has all the hullabaloo of baseball; it's not like standing in the sleet watching Bradford City draw nil-nil with Middlesborough.

Catch a game at *Saitama Super Arena*, *Yokohama International Stadium* or *Tokyo Dome*.

Horse Racing

There are two big racing tracks in the Tokyo area. They host some pretty major races and offer the punter a good chance to wager (and lose) some money. Races are generally held on weekends from 11am to 4pm.

Tokyo Keibajō (☎ 0423-63 3141) is near Fuchū-Keibajō-Nishinomae station on the Keiō line.

Ōi Keibajō (☎ 3763 2151) is near Ōi-Keibajō-mae station on the monorail from Hamamatsuchō.

Shopping

Even more than its Asian neighbours Hong Kong and Singapore, Tokyo is the shopper's city *par excellence*. There is something about consumer culture in Tokyo that is definitive of the city itself. The near-sacred halls in contemporary Tokyo are the enormous, opulent *depāto*, or department stores. These are usually open six days a week until about 7pm, and are always crowded. Service standards are very high and products are presented quite strikingly. With so much on offer and such excellent service, it is easy to get infected with the shopping syndrome. It's hard to leave Tokyo without having bought *something*.

Shopping in Tokyo is a simple matter of going out and looking around; the area around the next railway station on your sightseeing route will offer hours of potential window shopping. Choosing what to buy may take a little more effort; it's been a while since Japan regularly stunned the consumer world with new products and innovative designs. Lately a lot of effort seems to have gone into items that fill a void in Japanese life, like automated pets – 'Daddy's home kids, turn on the dog!'. If you want a toaster that looks like a cute pig, hand deodorant or a device to detect bad breath, Tokyo will supply it.

That said, Japan is still the land of quality manufacturing, though a lot of it is now done 'offshore', where labour costs and legal work standards are much lower, and new products (eg, compact digital cameras) and designs appear constantly. Keep your eyes open, and keep prices in perspective – a beautiful *nō* mask may be ¥6000, but what are the chances of finding one like it at home? Although Tokyo is an expensive city, certain things can be considerably cheaper than in other countries, eg, many electrical items in Akihabara can be very reasonably priced. The same applies for camera accessories. There are also numerous shops around selling second-hand cameras and lenses (especially in Ginza and Shinjuku).

Vending Machines

There are no prizes for guessing that Japan has the most vending machines per capita on the planet. Estimates are in the range of 20 million machines, and you'd swear they were all in Tokyo. A major reason for the numbers is that in Japan they go unmolested – in most countries, plonking a beer vending machine on a suburban street corner would be inviting disaster, or at least a free street party.

You can buy almost anything from vending machines – soft drinks, coffee, cigarettes, beer, sake and whisky, of course, but also everything from rice and vegetables to cup noodles, burgers (yuck!), jeans, neckties and computer software. Machines outside some pharmacies dispense condoms (conveniently matched to your blood type, the key to your personality); porno (magazines and videos) machines can be found in some areas.

Vending machines can be socially responsible, too. New vending systems are ecologically correct: 'eco vender' is a system that keeps drinks cool even when switched off; 'eco ice' uses the drinks' own liquid to cool the machine.

Then there's recycling, as with the used panties machine. Ostensibly once owned and worn by female high-school students, undies come in vacuum-sealed packs of three (with a photo of the erstwhile owner) and are targeted at the average fetishistic man about town. The cost? Around ¥3000 to ¥5000, making them an ideal souvenir.

東京 東京 東京 東京 東京 東京 東京

For souvenir items, almost all the big department stores have good selections of traditional crafts such as Japanese dolls, ceramics, lacquerware, kimonos, fans etc. But department stores often sell their goods at inflated prices, unless you are lucky enough to be around during a sale. You're likely to find less glamorous but possibly more interesting souvenirs in Tokyo's flea markets, where you can buy Japanese antiques and curiosities (see the Antique Fairs & Flea Markets boxed text in this chapter).

WHERE TO SHOP

If you don't have a hectic schedule, before doing any shopping go and watch how the locals do it. Some of Tokyo's major department stores are experiences in themselves, and the energy levels inside run very high. Ikebukuro has a couple of the largest department stores in Japan, if not the world. You could spend a day exploring the Ikebukuro branches of either Seibu or Tōbu.

For a total shopping experience, visit Shibuya. The Parco I, II and III stores are quite remarkable, featuring the latest in fashion, traditional Japanese items, art galleries and restaurant floors. There is also a branch of Seibu in Shibuya, with one building for women's clothing and another for men's. Other Shibuya high points include the Seibu Seed building (boutiques), the 109 building (fashion), Loft (indescribable youth-oriented items – great browsing), Tōkyū Plaza (boutiques), HMV Records and Tower Records, and last but not least, Tōkyū Hands, perhaps the biggest do-it-yourself shop in the world.

Most of Tokyo's major urban hubs have their own distinct mercantile character. While areas like Shinjuku and Ikebukuro have the lot, most other areas tend to specialise. Shibuya, for example, has a high-fashion orientation, but is dominated by the large department stores. Harajuku and Aoyama are also fashion centres, but the emphasis is on boutiques or collections of boutiques, as in the Laforet building. Akihabara is an area given over almost entirely to cut-price electrical stores; Jimbōchō (in Kanda) is an area of bookshops; Kappabashi (see the Asakusa section of the Things to See & Do chapter) is where you buy the mouth-watering plastic food that graces restaurant window displays; Ueno is the place for motorbikes; and Asakusabashi is well known for its traditional Japanese dolls.

What about Ginza? It's true Ginza is the most famous Tokyo shopping district, and it's still recommended for a browse, but it's worth remembering that Ginza is about prestige, respectability and having the money to spend there. Check the prices elsewhere before you do any buying, but relax: window-shopping is free.

WHAT TO BUY

If there's any market for it whatsoever, you can buy it in Tokyo. The question comes down to whether the price that's being asked for it is reasonable or not.

Arts, Crafts & Antiques

As much for the convenience of being able to look at a wide range of traditional arts and crafts in one location as anything else, it's worth taking a look in some of the big department stores. You may find a deal or two as well, since there are often sale bins in the department stores, especially for Japanese-style dining ware.

Japanese ceramics make beautiful, if fragile, gifts.

For genuine antiques, there are a few places in Harajuku and Aoyama that you should visit.

Hanae Mori building (☎ 3406 1021) **Map 4** Open daily. One of the best spots to look is the basement in this building, where there are more than 30 antique shops.

Oriental Bazaar (☎ 3400 3933) **Map 4** Open daily except Thur. Not far from the Hanae Mori building, the bazaar has a wide-ranging selection of antiques and tourist items, some at very reasonable prices. Items on sale include fans, folding screens, pottery, porcelain and kimonos.

Japan Traditional Crafts Center (☎ 3403 2460) **Map 4** The centre, right on the corner of Aoyama-dōri and Killer-dōri, has changing displays of Japanese crafts as well as items for sale. Also in Aoyama is the so-called **Antique Street**, a side street to the left of Aoyama-dōri as you move in the direction of Shibuya. Hidden among the trendy boutiques are some 30 antique shops.

Inachu Lacquerware (☎ 3582 4451) **Map 7** This shop in Akasaka is a renowned lacquerware shop, but it's strictly for those who want the genuine item and are prepared to pay for it.

Satomi building (☎ 3980 8228) **Map 2** Open 10am-6pm Mon-Sat. There are more than 30 antique dealers on the 1st floor of this building not far from Ikebukuro station's eastern exit.

International Arcade in Ginza **Map 7** This arcade is definitely along more touristy lines.

Also in Ginza are a couple of small shops with high-quality Japanese souvenirs.

Takumi (☎ 3571 2017) Takumi has been around for some 60 years, and has acquired an elegant selection of traditional crafts from around Japan.

Nakamise-dōri **Map 9**, in front of Sensō-ji temple in Asakusa is also worth a look. Among the items on sale here are traditional wigs, combs, fans and dolls. After exploring Nakamise-dōri, another fun possibility for picking up traditional souvenirs is to try out some of the flea markets and antique fairs held around the city.

Antique Fairs & Flea Markets

After days of perfectly ordered department stores, one longs for the colourful anarchy of a good flea market. Tokyo has loads of flea markets and antique fairs – many held on temple or shrine grounds – where you can spend hours among the bric-a-brac.

Don't get your hopes up about treasures though, for gone are the days when astute buyers could turn up at a flea market and cart off antique *tansu* (wooden chests) worth thousands of dollars. More likely, you'll find some quirky gifts at considerable savings over department store prices. Things to look for include old kimonos, scrolls, pottery, Chinese snuff bottles, old Japanese postcards, antique toys and costume jewellery.

The joy of these markets and fairs is that bargaining is permitted. Remember: have a good time at it and never drive too hard a bargain. If your Japanese is lacking, bring a pad of paper and a pencil.

The following are some of Tokyo's better flea markets and antique fairs. Check with the TIC before going, as shrine and temple events sometimes interfere with the scheduling of markets.

Arai Yakushi-ji antique market five minutes from Arai-yakushi-mae station on the Seibu Shinjuku Line; 8th, 18th and 28th of every month, dawn to dusk

Hanazono-jinja flea market five minutes from Shinjuku Sanchōme station on the Marunouchi subway line; Sunday, dawn to dusk

Kawagoe Narita Fūdo antique fair 15 minutes from Hon-Kawagoe station on the Seibu Shinjuku Line; 28th of every month, dawn to dusk

Nogi-jinja flea market one minute from Nogizaka station on the Chiyoda subway line; 2nd Sunday of every month, dawn to dusk

Salvation Army Bazaar 10 minutes from Nakano Fujimichō station on the Marunouchi subway line; Saturday, 9am to 1pm

Tōgo-jinja flea market three minutes walk from Harajuku station; 1st and 4th Sunday of every month, dawn to 2pm

東京 東京 東京 東京 東京 東京 東京

The large **Tokyo Antique Fair** takes place three times a year and brings together more than 200 antique dealers. The schedule changes annually; for information on this year's schedule, ring the Tokyo TIC.

Audio

Japanese recordings are renowned for their high fidelity, and Tokyo has numerous music stores with enormous collections of discs and tapes to sift through. Some of the best places to check out are the *Virgin Megastores* **Map 2** also in Shinjuku and Ikebukuro; *HMV Records* **Map 7** in Harajuku, Shibuya, Shinjuku and Ikebukuro; *Wave* in Roppongi, Shibuya and Ikebukuro; *Tower Records* in Shibuya; and *Yamaha* in Ginza. Wave, in particular, is notable for its AV displays (including hi-definition TV) and extensive audio selections. Tokyo also has lots of used record stores and you can find old LPs here that are difficult to find back home, usually in excellent condition. The best places to look for used record shops are in the streets of Shibuya, Aoyama, Harajuku and Nishi-Azabu.

Cameras & Film

Apart from wandering around straining your neck at concrete monoliths, Shinjuku's west side (Map 3) is the best place in Tokyo to buy photographic supplies. The city's largest camera stores can be found here.

Yodobashi Camera (☎ 3346 1010) **Map 3.** One of Tokyo's most famous camera stores, this emporium stocks anything and everything remotely connected with photography – from lenses to digital cameras to second-hand enlargers. Its prices are very competitive and foreigners are waived Japanese consumption tax (you may be asked to show your passport to prove you're not a resident, but the 'Oh-I-left-it-in-my-hotel' ploy often works).

Sakuraya Camera (☎ 3354 3636) **Map 3.** Yodobashi's rival offers much the same product range at similar prices. Comparison shopping is essential.

There are many places dealing in second-hand photographic equipment. Foreign-made large-format equipment is usually ridiculously expensive, but Japanese equipment can often be had at very good prices.

Surprisingly, one of the best areas in which to look for used cameras is Ginza (Map 7) – maybe it's all the photo galleries in the neighbourhood. On Harumi-dōri there's a good place opposite the Sony building on the Sukiyabashi crossing. There are a couple more places on the same side as the Sony building, towards the Kabuki-za Theatre. They're all on ground level and the windows are full of cameras and lenses.

Photographic film and processing in Japan are very expensive. It's advisable to bring your own film and process it after you leave if possible.

Bic Camera (☎ 3988 0002) **Map 2** You might try this place on the east side of Ikebukuro, where there are big bargain bins of film that is approaching its expiry date – the merchandise is usually fine. Bic Camera claims to be the cheapest camera store in Japan, a claim hotly disputed by Yodobashi and Sakuraya camera stores. There's also a branch in Shibuya. The big camera shops on the west side of Shinjuku station also have enormous selections of film, some at cut-rate prices.

Clothes & Shoes

Tokyo is a very fashionable city, and the range of clothes and shoes is enormous. Where you shop, however, depends on your budget. Shinjuku, Ikebukuro and Ueno are good areas for picking up clothes and shoes at discounted prices. Harajuku, Aoyama, Shibuya and Ginza are good for boutique browsing and making quality purchases.

Reasonably priced clothing stores are scattered all over the east side of Shinjuku (Map 3) – there are quite a few around Kinokuniya bookshop. In Harajuku (Map 4), Omote-sandō and Takeshita-dōri make good hunting grounds, although the market here is very youth oriented. These are also both good areas for buying shoes.

In Ikebukuro (Map 2), around the western exit of the station, there are many discount fashion shops. You might also take a look at Ueno's Ameyoko arcade (Map 9), which has a number of shops selling clothes and shoes at cheaper prices than other parts of Tokyo.

If you want to make a fashion statement and spend some money, head for the boutiques of Harajuku and Aoyama or the department stores of Shibuya.

Laforet building (☎ 3472 0411) **Map 4** This building in Harajuku houses a number of designer boutiques.

Bell Commons (☎ 3475 8121) **Map 4** One of the more famous of Aoyama's boutique buildings is right on the corner of Killer-dōri.

In Shibuya (Map 4), the Mark City Shibuya, Parco stores, Seibu, Seibu Seed and the 109 building are all rated highly by shoppers with style.

Venus Fort (☎ 3599 0700) **Map 6** Down in Ōdaiba, this place is a marvel. A collection of 137 boutiques and restaurants are all aimed at young women. Set in a building that mimics 17th-century Rome, it comes complete with marble fountains, illuminated ceilings that constantly change colour, and Japan's biggest lavatory (64 stalls with the promise 'you'll never need to wait in line'). Perfect for the credit-card-toting Renaissance Woman, and pretty good fun for the rest of us too. A good English pamphlet is available.

The high prices asked for new kimonos (¥100,000 and up) and other traditional Japanese clothing make second-hand shops the best option. Both the Oriental Bazaar and the basement of the Hanae Mori building in Harajuku are good places to look (see the Arts, Crafts & Antiques section). If you've got money to burn and are set on getting a new kimono or a similar item, check the big department stores like Isetan and Seibu. In March and September, there are big sales of rental kimonos at Daimaru. January and July are generally the other big sales months for the retail industry. Also look for the bargain sales listing in the *Tokyo Journal* to learn what off-season sales are on.

Western-Size Clothes If you require large-size shoes and clothes (which by Japanese standards means shoes over 27cm in length and anything long enough to fit a person over 180cm tall) the first rule is: get

it before you come. If, by some unlucky turn of events, you need something new while you're here, the best advice is to avoid the regular stores altogether – they don't have the larger sizes in stock.

This leaves two choices. If you're in town long enough, you can order from an overseas company. Two mail-order companies with Tokyo numbers are REI (☎ 5424 3471) and LL Bean (☎ 5350 8801). Or, you can visit one of Tokyo's big-and-tall stores.

Perche (☎ 5467 5586) **Map 4** Shibuya's Perche has a good selection of large shoes and clothes. Don't expect any bargains, however, as large-size items tend to be about double the price of comparable regular-size ones.

Computers

Tokyo is not the world's cheapest place to buy computers. Prices tend to be higher here than in Hong Kong, Taiwan and Singapore – and higher even than in the West. However, second-hand equipment is usually in good shape.

Linc Computer (☎ 3409 6510) **Map 4** Try giving this shop in Shibuya a ring. English is spoken and there's a wide range of computers, both Apple and PC, and software.

T Zone Computers (☎ 3257 2650) **Map 3** In west Shinjuku, you can check out T Zone's good selection of software, computer goods and new computers at prices about average for Tokyo.

Electronics

Ideally, you should have an idea of prices back home or in other places on your travel agenda before you buy any electronic goods in Tokyo. Nevertheless, there are some good bargains, and Akihabara (Map 8) is the place to get them. The range of products is mind boggling, but before you rush into buying remember that most Japanese companies use the domestic market as a testing ground. Many products end their days in Japan without ever making it onto overseas markets. This may pose difficulties if you take something home and later need to have a fault repaired. Check the voltage, too. Some larger stores (Laox is a reliable option) have tax-free sections with export models for sale. For audio goods, try Laox or Shintoku Echo; for TV and video, Hirose Musen has a good selection that includes export models.

Though it is unusual to find prices that match those of dealers in Hong Kong or Singapore, you should be able to knock 10% off the marked prices by bargaining in Akihabara. To find the shops, take the 'Electric Town' exit at Akihabara station. You will see the sign on the platform if you come in on the Yamanote line.

Food & Alcohol

Japanese food and alcohol are often overlooked as souvenir choices. Check out any of the food floors of the larger department stores for a great selection of things like Japanese tea, sweets, spices and alcohol. While *sake* tends to be an acquired taste, folks back home will usually be delighted by a bottle of good Japanese *ume-shu* (plum wine). As for spices, traditional Japanese ones should please anyone interested in cooking. The best choices are *shichimi* (a mix of seven spices) and *sanshō* (a three spice mix). These can be bought in interesting bamboo dispensers, which can be recycled as salt and pepper shakers (full of spice these can be had for less than ¥2000 at department stores). Japanese tea also comes in interesting containers and makes a great gift item.

Japanese Dolls

Edo-dōri, next to the Toei Asakusa line, is the place to go if you're interested in Japanese dolls. Both sides of the road have many shops specialising in traditional Japanese dolls as well as their contemporary counterparts. This is actually an area for retailers to buy their goods, so the prices should be substantially lower than buying in the department stores. It's also acceptable to bargain a little.

Yoshitoku (☎ 3863 4419) Doll-maker to the Emperor, this place next to exit A2 of Asakusabashi JR station has been in business here since 1711. It's possible to buy a smaller piece for around ¥2000. For the larger ones? The sky's the limit.

Kids' Stuff

The Japanese are an inventive lot; consequently Tokyo can be a wonderful place to pick up toys and games.

Loft (☎ 3462 3807) **Map 4** This Shibuya shop has a great selection of wacky kids' stuff.

Kiddyland (☎ 3409 3431) **Map 4** In Harajuku, Kiddyland has five floors of products that your children would probably be better off not knowing about.

Hakuhinkan Toy Park (☎ 3571 8008) **Map 7** Along similar lines is this place in Ginza. It claims to be the biggest toy shop in Japan, and even has a theatre and restaurants on its upper floors.

Pearls

It was in Japan that cultured pearls were first developed, and pearls are still cheaper here than in many other parts of the world.

Mikimoto Pearl (☎ 3535 5511) **Map 7** In Ginza, this is perhaps the most famous of Tokyo's pearl shops. It was founded by the man who first developed the cultured pearl, Mikimoto Kokichi, and has been running since 1899. It's next to Wakō department store, opposite Mitsukoshi.

Takasaki Shinju (☎ 5561 8880) Another store worth your while checking out is this one in Akasaka.

Washi (Japanese Paper)

Japanese hand-made paper is one of the cheaper and more interesting souvenir possibilities. A sheet of colourfully dyed paper about 1m square can often be bought for ¥1000 or less. Most people find this paper too beautiful for writing on, and wind up using is as a decoration or as wrapping paper.

Haibara (☎ 3272 3801) **Map 8** This place in Ginza stocks a good selection of *washi*. All the major department stores also have a section devoted to washi.

Itoya (☎ 3561 8311) **Map 7** Open 9.30am-7pm Mon-Sat, to 6pm Sun. Also in Ginza, Itoya has nine floors of every kind of stationery item you can imagine. What's more, it stocks washi. You can also get things printed or copied here.

Ideas

If you're at a loss for what to buy, here are a few suggestions.

Odds & Ends *Tsukiji External Market* **Map 7** Open all day Mon-Sat, closed Sun and holidays. One fascinating place which offers the imaginative souvenir hunter a wide range of inexpensive Japanese goods is this place, also known as 'Tsukijijō-gaishijō', outside the Tsukiji Central Fish Market. There are hundreds of little stalls here selling pottery, cooking equipment, food supplies, baskets and cutlery for a fraction of the prices charged by department stores.

Another area to explore for ideas is Asakusa's Kappabashi-dōri (Map 9), where all manner of restaurant and gourmet tools and supplies are sold wholesale.

Comics & Books Fans of *manga* comics might want to pick up some used ones in the bookstores of Jimbōchō (Map 8) in the Kanda area. Several shops here specialise in used manga. You can choose from valuable 1st edition classics and more common editions that can be had for less that ¥100. You can also find a wide range of old Japanese calendars, postcards and picture books. Tuttle editions of translated Japanese novels and poetry can make nice gifts as well.

For information on bookshops which sell a range of English-language texts from art to Zen, see the Tokyo Bookshops boxed text in the Facts for the Visitor chapter.

Traditional Clothes & Crafts For a variety of traditional Japanese clothes and craft items, the shopping arcade known as Hisago-dōri (Map 9), just north of Rokku-Broadway-dōri in Asakusa, is an excellent choice.

Takumi Crafts Gallery (☎ 3842 1990). See displays on the history and production of Shitamachi crafts, and browse through the traditional goods for sale. The stores alongside the gallery sell *happi* (half-length coats), *yukata* (summer-weight kimonos), *geta* (wooden shoes), and a whole range of crafts from combs to writing supplies.

Offbeat Items For non-traditional and off-the-wall gift ideas, head to Shibuya (Map 4).

Tōkyū Hands (☎ 5489 5111) Open 10am-8pm, closed the second and third Wed of every month. Tōkyū Hands is the do-it-yourself capital of Tokyo, selling everything from sewing repair kits to chainsaws. The toy department is certainly also worth a browse. There's a branch in Ikebukuro too.

Seibu's Loft store (☎ 3462 3807) This store offers an enormous range of goodies that most sensible people would never even consider shopping for (there is also a branch in Ikebukuro).

Axis building (☎ 3587 2781) **Map 7** Open 11am-7pm Mon-Sat. This complex in Roppongi is an excellent place to catch up on some of Japan's most innovative design ideas and interior design goods. Comprising 20 or so retail shops and galleries, it's on Gaien-higashi-dōri.

Wrapping It Up

So where do you get all these goodies wrapped up to give to the folks back home?

Tsutsumu Factory (☎ 5478 1330) **Map 4** Tsutsumu means 'to wrap' in Japanese and this store in Shibuya is devoted entirely to wrapping things up. Choose your materials and the staff will do the wrapping for you.

Excursions

Tokyo may be a tangled sprawl of express-ways, railway lines, office buildings and housing estates, but an hour or so away by train are some of Japan's best travel destinations. The places in this chapter can be visited as day trips, although in several cases an overnight stay is worthwhile.

Foremost among these is Nikkō, which is a must-see on any trip to Tokyo. Kamakura's peaceful temples are a lovely break from the big city; Hakone and the Mt Fuji region can provide magnificent views of Mt Fuji.

Fans of modern architecture, the World Cup and John Lennon will want to take the short train ride out to Saitama Shintoshin, home to the **Saitama Super Arena** and the controversial **John Lennon Museum**.

Most other destinations around Tokyo are less interesting to short-term visitors, despite heavy promotion by the Tourist Information Center (TIC). Izu-hantō and Dogashima are pleasant retreats from Tokyo, but they are geared to Japanese tourists – with entry fees, roped walkways and orderly queues.

The three main tour operators with English guides are Sunrise Tours (☎ 03-5260 9500), Gray Line Tours (☎ 03-3433 5745) and Odakyu Q-Tours (03-5321 7887). Some Sunrise one-day deals (including lunch) are Mt Fuji and Hakone (¥12,000), Nikkō (¥13,500) and Kamakura (¥13,000). Q-Tours do Kamakura (¥6,800) and Hakone (¥9,500). They depart from Shinjuku station's west exit.

YOKOHAMA 横浜

☎ 045 • pop 3.38 million

One hundred and fifty years ago Yokohama was mud-flats. Today it's Japan's second-largest city. Yokohama's fortunes are very much those of modern Japan. It was opened to foreign trade in 1858; in 1872 the city's first railway was laid, connecting it with Tokyo. By the early 20th century the city had embarked on a course of industrialisation. Nowadays its massive port facilities are complemented by huge steel-making, automobile, oil refining and chemical industries.

For the Japanese, its close proximity to the sea and international trading connections have lent it a certain cosmopolitan sheen and made it a popular tourist destination.

Attractions that appeal to Western visitors include Chinatown, the greenery of Sankei-en and the Minato Mirai 21 complex. Also worth a look is the elegant 860m Yokohama Bay Bridge, south of Yamashita-kōen. It is also home to an interesting, off-the-beaten-track tattoo museum, run by a legendary tattoo master – see the boxed text 'Horiyoshi' for more information.

Despite its fame, Yokohama is best considered a lower priority for visitors to Tokyo – Kamakura, Nikkō and Hakone are far more worthwhile day trips.

Orientation

Arriving in Yokohama can be slightly confusing. Most sights are on the harbour-front, quite a way from Yokohama station. It makes more sense to go to Sakuragi-chō, Kannai or Ishikawa-chō station. From Sakuragi-chō station the Minato Mirai 21 development, with the enormous Landmark Tower, is 5 minutes away by moving walkway. Kannai station is closer to Yamashita-kōen, the harbour area and a number of sights, like the Silk Museum. Ishikawa-chō station is convenient for the fashionable Motomachi shopping district, Chinatown and the Foreigners' Cemetery.

Information

The Tourist Information Center (☎ 211 0111), open from 9am to 6pm, is in front of the north exit of Sakuragi-chō station. The English speakers here give excellent information. Make sure to pick up their *English Map of Yokohama*. It's also worth picking up a copy of the TIC's excellent *Yokohama* handout before leaving Tokyo.

There's a Citibank with a 24-hour ATM outside the western exit of Yokohama station

Cherry blossom viewing – Ueno-kōen park

Street scene in Shinjuku

Shinjuku-gyoen blossoms

Stone statues of Jizō – guardian of travellers and children – at Zōjō-ji temple

Well-positioned advertising

Tunnel of orange *torii* (gates) at Hie-jinja shrine – Akasaka

Urban *samurai* negotiate Tokyo traffic

Postures and gestures take on new meanings in *nō* drama

King Kong *pachinko* parlour

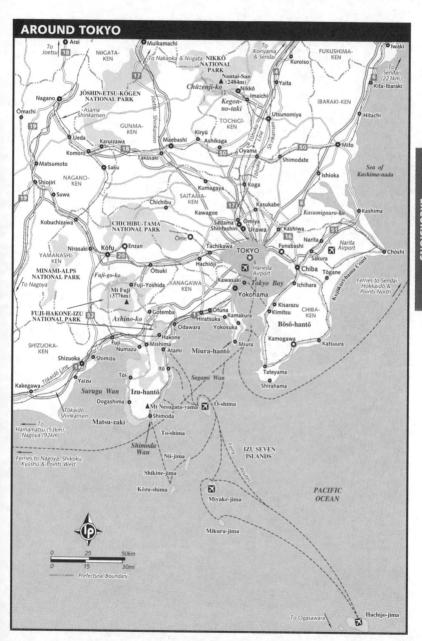

AROUND TOKYO

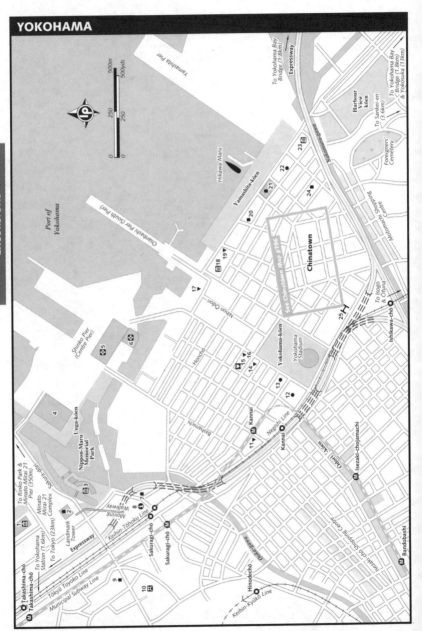

YOKOHAMA

EXCURSIONS

YOKOHAMA

PLACES TO STAY

2 Yokohama Royal Park
Hotel Nikkō
横浜ロイヤルパーク
ホテルニッコー

7 Sakuragi-cho
Washington Hotel
桜木町ワシントン
ホテル

9 Kanagawa Youth
Hostel
神奈川ユース
ホステル

20 Hotel Yokohama
ホテルヨコハマ

21 Hotel New Grand
ホテルニュー
グランド

24 Yokohama
International
Seaman's Hall
海員会館

PLACES TO EAT

11 Victoria Station
ビクトリア
ステーション

14 Pot Luck Bar
ポットラック

16 Baiko Emmie's
梅香亭

17 Suginoki; Scandia
杉の木

19 Parkside Gourmet
Plaza
パークサイドグルメ

OTHER

1 Yokohama Museum
of Art
横浜美術館

3 Yokohama Maritime
Museum
横浜マリタイム
ミュージアム

4 Yokohama Cosmo
World
横浜コスモワールド

5 Yokohama World
Porters
横浜ワールド
ポーターズ

6 Navio
ナヴィオ

8 Tourist Information
観光案内所

10 Iseyama-jinja
伊勢山神社

12 Yokohama City Hall
横浜市役所

13 JTB Travel Agent

15 Cape Cod Bar
ケープコッド

18 Silk Museum
シルク博物館

22 Marine Tower
マリンタワー

23 Ningyo-no-ie
人形の家

25 Empei-mon
延平門

東京 東京 東京 東京 東京 東京 東京 東京 東京 東京 東京 東京 東京 東京 東京

on the 2nd floor of the First Building, which is on the south-west side of the Yokohama Bay Sheraton.

Sankei-en

This lakeside garden (☎ 621 0635; admission ¥300; open 9am-4.30pm) is foremost among Yokohama's attractions. It's beautifully landscaped, featuring a three-storey pagoda that is 500 years old. The No 8 or 25 bus, from the road running parallel to the harbour behind the Marine Tower, operates with less than commendable frequency; but if one does happen along, ask for Honmoku Sankei-en-mae. Sankei-en is also accessible from JR Negishi station, where you can catch a bus bound for Sakuragi-chō (No 54, 58, 99, 101 or 108).

Minato Mirai 21

The '21' stands for '21st century', and this complex (☎ 222 5015; admission ¥1000; open 10am-9pm Mon-Fri & Sun, 10am-10pm Sat, 10am-10pm daily July-Aug)

represents Yokohama's vision of its future. Its most impressive feature is the Landmark Tower (296m), the tallest building in Japan, complete with the world's fastest lift and a viewing platform on the 69th floor.

Chinatown

Close to the harbour is Yokohama's Chinatown, the largest in Japan. 'Chūkagai', as it's known, is an interesting area in which to stroll and absorb the slightly synthetic ambience. But the best reason to come is to sample the excellent Chinese food.

To get there, go to Ishikawa-chō station, exit and head north along the tracks about 100m before heading east toward the harbour. You'll soon see Empei-mon. Pass through and continue straight; Chinatown is about 200m ahead.

Other Sights

Clustered around the Landmark Tower are a number of attractions. One of the best is the **Yokohama Maritime Museum** (☎ 211 1923;

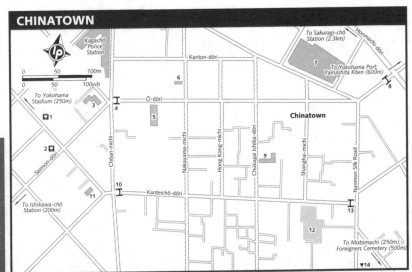

CHINATOWN

CHINATOWN

1 The Tavern
2 Windjammer
3 Taishinrō
　太新楼
4 Zenrin-mon
　善隣門
5 Kanton Hanten
　広東飯店
6 Raishanson
　苓香尊

7 Hotel Holiday Inn
　Yokohama;
　Jūkeihanten
　ホテルホリデーイン
　横浜；重慶飯店
8 Higashi-mon
　東門
9 Suuroku Saikan
　Shinkan
　四五六菜館新館

10 Jikyū-mon
　地久門
11 Keifukurō
　慶福楼
12 Yamashitachō-kōen
　山下町公園
13 Tenchō-mon
　天長門
14 Garlic Jo's

admission ¥600; open 10am-5pm Tues-Sun), which houses the handsome *Nippon Maru* sailing ship.

Another great attraction is **Cosmo World Amusement Park** (☎ 641 6591; *price varies according to ride; open 1pm-9pm Mon-Fri, 11am-10pm Sat & Sun*). Cosmo World features the world's second-highest Ferris wheel, Cosmo Clock. It was knocked into second spot only recently by the big feller in Ōdaiba.

The **Yokohama Museum of Art** (☎ 221 0300; *admission ¥500; open 10am-5pm, closed Thur*) is devoted to modern art.

Near Yamashita-kōen, the **Marine Tower** (☎ 641 7838; *admission ¥700; open 10am-9pm*) is a 1960s lighthouse offering an unimpressive viewing platform.

The **Silk Museum** (☎ 641 0841; *admission ¥300; open 9am-4.30pm Tues-Sun*) deals with every aspect of silk and silk production with Japanese thoroughness.

Yamashita-kōen (*admission free; open 24 hours*) itself is an average park; next to it is the *Hikawa Maru* (☎ 641 4361; *admission ¥800; open 9.30am-10pm*), a passenger liner that you can board and explore. There's a beer garden.

All You Need Is Cash

The small crowd of reverential visitors is ushered into a tiny auditorium, the lights dim, the curtains part and the strains of John Lennon's ballad 'Love' fill the room. A projector clatters into life and a familiar face appears on the screen, but it's not that of Liverpool's most beloved and notorious flop-top son. Rather, it's the owner of the Lennon copyright, and now the merchandiser of the Lennon myth, Yoko Ono. Welcome to the John Lennon Museum Incorporated.

Many Beatle devotees in the West have long, and probably unfairly, pilloried John's widow as the woman responsible for Fab Four's demise. Her decision, as owner of the Lennon estate and curator of this museum, to construct this would-be mausoleum out in the sticks in Saitama, not Merseyside or even Hamburg, will have won her no extra supporters. She defended her decision at the John Lennon fan Web site (W www.instantkarma.com/iknews_091900_museum.html) by claiming that the organisers are 'responsible and good people…this is the card that's been dealt to us now'.

The card dealer is none other than corporate giant Taisei (construction, real estate), and the JLM is a calculated, corporate, merchandising exercise, make no mistake. It is set on the 4th and 5th floors of the brand-spanking-new, architecturally spectacular Saitama Super Arena (see also the 'Soccer World' boxed text in the Facts for the Visitor chapter) and from the moment you cough up the hefty entrance fee to the moment you spill out into the ubiquitous souvenir shop (Roll up! Get your 'War Is Over' toothbrush holder here) there's a pervading sense that we're being spoon-fed a sanitised version of history.

Divided into nine zones ranging from childhood history, through The Beatles, Imagine, The Lost Weekend and, er, House Husband, the major landmarks of John's life – carefully edited for minimum offence – are delineated. However, there are several notable omissions. His caustic and often controversial wit – Beatles Bigger than Jesus, and the Nazi salute on the steps of Liverpool Town Hall to a crowd of 200,000 – receive no mention. Tellingly John Lennon's first wife, Cynthia Powell, has been Yoko'd out of the picture altogether.

Yet for the tourist, the Beatle nut, the casual student of 20th-century pop history, and the visiting youths and grandmas of Tokyo's dormitory towns, there are rewards here. One of the scurrilous 'newspaper' articles John wrote in junior school, in 1952, contains some lovely Goon-show-style dialogue – 'Our late editor is dead, he died of death, which killed him', and 'Four thousand Hindu carrots have been found eaten by the dreaded IRA', a line you could almost slip into 'A Day in the Life'. There's mildly diverting Japanese memorabilia from his time spent with Yoko in Karuizawa, an excellent Mickey Mouse watch, his JCB credit card 'for use in Japan only' and his lacquered Yamaha Dragon custom folk guitar.

And the visitors lap it up, right down to the Shrimp and Watercress Shiffonard with Strawberry Sauce in the restaurant designed to mimic John's fave hostelry in Karuizawa. It is a museum for the 21st century, stylishly built, seamlessly marketed, and undoubtedly it will pay its way.

But what would Fred and Alice's lad have made of it all? Is this Lennon Cloud Cuckoo Land, scripted by a revisionist widow, paid for by Japan Inc and aimed at Tokyo's suburban mass-market? Or is it a suitable epitaph for the man who, when once asked what he'd do when Beatlemania subsided, answered 'Count the money'?

John Lennon Museum (☎ 048-601 0009; W www.taisei.co.jp/museum/index_e.html; admission ¥1500; open 11am-6pm, closed Tues) is a few minutes' walk from Saitama Shintoshin station on the JR Keihin Tohoku, Utsunomiya and Takasaki lines, around 40 minutes from central Tokyo.

東京 東京 東京 東京 東京 東京 東京 東京 東京 東京 東京 東京 東京 東京 東京 東京

Harbour cruises operate from the pier next to the *Hikawa Maru* and take from 40 minutes (¥900) to 1½ hours (¥2000).

Close to the Marine Tower, the **Yokohama Doll Museum** (☎ 671 9361; admission ¥300; open 10am-5pm Tues-Sun) has

EXCURSIONS

Horiyoshi

LPP

Tucked away in the backstreets of Yokohama is the studio of one of Japan's greatest living artists. He is known as Yoshihito Nakano to his mum, but to those in the shadowy world in which he is the unparalleled master, he is Horiyoshi III. Horiyoshi is a *horishi* tattooist. An amiable, gentle character, he peers through thick glasses as he crafts the outline of a demon onto the thigh of a prostrate *yakuza*, using the ancient technique of *tebori*, tattooing by hand. His tattoos are all drawn freehand, representing the pantheon of Japanese and Chinese religious and mythological heroes and villains.

Horiyoshi's fame has taken him to tattoo conventions the world over, and brings a small stream of acolytes to his two studios and the small museum, the *name*, that he and his wife Mayumi run in Yokohama's Nishi-ku. A small space, crowded with the paraphernalia of tattooing from Ainu to Oceania, it's worth a visit for avid tattoo fans; but the real attraction is to meet the master himself, who will gladly chat in his best English about his art. You can even get emblazoned with a hero from *Suikoden*, the Water Margin, his depictions of which are the subject of a limited-edition artbook to be published by Nihon Shuppansha in Autumn 2001. But start saving now. His upper body pieces range from ¥1000,000 to a cool ¥8000,000.

Bunshi Rekishi Shiryokan (☎ 045-323 1073; admission ¥1000; open noon-7pm, closed Fri & 10th of each month) is a few minutes' walk from Tobe station on the Keihin Kyūko line, five minutes by *futsu* slow train (¥130) from Yokohama station. Cross the road in front of the station's only exit, walk past the fire station and turn left at the next corner, alongside the police station. Cross a small river and the museum is 100m ahead of you, on the right.

東京 東京 東京 東京 東京 東京 東京 東京 東京 東京 東京 東京 東京 東京 東京

1200 dolls and puppets from countries all around the world.

Just beyond the expressway and in the Yamate hill area is the **Harbour View Park** *(admission free; open dawn till dusk)* and, close by, the **Foreigners' Cemetery** *(admission free; open dawn till dusk)*, containing the sombre graves of more than 4000 foreigners. This area is best reached by walking through the trendy Motomachi shopping street from Ishikawa-chō station.

The sprawling **Yokohama Hakkeijima Sea Paradise** (☎ 788 8888; admission free, most entertainment ¥500-1000; open 8.30am-10.30pm) complex has a great aquarium, amusement park rides, restaurant areas, upmarket shopping – even a yacht harbour and expensive accommodation. The complex is best reached from Minato Mirai 21 pier by the Paradise Line Ferry (¥2000). Or, take the Keihin-Kyūkō line to Kanazawa-hakkei station, change to the Kanazawa Seaside Line and get off at Hakkeijima.

The gargantuan **Wild Blue Yokohama** (☎ 511 2323; adults/students/children ¥3900/ 3100/2600; open 10am-9pm) is a water sports park. Unlike many such parks around Tokyo, it is open year-round. Attractions include surfing on artificial waves, water slides and artificial rivers. It can be reached by shuttle bus from Tsurumi station on the Keihin-Tōhoku line.

Shin-Yokohama Rāmen Hakubutsukan (☎ 471 0503; admission ¥300; open 11am-11pm) is a noodle-nut's paradise. The museum is a kind of *rāmen* theme park that tells the history of the cuisine – and houses, in a replica of 1958 Shitamachi, eight rāmen shops run by masters of the trade from across the country. Currently the most popular eatery is **Sumire**. A bowl of rāmen costs around ¥900. Avoid this place on public holidays unless you want to wait in line for up to 70 minutes. It's a seven-minute walk from Shin-Yokohama station and is clearly signposted in English.

Places to Stay

It makes most sense to visit Yokohama from Tokyo, as the longest the journey will take is 40 minutes. Those determined to make a night of it will generally find Yokohama accommodation either expensive or inconveniently located.

Kanagawa Youth Hostel (☎ *241 6503*) Beds ¥2730. This is your cheapest option. From Sakuragi-chō station, exit on the opposite side to the harbour, turn right and follow the road alongside the railway tracks. Cross the main road and turn left into the steep street with a bridge and cobblestoned section. The youth hostel is up the road on the right.

Most other accommodation is aimed at business travellers. These hotels are located near Yamashita-kōen.

Yokohama International Seamen's Hall (☎ *681 2358, fax 681 2032*) Singles/doubles ¥7350/10,920. Handily placed spot not just for salty types – anyone can stay. It's bar gets quite noisy.

Hotel Yokohama (☎ *662 1321, fax 662 3536*) Singles/doubles/twins from ¥13,000/18,000/26,000 (rooms without a seaside view are slightly less). This is an upmarket option by the waterfront.

Hotel New Grand (☎ *681 1841, fax 681 1895*). Singles/doubles ¥12,000/20,000. It's not new but it is quite grand, having occupied its harbourside location since 1920. Price includes breakfast.

Sakuragi-chō Washington Hotel (☎ *683 3111, fax 683 3112*). Singles/doubles ¥9500/16000. Smack dab in front of Sakuragi-chō station, this new upmarket business hotel is a convenient, if unremarkable, option. Its prices go up on Saturdays.

Places to Eat

Chinatown is undoubtedly the place for a meal in Yokohama. Front window displays are common in the many restaurants, and long queues of patient Japanese pinpoint the best places.

Kanton Hanten (☎ *681 7676*) Servings ¥500. A good spot for dim-sum (*yumu-cha* or *ten-shin* in Japanese). Order from a wide selection of small dishes including dumplings, fried *yuba* rolls and sliced pork. While dim-sum is traditionally a Sunday lunch meal in China, here you can try it all day, every day.

Daichinrō (☎ *681 3277*) Servings ¥800. Across from Zenrin-mon; look for a gaudy Chinese-style facade with steamed dumplings and buns for sale outside. Its yumu-cha course takes the pain out of ordering and includes eight small servings of dim-sum and your choice of Chinese tea.

Suuroku Saikan Shinkan (☎ *664 4569*) Servings ¥600. There are nine varieties of dumplings here. Try the *fukahire* (shark fin) dumpling or the *shūmai* with crab and pork filling.

Raishanson (☎ *651 5055*) Lunch specials ¥1000, dinner ¥4000. A good, unpretentious choice for varied sets of Cantonese at reasonable prices.

Keifukurō (☎ *681 5256*) Mains ¥4000. Good Beijing-style cooking in casual surroundings. A large picture menu displays spicy fried beef, sweet-and-sour frog legs etc.

Jūkeihanten (☎ *641 8288*) Lunch ¥4000, dinner up to ¥10,000. Jūkeihanten is more upmarket, and located in the Hotel Holiday Inn Yokohama (3rd floor). Try the delicious sliced pork with spicy Shisen-style sauce.

Garlic Jo's (☎ *629 5222*) Mains ¥3000. A great place to eat as long as you don't have a date later.

Yokohama's reputation doesn't just rest on Chinese food – the area between Kannai station and Yamashita-kōen is packed with bars, coffee shops and restaurants. Good for wandering.

Baiko Emmie's (☎ *681 4870*) Servings ¥750. Closed Sun. A wonderful little place, with its rather touching sign outside promising 'English spoken'. Established in 1924, it was moved to its current spot in the '50s. Try the *hayashi* or curry rice.

Pot Luck (☎ *662 0525*) Mains ¥1500. For salads, fries and the like, call into this American-style kitchen (complete with a Budweiser sign outside); the 'trucker salad' is enough for three.

Victoria Station (☎ *631 0393*) Mains ¥1500. The Yokohama branch of Victoria Station is another good salad-and-steak stop.

Yamashita-kōen also has some interesting options, though much is Western food at marked-up prices. Go at lunch for some good specials.

Scandia (☎ *201 2262*) Mains ¥2000. Just across the road from the Silk Museum, this is probably the only Danish restaurant in Japan.

Suginoki (☎ *212 4143*) Mains ¥1500. Around the corner, Suginoki serves what it alleges is Spanish cuisine for reasonable prices.

In the Yokohama station area, try the *basement mall* that leads out from the station or the 10th floor of Sogō department store. In Sakuragi-chō the Yokohama World Porters, Navio and Landmark Tower building all teem with eateries.

Entertainment
Some of the city's best bars are on the edge of Chinatown. The bar-restaurant *Windjammer* (☎ *662 3966*) is a good spot for a few drinks and the occasional live jazz (for which you'll pay a ¥300 'music charge'). Far rowdier is the *Mission to Seamen*, the International Seaman's Hall bar, which has cheap beer and billiards.

There are two good bars in the centre of town: *Cape Cod* (☎ *661 0700*), which attracts a lot of foreigners, and *Bar Bar Bar* (☎ *662 6868*). The latter has a long saloon-style bar on the 1st floor and live music upstairs.

Getting There & Away
There are numerous trains from Tokyo, the cheapest being the Tōkyū Tōyoko line from Shibuya station to Sakuragi-chō station for ¥290. The trip takes 44 minutes by ordinary train and 35 minutes by limited express (same price).

The Keihin-Tōhoku line goes to Yokohama (¥450) and Kannai (¥540) stations from Tokyo and Shinagawa stations. If you only want to go as far as Yokohama station, you can save 10 minutes by taking the Tōkaidō line from Tokyo, Shimbashi or Shinagawa stations (¥470, 30 minutes).

The Yokosuka line can also take you from Tokyo, Shimbashi or Shinagawa station to Yokohama station. This is a convenient line to continue on to Kamakura from Yokohama (¥330). There is also a *shinkansen* connection to the Kansai region at Shin-Yokohama station, a fair way to the north-east of town.

Getting Around
Shin-Yokohama station connects to Yokohama, Sakuragi-chō and Kannai stations via the Yokohama municipal subway line. Yokohama, Sakuragi-chō and Kannai stations are also linked via the JR Negishi line. Buses around town cost a flat ¥210 each trip; a day pass costs ¥600.

KAMAKURA 鎌倉
☎ 0467 • pop 181,000
Kamakura had a spell of glory as the nation's capital from 1192 to 1333. The Minamoto and later the Hōjo clans ruled Japan from Kamakura for more than a century, until finally in 1333, weakened by the heavy cost of maintaining defences against threats of attack from Kublai Khan in China, the Hōjo clan fell from power at the hands of the forces of Emperor Go-Daigo. Though the restoration of imperial authority was somewhat illusory, the capital nevertheless shifted back to Kyoto and Kamakura disappeared from the history books.

Today Kamakura may not offer as much as Kyoto or Nara, but a wealth of notable temples and shrines make it one of Tokyo's most rewarding day trips. The town offers relaxing walks and a peacefulness that is hard to come by in Kyoto, where the sights are so often swamped with tourists.

Orientation & Information
The sights are spread over a fairly wide area, although most of them can be visited by foot. At worst you may have to catch a bus. There's not much chance of getting lost, however, as the temples are well signposted in English and Japanese. Pick up the Tokyo TIC's *Hakone and Kamakura* pamphlet, which has details on transport and some of the attractions. There is a TIC at the east exit of Kamakura station.

Things to See

Kita-Kamakura Station Area The best route is to start at Kita-Kamakura station and visit the temples between there and Kamakura on foot. As you exit the station, there are vendors selling useful bi-lingual maps.

Engaku-ji *(admission ¥200; open 8am-5pm)* is on your left as you exit Kita-Kamakura station. It is one of the five main Rinzai Zen temples in Kamakura, and dates from 1282.

Across the railway tracks from Engaku-ji is **Tōkei-ji** *(admission ¥100; open 8.30am-5pm)*, notable for its grounds as much as for the temple itself. On weekdays, when there are few visitors, it can be a very relaxing place. Walk up to the cemetery and wander around. Women were once officially recognised as divorced if they spent three years as nuns here.

A couple of minutes further from Tōkei-ji is **Jōchi-ji** *(admission ¥100; open 9am-4.30pm)*, another temple with tranquil surroundings. Founded in 1283, this is considered one of Kamakura's five great Zen temples.

Kenchō-ji *(admission ¥300; open 9am-4.30pm)* is about a 10-minute walk beyond Jōchi-ji. It is on the left after you pass through a tunnel. This is not only Kamakura's most important Zen temple but something of a showcase generally. The grounds and the buildings are well maintained and still in use. The first of the main buildings, the Buddha Hall, was moved to its present site and reassembled in 1647. The second building, the Hall of Law, is used for *zazen* meditation. Further back is the Dragon King Hall, a Chinese-style building with a garden to its rear. The temple bell, the second largest in Kamakura, is a 'National Treasure'.

Across the road from Kenchō-ji is **Ennō-ji** *(admission ¥300; open 9am-4pm)*, distinguished primarily by its collection of statues depicting the judges of hell.

Further down the road is **Tsurugaoka Hachiman-gū**. Hachiman, the deity to whom this shrine is dedicated, is both the god of war and the guardian deity of the Minamoto clan. It's a dramatic contrast to the quiet repose of the Zen temples around Kita-Kamakura station. Notice the gingko tree at the foot of the stairs leading to the square. An assassination was carried out beneath it in 1219, making it one very old tree. Nearby, the steeply arched bridge was once reserved for the passage of the *shōgun* alone.

The **National Treasure Museum** *(☎ 0467-22 0753; admission ¥150; open 9am-4pm Tues-Sun)* is recommended, as it is a unique opportunity to see Kamakura art, most of which is cloistered away in temples.

Kamakura Station Area Apart from Hachiman-gū, there aren't any sites of historic importance in the immediate vicinity; most places require a short bus trip from in front of the station. The most worthwhile trip is to the Great Buddha.

The **Daibutsu** *(Great Buddha; admission ¥200; open 7am-5.30pm)* was completed in 1252 and is Kamakura's most famous sight. Once housed in a huge hall, the statue today sits in the open, its home having been washed away by a *tsunami* (tidal wave) in 1495. Cast in bronze and weighing close to 850 tonnes, the statue is 11.4m tall. Its construction was inspired by the even bigger Daibutsu in Nara, though it is generally agreed that the Kamakura version is artistically superior. To get there, take a bus from the No 2, 7 or 10 bus stop in front of Kamakura station to Daibutsu-mae bus stop.

Back towards Kamakura station and right at the intersection where the bus goes left is the small street leading to **Hase-dera** *(Hase Kannon-dō Temple; admission ¥300; open 8am-4.30pm)*. There is a garden and an interesting collection of statues of Jizō, the protector of travellers and souls of departed children. The main point of interest, however, is its **Kannon statue**.

Kannon is the goddess of mercy, and her compassion is often invoked as a source of succour to the bereaved and aggrieved. The 9m wooden *jūichimen* (11-faced Kannon) is believed to date from the 8th century. The 11 faces are actually one major face and 10 minor faces, the latter representing 10 stages of enlightenment.

EXCURSIONS

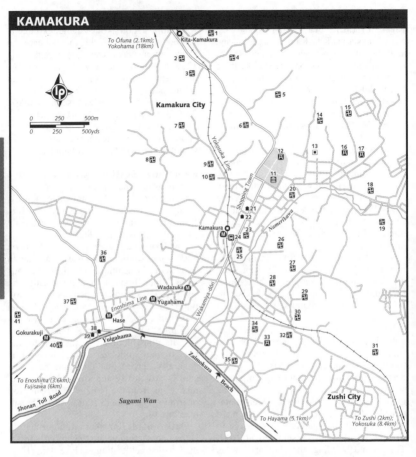

KAMAKURA

To Ōfuna (2.1km);
Yokohama (18km)

Kita-Kamakura

Kamakura City

Yokosuka Line

Kamakura

Shopping Town

Namerikawa

Wadazuka

Enoshima Line

Yugahama

Hase

Gokurakuji

Yuigahama

Wakamiya-dōri

Zaimokuza Beach

To Enoshima (3.6km);
Fujisawa (6km)

Shonan Toll Road

Sugami Wan

Zushi City

To Hayama (5.1km)

To Zushi (2km);
Yokosuka (8.4km)

Unfortunately, though the hall containing this statue is open to the public, the statue itself is normally off-limits.

Other Shrines & Temples There are something like 70 temples and shrines (the Kamakura map indicates the main ones) around this area. From the Great Buddha, it's best to return to Kamakura station by bus and take another bus out to the less-touristy temples in the eastern part of town.

Egara Ten-jin *(admission free; open dawn till dusk)* is popular with students, who pray here for academic success. Many write their academic aspirations on *ema* (small wooden plaques), which are then hung to the right of the shrine. Buses from stop No 6 in front of Kamakura station run out to Egara Ten-jin; get off at the Tenjin-mae bus stop.

Zuisen-ji *(admission ¥100; open 9am-5pm)* is a pleasant Zen temple which affords relaxing strolls through its gardens (laid out by the temple's founder, Musō Kokushi, during the Kamakura era). It's 15 minutes on foot from Egara Ten-jin; turn right where the bus turns left in front of the shrine, take the next left and keep following this road.

KAMAKURA

PLACES TO STAY

21 City Pension Shangri
   La
   シティーペンション
   シャングリラ
22 Tsurugaoka Kaikan
   Hotel
   鶴ヶ岡会館
38 BB House
   ＢＢハウス
39 Kamakura Kagetsuen
   Youth Hostel
   鎌倉花月園ユース
   ホステル

OTHER

1 Engaku-ji
   円覚寺
2 Tōkei-ji
   東慶寺
3 Jōchi-ji
   浄智寺
4 Meigetsu-in
   明月院
5 Kenchō-ji
   建長寺
6 Ennō-ji
   円応寺
7 Kaizō-ji
   海蔵寺
8 Zeniarai-benten
   銭洗弁天

9 Eishō-ji
   英勝寺
10 Jufuku-ji
   寿福寺
11 National Treasure
   Museum
   鎌倉国宝館
12 Hachiman-gū
   鶴岡八幡宮
13 Tomb of Minamoto
   Yoritomo
   源頼朝の墓
14 Raigō-ji
   来迎寺
15 Kakuen-ji
   覚園寺
16 Egara Tenjin
   荏柄天神
17 Kamakura-gū
   鎌倉宮
18 Sugimoto-dera
   杉本寺
19 Hōkoku-ji
   報国寺
20 Hōkai-ji
   宝戒寺
23 Daigyō-ji
   大巧寺
24 Bus Station
   バスターミナル
25 Hongaku-ji
   本覚寺

26 Myōhon-ji
   妙本寺
27 Daihō-ji
   大宝寺
28 Anyō-in
   安養院
29 Myōhō-ji
   妙法寺
30 Ankokuron-ji
   安国論寺
31 Hosshō-ji
   法性寺
32 Chōshō-ji
   長勝寺
33 Gosho-jinja
   五所神社
34 Myōchō-ji
   妙長寺
35 Kyūhin-ji
   九品寺
36 Daibutsu
   (Great Buddha)
   鎌倉大仏
37 Hase-dera
   長谷寺
40 Jÿju-in
   成就院
41 Gokuraku-ji
   極楽寺

EXCURSIONS

東京 東京 東京 東京 東京 東京 東京 東京 東京 東京 東京 東京 東京 東京 東京

Sugimoto-dera *(admission ¥200; open 8.30am-4.30pm),* founded in AD 734 by the Buddhist Tendai sect, is the oldest temple in Kamakura. Ferocious guardian figures are poised at the entrance and the main hall houses three Kannon statues, which are not quite on a par with the one at Hase-dera. To get there, take a bus from the No 5 bus stop in front of Kamakura station and get off at Sugimoto Kannon.

Hōkoku-ji *(admission ¥100; open 9am-4.30pm)* is down the road (away from Kamakura station) from Sugimoto-dera. This is a Rinzai Zen temple with quiet landscaped gardens where you can relax under a parasol with a cup of green tea. It regularly holds *zazen* meditation classes for beginners.

Places to Stay

Kamakura Kagetsuen Youth Hostel (☎/fax 0467-25 1238) Beds ¥3150 (membership required). You can walk to the hostel from Hase-dera or take an Enoden train to Hase station and walk five minutes south-west of the station (just north of the seafront). Breakfast costs ¥600.

BB House (☎/fax 0467-25 5859) Beds ¥5000 including breakfast. Not far from the youth hostel this place provides accommodation for women only.

City Pension Shangri La (☎ 0467-25 6363, fax 25 6456) Twins ¥6000. Look for the modern white building on the left as you walk up the road from the station. Four-person rooms go for economical rates.

Buddhism in Kamakura

Though Buddhism came to Japan in the 6th century AD, it was 500 years later, during the Kamakura period, that Buddhism spread to all of Japan. Initially the Kamakura period was marked by secular disillusionment with Buddhist institutions and the monastic orders, and a widespread belief that the world had entered Mappō (the Later Age), a period of Buddhist decline when individuals would no longer be able to achieve enlightenment through their own efforts alone. This led to the flourishing of alternatives to established Buddhist doctrine – notably Zen and the 'Pure Land' school of Buddhism.

The Pure Land school preached that in the Later Age salvation could only be achieved through devotion to the transcendent Buddha Amida – all who called on him sincerely would achieve salvation in the Pure Land after death. This populist stroke opened Buddhism in Japan to the masses, who had been largely excluded from the more esoteric branches of Buddhism. This also contrasted with Zen, which sought Buddhahood through meditative practice aimed at the empty centre of the self.

With its rigorous training and self-discipline, Zen found support among an ascendant warrior class and made a considerable contribution to the samurai ethic. Differences on the question of whether *satori* (enlightenment) could be attained suddenly or whether it was a gradual process accounted for Zen breaking into the Rinzai and Sōtō sects.

The contending schools of Pure Land and Zen, along with the views of charismatic leaders such as the influential 13th century priest Nichiren, led to revitalisation of Buddhism within Japan during the Kamakura period. The major Japanese Buddhist sects can trace their antecedents to that era.

東京 東京 東京 東京 東京 東京 東京

Tsurugaoka Kaikan Hotel (☎ 0467-24 1111, fax 24 1115) Rooms ¥16,000 with two meals. This pricey hotel offers questionable value for money. It's a few doors down from the City Pension Shangri La.

Places to Eat

Around the square facing Kamakura station are some fast-food places. If you are after some more palatable food, head up to Shopping Town street or the main road to Hachiman-gū, both of which run north-east of the station.

Sakuraya (☎ 22 1077) Lunch ¥800. On the main road, just north of Tsurugaoka Kaikan Hotel, this no-frills lunch stop has generic dishes like katsudon and soba. It's inexpensive and tasty.

Riccione Milano (☎ 24 5491) Lunch ¥900. This Italian place does a decent pasta lunch.

On Shopping Town street there's a branch of the *izakaya* chain *Yōrōnotaki* on the right just before you enter the station square.

Hirano Rāmen (☎ 23 1862) Noodles ¥650. This basic shop is just opposite Riccione Milano.

Niraku-sō (☎ 22 0211) Dishes ¥1500. Further up the road, close to Ryokan Ushio, is this good Chinese restaurant.

Getting There & Away

Trains on the Yokosuka line run to Kamakura and Kita-Kamakura stations. The trip takes 55 minutes from Tokyo; fares to Kamakura are ¥890 from Tokyo station, ¥770 from Shimbashi and ¥690 from Shinagawa. You can also catch a train from Yokohama on the Yokosuka line, which costs ¥300 to Kita-Kamakura, or ¥380 to Kamakura, and takes 27 minutes. If you're getting off at Kita-Kamakura station, it's the stop after Ōfuna.

You can go on to Enoshima via the scenic Enoden (Enoshima Dentetsu) line from Kamakura station or by bus from stop No 9 in front of the station. The train (¥250, 25 minutes) is the simpler and cheaper option.

Getting Around

The transportation hub here is Kamakura station. A lack of English-language signposting makes the bus network hard to use, but the station's TIC has the latest details on which *noriba* (bus stops/boarding points) serve which destinations. Local bus trips cost either ¥170 or ¥190.

ENOSHIMA 江ノ島

It's best to avoid this popular beach on weekends, when it's completely packed with day-trippers. At the end of the beach is a bridge to **Enoshima Island**, where the **Enoshima-jinja** (☎ 22 4020; open 9am-4pm) is reached by an 'outdoor escalator' that costs ¥350, but you *can* walk through. It houses a *hadaka-benzaiten* – a nude statue of the Indian goddess of beauty. Other sights around the island include the **Enoshima Shokubutsu-en** (*Tropical Garden*; ☎ 22 0209; admission ¥200; open 9am-5pm). A set ticket for escalator, garden and an observation point is ¥720.

Enoshima's beaches are good for a bit of meditative wandering, particularly around the rocky headlands on the southern side of the island. On fair days, Mt Fuji is clearly visible from the south and west sides of the island. In the late afternoon, stop for a drink in one of the cliff-side restaurants and watch the sun set over the mountain.

Getting There & Away

Buses and trains run frequently between Kamakura and Enoshima (see the previous Kamakura Getting There & Away section). The Tōkaidō line goes to Ōfuna station from Tokyo station (¥780). At Ōfuna, change to the Shōnan monorail and go to Shōnan-Enoshima station (¥300). Trains also run on the Odakyū line from Shinjuku station to Katase-Enoshima station. The Romance Car runs direct and takes 70 minutes (¥1220); an express takes 10 minutes longer and involves changing trains, but costs only ¥610.

IZU-HANTŌ 伊豆半島

Izu-hantō is noted for its abundant *onsen* (hot springs) and rural landscapes. You can get around the peninsula in one long and very hurried day or stay overnight at a halfway point such as Shimoda. If you decide to stay overnight, treat yourself to a hot-spring hotel.

A suggested itinerary is to start at Atami and travel down the east coast to Shimoda; from there you can cut across to Dogashima

and travel up to Mishima or Numazu, where there are railway stations with direct access to Tokyo. Buses frequently connect the peninsula's main towns, and some towns are also serviced by ferries.

Atami
☎ 0557 • pop 46,000

Atami is known as a naughty hot-spring weekend destination for Japanese couples, though one well-known gaijin, John Wayne, got off his horse and drank his sake here for the filming of *The Barbarian & the Geisha*. It's an expensive place to spend the night – Itō or Shimoda are far cheaper. There's an information counter at Atami station (☎ 81 6002).

Atami's prime attraction is **MOA Art Museum** (☎ 84 2511; admission ¥1500; open 9.30am-4.30pm Fri-Wed), with a collection of Japanese and Chinese art that includes a few 'National Treasures' and a good number of 'Important Cultural Properties'. Take a bus from the No 4 bus stop outside the station to the 'MOA Bijitsukan' (10 minutes, ¥140).

Getting There & Away An ordinary Tōkaidō line train from Tokyo station to Atami is one hour 50 minutes and ¥1850. The shinkansen takes only 50 minutes, but costs ¥4080. Ordinary trains leave Tokyo every 40 minutes during the day. It is also possible to approach Atami via Shinjuku by taking the Odakyū line to Odawara (one hour 10 minutes, ¥1550), then connecting with the Tōkaidō line to Atami (20 minutes, ¥400).

By far the most comfortable way to travel down to Izu-hantō is by *Odoriko*, a state-of-the-art express service, which departs Tokyo station regularly during the day and stops at Atami, Itō, Izu-Inatori and Shimoda. To Atami, the standard Odoriko costs ¥3770; it's ¥4070 for the deluxe *Super Odoriko*.

Itō
☎ 0557 • pop 74,000

Itō, a hot-spring resort, is famous as the place where Anjin-san (William Adams), the hero of James Clavell's book *Shogun*, built a ship for the Tokugawa *shōgunate*.

Among the sights in and around Itō are the gourd-shaped **Ippeki-ko**; the **Cycle Sports Centre** (☎ 79 0001; admission ¥800; open 9.30am-4pm), complete with *rotemburo*, heated swimming pool and maze; and the **Izu Shaboten-kōen** (☎ 51 1111; admission ¥1800; open 8.40am-4pm), a prickly priced cactus-park, 35 minutes by bus from Izu station.

The **Ikeda 20th Century Art Museum** (☎ 45 2211; admission ¥900; open 10am-4.30pm) has a collection of paintings and sculptures by Matisse, Picasso, Dali and others. The block-like museum is 25 minutes from Itō station.

Places to Stay *Business Hotel Itō* (☎ 36 1515, fax 36 7607) Singles/twins ¥5250/9450. One of the cheapest deals in town, look for the four-storey building around 300m east of the railway station. It's close to the waterfront.

The Ippeki-ko area is good for pensions – small Western-style places based on the European pension.

Getting There & Away Itō is about 25 minutes from Atami station on the JR Itō line, and the fare is ¥320. There is also a JR limited express *Odoriko* service from Tokyo station to Itō (1¾ hours, ¥4090). Direct ordinary trains from Tokyo station are quite a bit cheaper at ¥2180 and take about two hours and 10 minutes.

Shimoda
☎ 0558 • pop 30,000

This area boasts the most pleasant of the hot-spring resorts and the former residence of the American Townsend Harris, the first Western diplomat to live in Japan. Incidentally, it was also the site of Japan's first ever seance (*kokkuri-san* in Japanese). It's a peaceful place with a few historical sites in addition to the usual touristy stuff.

Things to See Look for the cable cars in front of the station that lurch their way up 200m-high **Nesugata-yama** every 10 minutes. The park (open 9am-5pm) on the top has good views of Shimoda and Shimoda Bay, and a reasonably priced restaurant. A return cable-car trip, including admission to the park, costs ¥1000.

About a 25-minute walk from Shimoda station is **Ryōsen-ji** (admission free), famous as the site of a treaty signed by Commodore Perry and representatives of the Tokugawa shōgunate in 1854.

Next to the temple is a small museum (admission ¥500; open 8.30am-5pm) with exhibits relating to the arrival of Westerners in Japan. These include a series of pictures depicting the tragic life of Okichi-san, a courtesan who was forced to give up the man she loved in order to attend to the needs of the barbarian Harris. When Harris left Japan five years later, Okichi was stigmatised for having had a relationship with a foreigner and was eventually driven to drink and suicide. Downstairs there's an interesting collection of erotic knick-knacks – pickled turnips with suggestive shapes, stones with vagina-like orifices etc.

Next door to Ryōsen-ji is **Chōraku-ji**, a pleasant little temple worth a quick look. Nearby **Hōfuku-ji** (admission ¥300; open 8am-5pm) has a museum that commemorates the life of Okichi-san.

Places to Stay There is a small information counter (☎ 22 1531) across the square from the station where staff will help you book accommodation.

Places to stay in and around Shimoda include the following:

Gensu Youth Hostel (☎ 62 0035) Beds ¥3145. The hostel is 25 minutes by bus from town (¥630). Get off at the Yakubamae stop. Check-in is from 4pm to 8pm.

Amagi Harris Court Youth Hostel (☎ 35 7253, fax 36 8931) Beds ¥3200. Check-in is from 4pm to 8pm. This is even farther from town, around 5km inland from Kawazu station, between Itō and Shimoda.

Station Hotel Shimoda (☎ 22 8885) Singles/twins ¥5800/9800. Right next to the station, this is a reasonably priced business hotel.

Getting There & Away Shimoda is as far as you can go by train on the peninsula; the limited express from Tokyo station takes 2¾ hours (¥6160). An Izu Kyūkō line train from Itō station takes about an hour (¥1570). There are a few express services each day from Atami station, but the surcharges make them expensive. The deluxe *Odoriko* from Tokyo will cost ¥6160, and the *Super Odoriko* service is ¥6460.

Bus platform No 5 in front of the station is for buses going to Dogashima, while platform No 7 is for those bound for Shuzenji.

West to North Izu-hantō

From Shimoda's No 5 bus stop in front of the station, it's a very scenic bus journey to **Dogashima**, a small, charming fishing town on the other side of the peninsula. Along the way is **Matsu-zaki**, a cape recommended for its traditional-style houses and quiet sandy beach. The bus to Dogashima takes about 30 minutes (¥1300).

The unusual cave and rock formations lining the shore are Dogashima's main attraction. Boat trips allow better views: A 20-minute trip costs ¥920, while two-hour tours are ¥1840.

To complete the circuit, there are a number of bus stops in Dogashima on the road opposite the jetty. The fare to **Shuzenji** – another resort town with a rail link via the Tōkaidō line to Tokyo – from stop No 2 is ¥2030. There are many *ryokan* and *minshuku* in this area.

A more interesting and not much more expensive alternative is to catch a high-speed ferry to **Numazu**, also on the Tōkaidō line (¥3400, 1¼ hours; six departures a day from 10am to 4.45pm). Boats also go to **Tōi** (¥820, 25 minutes), where you could stay at the *Takasagoya Youth Hostel* (☎/fax 98 0200) for ¥2900, continue on to Shuzenji by bus or take another boat to Numazu.

Half an hour by rail from Shuzenji is **Mishima**, a town that is short on interesting sights but serviced by the Tōkaidō line. The shinkansen from Mishima to Tokyo station takes 65 minutes and costs ¥4400. Ordinary trains take twice as long and cost ¥2160. Ten minutes by train from Mishima is Numazu, from where you can continue into Izu-hantō by boat or bus.

HAKONE 箱根
☎ 0460 • pop 22,000

If the weather cooperates and Mt Fuji is clearly visible, the Hakone region can make a memorable day trip from Tokyo. You can enjoy cable-car rides, visit an open-air museum, poke around smelly volcanic hot-water springs and cruise Ashino-ko. The weather, however, is crucial. Without Mt Fuji hovering in the background, Hakone loses some sparkle.

A good loop through the region takes you from Tokyo to Hakone-Yumoto station by train and then 'toy train' (a two-car mountain train) to Gōra; by funicular and cable car up Sōun-zan and down to Ashino-ko; by boat around the lake to Moto-Hakone, where you can walk a short stretch of the Edo-era Tōkaidō Hwy; and from there by bus back to Odawara, where you catch the train to Tokyo. (If you're feeling energetic, you could spend 3½ hours walking the old highway back to Hakone-Yumoto, which is connected to Tokyo by rail.)

Information

The Tokyo TIC has some useful pamphlets, particularly if you're planning on staying. If you want to try some of the area's onsen, definitely get the TIC's *Open-Air Hot Springs in Hakone*. Note that Hakone gets busy on weekends and during the holiday season – reservations are recommended.

Hakone Free Pass The Odakyū line offers a Hakone *furii pasu* (free pass), which costs ¥5500 for adults and ¥2750 for children; it allows you to use any mode of transport within the Hakone region for three days and provides discounts on some sights. The fare between Shinjuku and Hakone-Yumoto station is also included in the pass, although you'll have to pay an ¥850 surcharge to take the Romance Car. If you have a Japan rail pass, you'd be advised to buy a Free Pass in Odawara for ¥4050 (¥2030 for children), as this doesn't include the fare from Shinjuku. Altogether it's a good deal for a Hakone circuit, as the pass will save you at least ¥1000 even on a one-day visit.

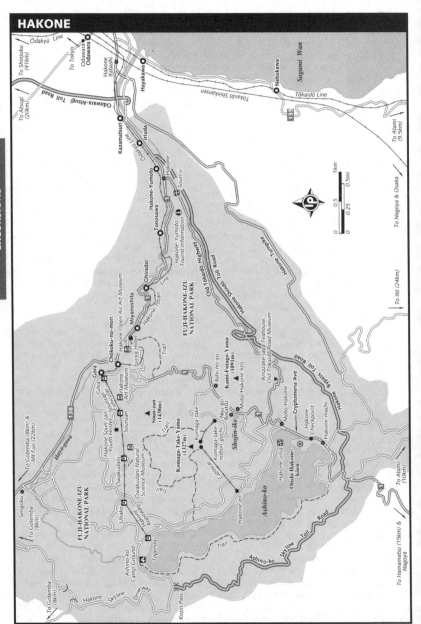

Fuji-san (Mt Fuji) from Yamanako-ko lake

Competitive fishermen on Fuji-go-ko (Fuji Five Lakes)

CHRIS ROWTHORN

Bathers at an *onsen* (mineral hot spring)

BOB CHARLTON

Amongst the marigold flowers – Chiba-ken ward

BOB CHARLTON

Autumn forest near Chuzenji-ko lake

CRAIG McLACHLAN

Getting away from the urban crush at Motosu-ko

Things to See & Do

Between Odawara and Gōra on the toy-train Hakone-Tōzan line is the **Hakone Open-Air Art Museum** (☎ *0460-2 1161; admission ¥1600, discounted with Hakone Free Pass; open 9am-5pm Mar-Oct, 9am-4pm Nov-Feb*). The art museum is next to Chōkoku-no-mori station, a little before Gōra. As well as paintings, the museum features sculptures by famous Western artists such as Auguste Rodin and Henry Moore in a 30-sq-km park.

The end of the Hakone-Tōzan line and the start of the funicular and cable-car trip to Togendai on Ashino-ko is **Gōra**. This small town also has a couple of attractions, including **Gōra-kōen**, just a short walk beside the funicular tracks up Sōun-zan. Further up the hill, 10 minutes from Gōra station, is **Hakone Art Museum** (☎ *2 2623; admission ¥900; open 9am-4.30pm, closed Thur*), which has a moss garden and a collection of ceramics from Japan and other Asian nations.

Take the funicular from Gōra up **Sōun-zan**. If you don't have a Hakone Free Pass, you'll need to buy a ticket at the booth to the right of the platform exit for ¥400. The ride takes 10 minutes.

Sōun-zan is the starting point for what the Japanese refer to as a 'ropeway', a 30-minute, 4km cable-car ride to **Togendai**, next to Ashino-ko. On the way, the gondolas pass through Ōwakudani. Get out at this point and take a look at the volcanic hot springs. If the weather is fine, there are great views of Mt Fuji, both from the gondolas and from Ōwakudani. The journey from Gōra to Togendai costs ¥1300 one way, ¥2300 return; hold on to the ticket if you pause at Ōwakudani. The **Ōwakudani Natural Science Museum** (☎ *4 9149; admission ¥400; open 9am-4.30pm*) has displays on the geography and natural history of Hakone.

From Ōwakudani, the cable car continues to **Ashino-ko**, touted as the primary attraction of the Hakone region. Majestic Mt Fuji rises above the surrounding hills, its snow-clad slopes shimmering on the mirror-like surface of the lake. That is, if the venerable volcano is not hidden behind a dirty grey bank of clouds.

From Togendai there are ferry services to Hakone-en, Moto-Hakone and Hakone-machi. At **Hakone-en**, you can take a cable car (¥620 one way, ¥1050 return) to the top of **Komaga-take**, where you get good views of the lake and Mt Fuji. You can leave the mountain by the same route or by taking a five-minute funicular descent (¥360) to Komaga-take-nobori-guchi. Buses run from there to Odawara for ¥770.

Most people take the ferry from Togendai to Moto-Hakone (¥970). **Moto-Hakone** has a few places to eat or get an overpriced cup of coffee, and there are a couple of interesting sights within an easy walk of the jetty. These include **Hakone-jinja** (*admission ¥300; open 9.30am-4pm*), which is impossible to miss, with its red *torii* (gates) rising from the lake. The shrine is nothing special, but the effect is quite evocative.

Up the hill from the lakeside Moto-Hakone bus stop runs the **Old Tōkaidō Hwy**, the road that once linked the ancient capital Kyoto with Edo (Tokyo). It's a 3½-hour walk on the old road to Hakone-Yumoto station, passing **Amazake-jaya Teahouse** (☎ *3 6418; open 7am-5.30pm*), the **Old Tōkaidō Road Museum** (☎ *3 6635; admission ¥300; open 9am-5pm*) and **Soun-ji** (☎ *5 5133; admission free; open dawn till dusk*) along the way.

A rather less arduous walk follows **Cryptomeria Ave**, or Sugi-namiki, a 500m-long path between Moto-Hakone and Hakone-machi, lined with cryptomeria trees planted some 360 years ago. The path runs behind the lakeside road used by the buses and other traffic.

Hakone-machi (*open 8.30am-4.30pm*) itself was once the **Hakone Checkpoint** (*admission included in museum ticket; open 8.30am-4.30pm*), run by the Tokugawa regime (see History in the Facts about Tokyo chapter) from 1619 to 1869 as a means of controlling the movement of everything from people to ideas in and out of Edo. The present-day checkpoint is a recent reproduction.

Buses run from Moto-Hakone back to **Odawara** for ¥1070. Odawara is billed as an 'old castle town', which it is, except that the castle is an uninspiring reconstruction of the original. If you're still interested, Odawara castle (☎ 0465-23 1373; admission ¥300; open 9am-4.30pm) is a 10-minute walk from Odawara station.

There are many bathing options around Hakone's numerous onsen areas – Yumoto Onsen, Gōra Onsen, Sengokuhara Onsen and Ashino-ko Onsen – which contain many onsen and onsen ryokan, some of which welcome day visitors.

Oku Yumoto Tenzan Notemburo (☎ 6 4126, admission ¥900, 9am-10pm) is a large, modern luxurious bath-fest, 2km south-west of town. A free shuttle bus ferries customers from the bridge near Hakone-Yumoto station. Contact the Tokyo TIC for other bath details.

Places to Stay

Hakone's popularity with Japanese weekenders is reflected in the high price of most accommodation in the area. With the exception of two youth hostels and a couple of Welcome Inns, there are few really cheap options.

Ashino-ko Campground (☎ 4 8279) Tent site ¥1000, six-person hut ¥10,000.

Hakone Sengokuhara Youth Hostel (☎ 4 8966, fax 4 6578) Beds ¥2900. Check-in is from 4pm to 6pm.

Fuji Hakone Guest House (☎ 4 6577, fax 4 6578) Singles ¥5000-6000, doubles ¥10,000-12,000. To get to both the hostel and guesthouse, take a bus from stand No 4 of Odawara station to the Senkyōrō-mae bus stop (50 minutes, ¥1020). There is an English sign close by. A natural hot spa is available for bathing.

Moto Hakone Guest House (☎ 3 7880, fax 4 6578) ¥5000 per person. This pleasant guest house is conveniently located in Moto-Hakone.

Fujiya Hotel (☎ 2 2211, fax 2 2210) Singles/doubles around ¥16,900/25,000. Fujiya is famous as one of Japan's earliest Western-style hotels and is highly rated on all fronts. There's a weekday special for foreign travellers of US$120 for double rooms. The hotel is a five-minute walk from Miyanoshita station on the Hakone-Tōzan line; if you ring from the station, someone will give you directions in English.

Getting There & Away

There are three ways of getting to the Hakone region: the Odakyū express bus service from the Shinjuku bus terminal on the western side of Shinjuku station; JR from Tokyo station; and the private Odakyū line from Shinjuku station.

Train JR trains run on the Tōkaidō line between Tokyo station and Odawara. Ordinary trains (¥1450, 1½ hours) run every 15 minutes or so. Limited express trains take 70 minutes (the express surcharge is ¥1450). Shinkansen (¥3640, 40 minutes) leave Tokyo station every 20 minutes – but make sure you are on a train that stops at Odawara (the *kodama* does).

Trains run to Odawara from Shinjuku station on the Odakyū line. Quickest and most comfortable is the Romance Car (one hour 25 minutes, ¥1690), which leaves every half hour. There's also an express service (¥850, one hour 35 minutes), which is by far the cheapest way of reaching Odawara.

At Odawara, you can change to the Hakone-Tōzan line, which takes you to Gōra (¥650). Alternatively, if you are already on the Odakyū line, you can continue on to Hakone-Yumoto and change to the Hakone-Tōzan line (¥390 to Gōra) simply by walking across the platform.

Bus The Odakyū express bus service has the advantage of running directly into the Hakone region, to Ashino-ko and to Hakone-machi for ¥1950 (two hours). The disadvantage is that the bus trip is much less interesting than the combination of Romance Car, toy train (Hakone-Tōzan line), funicular, cable car (ropeway) and ferry. Buses leave from bus stop No 35 in front of Odakyū department store on the west side of Shinjuku station.

[continued on page 214]

MT FUJI AREA

Mt Fuji, Japan's highest mountain, stands 3776m high, and when it's capped with snow, it's a postcard-perfect volcano cone. Fuji-san, as it's known in Japanese (*san* is the Chinese reading of the *kanji*, or character, for mountain), last blew its top in 1707, when streets in Edo were covered in volcanic ash. Unfortunately, Mt Fuji is a notoriously reclusive mountain, often hidden by cloud. Views are usually best in winter and early spring, when the snow cap adds to the scene.

Information

Climbing Mt Fuji, *Mt Fuji Climber's Guidebook* and *Mt Fuji & Fuji Go-ko* brochures are available from the Tourist Information Center (TIC) and provide exhaustive detail on transport to the mountain and how to climb it, complete with climbing schedules worked out to the minute.

During the climbing season, there is a 24-hour taped climbing information line on ☎ 23 3000 (English-language). Alternatively, contact the Kawaguchi-ko TIC (☎ 0555-72 6700).

Fuji Views

You can get a classic view of Mt Fuji from the *shinkansen* as it passes the city of Fuji. There are also good views from the Hakone area and the Nagao-tōge Pass on the road from Hakone to Gotemba. The road that encircles the mountain offers good views, particularly near Yamanaka-ko and Sai-ko lakes.

Climbing Mt Fuji

Officially the climbing season on Fuji is July and August, and the Japanese pack in during those busy months. Climbing may be just as good either side of the official season, but transport services to and from Mt Fuji are less frequent then and many of the mountain huts are closed. You can climb Mt Fuji at any time of year, but a mid-winter ascent is strictly for experienced mountaineers.

Bear in mind that although this is a popular climb, Mt Fuji is high enough for altitude sickness, and the weather can be viciously changeable. On the summit it can quickly go from clear but cold to cloudy, wet, windy and freezing cold – not just miserable but downright dangerous. Don't climb without adequate clothing for cold and wet weather – even on a good day in summer, the temperature on top is likely to be close to freezing.

The mountain is divided into 10 'stations' from base to summit, but these days most climbers start from one of the 'fifth stations', which you can reach by road. Count on a 4½ hour ascent and about 2½ hours to descend. Once you're on the top, it takes about an hour to make a circuit of the crater.

You should try to reach the top at dawn – both to see the *Goroke* (sunrise), and because early morning is the time when the mountain is least likely to be shrouded in cloud. You can either start up in the afternoon, stay overnight in a mountain hut and continue early in the morning, or climb the whole way at night. You do not want to arrive on the top too long before dawn, as it's likely to be very cold and windy.

Fifth Stations There are four fifth stations around Fuji, and it's quite feasible to climb from one and descend to another. On the northern side of Fuji is Kawaguchi-ko Fifth Station, at 2305m, which is reached from the town of Kawaguchi-ko. This station is very popular with climbers starting from Tokyo. The Yoshida route, which starts much lower down, close to the town of Fuji-Yoshida, is the same as the Kawaguchi-ko route for much of the way.

Subashiri Fifth Station is at 1980m, and the route from there meets Kawaguchi-ko just after the eighth station. Gotemba Fifth Station is reached from the town of Gotemba and, at 1440m, is much lower than the other fifth stations. From Gotemba Fifth Station it takes seven or eight hours to reach the top, as opposed to the 4½ to five hours it takes on the other routes. Fujinomiya/Mishima Fifth Station, at 2380m, is more convenient for climbers approaching from the west than for those coming from Tokyo. It meets the Gotemba route right at the top.

Equipment Make sure you have clothing suitable for cold and wet weather, including a hat and gloves. Bring drinking water and some snack food. If you're going to climb at night, bring a torch (flashlight). Even at night it would be difficult to get seriously lost, as the trails are very clear, but it's easy to put a foot wrong in the dark.

Mountain Huts There are 'lodges' dotted up the mountainside but they're expensive – ¥4000 to ¥4500 for a mattress on the floor squeezed between countless climbers – and you don't get much opportunity to sleep anyway, as you have to be up well before dawn to start the final slog to the top. No matter how miserable the nights, don't plan to shelter or rest in the huts without paying. The huts also prepare simple meals for their guests and for passing climbers, and you're welcome to rest inside as long as you order something. If you're not hungry, an hour's rest costs ¥400. Camping on the mountain is not permitted.

Getting There & Away See the Fuji Go-ko section, following, for details on transport to Kawaguchi-ko, the most popular arrival point for Tokyo Fuji-climbers.

From Kawaguchi-ko, there are bus services up to Kawaguchi-ko Fifth Station (¥1700, 55 minutes) from April to mid-November. The schedule varies considerably. Call Fuji Kyūkō bus on ☎ 72 2911 for details. At the height of the climbing season buses run until quite late in the evening – ideal for climbers intending to make an overnight ascent.

There are also direct buses from the Shinjuku bus terminal to Kawaguchi-ko Fifth Station (¥2600, 2½ hours). This is by far the fastest and cheapest way of getting here from Tokyo.

From Gotemba, buses to the Gotemba Fifth Station (¥1220, 55 minutes) operate four to six times daily.

From Subashiri, buses to the Subashiri Fifth Station (¥1080, 45 minutes) follow a similar schedule.

Fuji-go-ko

The five lakes scattered around the northern side of Mt Fuji are major attractions for Tokyo day-trippers, offering water sports and some good views of Mt Fuji. For visitors to Tokyo, the views of the lakes and Mt Fuji are the area's biggest draw cards.

Perhaps the best way to make the most of this is to avail yourself of the area's comprehensive bus network, which includes regular buses from Fuji-Yoshida station. These buses pass the four smaller lakes and travel around the mountain to the city of Fujinomiya on the south-western side. From Kawaguchi-ko, there are nine to 11 buses daily making the two-hour trip to Mishima, which is on the shinkansen line.

Places to Stay *Fuji-Yoshida* (☎ 0555-22 0533) and *Kawaguchi-ko* (☎ 0555-72 1431) are the two youth hostels in the Fuji area. Fuji-Yoshida costs ¥2700 a night and is about 1km south of Fuji-Yoshida station, just off Route 139 (look out for the Lawson's convenience store on the left-hand corner if you're walking north). Kawaguchi-ko costs ¥2900 a night and is about 500m south-east of Kawaguchi-ko station.

There are numerous hotels, *ryokan, minshuku* and pensions in the Fuji-go-ko area, particularly at Kawaguchi-ko. The TIC at Kawaguchi-ko station (☎ 0555-72 6700) can make reservations.

Hotel Ashiwada (☎ 0555-82 2321) Singles ¥7000. Hotel Ashiwada represents the Japanese Inn Group and is located at the western end of Kawaguchi-ko. Only single rooms are available.

Petit Hotel Ebisuya (☎ 0555-72 2587) Per-person rates ¥5000 or ¥6000. The Petit Hotel Ebisuya is handily placed outside Kawaguchi-ko station.

Getting There & Away Fuji-Yoshida and Kawaguchi-ko are the two main travel centres in the Fuji-go-ko area. Frequent buses run directly to Kawaguchi-ko (¥1740, 1¾ hours) from the Shinjuku bus terminal in the Yasuda Seimei second building, beside the main Shinjuku station in Tokyo. Some buses continue on to Yamanaka-ko and Motosu-ko lakes.

You can also get to the lakes by train, although it takes longer and costs more. JR Chūō line trains go from Shinjuku to Otsuki (¥2930, one hour by limited express; ¥1300 by local train). At Otsuki you cross the platform to the Fuji Kyūkō line local train, which takes about 50 minutes and costs ¥1510 to Kawaguchi-ko. The train actually goes to Fuji-Yoshida first, then reverses out for the short leg to Kawaguchi-ko. On Sunday and holidays from March to November, there is a direct local train from Shinjuku (¥2370, two to 2½ hours).

{continued from page 210}

NIKKŌ 日光

☎ 0288 • pop 19,000

Nikkō is not only one of the most popular day trips from Tokyo, it's also one of Japan's major tourist attractions, due to the splendour of its shrines and temples. You should pick a weekday to visit, when the crowds are lighter, but whatever you do, don't miss it. Nikkō should be included on even the most whirlwind tour of Japan.

History

Nikkō has been a sacred site since the middle of the 8th century, when Buddhist priest Shōdō Shōnin established a hermitage there. In 1617 it was chosen as the site for the mausoleum of Tokugawa Ieyasu. In 1634, Tokugawa Iemitsu, the grandson of the deceased Ieyasu, commenced work on the shrine that can be seen today. Tōshō-gū was built using a huge army of some 15,000 artisans from all over Japan.

British art historian Gordon Millar described Nikkō's shrines as 'pure 17th-century Disneyland'. Every available space of Ieyasu's shrine and mausoleum is crowded with detail; not a single centimetre hasn't been used to remind you of its creator's munificence and power. Dragons, lions and peacocks jostle with gods and demi-gods among

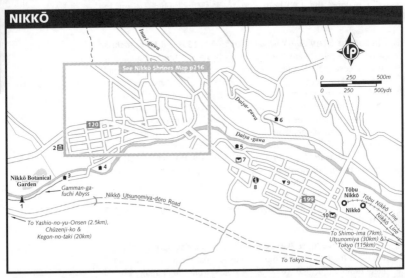

NIKKŌ

1	Bake-jizō 化け地蔵	4	Turtle Inn Nikkō タートルイン日光	7	Nikkō Post Office 日光便局
2	Nikkō Museum 日光博物館	5	Nikkō Daiyagawa Youth Hostel 日光大谷川ユース ホステル	8	Nikkō Kyōdo Center 日光郷土センター
3	Annex Turtle Hotori-an アネックスタートル ほとり庵	6	Kōryu Sokushin Centre 日光交流促進センター	9	Yūrō-no-Taki 養老の滝
				10	Post Office 郵便局

the glimmering gold-leaf and red lacquer-work. This is as far as you can get from the minimalism of Zen architecture, but don't let this put you off – Tōshō-gū is a grand sensory roller-coaster ride.

Orientation
It's a straight 30-minute walk uphill from the JR and Tōbu stations to the shrine area. You can also take bus No 1, 2, 3 or 4 up to the Shin-kyō-bashi bus stop for ¥190.

Information
The Kyōdo Centre (☎ 53 3795), open from 9am to 5pm, with its useful Tourist Information Center and great video of the city's attractions and cuisine, can be found on the road up to Tōshō-gū. There is another TIC in the Tōbu Nikkō station (☎ 53 4511), open from 8.30am to noon and 1pm to 5pm. At both offices English is spoken.

Hikers should pick up a copy of the *Nikkō-Yumoto-Chuzenji Area Hiking Guide* (¥180), available from some of the area's pensions and from information counters in Nikkō.

Tickets Admission to Futara-san-jinja is ¥200, to Rinnō-ji ¥380 and to Tōshō-gū ¥1350. However, it makes more sense to buy the combination ticket (ask for 'kyōtsū-haikan-ken') for ¥1350. The ticket covers all three of the above sights, plus the Hōbutsuden Treasure House and Shōyō-en though not the Nemuri-neko in Oku-miya. Entry to the latter is a further ¥500. Even so, this is a considerable saving on buying each of the tickets separately.

Things to See
Close to the Tōshō-gū area is **Shin-kyō-bashi**. Shōdō Shōnin, who first established a hermitage in Nikkō in 782, was carried across the river at this point on the backs of two huge serpents. Non-reptilian-toting tourists can cross the bridge on foot, but not until it opens after repairs in 2002.

The next stop is **Rinnō-ji** *(admission ¥380; open 8am-4pm)*, also founded by Shōdō Shōnin (of the Buddhist Tendai sect). **Sambutsu-dō** (Three Buddha Hall) has a trio of huge, remarkable gold-lacquered images –

a *senjū* (1000-armed Kannon); the central image, Amida Nyorai; and Batō, a horse-headed goddess of mercy.

Hōbutsu-den *(Treasure Hall; admission ¥300; open 8am-4pm)*, also on the temple grounds, has a splendid collection of temple artefacts, sculptures and scrolls. Admission includes entry to the lovely Edo-period garden Shōyō-en.

A huge stone torii marks the entrance to **Tōshō-gū** *(admission ¥1250; open 8am-4.30pm)*, while to the left is a five-storey **pagoda**, dating from 1650 but reconstructed in 1818. The pagoda is remarkable for its lack of foundations – the interior contains a long suspended pole that apparently swings like a pendulum in order to maintain equilibrium during an earthquake.

The true entrance to Tōshō-gū is through the torii at **Omote-mon**, protected on either side by Deva kings. Through the entrance to the right is **Sanjinko** (Three Sacred Storehouses), the upper storey of which is renowned for the imaginative relief carvings of elephants by an artist who had never seen the real thing. To the left of the entrance is the **Sacred Stable**, a suitably plain building housing a carved white horse. The stable's only adornment is an allegorical series of relief carvings depicting the life-cycle of the monkey. They include the famous 'hear no evil, see no evil, speak no evil' trio that is now emblematic of Nikkō.

Pass through another torii and climb another flight of stairs, and on the left and right are a drum tower and a belfry. To the left of the drum tower is **Honji-dō**, with its huge ceiling painting of a dragon in flight known as the Roaring Dragon. The dragon will roar if you clap your hands beneath it.

Next comes **Yōmei-mon**, adorned with a multitude of reliefs of Chinese sages, children, and dragons and other mythical creatures. So much effort and skill went into the gate that its creators worried that its perfection might arouse envy in the gods, so the final supporting pillar on the left side was placed upside down as a deliberate error.

Through Yōmei-mon and to the right is **Nemuri-neko** (Sleeping Cat). **Sakashita-mon** here opens onto a path that climbs up

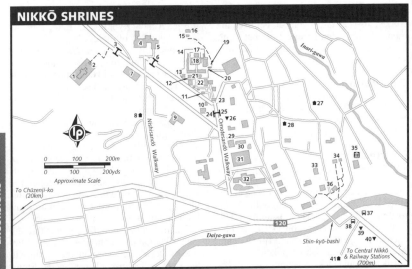

NIKKŌ SHRINES

through towering cedars to **Ieyasu's Tomb**, a relatively simple affair. If you are using the ¥900 ticket, it will cost an extra ¥430 to see the cat and the tomb. To the left of Yōmei-mon is Jinyōsha, a storage depot for Nikkō's *mikoshi* (portable shrines), which come alive during the May and October festivals. The Honden (Main Hall) and Haiden (Hall of Worship) can also be seen in the enclosure.

Nearby is **Futara-san-jinja** *(admission ¥200; open dawn till dusk)* dedicated to Nantai-san, its consort Nyotai and their mountainous progeny Tarō. Also in the vicinity is **Taiyūin-byō** *(admission ¥500; open 8am-4.30pm)*, which enshrines Ieyasu's grandson Iemitsu (1604–51) and is a smaller version of Tōshō-gū. The smaller size gives it a less extravagant air, and some consider it more aesthetically worthy than its larger neighbour.

The **Kosugi Hōan Museum of Art** *(☎ 50 1200; admission ¥700; open 9.30am-4.30pm Tues-Sun)* has a collection of landscape paintings by local artist Kosugi (1920–64) and is a good rainy-day option.

Gamman-ga-Fuji Abyss

To get away from the tourist hordes, take a 20-minute walk over to Gamman-ga-Fuji Abyss and its collection of statues of Jizō, protector of travellers and the souls of departed children. One of the statues Bake-jizō mocks travellers foolish enough to count the number of statues (it's said to be constantly changing).

Yashio-no-yu Onsen

This modern hot-spring complex *(☎ 53 6611; adult/child ¥500/free; open 10am-8.30pm Fri-Wed)* has open-air baths, saunas and a large indoor bath. It's a 12-minute bus ride from Nikkō station. Take the bus bound for Kiyotaki 1-chome.

Chūzenji-ko

On a quiet day it's a 50-minute bus trip from Nikkō up to Chūzenji-ko lake along a winding road. There's some beautiful scenery, including the 97m waterfall Kegon-no-taki and the lake, but don't cut short a visit to the shrine area just to fit in Chūzenji-ko. There's an elevator (¥530 return) down to a platform where you can observe the full force of the plunging waterfall. Also worth a visit is the third of the Futara-san-jinjas *(admission ¥200; open dawn till dusk)*, complementing the ones near Tōshō-gū and on Nantai-san.

NIKKŌ SHRINES

PLACES TO STAY

8 Nikkō Pension
   Green Age
   日光ペンション
   グリーンエイジ
27 Nikkō Tōkan-sō
   Ryokan
   日光東観荘旅館
28 Hotel Seikōen
   ホテル清晃苑
41 Nikkō Kanaya Hotel
   日光金谷ホテル

PLACES TO EAT

26 Musubijaya
   むすび茶屋
39 Sawamoto
   さわもと
40 Hippari Dako
   ひっぱりだこ

OTHER

1 Taiyūin-byō
   大猷院廟
2 Yasha-mon
   夜叉門
3 Niō-mon
   仁王門
4 Futara-san-jinja
   二荒山神社
5 Kara-mon
   唐門

6 Bronze Torii
   銅鳥居
7 Hokke-dō; Jōgyō-dō
   法華堂；常行堂
9 Treasury
   東照宮宝物館
10 Ticket Office
   券売所
11 Sacred Stable
   神厩舎
12 Drum Tower
   鼓楼
13 Honji-dō
   本地堂
14 Tōshō-gū
   東照宮
15 Tomb of Ieyasu
   奥社
16 Honden
   本殿
17 Honden
   本殿
18 Haiden
   拝殿
19 Sakashita-mon
   坂下門
20 Nemuri-neko
   眠猫
21 Yōmei-mon
   陽明門

22 Sanjinko
   三神庫
23 Omote-mon
   表門
24 Pagoda (5 stories)
   五重塔
25 Granite Torii
   一ノ鳥居
29 Goma-dō
   護摩堂
30 Gohōten-dō
   護法典堂
31 Rinnō-ji; Sambutsu-dō
   輪王寺；三仏堂
32 Hōbutsuden ;
   Shōyōen
   宝物殿；逍遙園
33 Nanshō-in
   南照院
34 Shihonryū-ji
   四本竜寺
35 Kosugi Hōan Museum
   of Art
   小杉放菴記念美術館
36 Hongū
   本宮神社
37 Bus Stop
   バス停
38 Bus Stop
   バス停

EXCURSIONS

東京 東京 東京 東京 東京 東京 東京 東京 東京 東京 東京 東京 東京 東京 東京 東京

Buses run frequently from Tōbu Nikkō station to Chūzenji Onsen from 6.20am to 6.30pm (50 minutes, ¥1100).

Places to Stay

Because of Nikkō's importance as a tourist attraction, it is one of the few places outside Tokyo and Kyoto where travellers on a budget get some choice. If you're willing to spend ¥2000 or so over standard youth hostel rates, there are some very good options close to the central shrine and temple area.

Youth Hostels *Nikkō Daiyagawa Youth Hostel (☎/fax 54 1974)* Beds ¥2450-2650, depending on the time of year. Closed 28 Dec-3 Jan. A pleasant if unspectacular hostel. It's just to the rear of the post office opposite the Shiyakusho-mae bus stop.

Kōryu Sokushin Centre (☎ 54 1013, fax 50 1030) Dormitory bed ¥3100, singles/twins ¥4100/8200. This newly refurbished, very popular hostel is a 10-minute walk from the Shiyakusho-mae bus stop, on the other side of the Daiya-gawa.

Pensions & Ryokan Nikkō's many pensions offer very reasonable rates and clean, comfortable surroundings. Per-person costs are around ¥5000, but you can often reduce this by sharing rooms with other travellers. Nikkō is very popular, so book well in advance. All the following pensions have someone who can speak a little English.

Turtle Inn Nikkō (☎ 53 3168, fax 53 3883) From ¥4200/5000 per person without/with bath, prices vary seasonally. Breakfast ¥1000, dinner ¥2000. Far and away the most popular of Nikkō's pensions is the Turtle Inn Nikkō, located by the river, beyond the shrine area. From the station, take a bus to the Sōgo-kaikan-mae bus stop, backtrack around 50m to the fork in the road and follow the river for around five minutes.

Annex Turtle Hotori-An (☎ 53 3663, fax 53 3883) Japanese and Western-style rooms from ¥5800. Breakfast ¥1000, dinner ¥2000. This place is to the west, over the river but on the same road.

Nikkō Pension Green Age (☎ 54 3636) From ¥9800 with two meals, ¥5800 without. The Green Age looks like a Tudor mansion.

Nikkō Tōkan-sō Ryokan (☎ 54 0611, fax 53 3914) From ¥10,000 with two meals. This is a great place for a Japanese-inn experience. Neither of these places offer single occupancy.

Hotels *Hotel Seikōen (☎ 53 5555, fax 53 5554)* Rooms from ¥13,000 with two meals. Hotel Seikōen is in a fairly uninspiring spot, although it is handy for the shrines.

Nikkō Kanaya Hotel (☎ 54 0001, fax 53 2487) Twins ¥12,000-50,000, doubles ¥15,000-32,000. This is Nikkō's classiest hotel, and decent value if you feel like a little civilised splendour. It's above Shin-kyōbashi. During peak holiday periods room prices nearly double.

Places to Eat

Nikkō is something of a gourmet black hole, thus many travellers prefer to eat at their ryokan or pension. However, there are some options on the main road between the stations and shrines.

Opposite the fire station the izakaya chain *Yōrō-no-taki* has cheap beer and so-so food, but the staff look like they can hardly be bothered.

Hippari Dako (☎ 53 2933) From ¥800. Open until 7pm. Close to Shin-kyō-bashi, Hippari Dako has long been a backpacker's favourite, though recent reports suggest it might be going downhill. The greeting, however, remains warm and there's an English menu. Try the yaki-udon.

Sawamoto (☎ 54 0163) From ¥1700. Open 11am-2pm & 5pm-7pm. If you don't

mind eel, this friendly spot is the best choice of the lot, up the hill between Yakitori-ya and the Kanaya Hotel.

In the shrine area, some shops sell inexpensive food and have English menus.

Musubijaya Dishes ¥800. Open 9am-4pm. This place serves the local speciality, Yuba soba buckwheat noodles.

Nikkō Kanaya Hotel Mains ¥3000-8000. For a more upmarket lunch or dinner, this hotel restaurant is recommended both for its atmosphere and for its meals.

Getting There & Away

The best way to visit Nikkō is via the Tōbu Nikkō line from Asakusa station in Tokyo. The station, which is separate from Asakusa subway station, is in the basement of Tōbu department store, but it is well signposted and easy to find from the subway. Limited express trains take one hour 55 minutes (¥2740). They require a reservation (on a quiet day you'll probably be able to organise this before boarding the train) and run every 30 minutes or so from 7.30am to 10am; after 10am they run hourly. Rapid trains don't require reservations, take 15 minutes longer and cost ¥1320. They run once an hour from 6.20am to 4.30pm. Buy tickets from a vending machine or the ticket office.

As usual, travelling by JR trains is time-consuming and expensive; it is only of interest to those on a Japan Rail Pass. Best go by shinkansen from Tokyo or Ueno to Utsunomiya (¥4510, 53 minutes), changing there for an ordinary train (no other options) for the 45-minute, ¥740 trip to Nikkō. Trains from Utsunomiya to Nikkō leave about once every 30 minutes. Not all trains go all the way to Nikkō – unless you checked beforehand, you may have to get off part way and wait for a train that makes the whole journey.

MASHIKO 益子
☎ 0285 • pop 26,000

Mashiko, a centre for country-style pottery, has about 50 resident potters, some of whom you can see working at their kilns. The town achieved fame when the esteemed potter Hamada Shōji settled there and, from 1930, produced his Mashiko pottery. Today he is designated as a 'Living National Treasure' and has been joined by a legion of potters.

Mashiko's kilns are spread out over a wide area; getting to them requires a lot of footwork. Get a copy of the *Tourist Map of Mashiko* from the information counter at Utsunomiya station (see the following Getting There & Away section) or the Tokyo TIC. **Hamada House** *(☎ 72 7555; admission ¥1200; open 9am-4pm)* and **Tsukamoto Kiln** *(☎ 72 3223)* are recommended, but there are some 300 kilns in the area and you could spend weeks seeking them out.

Hamada House has both wood-fired kilns and modern automated ones, and visitors can play around with the machinery. One-hour introductory courses at the Tsukamoto Kiln cost ¥3570, but a reservation is required. The **Mashikoyaki Kyōhan Centre** *(72 4444)* also has a one-hour course, but firing the items produced takes a month.

Getting There & Away

It is possible to combine Mashiko with a visit to Nikkō if you set off from Tokyo very early and use the JR route. See the earlier Nikkō Getting There & Away section for travel details to Utsunomiya. From Utsunomiya, buses run regularly during the day to Mashiko (¥1200, one hour).

Ask at TIC Utsunomiya station for how to get to the bus stop and for bus times.

FURTHER AFIELD

Domestic travel in Japan is a painless affair. You can hop on the shinkansen at Tokyo station in the morning and be sightseeing in some of the county's most famous cities by early afternoon. There is no doubt, however, that extensive use of trains of any kind in Japan can eat through a travel budget in little time. Those who plan extensive sightseeing would be well advised to get a Japan Rail Pass before coming to Japan.

For most visitors, Kyoto is the single most rewarding destination in Japan. With more than 2000 temples and shrines, and endless reminders of traditional Japan, Kyoto is the perfect counterpoint to the restless hyper-modernity of Tokyo. Those with the time (three hours on the shinkansen) and money (about ¥25,000 for a round trip) should make every effort to visit, even if it's just a quick two-day trip.

An hour from Kyoto by local train, Nara is the second of Japan's great cultural mecas, boasting several splendid temples and shrines. Moreover, the pleasant layout of the city makes it perfect for aimless strolling and temple hopping.

An hour west of Kyoto by local train (17 minutes by shinkansen), Osaka is Japan's second largest city and a rival to Tokyo for sheer bustling urban energy. While Tokyo citizens pride themselves on their sophisticated manners, Osakans are a down-to-earth lot who enjoy hearty food and rough humour. Its casual atmosphere and warm people make Osaka a worthwhile day trip if you're in the Kansai area.

Heading west from Osaka, the shinkansen and regular JR trains continue to Kōbe, Himeji, Hiroshima and on into the southern island of Kyūshū, with its wonderful hot springs and natural sights.

North and north-west of Tokyo are deep mountains and traditional villages to lure the adventurous traveller. Further north, the island of Hokkaidō has some of Japan's most unspoiled nature as well as the city of Sapporo, with its friendly locals and excellent seafood. For more information on these and many other places, see Lonely Planet's comprehensive *Japan* guidebook.

HIKING AROUND TOKYO

Those interested in hiking in the Tokyo area should visit the TIC and pick up a copy of its excellent *One Day Hiking Courses from Central Tokyo* pamphlet. See the Guidebooks entry under Books in the Facts for the Visitor chapter for more resources.

ONSEN (HOT SPRING BATHS)

If you have a yen for a Japanese hot springs diversion, pick up the TIC's *Japanese Hot Springs* pamphlet, which lists onsen in Hakone, Nikkō, and Shimoda and Itō on Izu-hantō, as well as three onsen in Tokyo itself. See also Public Baths & Onsen in the Entertainment chapter.

Language

It is something of a cliché that Japanese spend years studying English and end up unable to string a coherent English sentence together. This is partly due to the language-teaching techniques employed in Japanese classrooms, but it also reflects the difficulty of translation. Structurally, Japanese and English are so different that word-for-word translations will often produce almost incomprehensible sentences.

Grammar

To English speakers, Japanese language patterns often seem to be back to front and lacking in essential information. For example, where an English speaker would say 'I'm going to the shop' a Japanese speaker would say 'shop to going', omitting the subject pronoun (I) altogether and putting the verb at the end of the sentence. To make matters worse, many moods which are indicated at the beginning of a sentence in English occur at the end of a sentence in Japanese, as in the Japanese sentence 'Japan to going if' – 'if you're going to Japan'.

Fortunately for visitors to Japan, it's not all bad news. Unlike other languages in the region (Chinese, Vietnamese and Thai among others), the Japanese pronunciation system is fairly easy to master. In fact, with a little effort, getting together a repertoire of travellers' phrases should be no trouble – the only problem will be understanding the replies you get.

Written Japanese

Japanese has one of the most complex writing systems in the world, using three different scripts (four if you include the increasingly used Roman script *romaji*). The most difficult of the three, for foreigners and Japanese alike, is *kanji*, the ideographic script developed by the Chinese. Not only do you have to learn a couple of thousand of them, but unlike Chinese many Japanese kanji have wildly variant pronunciations depending on context.

Because of the differences between Chinese grammar and Japanese grammar, kanji had to be supplemented with an alphabet of syllables, or a syllabary, known as *hiragana*. And there is yet another syllabary that is used largely for representing foreign-loan words such as *terebi* (TV) and *biiru* (beer); this script is known as *katakana*. If you're serious about learning to read Japanese you will have to set aside several years.

If you're thinking of tackling the Japanese writing system before you go or while you're in Japan, your best bet would be to start with hiragana or katakana. Both syllabaries have 48 characters each, and can be learned within a week – although it will take at least a month to consolidate them. You can practise your katakana on restaurant menus, where such things as *kōhii* (coffee) and *kēiki* (cake) are frequently found, and practise your hiragana on train journeys, as station names are usually indicated in hiragana (in addition to English and kanji).

The romaji used in this book follows the Hepburn system of romanisation. Macrons are used to indicate long vowels.

Language Guides

The new edition of Lonely Planet's *Japanese phrasebook* offers a convenient collection of survival words and phrases for your trip to Japan, plus a section on grammar and pronunciation. If you'd like to delve deeper into the intricacies of the language, we recommend *Japanese for Busy People* (Kodansha) for beginners, *Introduction to Intermediate Japanese* (Mizutani Nobuko, Bojinsha) for intermediate students, and *Kanji in Context* (Japan Times) for more advanced students. One of the best guides to the written language, for both study and reference, is *Kanji & Kana* (Wolfgang Hadamizky and Mark Spahn, Tuttle).

Pronunciation

Unlike Chinese, Vietnamese and Thai, among others, Japanese is not tonal and the pronunciation system is fairly easy to master.

The following examples reflect British pronunciation:

a	as in 'father'
e	as in 'get'
i	as in 'pin'
o	as in 'bone', but shorter
u	as in 'flu'

Vowels appearing in this book with a macron (or bar) over them (ā, ē, ō, ū) are pronounced in the same way as standard vowels except that the sound is held twice as long. You need to take care with this as vowel length can change the meaning of a word, eg, *yuki* means 'snow', while *yūki* means 'bravery'.

Consonants are generally pronounced as in English, with the following exceptions:

f	this sound is produced by pursing the lips and blowing lightly
g	as the 'g' in 'goal' at the start of word; and nasalised as the 'ng' in 'sing' in the middle of a word
r	more like an 'l' than an 'r'

Greetings & Civilities
The all-purpose title **san** is used after a name as an honorific and is the equivalent of Mr, Miss, Mrs and Ms.

Good morning.
ohayō gozaimasu
おはようございます。
Good afternoon.
konnichiwa
こんにちは。
Good evening.
kombanwa
こんばんは。
Goodbye.
sayōnara
さようなら。
See you later.
dewa mata
ではまた。
Please/Go ahead. (when offering)
dōzo
どうぞ。

Please. (when asking)
onegai shimasu
お願いします。
Thanks. (informal)
dōmo
どうも。
Thank you.
dōmo arigatō
どうもありがとう。
Thank you very much.
dōmo arigatō gozaimasu
どうもありがとうございます。
Thanks for having me.
(when leaving)
o-sewa ni narimashita
お世話になりました。
You're welcome.
dō itashimasite
どういたしまして。
No, thank you.
iie, kekkō desu
いいえ、けっこうです。
Excuse me/Pardon.
sumimasen
すみません。
Excuse me. (when entering a room)
o-jama shimasu/shitsurei shimasu
おじゃまします。／失礼します。
I'm sorry.
gomen nasai
ごめんなさい。
What's your name?
o-namae wa nan desu ka?
お名前は何ですか？
My name is ...
watashi wa ... desu
私は…です。
This is Mr/Mrs/Ms (Smith).
kochira wa (Sumisu) san desu
こちらは（スミス）さんです。
Pleased to meet you.
dōzo yoroshiku
どうぞよろしく。
Pleased to meet you too.
hajimemashite, kochira koso dōzo yoroshiku
はじめまして、こちらこそどうぞよろしく。
Where are you from?
dochira no kata desu ka?
どちらのかたですか？

How are you?
o-genki desu ka?
お元気ですか？

Fine.
genki desu
元気です。

Is it OK to take a photo?
shashin o totte mo ii desu ka?
写真を撮ってもいいですか？

Cheers!
kampai!
乾杯！

Basics

Yes.
hai
はい。

No.
iie
いいえ。

No. (for indicating disagreement)
chigaimasu
違います。

No. (for indicating disagreement; less emphatic)
chotto chigaimasu
ちょっと違います。

OK.
daijōbu (desu)/ōke
だいじょうぶ（です）。/ オーケー。

What?
nani?   なに？

When?
itsu?   いつ？

Where?
doko?   どこ？

Who?
dare?   だれ？

Requests

Please give me this/that.
kore/sore o kudasai
（これ / それ）をください。

Please give me a (cup of tea).
(o-cha) o kudasai
（お茶）をください。

Please wait (a while).
(shōshō) o-machi kudasai
（少々）お待ちください。

Please show me the (ticket).
(kippu) o misete kudasai
（切符）を見せてください。

Language Difficulties

Do you understand English/Japanese?
ei-go/nihon-go wa wakarimasu ka?
（英語 / 日本語）はわかりますか？

I don't understand
wakarimasen
わかりません。

Do you speak English?
eigo ga hanasemasu ka?
英語が話せますか？

I can't speak Japanese.
nihongo wa dekimasen
日本語はできません。

How do you say ... in Japanese?
nihongo de ... wa nan to iimasu ka?
日本語で…は何といいますか？

What does ... mean?
... wa donna imi desu ka?
…はどんな意味ですか？

What is this called?
kore wa nan to iimasu ka?
これは何といいますか？

Please write in Japanese/English.
nihongo/eigo de kaite kudasai
（日本語 / 英語）で書いてください。

Please speak more slowly.
mō chotto yukkuri itte kudasai
もうちょっとゆっくり言ってください。

Please say it again more slowly.
mō ichidō, yukkuri itte kudasai
もう一度、ゆっくり言ってください。

What is this called?
kore wa nan to iimasu ka?
これは何といいますか？

Getting Around

What time does the next ... leave?
tsugi no ... wa nanji ni demasu ka?
次の…は何時に出ますか？

What time does the next ... arrive?
tsugi no ... wa nanji ni tsukimasu ka?
次の…は何時に着きますか？

boat
bōto/fune   ボート / 船

bus (city)
shibasu   市バス

bus (intercity)
chōkyoribasu   長距離バス

bus stop
basutei   バス停

tram
  romen densha   路面電車
train
  densha   電車
subway
  chikatetsu   地下鉄
station
  eki   駅
ticket
  kippu   切符
ticket office
  kippu uriba   切符売り場
timetable
  jikokuhyō   時刻表
taxi
  takushī   タクシー
entrance
  iriguchi   入口
exit
  deguchi   出口
left-luggage office
  nimotsu azukarijo 荷物預かり所
one way
  katamichi   片道
return
  ōfuku   往復
non-smoking seat
  kin'en seki   禁煙席

Where is the ... ?
  ... wa doko desu ka?
  …はどこですか？
How much is the fare to ...?
  ... made ikura desu ka?
  …までいくらですか？
Does this (train, bus, etc) go to ...?
  kore wa ... e ikimasu ka?
  これは…へ行きますか？
Is the next station ...?
  tsugi no eki wa ... desu ka?
  次の駅は…ですか？
Please tell me when we get to ...
  ... ni tsuitara oshiete kudasai
  …に着いたら教えてください。
Where is the ... exit?
  ... deguchi wa doko desu ka?
  …出口はどこですか？
How far is it to walk?
  aruite dono kurai kakarimasu ka?
  歩いてどのくらいかかりますか？

I'd like to hire a ...
  ... o karitai no desu ga.
  …を借りたいのですが。
I'd like to go to ...
  ... ni ikitai desu
  …に行きたいです。
Please stop here.
  koko de tomete kudasai
  ここで停めてください。
How do I get to ...?
  ... e wa dono yō ni ikeba ii desu ka?
  …へはどのように行けばいいですか？
Where is this address please?
  kono jūsho wa doko desu ka?
  この住所はどこですか？
Could you write down the address for me?
  jūsho o kaite itadakemasen ka?
  住所を書いていただけませんか？
Go straight ahead.
  massugu itte   まっすぐ行って。
Turn left/right.
  hidari/migi e magatte
  （左 / 右）へ曲がって。
near/far
  chikai/tōi   近い / 遠い

Around Town
bank
  ginkō   銀行
embassy
  taishi-kan   大使館
post office
  yūbin kyoku   郵便局
market
  ichiba   市場
a public telephone
  kōshū denwa   公衆電話
toilet
  o-tearai/toire   お手洗い / トイレ
the tourist office
  kankō annaijo   観光案内所

What time does it open/close?
  nanji ni akimasu/shimarimasu ka
  何時に（開きます / 閉まります）か？

Accommodation
I'm looking for a ...
  ... o sagashite imasu
  …を探しています。

Signs

Information		
	annaijo	案内所
Open		
	eigyōchū	営業中
Closed		
	junbichū	準備中
Toilets		
	o-tearai/toire	お手洗い / トイレ
Men		
	otoko	男
Women		
	onna	女

hotel
  hoteru ホテル
guesthouse
  gesuto hausu ゲストハウス
inn
  ryokan 旅館
youth hostel
  yūsu hosuteru ユースホステル
camping ground
  kyampu-jō キャンプ場
Japanese-style inn
  ryokan 旅館
family-style inn
  minshiku 民宿

Do you have any vacancies?
  aki-beya wa arimasu ka?
  空き部屋はありますか？
I don't have a reservation
  yoyaku wa shiteimasen
  予約はしていません。

single room
  shinguru rūmu シングルルーム
double room
  daburu rūmu ダブルルーム
twin room
  tsuin rūmu ツインルーム
Japanese-style room
  washitsu 和室
Western-style room
  yōshitsu 洋室
Japanese-style bath
  o-furo お風呂
room with a (Western-style) bath
  basu tsuki no heya
  バス付きの部屋

How much is it per night/per person?
  ippaku/hitori ikura de suka?
  （一泊 / 一人）いくらですか？
Does it include breakfast/a meal?
  chōshoku/shokuji wa tsuite imasu ka?
  （朝食 / 食事）は付いていますか？
I'm going to stay for one night/two nights.
  hito-ban/futa-ban tomarimasu
  （一晩 / 二晩）泊まります。
Can I leave my luggage here?
  nimotsu o azukatte itadakemasen ka?
  荷物を預かっていただけませんか？

Shopping

I'd like to buy ...
  ... o kaitai desu
  …を買いたいです。
How much is it?
  ikura desu ka?
  いくらですか？
I'm just looking.
  miteiru dake desu
  見ているだけです。
It's cheap.
  yasui desu
  安いです。
It's too expensive.
  taka-sugi masu
  高すぎます。
I'll take this one.
  kore o kudasai
  これをください。
Can I have a receipt?
  ryōshūsho o itadakemasen ka?
  領収書をいただけませんか？

big
  ōkii 大きい
small
  chiisai 小さい
shop
  mise 店
supermarket
  sūpā スーパー
bookshop
  hon ya 本屋
camera shop
  shashin ya 写真屋
department store
  depāto デパート

Food

breakfast
chōshoku/asa gohan 朝食 / 朝ご飯
lunch
ranchi/chūshoku/ ランチ / 昼食 /
hiru gohan 昼ご飯
dinner
yūshoku/ban gohan 夕食 / 晩ご飯

I'm a vegetarian.
watashi wa bejitarian desu
私はベジタリアンです。
Do you have any vegetarian meals?
bejitarian-ryōri wa arimasu ka?
ベジタリアン料理はありますか？
What do you recommend?
o-susume wa nan desu ka?
おすすめは何ですか？
Do you have an English menu?
eigo no menyū wa arimasu ka?
英語のメニューはありますか？
I'd like the set menu please.
setto menyū o o-negai shimasu
セットメニューをお願いします。
Please bring the bill.
o-kanjō o onegai shimasu
お勘定をお願いします。
This is delicious.
oishii desu
おいしいです。

Health

I need a doctor.
isha ga hitsuyō desu
医者が必要です。
How do you feel?
kibun wa ikaga desu ka?
気分はいかがですか？
I'm ill.
kibun ga warui desu
気分が悪いです。
It hurts here.
koko ga itai desu
ここが痛いです。

I have diarrhoea.
geri o shiteimasu
下痢をしています。
I have a toothache.
ha ga itamimasu
歯が痛みます。

Emergencies

Help!
tasukete!
助けて！
Call a doctor!
isha o yonde kudasai!
医者を呼んでください！
Call the police!
keisatsu o yonde kudasai!
警察を呼んでください！
I'm lost.
michi ni mayoi mashita
道に迷いました。
Go away!
hanarero!
離れろ！

I'm ...
watashi wa ... 私は…
diabetic
tōnyōbyō desu 糖尿病です。
epileptic
tenkan desu てんかんです。
asthmatic
zensoku desu 喘息です。

I'm allergic to antibiotics/penicillin.
kōsei-busshitsu/penishirin ni arerugī ga arimasu
（抗生物質 / ペニシリン）に
アレルギーがあります。

antiseptic
shōdokuyaku 消毒薬
aspirin
asupirin アスピリン
condoms
kondōmu コンドーム
contraceptive
hinin yō piru 避妊用ピル
dentist
ha-isha 歯医者
doctor
isha 医者
hospital
byōin 病院
medicine
kusuri 薬
pharmacy
yakkyoku 薬局
tampons
tampon タンポン

(a) cold
kaze 風邪
diarrhoea
geri 下痢
fever
hatsunetsu 発熱
food poisoning
shoku chūdoku 食中毒
migraine
henzutsū 偏頭痛

Time, Days & Numbers

What time is it?
ima nan-ji desu ka?
今何時ですか？
today
kyō 今日
tomorrow
ashita 明日
yesterday
kinō きのう
morning/afternoon
asa/hiru 朝 / 昼

Monday
getsuyōbi 月曜日
Tuesday
kayōbi 火曜日
Wednesday
suiyōbi 水曜日
Thursday
mokuyōbi 木曜日
Friday
kinyōbi 金曜日

Saturday
doyōbi 土曜日
Sunday
nichiyōbi 日曜日

Numbers

0	*zero/rei*	ゼロ / 零
1	*ichi*	一
2	*ni*	二
3	*san*	三
4	*yon/shi*	四
5	*go*	五
6	*roku*	六
7	*nana/shichi*	七
8	*hachi*	八
9	*kyū/ku*	九
10	*jū*	十
11	*jūichi*	十一
12	*jūni*	十二
13	*jūsan*	十三
14	*jūyon/ jūshi*	十四
20	*nijū*	二十
21	*nijūichi*	二十一
30	*sanjū*	三十
100	*hyaku*	百
200	*nihyaku*	二百
1000	*sen*	千
5000	*gosen*	五千
10,000	*ichiman*	一万
20,000	*niman*	二万
100,000	*jūman*	十万

one million
hyakuman 百万

Glossary

anime – animated films
annai-jo – information office
arubaito – from the German 'arbeit', meaning 'to work', adapted into Japanese to mean part-time work

basho – *sumō* wrestling tournament
bentō – boxed lunch or dinner, usually of rice, fish or meat and vegetables
bijutsukan – art museum
biru – building
bodhisattva – Sanskrit term; Buddhist monks who have postponed enlightenment in order to help others along the same path; *Kannon* and *Jizō* are popular examples
bonkei – the art of miniaturising entire landscapes
bonsai – the art of cultivating miniature trees by careful pruning of the branches and roots
bottle keep – system that allows you to buy a bottle of liquor and leave it at the bar for subsequent visits
bugaku – dance pieces played by court orchestras in ancient Japan
bunraku – classical puppet theatre using life-size puppets to enact dramas similar to those of *kabuki*
bushidō – literally, 'way of the warrior'; esoteric ethos of the *samurai* class
butsu/butsu-zō – Buddha statue (as in Kamakura's Daibutsu, or Great Buddha)

carp – see *koi*
chaniwa – tea garden
chanoyu – tea ceremony
chizu – map
chō – city area between a ward *(ku)* and *chōme* in size
chōme – city area of a few blocks

dai – great; large
daifuku – literally, 'great happiness'; sticky rice cakes filled with red bean paste and eaten on festive occasions
daimyō – regional lords under the *shōgun*
deguchi – exit, as at a railway station
densha – train

denshi mēru – E-mail
depāto – department store
dōri – avenue or street (also *dōro*)

Edo – pre-Meiji Restoration name for Tokyo
eki – train station
ekiben – *bentō* lunch boxes sold at train stations
ema – small votive plaques hung in shrine sanctuaries as petitions to resident deities
en – garden (also *teien* or *niwa*)
enka – often referred to as Japanese country and western; ballads about love and loss that are popular with the older generation

fugu – poisonous blowfish or pufferfish, elevated to haute cuisine with a bite
furigana – Japanese syllabic script *(hiragana)* used as an aid to pronouncing *kanji*
furii kippu – all-day open ticket
futon – cushion-like mattress that is rolled up and stored away during the day
futsū – literally, 'ordinary'; a basic stopping-at-all-stations train service

gagaku – music of the imperial court
gaijin – literally, 'outside person'; the usual term for a foreigner; contracted form of *gaikokujin* (outside country person)
geisha – a 'refined person'; a woman versed in the arts and other cultivated pursuits who entertains guests
genkan – foyer area where your shoes are exchanged for slippers before entering the interior of a building
geta – traditional wooden sandals
gochisō-sama – after-meals expression of thanks

haiden – hall of worship in a shrine
haiku – 17-syllable poem
hakubutsukan – museum
hanami – cherry blossom viewing
hanko – personal stamp or seal used to authenticate documents; carries the same weight as a signature in the west

hantō – peninsula
hashi/bashi – bridge
hashi – chopsticks
hichiriki – Japanese oboe
higashi – east
hiragana – phonetic syllabary used to write Japanese words
honden – main building of a shrine
hondō – main building of a temple

ichiba – market
ike – pond
ikebana – art of flower arranging
innen – karma
itadakimasu – literally, 'I will receive'; before-meals expression
izakaya – Japanese version of a pub; beer, *sake* and lots of snacks available in a rustic, boisterous setting

ji – temple; see also *tera*
jikokuhyō – book of timetables; usually for trains
jinja – shrine (also *jingū* or *gū*)
jitensha – bicycle
Jizō – *bodhisattva* whose special charges are travellers and children

kabuki – form of Japanese theatre drawing on popular tales and characterised by elaborate costumes, stylised acting and the use of male actors for all roles
kaikan – hotel-style accommodation sponsored by the government
kaiseki – Japanese banquet cuisine in which every small detail of the repast is carefully controlled
kaisha – a company or firm
kaisoku – rapid train
kamemono – hanging pictures
kami – Shintō gods or spirits associated with natural phenomena
kami – above, or upper. Used in geographical terms and place names
kamikaze – literally, 'wind of the gods'; the typhoon that sank Kublai Khan's 13th-century invasion fleet and the name adopted by Japanese suicide bombers in the waning days of WWII
kampai – 'cheers', as in a drinking toast
kan – building/hall

kana – the two Japanese syllabaries (*hiragana* and *katakana*) used to supplement *kanji* in the Japanese writing system
kanji – literally, 'Chinese writing'; Chinese ideographic script used for writing Japanese
Kannon – Buddhist goddess of mercy (Guanyin in Chinese, Avalokiteshvara in Sanskrit and a camera company in Japanese)
karaoke – a famous export where revellers sing along to taped music minus the vocals
katakana – phonetic syllabary used to write foreign loan words, among other things
katamichi – one-way ticket
katana – Japanese sword
kawa/gawa – river
keigo – honorific language used in formal situations and to show respect to elders
ken – prefecture
kendō – 'the way of the sword'; fencing technique based on the two-handed samurai sword
kimono – robe-like outer garment, traditionally made of bast fibres or fine silk
kissaten – coffee shop
kita – north
ko – lake
kōban – local police box; a common sight in urban Japan
kōen – park
koi – carp; considered a brave, tenacious fish; *koinobori* windsocks are flown in honour of sons whom it is hoped will inherit these virtues
kokuminshukusha – 'peoples' lodges'; an inexpensive form of accommodation found in rural Japan
kokutetsu – Japan Railways (JR); literally, 'national line'
konb□ni – convenience store
kotatsu – heated table with quilt or cover over it to keep the lower body warm in the winter
koto – 13-stringed zither-like instrument
ku – city ward, an administrative area
kyūkō – ordinary express train (faster than *futsū*, stopping only at certain stations)

live house – nightclub or bar with performances of modern music by bands and solo performers

machi – town; the city area between a *ku* (ward) and *chōme* (a few blocks)

mama-san – occupation-era term that has survived: a woman who manages a snack or hostess bar; otherwise a matronly proprietor of a bar

manga – Japanese comic books or magazines

matsuri – festival

meishi – business card; very important in Japan

miko – shrine maidens

mikoshi – portable shrines carried around by phalanxes of sweaty half-naked *salarymen* during festivals

minami – south

minshuku – Japanese equivalent of a B&B; family-run budget accommodation usually found in rural Japan

mizu-shōbai – see *water trade*

mochi – pounded rice made into cakes and eaten on festive occasions

mon – gate, as at a shrine or temple

morning service – *mōningu sābisu*; a light breakfast served by coffee shops until around 10am; usually a doorstep slice of bread, a boiled egg, and jam and butter

Nihon or **Nippon** – Japanese word for Japan; literally, 'Source of the Sun'. The latter version sometimes carries a whiff of nationalism

ningyō – Japanese doll

niō – temple guardians

nishi – west

nō – classical Japanese mask drama performed on a bare stage

nomiya – traditional Japanese pub; see also *izakaya*

noren – door curtain for restaurants, usually with the name of the establishment

noriba – bus stop/boarding point

o- – prefix used to show respect, eg o-tōsan (father); see also *san*.

obi – sash or belt worn with *kimono*

o-cha – Japanese tea

Odoriko – state-of-the-art express train

ofuku – return ticket

o-furo – traditional Japanese bath

OL – common term which stands for office lady; female employee of a large firm; usually a clerical worker

o-miyage – souvenir; an obligatory purchase on any trip for Japanese

onsen – mineral hot spring with bathing areas and accommodation

origami – art of paper folding

pachinko – vertical pinball game which is a Japanese craze (estimated to take in ¥6 trillion a year) and a major source of tax evasion, *yakuza* funds and noise

pink salon – seedy hostess bar; pink is the Japanese equivalent of blue, as in pornography and the like

prepaid card – *puriipeido kādo*; magnetically coded card for a given sum of money which can then be spent on telephone calls, railway tickets and so on

rakugo – performances of stand-up comedy or long tales; a traditional art that is dying out

robotayaki – *yakitori* and the like, served in a boisterous, homey, rustic atmosphere; see also *izakaya*

romaji – roman script, as used in English

ryokan – traditional Japanese inn

sakura – cherry blossoms

salaryman – male employee of a large firm

sama – even more respectful than *san* (see below)

samurai – Japan's traditional warrior class; largely employed as Customs officials at Narita Airport nowadays

san – a respectful suffix applied to personal names; similar to Mr, Mrs or Ms, but more widely used

sanshō – Japanese three-spice powder

sekitori – a *sumō* who is in the top 50

sembei – soy-flavoured crispy rice crackers often sold in tourist areas

sen – line, usually train line

sensei – teacher, but also anyone worthy of respect

sentō – public bath

setto – set meal; see also *teishoku*

shakuhachi – wooden flute-like instrument

shamisen – traditional three-stringed banjo-like instrument

shi – city

shichimi – Japanese seven-spice powder

shikata ga nai – catch-all phrase, freeing individuals of responsibility or blame. Usually translated as 'It can't be helped', more liberal interpretations could run from 'someone stuffed up' to 'we're screwed now'
shin – new, as in *shinkansen* (new trunk line)
shinkansen – bullet train
shita-/shimo- – prefixes meaning down or lower. Used in geographical terms and place names
Shitamachi – low-lying plebeian quarters of old Edo, centred around Ueno and Asakusa
shodō – Japanese calligraphy; literally, 'the way of writing'
shōgun – military ruler of pre-Meiji Japan
shokudō – Japanese-style cafeteria/cheap restaurant
soba – buckwheat noodles
sumi-e – black ink-brush paintings
sumō – Shintō-derived sport where two immovable objects in ritual diapers collide in a ring

tabi – split-toed socks used when wearing *geta*
tako – traditional Japanese kite
tanka – poem of 32 syllables
tatami – tightly woven floor matting on which shoes should not be worn
teiki-ken – discount commuter tickets between two designated stops
teishoku – a set meal in a restaurant (usually lunch)
tera – temple (also *o-tera*, *dera* and *ji*)
to – metropolis, as in Tokyo-to
tokkyū – limited express train; faster than ordinary express *(kyūkō)*
torii – entrance gate to a Shintō shrine
tsunami – huge 'tidal' waves caused by an earthquake

ukiyo-e – wood-block prints; literally, 'pictures of the floating world'

uyoku – right-wing groups that yearn for the good old imperial days

wafuku – Japanese-style clothing
waka – 31-syllable poem
warikan – custom of sharing the bill (among good friends)
washi – Japanese paper
water trade – the world of bars, entertainment and sex for sale

yakitori – grilled chicken on a stick
yakuza – Japanese mafia
Yamanote – historically refers to the high city region of old Edo
yamato – a term of much debated origins that refers to the Japanese world, particularly in contrast to things Chinese
yatai – festival floats
yōfuku – Western-style clothing
yukata – like a dressing gown, worn for lounging after a bath; standard issue at *ryokan* and some budget business hotels

ACRONYMS
IDC – International Digital Communication
ITJ – International Telecom Japan
JETRO – Japan External Trade Organization
JNTO – Japan National Tourist Organization
JR – Japan Railways
JTB – Japan Travel Bureau
KDD – Kokusai Denshin Denwa
MIPRO – Manufactured Imports Promotion Organization
MITI – Ministry of International Trade & Industry
N'EX – Narita Express
NHK – Japan Broadcasting Corporation
NTT – Nippon Telegraph & Telephone Corporation
TCAT – Tokyo City Air Terminal
TIC – Tourist Information Center
YCAT – Yokohama City Air Terminal

LONELY PLANET

You already know that Lonely Planet produces more than this one guidebook, but you might not be aware of the other products we have on this region. Here is a selection of titles that you may want to check out as well:

Lost Japan
ISBN 0 86442 370 5
US$10.95 • UK£5.99

World Food Japan
ISBN 1 74059 010 4
US$13.99 • UK£8.99

Japan
ISBN 0 86442 693 3
US$25.99 • UK£15.99

Hiking in Japan
ISBN 1 86450 039 5
US$19.99 • UK£12.99

Japanese phrasebook
ISBN 0 86442 616 X
US$6.95 • UK£4.50

Read this First: Asia & India
ISBN 1 86450 049 2
US$14.95 • UK£8.99

Kyoto
ISBN 0 86442 564 3
US$14.95 • UK£8.99

Healthy Travel Asia & India
ISBN 1 86450 051 4
US$5.95 • UK£3.99

Tokyo Condensed
ISBN 1 74059 069 4
US$11.99 • UK£5.99

Chasing Rickshaws
ISBN 0 86442 640 2
US$34.95 • UK£19.99

Available wherever books are sold

Index

Text

Boxed Text

Places to Stay

Places to Eat

Locality Guide

Tokyo Map Section

MAP 1 – TOKYO

Map 2
Map 9
Map 3
Map 8
Map 4
Map 7
Map 5
Map 6

Senkawa
Kōshin-Zuka
Shin Mikawashima
Mikawashima
Tabata
Jōban Line
Shugamo-Shinden
17
Rikugi-en
Sugamo
Yamanote, Keihin-Tōhoku & North-bound Lines
Toshima-ku
Otsuka
Sugamo
Yamanote Line
Ikebukuro
Mukōhara
Sendagi
Yanaka Cemetery
Seibu Ikebukuro Line
Shin-Otsuka
Sengoku
Honkomagome
Saikyō Line
Bunkyō-ku
Ueno-kōen
Gokokuji
Hakusan
Ueno
Shuto Expressway No 5
Myōgadani
Todaimae
Takadanobaba
Takadanobaba
Kasuga
Hongō 3-chōme
Higashi-Nakano
Edogawabashi
Koshikawa Kōraku-en
Chūō Line
Kagurazaka
Seibu Shinjuku Line
Yamanote & Saikyō Lines
Ushigome Yanagi-chō
Sōbu Line
Kanda
Wakamatsu Kawada
Ushigome Kagurazaka
Shinjuku-ku
To Nerima
Ichigaya
Ichigaya
Chiyoda-ku
Kanda
Akebonobashi
Belgian Embassy
Imperial Palace
Shinjuku
Yotsuya
Yotsuya-Sanchōme
Yotsuya
Imperial Palace Gardens
Shinjuku-gyōen
Shinanomachi
Tōkyo
Japan Foundation Library
Shuto Expressway No 4
National Stadium
Akasaka Goyōchi
Sangūbashi
Jingū Gaien Gardens
Akasaka
Yoyogi-kōen
Shibuya-ku
Ginza
Yoyogi-Hachiman
Aoyama Cemetery
Roppongi
Tsukiji
Odakyū Line
New Zealand Embassy
Shibuya
Shuto Expressway No 3
Minato-ku
Komaba-Tōdaimae
Yamanote Line
Hama Rikyū Onshi-teien
Chūō-
Malaysian Embassy
Hiro-o
South Korea Embassy
Australian Embassy
Hinode Pier
Nakameguro
German Embassy
Italian Embassy Mita
Hinode
Map 5
Ebisu
French Embassy
Shuto Expressway No 2
Tamachi
Shirokane-Takanawa
Sengaku-ji
Shibaura Futō
Yütenji
Shizen Kyoiku-En
Takanawadai
Sengakuji
Tōyoko Line
Meguro-ku
New Takanawa Prince Hotel
Takanawadai
Tōkyo Monorail
Yurikamome Line
Gakugei-Daigaku
1
Hotel Pacific Meridien
Shinagawa
Shinkansen Line
Shuto Expressway No 1
To Den-en-chōfu
Gotanda
To Hara Museum of Contemporary Art, Yokohama & Kamakura
Yamanote, Keihin-Tōhoku & South-bound Lines
Rinkai Line
To Haneda Airport

Arakawa-ku
Arakawa
Kuyakushomae
Minami-Senju
Minowabashi

Kangafuchi

Keisei-Tateishi

Yotsugi

Koiwa

Katsushika-ku

Yahiro

Higashi-
Mukōjima

Hikifune

6

Keisei-
Hikifune

Shin-Koiwa

Taitō-ku

Asakusa

Oshiage

Narihirabashi

Omurai

Hirai

Sumida-ku

Kokugikan Sumō Hall
Ryōgoku
Ryōgoku

Kinshichō

Kameido

Edo-Tokyo
Museum

Shuto Expressway No 7

Higashi-
Ojima

Hamachō

Morishita

Kikukawa

Sumiyoshi

Nishi-
Ojika

Ojima

Tokyo City
Air Terminal
(TCAT)

Kiyosumi
Shirakawa

Funabori

Ichinoe

Kiyosumi-
teien

Fukagawa-Edo
Museum

Kōtō-ku

Monzen-nakachō

Kiba

Tōyōchō

Minami-Sunamachi

Edogawa-ku

Etchūjima

Keiyō Line

Nishi-Kasai

Kasai

Shiomi

Toyosu

Tatsumi

Shuto Expressway Chuo Loop Line

Shuto Expressway Wangan Line

Shin-Kiba

Shin-Kiba

Kasai-Rinkai-Kōen

Shinonome

Tokyo
Disneyland

Tokyo Bay

Tokyo International Pier

Shuto Expressway No 6

Transport

Railway Lines

Japan Railway

Private Railway

Shinkansen

Metro Lines

Ginza Lines

Marunouchi Line

Hibiya Line

Tōzai Line

Chiyoda Line

Yūrakuchō Line

Yūrakucho Line
(New Line)

Hanzōmon Line

Namboku Line

Toei Asakusa Line

Toei Mita Line

Toei Shinjuku Line

Toei Ōedo Line

0   0.5   1km
0   0.25   0.5mi

MAP 2 – IKEBUKURO, TAKADANOBABA

Senkawa

Takamatsu

Kanamechō

Senkawa

Kanamechō

Yurakuchō Line (New Line)

To Nerima (3km)

Seibu Ikebukuro Line

Toshima-ku

Ikeburo

See Enlargement

Tōbu Tōjō Line

Saikyō Line

Yamanote Line

Kita-Ikebukuro

Kami-Ikebukuro

Meiji-dōri

254

Higashi-Ikeburo

Kasuga-dōri

Marunouchi Line

To Ueno (5km)

Rokujikkai-dōri

49
50 51 52
53 54 55 56
Sunshine City Alta
World Import Mart
Sunshine 60

Green-dōri

Minami-Ikeburo-kōen

Higashi-Ikebukuro
To Otsuka Station (950m)

Shuto Expressway No 5

305

Minami-Ikeburo

Meiji-dōri

Kijakuchō Line

Zōshigaya (Streetcar Stop)

Zōshigaya Cemetery

Kishibojin-mae (Streetcar Stop)

To Gokoku-ji Temple (400m)

Kishimojinmae

2
10
1
Sakashita-dōri 6 9 Tokiwa-dōri
4 5 7
20 8
19 18 16 Bunka-dōri
17 Shinsen Ikeburo 12
21 13
11
15 42 43
22 24 4 14 West North 46 44
23 35 Exit Exit
27 36 41 45
26 Ikebukuro
28 29 25 Nishi-guchi 39 48
30 40 47
Nishi-Ikebukuro-kōen
31 34 Ikebukuro
33
32 38 East Exit
South Exit
Seibu Ikebukuro

Metropolitan-dōri
Gekijō-dōri

To Nakai (500m)

Shimo-Ochiai

Ochiai Central Park

Waseda-dōri

Kanda-gawa

Seibu Shinjuku Line

Saikyō Line

Yamanote Line

Shin-Mejiro-dōri

Takadanobaba
Takadanobaba
Takadanobaba

58

57
Nishi-Waseda
62 63 64
59 65
60 66
61 67 68

Tōzai Line

Takadanobaba

Gakushūin University

Gakushi-In-shita

Kanda-gawa

Omokagebashi

69
Waseda University

Waseda

Waseda

Toyama Park

0   125   250m
0   125   250yd

0   250   500m
0   250   500yd

MAP 2 – IKEBUKURO, TAKADANOBABA

PLACES TO STAY
3 Kimi Ryokan
貴美旅館
4 Hotel Star Plaza
Ikebukuro
ホテルスタープラザ
池袋
9 Ikebukuro Royal
Hotel
池袋ロイヤルホテル
13 Hotel Sun City
Ikebukuro
ホテルサンシティ池袋
20 House Ikebukuro
ハウス池袋
32 Hotel Metropolitan
ホテルメトロポリタン
37 Business Hotel
Ikebukuro Park
ビジネスホテル
池袋パーク
43 Hotel Sunroute
Ikebukuro
ホテルサンルート池袋
51 Hotel Grand City
ホテルグランド
シティー
52 Ark Hotel
アークホテル
55 Sunshine City Prince
Hotel
サンシャインシティ
プリンスホテル

PLACES TO EAT
1 Taiwan Hsiao Tiao
台湾小調
2 Joidar
ジョイダー
5 Sushi Kazu
寿司和
7 Tonerian
舎人庵
11 Doutor Coffee;
Tenkaippin Rāmen
天下一品ラーメン
14 McDonald's
16 Sasashū
笹周
17 Subway
18 Doutor Coffee
25 Mekong
メコン

26 Capricciosa
カプリチョーサ
27 Akiyoshi
秋吉
28 Malaychan
マレーチャン
29 Chez Kibeau
シェ・キーボウ
30 Tonbo
とんぼ
33 Yōrōnotaki
養老乃瀧
35 Pekin-tei
北京亭
48 Komazushi
こま寿司
50 Oriental Kitchen
オリエンタルキッチン
57 Cambodia
カンボジア
58 McDonald's
60 KFC
62 Yeti; Mingalaba
63 Kao Thai
カオ・タイ
65 Wendy's
ウエンディーズ
67 Capricciosa
カプリチョーサ

OTHER
6 Ikebukuro Post Office
池袋郵便局
8 Cinema Rosa
シネマロサ
10 Kimi Information
Center
貴美インフォ
メーションセンター
12 Bic Camera
ビックカメラ
15 Bobby's Bar
19 Hard Internet Cafe T&T
ハードインターネット
21 Police
警察署
22 Marui in the Room
マルイ・イン・ザ・
ルーム
23 Marui Department
Store; Virgin Megastore
丸井百貨店
バージンメガストア

24 Kinko's
31 Tokyo Metropolitan Art
Space
東京芸術劇場
34 The Dubliners
ザ・ダブリナーズ
36 Marui Field Sports Store
丸井フィールド
スポーツ館
38 Metropolitan Plaza
メトロポリタンプラザ
39 Tōbu Department Store
東武百貨店
40 Seibu Loft
西武ロフト
41 Parco Department Store
パルコ
42 Bic Camera (Main
Store)
ビックカメラ本店
44 The Black Sheep
ザブラックシープ
45 Mitsukoshi Department
Store
三越百貨店
46 Bic Camera PC Store
ビックカメラＰＣ
ストア
47 BicCamera
ビックカメラ
49 Toshima-ku Ward
Office
豊島区役所
53 Tōkyū Hands
東急ハンズ
54 Toyota Amlux
トヨタアムラックス
56 Toshima Post Office
豊島郵便局
59 Biblos Bookshop
洋書ビブロス
61 Daimaru Peacock
Department Store
大丸ピーコック
64 Mickey House
ミッキーハウス
66 Starbucks
68 Billy Barew's Beer Bar
ビリー・バリューズ・
ビア・バー
69 Sankus

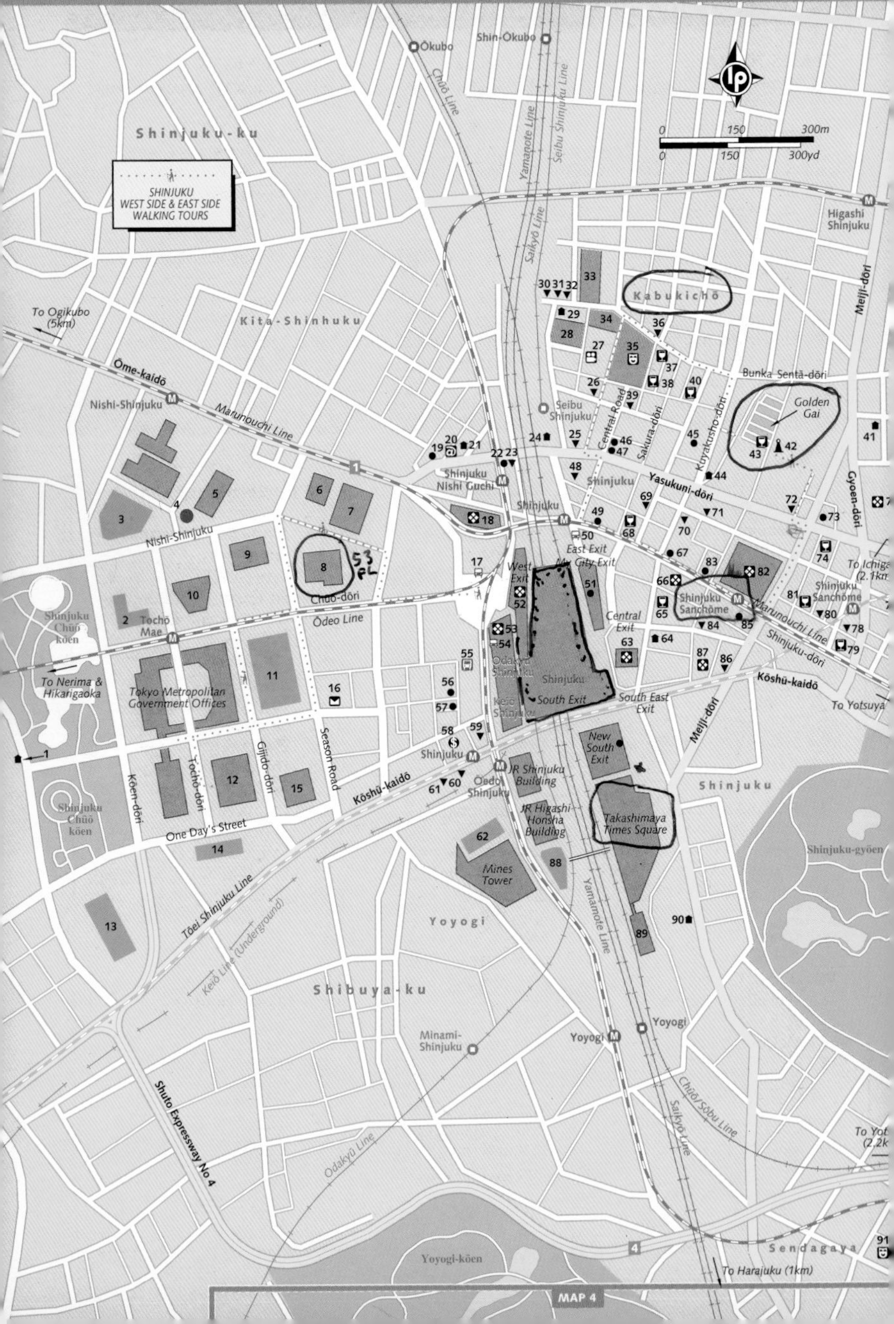

MAP 3 – SHINJUKU

Ōkubo

Shin-Okubo

Shinjuku-ku

SHINJUKU
WEST SIDE & EAST SIDE
WALKING TOURS

Chūō Line

Yamanote Line

Seibu Shinjuku Line

Saikyō Line

Higashi
Shinjuku

Meiji-dōri

To Ogikubo
(5km)

Ōme-kaidō

Marunouchi Line

Nishi-Shinjuku

Kita-Shinhuku

Kita-Shinjuku

Kabukichō

30 31 32   33

29   34

28   27   37

26   35   36

38   40

Bunka Sentā-dōri

Seibu
Shinjuku

Golden
Gai

19 20 21   24   25   46   45   43 42   41

Shinjuku
Nishi Guchi

22 23   48   47   44

Shinjuku   49   69   72

Nishi-Shinjuku

5   6   7   18   50   70   73

3   9   Chūō-dōri   53   East Exit   67   71

8   52   51   City Exit   66   83   82   74

4   17   West   54   Central   65   84   85   81

Tōchō   10   Exit   53   Exit   64   87   86   78

Mae   2   Ōdeo Line   55   63   68   79

Tokyo Metropolitan   11   16   56   South Exit   Shinjuku   Kōshū-kaidō

Government Offices   57   58   59   Nishi   South East   To Yotsuya

Shinjuku Chūō   12   15   58   Shinjuku   Exit   Shinjuku

kōen   14   60 61   JR Shinjuku   New South   Takashimaya

To Nerima &   Building   Exit   Times Square

Hikarigaoka   13   62   JR Higashi

One Day's Street   Honma   88

Kōshū-kaidō   Building

Mines   89   90

Tower

Yoyogi

Shibuya-ku

Shinjuku-gyōen

Minami-
Shinjuku

Yoyogi

Toei Shinjuku Line

Keiō Line (Underground)

Shuto Expressway No 4

Odakyū Line

Chūō Sōbu Line

Saikyō Line

Yamanote Line

Yoyogi-kōen

To Harajuku (1km)

Sendagaya

91

To Yot
(2.2k

To Ichiga
(2.1km)

Shinjuku
Sanchōme

Shinjuku-dōri

Marunouchi Line

Yasukuni-dōri

Central Road

Sakura-dōri

Koyatachō-dōri

Gyoen-dōri

Kōen-dōri

Jūnichō-dōri

Seison Road

Ōdeo Line

Tōchō-dōri

Gijidō-dōri

Chūō-dōri

Odakyū
Shinjuku

Odakyū
Station

0   150   300m
0   150   300yd

MAP 4

MAP 3 – SHINJUKU

PLACES TO STAY

1 Shinjuku New City Hotel
新宿ニューシティーホテル

2 Century Hyatt Tokyo
センチュリーハイアット東京

3 Hilton Tokyo
ヒルトン東京

11 Keiō Plaza Inter-Continental; Aurora Lounge; New York Bar
京王プラザインターコンチネンタル；オーロララウンジ；ニューヨークバー

13 Park Hyatt Tokyo; New York Grill/Bar; Sky Bar
パークハイアット東京；ニューヨークグリル／バー；スカイバー

14 Shinjuku Washington Hotel
新宿ワシントンホテル

21 Star Hotel Tokyo
スターホテル東京

24 Shinjuku Prince Hotel
新宿プリンスホテル

29 Green Plaza Shinjuku; Ladies Sauna
グリーンプラザ新宿；レディースサウナ

41 Hotel Sunlite Shinjuku
ホテルサンライト新宿

44 Shinjuku Kuyakusho-Mae Capsule Hotel
新宿区役所前カプセルホテル

62 Hotel Sunroute Tokyo
ホテルサンルート東京

64 Central Hotel
セントラルホテル

77 City Hotel Lornstar
シティーホテルロンスター

88 Hotel Century Southern Tower
ホテルセンチュリーサザンタワー

90 Park Hotel
新宿パークホテル

PLACES TO EAT

23 Omoide Yokochō Arcade
思い出横丁

25 Suzuya
すずや

26 Doutor Coffee

30 Peking
北京

31 Shinjuku Negishi
新宿ねぎし

32 Tainan Taami
台南担仔ヒ

36 Tokyo Kaisen Ichiba
東京海鮮市場

39 Tenkaippin
天下一品

48 Ibuki
いぶき

59 Raobian Gyōzakan
老辺餃子館

60 Court Lodge

61 Rose de Sahara
ローズデサハラ

69 Kurumaya
車屋

70 El Borracho
エルブラッチォ

71 Irohanihoheto
いろはにほへと

72 Tokyo Dai Hanten
東京大飯店

78 Istanbul
イスタンブール

80 Keika Kumamoto Rāmen
桂花熊本ラーメン

84 Tsunahachi
つな八

86 Daikokuya
大黒屋

OTHER

4 Island Hall
アイスランドホール

5 Shinjuku Island Tower
新宿アイスランドタワー

6 Shinjuku Nomura Building
新宿野村ビル

7 Yasuda Kasai-Kaijo Building
安田火災ビル

8 Shinjuku Center Building
新宿センタービル

9 Shinjuku Mitsui Building
三井ビル

10 Shinjuku Sumitomo Building
新宿住友ビル

12 Shinjuku NS Building
新宿ＮＳビル

15 KDD Building
ＫＤＤビル

16 Shinjuku Main Post Office
新宿中央郵便局

17 Shinjuku Main City Bus Stop
新宿西口バスターミナル

18 Odakyū Department Store
小田急百貨店

19 T Zone Computers
ティーゾーンコンピューター

20 Gaiax Net Café

27 Joy Cinemas
ジョイシネマ

28 Shinjuku Tokyū Bunka Kaikan Building
新宿東急文化会館

33 Tokyo Kenkō Plaza Hygeia Building; LL Bean
東京康健プラザハイジヤ

34 Grand Odeon Building; Cinemas; Liquid Room
グランドオデオンビルシネマ；リキッドルーム

35 Koma Theatre
新宿コマ劇場

37 Asa

38 Loft
ロフト

40 Club X

42 Hanazono-jinja Shrine
花園神社

43 Bon's

45 Shinjuku Ward Office
新宿区役所

Discount Ticket Stores

MAP 3 – SHINJUKU

The Tokyo subway system – clean, fast, safe and cheap. The *only* way to travel.

Shinjuku shopping area – something for everyone

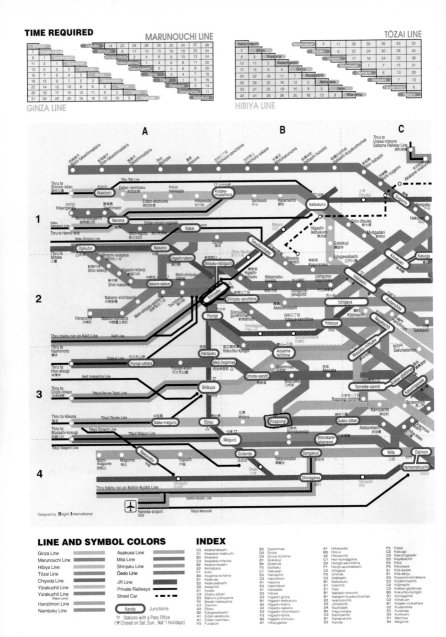

TIME REQUIRED

MARUNOUCHI LINE

TŌZAI LINE

GINZA LINE

HIBIYA LINE

LINE AND SYMBOL COLORS

Ginza Line
Marunouchi Line
Hibiya Line
Tōzai Line
Chiyoda Line
Yūrakuchō Line
Yūrakuchō Line (New Line)
Hanzōmon Line
Namboku Line

Asakusa Line
Mita Line
Shinjuku Line
Ōedo Line
JR Line
Private Railways
Street Car

Kanda   Junctions

▽ Stations with a Pass Office
(♥ Closed on Sat.,Sun., Nat'l Holidays)

INDEX

C3 Akabanebashi
C1 Akabane-iwabuchi
B3 Akasaka
C3 Akasaka-mitsuke
B2 Akebonobashi
C2 Akihabara
F1 Aoto
B3 Aoyama-itchōme
E1 Asakusa
E2 Asakusabashi
D2 Awajichō
A1 Ayase
C3 Azabu-jūban
E2 Bakuro-yokoyama
F2 Baraki-nakayama
C4 Daimon
A3 Ebisu
B2 Edogawabashi
A1 Eidan-akatsuka
A1 Eidan-narimasu
F3 Funabori

B3 Gaiemmae
D3 Ginza
D3 Ginza-itchōme
B1 Gokokuji
B4 Gotanda
F3 Gyōtoku
C1 Hakusan
E3 Hamachō
D3 Hanzōmon
A1 Hasune
E3 Hatchōbori
A1 Heiwadai
D3 Hibiya
B3 Higashi-ginza
B1 Higashi-ikebukuro
B1 Higashi-kōenji
A2 Higashi-nakano
F3 Higashi-nihombashi
F3 Higashi-ōjima
B2 Higashi-shinjuku
A1 Higarigaoka

A1 Hikawadai
B3 Hiro-o
A2 Hōnanchō
C1 Hon-komagome
D2 Hongō-sanchōme
F1 Honjo-azumabashi
C2 Ichigaya
F3 Ichinoe
C2 Iidabashi
B1 Ikebukuro
E1 Inarichō
C2 Iriya
B1 Itabashi-honchō
B1 Itabashi-kuyakushomae
E2 Iwamotochō
D2 Jimbōchō
D1 Kachidoki
B2 Kagurazaka
D2 Kamiyachō
E1 Kanamechō
E2 Kanda

F3 Kasai
C2 Kasuga
C2 Kasumigaseki
E3 Kayabachō
E4 Kiba
F3 Kikukawa
E1 Kita-ayase
C1 Kita-senju
E3 Kiyosumi-shirakawa
E3 Kodemmachō
C2 Kōjimachi
C3 Kokkai-gijidōmae
B3 Kokuritu-kyōgijō
C1 Komagome
C2 Kōrakuen
B3 Kotake-mukaihara
C2 Kudanshita
E2 Kuramae
E1 Kyōbashi
D1 Machiya
A4 Magome

Designed by Bright International

✈ Haneda-airport   Tōkyō Monorail

YŪRAKUCHŌ LINE

NAMBOKU LINE

CHIYODA LINE

HANZŌMON LINE

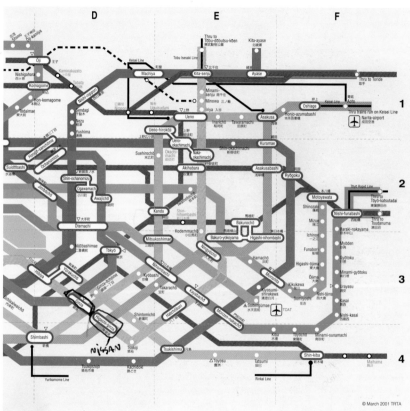

© March 2001 TRTA

B4 Meguro	A2 Nakano-sakaue	B3 Nogizaka
B3 Meiji-jingūmae	A4 Nakano-shimbashi	A1 Ochiai-minami-nagasaki
A2 Minami-asagaya	A4 Nakanobu	A1 Ochanomizu
F3 Minami-gyōtōku	E2 Naka-okachimachi	A1 Ochiai
E1 Minami-senju	A1 Nerima	D2 Ogawamachi
F4 Minami-sunamachi	A1 Nerima-kasugachō	A1 Ogikubo
C4 Minowa	D1 Nezu	D1 Ōji
E3 Mitsukoshimae	D3 Nihombashi	D1 Ōji-kamiya
F2 Mizue	D3 Nijūbashimae	F3 Ōjima
F2 Monzen-nakachō	D3 Ningyōchō	C3 Omote-sandō
A3 Morishita	F2 Nishi-funabashi	C3 Onarimon
B1 Motohasunuma	D1 Nishi-kasai	D2 Oshiage
F3 Motoyawata	A4 Nishi-magome	D2 Ōtemachi
F3 Myōden	D1 Nishi-nippori	B3 Roppongi
C2 Myōgadani	D1 Nishi-shinjuku	C3 Roppongi-itchōme
C2 Nagatachō	A2 Nishi-shinjuku-gochōme	F2 Ryōgoku
A1 Nakai	C1 Nishi-sugamo	C3 Sakuradamon
A3 Naka-meguro	A1 Nishi-takashimadaira	D1 Sendagi
A1 Nakano	A1 Nishidai	B4 Sengakuji
A2 Nakano-fujimichō	C1 Nishigahara	C1 Sengoku
		E1 Senkawa

C3 Shiba-kōen	B3 Shirokanedai	F4 Tōyōchō
B4 Shirokane-takanawa	B4 Shirokane-takanawa	E4 Toyosu
D4 Shimbashi	D2 Suehirochō	C4 Tsukiji
C1 Shimo	C1 Sugamo	D4 Tsukijishijō
B1 Shimura-sakae	C2 Suidōbashi	D4 Tsukishima
A2 Shin-egota	E3 Suitengūmae	E2 Uchisaiwaichō
C1 Shin-itabashi	F3 Sumiyoshi	E1 Ueno
F4 Shin-kiba	E1 Takadanobaba	E1 Ueno-hirokōji
A3 Shin-kōenji	B4 Takanawadai	E2 Ueno-okachimachi
A2 Shin-nakano	E3 Takarachō	F3 Urayasu
D2 Shin-ochanomizu	A1 Takashimadaira	B2 Ushigome-kagurazaka
C2 Shin-okachimachi	C2 Takebashi	B2 Ushigome-yanagichō
C1 Shin-ōtsuka	C3 Tameike-sannō	B2 Wakamatsu-kawada
A2 Shin-takashimadaira	E4 Tatsumi	B2 Waseda
A2 Shinjuku	E1 Tawaramachi	B2 Yotsuya
A2 Shinjuku-gyōemmae	A2 Tōchōmae	B2 Yotsuya-sanchōme
A2 Shinjuku-nishiguchi	C1 Tōdaimae	A2 Yoyogi
A2 Shinjuku-sanchōme	A4 Togoshi	A3 Yoyogi-kōen
F2 Shinozaki	D3 Tōkyō	D3 Yūrakuchō
D3 Shintomichō	C3 Toranomon	D1 Yushima
	A1 Toshimaen	

MAP 4 – SHIBUYA, ROPPONGI

MAP 3

Meiji-jingū Treasure Museum

To Shinjuku

North Gate

National Stadium

Meiji-jingū Shrine

Meiji-jingū Kaikan

Meiji-kōen

Sendagaya

Shrine Office

Yoyogi-kōen

5

Meiji-dōri

6

Southern Rest House

7

South Pond

Kitie-dōri

Harajuku

2 Takeshita-dōri

3

4

33

Jingūmae

Jingubashi

Meiji-jingu -mae

M 11

10 9

8

12

32

Harajuku

14

National Gymnasium

13

Aoyama-dōri

To Yoyogi (750m)

Jinnan

16 17

15

18

Omote-sandō

19

20

30

31

NHK Studio Plaza Building

TOKYU HANDS

127

126

29

Omote-sandō

M

21

Kamiyamachō

125

128

124

123

Jingū-dōri-kōen

Jingūmae

22

23

28

27

131

130

132

129

122

Shibuya

24

25

26

Udagawachō

Shōtō

137

138 139

140

Mitake-kōen

National Children's Castle

Hantōmon Line

Ginza Line

136

143

115

135

146

141

121

133 134

148 147

145

144

142

120

118 119

116

149 150 151

152

Shibuya

Miyamasu-zaka-dōri

Aoyama-dōri

Dōgenzaka

153

157

Hachikō Exit Shibuya

Shibuya

117

Shuto Expressway No 3

154

155

156

157

161

East Exit

160

162

Shibuya

163

South Exit

Tōkyū Shibuya

169

Shibuya-gawa River

To Shimokitazawa (3km) (underground)

159

Shibuya

168

To Daikanyama (900m)

Tamagawa-dōri

158

164

165

167

166

Shuto Expressway No 3

To Akasaka
Detached Palace

43

44

Roppongi

Toei Ōedo Line

55 56
52   57   Mikawadai-kōen
53 54   58   Roppongi-dōri
                      59
Roppongi-nishi-kōen 60   Hotel Baden
63   61 Roppongi (under construction)
64   Crossing 75
65 62   73 77 78
66   74 76   Roppongi
            72 79   Cemetery
            69 80   84 85
68   70 82 81
67   Roppongi 90 89 88 87 86
                  91 Roi
                  Building
                  92   To Axis
                          Building (100m)

0   100   200m
0   100   200yd

Meiji-jingū
Baseball
Diamond

Jingū Gaien

Prince Chichibu
Memorial
Rugby Stadium

Aoyama-ichome

39

Harzōmon Line

Ginza Line

Gaien-mae

37
34
36
35

Gaien-nishi-dōri

Minami-Aoyama

Aoyama
Cemetery

Chiyoda Line

Aoyama
Cemetery

113

110

109
108

114

111 Shuto Expressway No 3

112

Nishi-Azuma
Crossing

Nishi-Azabu

0   100   200m
0   100   200yd

100
99

To Hiroo (1.2km)

42

Akasaka

Tokyo
Broadcasting
Station (TBS)

Akasaka-dōri

45
46
47
48

Akasaka

MAP 7

Roppongi

To Ark
Hills (900m)

Gaien-higashi-dōri

40

41

Nogizaka

Toei Ōedo Line

51   50

Roppongi

Roppongi

See Enlargement

103

107

106
105 104

102

101

Roppongi-dōri

Hibiya Line

Teribi-Asahi-dōri

T.V. Asahi

Roppongi

93

94
95

96

97

98

Moto-Azabu

Azabu-Jūban

MAP 4 – SHIBUYA, ROPPONGI

PLACES TO STAY

1 Yoyogi Youth Hostel
代々木ユース
ホステル
40 Asia Center of Japan
アジア会館
43 Hotel New Ōtani
ホテルニュー
オータニ
47 Capsule Hotel Fontaine
Akasaka
カプセルホテル
フォーンテーン赤坂
54 Hotel Ibis
ホテルアイビス
93 International House of
Japan
国際文化会館
116 Shanpia Hotel Aoyama
シャンピアホテル青山
119 Shibuya Business Hotel
渋谷ビジネスホテル
120 Shibuya Tōkyū Inn
渋谷東急イン
128 Shibuya Tōbu Hotel
新宿東武ホテル
158 Hotel Sunroute
Shibuya
ホテルサンルート渋谷

PLACES TO EAT

2 McDonald's
3 Rat Ngon Store
5 Fonda de la
Madrugada
フォンダ・デ・ラ・マ
ドルガーダ
7 Ghee
ギー
8 Son of the Dragon
(Ryunoko)
龍子
11 Doutor Coffee
14 Tacos Del Amigo
タコス・デル・アミゴ
16 Fujimama's
17 Cafe de Rope
カフェ・ド・ロペ
19 Bamboo
バンブー
20 Apetito
アペティート
22 Home; Hiroba
ホーム；広場
23 Aux Sept Bonheurs
オー・セ・ボヌール
24 Las Chicas
ラス・チカス
25 Kinokuniya
International
Supermarket
紀ノ国屋

29 Subway
32 L'Amphore
アンフォーレ
35 Tony Roma's; Doutor
Coffee
38 Trattoria La Pecora
45 Ten-Ichi
天一
46 Fisherman's Wharf
48 Tendon Tenya
天丼天や
50 Inakaya
田舎屋
51 Gokoku
五穀
56 Havana Café
ハバナカフェ
58 Shōikiya
正直屋
65 McDonald's
67 Moti
モティ
71 Almond Coffee Shop
アーモンド
73 Johnny Rockets;
Cerveza
ジョニーロケッツ；
セルベザ
76 Moti Darbar
モティダールバリ
77 Seryna
瀬里奈
82 Bellini's Trattoria; Hub 2
ベリーニズピザ
83 Bikkuri Sushi
びっくり寿司
86 Hamburger Inn
ハンバーガーイン
88 McDonald's
89 Paco's Café
パコス・カフェ
91 Tony Roma's;
Hard Rock Café
トニーロマーズ；
ハードロックカフェ
92 Spago; Fukuzushi
スパゴ；
福寿司キッチン
99 Bistro de la Cite
ビストロ・ド・ラシテ
100 Casa Monnon
カサ・モンノン
102 Maenam
メナム
103 Bengawan Solo
ブンガワンソロ
107 El Mocambo
エル・モカンボ
108 Hokkaien
北海園
109 Monsoon Café
モンスーンカフェ

110 Rice Terrace
ライステラス
112 Bindi
ビンデ
124 New York
Kitchen
ニューヨークキッチン
126 Charlie House
145 Samrat
サムラート
147 Bougainvillea
ブーゲンビリア
149 Sakana-tei
酒菜亭
151 Reikyō
麗郷
159 Tainan Taami
台南担仔麺
165 Kantipur
カンティプール
166 Akiyoshi
秋吉
167 Court Lodge
169 Shizenkan
自然館

OTHER

4 Tōgo-jinja Shrine
東郷神社
6 Turkish Embassy
トルコ大使館
9 Do! Family Art
Museum
ドゥ！ファミリー
美術館
10 Ōta Memorial Art
Museum
大田記念美術館
12 Laforet Building
ラフォーレビル
13 Condomania
コンドーマニア
15 Oh God; Zest
18 Oriental Bazaar
オリエンタル
バザール
21 Hanae Mori Building;
L'Orangerie de Paris
ハナエモリビル
26 Maniac Love
27 Spiral Building;
Spiral Café
スパイラルビル
28 Mix; Topkapi
ミックス ；トプカピ
30 Zenkō-ji Temple
善光寺
31 Kiss
33 On Sundays;
Watari Museum of
Contemporary Art
ワタリウム美術館

34 Apollo
アポロ

36 Japan Traditional Craft Center
日本伝統工芸センター

37 Bell Commons
ベルコモンズ

39 Honda Welcome Plaza
ホンダビル

41 Nogi-jinja
乃木神社

42 Canadian Embassy
カナダ大使館

44 Suntory Museum of Art
サントーリ美術

49 Hikawa-jinja Shrine
氷川神社

52 Salsa Sudada
サルサ・スダーダ

53 Velfarre
ヴェルファーレ

55 Paranoia
パラノイア

57 People's Bar
ピープルズ・バ

59 Police Box

60 Netcafe Seishido
誠志堂

61 Geronimo
ジェロニモ

62 Dai-ichi Kangin Bank
第一勧業銀行

63 Tokyo Sports Cafe

64 Pylon

66 Meijiya International Supermarket
明治屋

68 Aoyama Book Centre
青山ブックセンター

69 Castillo
カスティーロ

70 Mogambo
モガンボ

72 Citibank; Tsukiji Sushiko
築地すし好

74 Milwaukee; Motown House
ミルウォーキー；モータウン・ハウス

75 Gas Panic Club
ガス・パニック・クラブ

78 Bar, Isn't it?; Cars
バーイズント イット；カーズ

79 Lexington Queen
レキシントンクィーン

80 Dusk Till Dawn

81 Manga Hiroba
マンガ広場

84 Gas Panic; Gas Panic Executive Lounge; Miller Bar Gas Panic

85 Déjà Vu
デジャブ

87 Paddy Foley's
パディフォーリーズ

90 Cavern Club
カバーンクラブ

94 Singaporean Embassy
シンガポール大使館

95 Luners

96 Azabu-jūban Onsen
麻布十番温泉

97 Austrian Embassy
オーストリア大使館

98 Chinese Embassy
中国大使館

101 328

104 Bul-Lets

105 Nishi-Azabu Post Office
西麻布郵便局

106 Club Oz
クラブオズ

111 Fuji Film Building
フジフィルムビル

113 Nezu Fine Art Museum
根津美術館

114 Blue
ブルー

115 Blue Note
ブルーノート東京

117 Gotō Planetarium; Tōkyū Bunka Kaikan
五島プラネタリウム；東急文化会館

118 Shibuya Post Office
渋谷郵便局

121 Marui Young Store
丸井ヤング館

122 Doi Camera
カメラのドイ

123 Tepco Electric Energy Museum (Denryokukan)
電力館

125 Tobacco & Sal Museum
たばこと塩の博物館

127 Eggman
エッグマン

129 Parco II
パルコパート2

130 Jazz Swing
ジャズスウィング

131 Tsutsumu Factory
つつむファクトリー

132 Kanze Nō-gakudō Theatre
観世能楽堂

133 Bunkamura
文化村

134 Tokyo Department Store
東急百貨店

135 The Cave
ザ・ケイブ

136 Beam Building
ビーム

137 Tōkyū Hands
東急ハンズ

138 Parco III; Fungo
パルコパート3

139 Parco I
パルコパート1

140 Marui Department Store
丸井百貨店

141 Seibu Department Store (Main Store)
西武百貨店（本店）

142 Seibu Department Store (A Building)
西武百貨店（A館）

143 Loft
ロフト

144 Hub Pub
ハブパブ

146 Club Quattro
クラブクアトロ

148 Cine Amuse
シネアミューズ

150 Click On
クリックオン

152 109 Building

153 Panama Joe's
パナマジョーズ

154 Club Asia

155 On Air West
オンエアーウエスト

156 Dr. Jeekan's
ドクタージーカンズ

157 On Air East
オンエアーイースト

160 Mark City West
マークシティウエスト

161 Mark City East;Shibuya Excel Hotel Tōkyū
マークシティイース ト；渋谷エクセルホテ ル東急

162 Shibuya Bus Terminal
渋谷バスターミナル

163 Tokyu Plaza
渋谷東急プラザ

164 Fujiya Honten
富士屋本店

168 Kirin City
キリンシティー

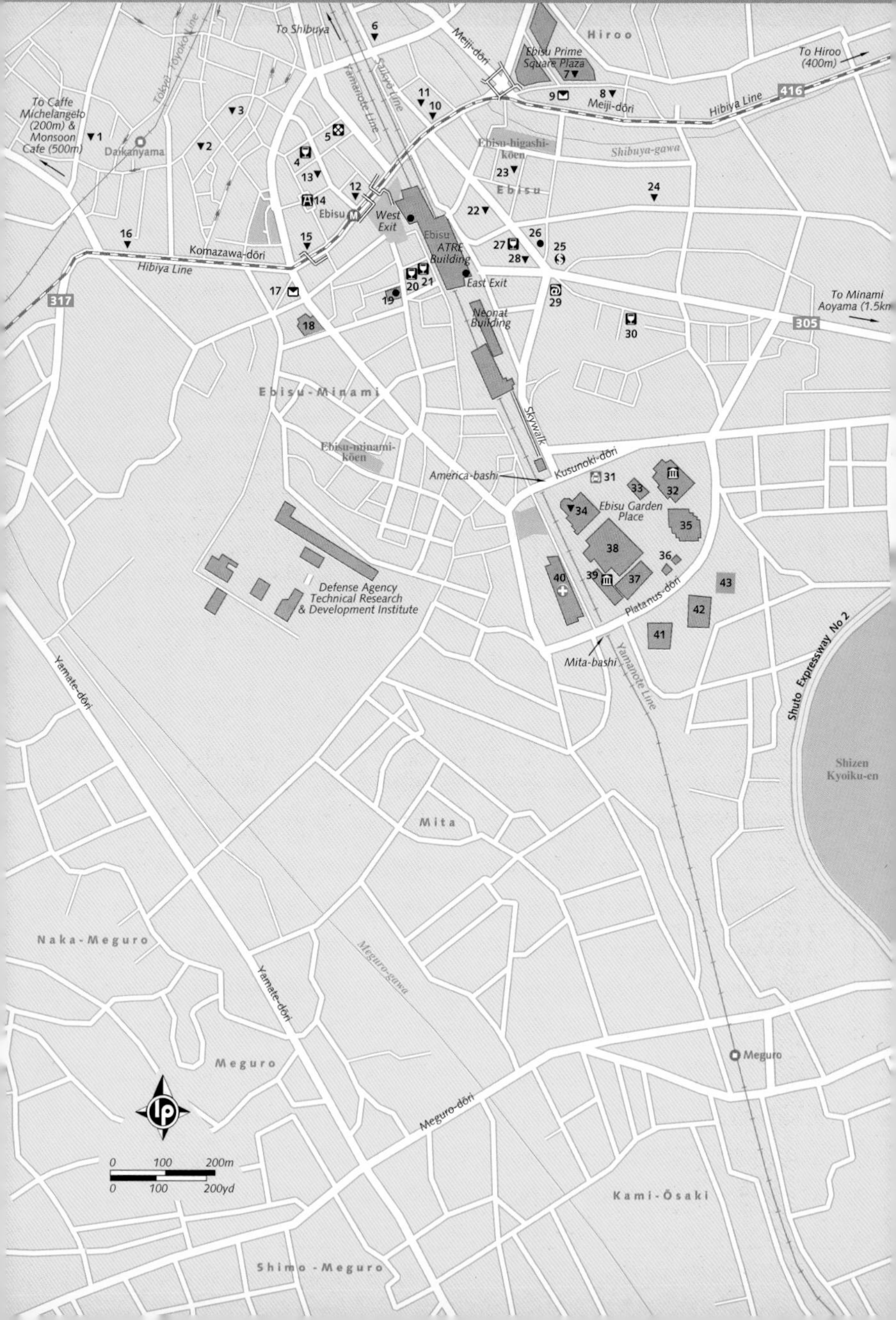

MAP 5 – EBISU

Hiroo

To Shibuya

Ebisu Prime
Square Plaza
7 ▼

To Hiroo
(400m)

Meiji-dōri

6 ▼

Meiji-dōri

9 ☐ 8 ▼
7 ▼

11 ▼
10 ▼

Hibiya Line
316

To Caffe
Michelangelo
(200m) &
Monsoon
Cafe (500m)

▼ 3

Daikanyama

Ebisu-higashi-
kōen

Shibuya-gawa

▼ 1

▼ 2

5 ☐

23 ☐

24 ▼

4 ☐

13 ☐

Ebisu

12 ☐

22 ☐

26 ●
27 ☐ 25
28 ☐

16 ▼

Komazawa-dōri

Ebisu Ⓜ

14 ☐

West
Exit

Ebisu
ATRE
Building

15 ▼

Hibiya Line

317

17 ☐

East Exit

29

30 ☐

Yebisu
Building

To Minami
Aoyama (1.5km)

305

19 20 21

18 ☐

Ebisu-Minami

Skywalk

America-bashi

Kusunoki-dōri

31 ☐

33 ☐ 🏛 32

Ebisu-minami-
kōen

34 ☐

Ebisu Garden
Place

35 ☐

Defense Agency
Technical Research
& Development Institute

38 ☐

36 ☐

Platanus-dōri

43 ☐

40 ☐ ✚
39 ☐ 🏛 37

42 ☐

Mita-bashi

Yamate-dōri

41 ☐

Shuto Expressway No 2

Shizen
Kyōiku-en

Mita

Meguro-gawa

Naka-Meguro

Yamate-dōri

Meguro Ⓜ

Meguro

Meguro-dōri

Kami-Ōsaki

0   100   200m
0   100   200yd

Shimo-Meguro

Traffic lights and office blocks

ERIC L WHEATER

MAP 6 – ŌDAIBA/TOKYO BAY AREA

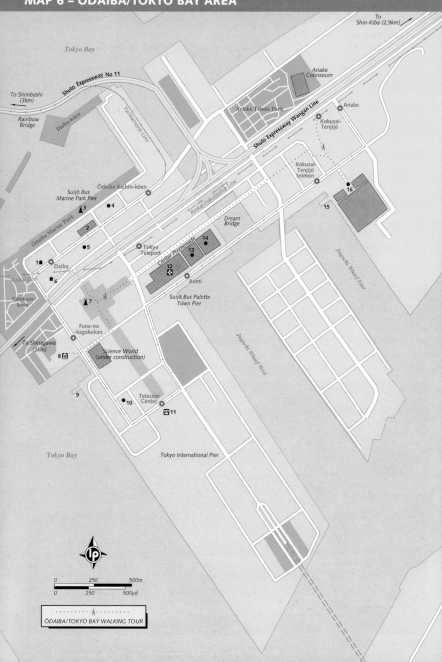

Tokyo Bay

To Shin-Kiba (2.9km)

Ariake Colosseum

To Shimbashi (3km)

Shuto Expressway No 11

Rainbow Bridge

Daiba-kōen

Ariake Tennis Park

Ariake

Shuto Expressway Wangan Line

Yurikamome Line

Kokusai-Tenjijō

Suijō Bus Marine Park Pier

Ōdaiba Kaihin-kōen

Kokusai-Tenjijō Seimon

3

4

Rinkai Fukutoshin Line

Ōdaiba Marine Park

2

Dream Bridge

16

15

5

Tokyo Teleport

Center Promenade

14

13

1

Daiba

12

6

Aomi

7

Suijō Bus Palette Town Pier

To Shinagawa (3km)

Rinkai Line

Shiokaze-kōen

Fune-no -kagakukan

8

Science World (under construction)

Jōnanjima Wharf East

Jōnanjima Wharf West

9

Telecom Center

10

11

Tokyo Bay

Tokyo International Pier

0   250   500m
0   250   500yd

ŌDAIBA/TOKYO BAY WALKING TOUR

MAP 6 – ŌDAIBA/TOKYO BAY AREA

PLACES TO STAY

1 Hotel Nikkō Tokyo
ホテル日航東京

6 Hotel Grand Pacific
Meridien
ホテルグランドパシ
フィックメリデイエン

OTHER

2 Aqua City Odaiba
アクアシティお台場

3 Statue of Liberty
自由の女神

4 Deck's Tokyo Beach;
Wakō; Hina Zushi;
Khazana
デックス東京ビーチ；
和幸；雛寿司；
カザーナ

5 Fuji Television Japan
Broadcast Centre
フジテレビ日本放送
センター

7 Flame of Liberty

8 Museum of Maritime
Science
船の科学館

9 Suijō Bus Aomi Pier
水上バス青海発着所

10 Time 24 Building
タイム２４ビル

11 Telecom Center
テレコムセンター

12 Palette Town;
Venus Fort
Soup Stock Tokyo
パレットタウン；
ビーナスフォート；
スープストック
トーキョー

13 Toyota Mega Web
メガウェブ

14 Neo Geo World
ネオジオワールド

15 Suijō Bus Ariake Pier
水上バス有明発着所

16 Tokyo International
Exhibition Center
東京ビッグサイト
（東京国際展示場）

Fuji Television Japan Broadcast Center in Ōdaiba, with the Yurikamome monorail in the foreground

MAP 7 – AKASAKA, GINZA, TSUKIJI

Hanzōmon Line

Shuto Expressway No 4

Sukibayashi Crossing

1

34

Nagatachō

Nagatachō

Nagatachō

35

Sakuradamon

Nagatachō

4

Yūrakuchō Line

3

5

33

Akasaka-mitsuke

Nagatachō

Marunouchi Line

Sakurada-dōri

6

7

11

31

32

Kasumigaseki

Kasumigaseki

8

9

10

16

30

Kokkai-gijidōmae

Kasumigaseki

Kasumigaseki

12

14

17

Kokkai-gijidōmae

Chiyoda Line

13

Kasumigaseki

15

18

29

27

28

Hibiya-kōen

TBS Building 19

Sotobori-dōri

Hibiya-dōri

20

21 22

26

Akasaka

24 25

Hikawa-kōen

Tameike-sannō

Shuto Expressway Loop Line

r

Toranomon

125

23

130 129

128

Akasaka

131

127

126

Toranomon

Ginza Line

Uchisaiwaichō

Roppongi-dōri

132

Toranomon

Hibiya Line

Uchibori-dōri

138

Shimbashi

141

139

Ark Hills

133

140

137

134

142

136

135

Azabudai

Roppongi

143

Kamiyachō

147

144

145 146

Onarimon

Toei Mita Line

149

Toei Asakusa Line

148

LP

Zōjō-ji

Daimon

Toei Ōedo Line

0   100   200m
0   100   200yd

To Roppongi (1km)

150

Azabu-jūban

Shiba-kōen

Shiba-Kōen

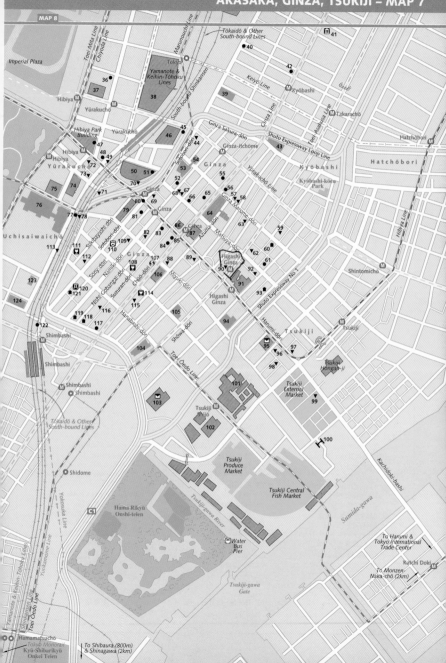

MAP 7 – AKASAKA, GINZA, TSUKIJI

PLACES TO STAY

1 Akasaka Prince Hotel
赤坂プリンスホテル
3 Akasaka Tōkyū Hotel
赤坂東急ホテル
13 Capsule Hotel Fontaine
Akasaka
カプセルホテル
フォンテーヌ赤坂
17 Capitol Tōkyū Hotel;
Keyaki Grill
キャピトル東急ホテル
39 Yaesu Fujiya Hotel
八重洲富士屋ホテル
43 Hotel Seiyō Ginza
ホテル西洋銀座
60 Hotel Ginza Dai-ei
ホテル銀座ダイエー
76 Imperial Hotel;
Old Imperial Bar
帝国ホテル
93 Hotel Alcyone
ホテルアルシオン
94 Ginza Tōkyū Hotel
銀座東急ホテル
104 Ginza Dai-Ichi Hotel;
Ichi-zushi
銀座第一ホテル
105 Ginza Tōbu Hotel
銀座東武ホテル
118 Ginza International
Hotel
銀座国際ホテル
119 Mitsui Urban Hotel;
Munakata
三井アーバンホテル
121 Ginza Nikkō Hotel
銀座日航ホテル
123 Dai-Ichi Hotel Annex
第一ホテルアネックス
124 Dai-Ichi Hotel
第一ホテル
133 Hotel Ōkura; Tohkalin;
Highlander
ホテルオークラ
134 Hotel Ōkura (South
Wing)
ホテルオークラ別館
138 ANA Hotel Tokyo
全日空ホテル東京
142 Roppongi Prince Hotel
六本木プリンスホテル
149 Tokyo Prince Hotel
東京プリンスホテル

PLACES TO EAT

7 Subway

8 Ten-Ichi
天一
9 Trattoria Marumo
トラットリアマルーモ
10 Moti
モティ
11 Tokyo Joe's
東京ジョーズ
12 Fisherman's Wharf
14 Sushi-sei
寿司清
15 Tendon Tenya
天丼天や
18 Tōfuya
豆腐屋
19 Starbucks
20 Moti
モティ
24 Mugyodon
ムギョドン
25 Chez Prisi
シェ・プリシィ
44 Wendy's
49 Shin-hi-no-moto
新日の基
57 Kaiten Sushi
回転寿司
58 Volks
フォルクス
59 Chichibu Nishiki
ちちぶにしき
62 Doutor Coffee
63 Tendon Tenya
天丼天や
67 Don Don Tei
どんどん亭
68 Subway
69 Jirō Sushi
次郎寿司
70 Buono Buono
ヴォノヴォノ
71 Yūrakuchō Yakitori Alley
焼き鳥屋
72 Tonton Honten
とんとん本店
73 Robata
炉端
78 Funachu
鮒忠
82 New Torigin
新鳥ぎん
88 Potohar
パトワール
89 Maharaja
銀座マハラジャ
90 Nair's
ナイル
92 Doutor Coffee

96 Tsukiji Sushikō
築地すし好
97 Sushi Iwa
寿司岩
98 Edogin Sushi
江戸銀寿司
99 Sushidai
寿司代
109 Ten-Ichi
天一
112 West
ウエスト
113 Shinjuku Negishi
新宿ねぎし
115 Ashoka
アショカ
116 Kyūbei
久兵衛
129 Doutor Coffee
143 Panic Café
146 Bernd's Bar

OTHER

2 Akasaka Tōkyū Plaza
赤坂東急プラザ
4 Argentina/Lebanon/
Jordan Embassies
アルゼンチン／
レバノン／
ヨルダン大使館
5 Mexican Embassy
メキシコ大使館
6 Citibank
16 Hie-jinja Shrine
日枝神社
21 Hobgoblin
22 Akasaka Post Office
赤坂郵便局
23 B-Flat
26 Akasaka Sakurado
赤坂桜堂
27 Prime Minister's
Residence
首相官邸
28 Prime Minister's Office
総理府
29 Diet Press Center
国会記者会館
30 Members of the House of
Representative's
No 1 Office Building
衆議院第一議員館
31 Members of the House of
Representative's
No 2 Office Building
衆議院第二議員館
32 National Diet Building
国会議事堂

33 Members of the House
of Councillor's Office
衆議院議員会館

34 Social Democratic Party
Headquarters; Social
Culture Building
社会民主党本部 ；
社会文化会館

35 Constitution
MemorialHall
憲政記念館

36 United Airlines

37 Imperial Theatre;
Idemitsu Art Museum
帝国劇場 ；出光美術館

38 Tokyo International
Forum/ (TIC) Tourist
Information Center
東京国際フォーラム ；
観光案内所

40 Yaesu Book Center
八重洲ブック
センター

41 Bridgestone Bijitsukan
Art Museum
ブリジストン美術館

42 Meijiya International
Supermarket
明治屋

45 HMV Record Store
ＨＭＶレコード店

46 Kōtsū Kaikan Building
(JNTO Overseas Office)
東京交通会館

47 American Pharmacy

48 American Express

50 Mullion Building
(Seibu &
Hankyū Department
Stores)
有楽町マリオンビル

51 Seibu Department Store
(Annex)
西武百貨店

52 Kodak Imagica
コダックイメージ

53 Printemps
Department Store
プランタン百貨店

54 Printemps Annex
プランタン別館

55 Meijiya
明治屋

56 Itōya
伊藤屋

61 World Magazine Gallery
マガジンハウス

64 Matsuya Department
Store
松屋百貨店

65 Nikon Salon
ニコンサロン

66 Kirin City
キリンシティー

74 Hibiya Chanter;
L'Attresco (Cinema)
日比谷シャンテ

75 Tokyo Disneyland Ticket
Center
Tokyo Takarazuka
Theatre
東京宝塚劇場

77 International Arcade
国際アーケード

79 Hankyū Department
Store (Sukiyabashi Store)
阪急百貨店

80 Sukiyabashi Crossing
数寄屋橋交差点

81 Sony Building;
Maxim's de Paris;
Sabatine di Firenze
ソニービル

83 Jena Bookshop
イエナ書店

84 Contax Gallery
コンタックスサン

85 San Ai Building
三愛ビル

86 Wakō Department Store;
Mikimoto Pearl
和光百貨店

87 Mitsukoshi Department
Store
三越百貨店

91 Kabuki-za Theatre;
Chichibu Nishiki
歌舞伎座

95 Kyōbashi Post Office
京橋郵便局

100 Namiyoke-jinja
波除神社

101 National Cancer Center
国立ガンセンター

102 Asahi Newspapers
朝日新聞社

103 Ginza Post Office
銀座郵便局

106 Matsuzakaya
Department Store
松坂屋百貨店

107 Citibank

108 Pilsen
ピルセンビアホール

110 Ginza Nō-gakudō
Theatre
銀座能楽堂

111 Henry Africa
ヘンリー・アフリカ

114 Lion Beer Hall
ライオンビアホル

117 Hakuhinkan Toy Park
博品館トーイパク

120 Hachiman-jinja Shrine
八幡神社

122 Daikokuya Discount
Tickets
大黒屋

125 Nihonshu Jōhōkan
日本酒情報館

126 Toranomon Hospital
虎の門病院

127 Japan External Trade
Organization (JETRO)
Main Office
日本貿易振興会

128 Inachū Laquerware
いなちゅう漆器

130 Akasaka Hospital
赤坂病院

131 Akasaka Twin Tower
Building
赤坂ツインタワー

132 US Embassy
アメリカ大使館

135 Swedish Embassy
スウェーデン大使館

136 Spanish Embassy
スペイン大使館

137 Suntory Building
サントリーホール

139 Ark Mori Building
アーク森ビル

140 Roppongi Post
Office
六本木郵便局

141 American Ambassador's
Residence
アメリカ大使館宿舎

144 Pit Inn

145 Axis Building

147 Netherlands
Embassy
オランダ大使館

148 Tokyo Tower
東京タワー

150 American Center

151 World Trade Center
Building
貿易センタービル

MAP 8 – KANDA, TOKYO STATION AREA, IMPERIAL PALACE

Iidabashi

To Kasuga
(600m)

405

Sotobori-dōri

Iidabashi

3

Iidabashi

2

1

To Tokyo Dome
(Big Egg)
(150m)

Suidōbashi

Chūō & Sōbu Line

Sarugakuchō

Tozai Line

5

Nihon
University

4

8

Hakusan-dōri

Toei Mita Line

Bookshop
Neighbourhood

Jimbōchō

39

36

Jimbōchō

38

37

Kudan-Kita

Yasukuni-dōri

Kudanshita

Jimbōchō

43

40

Toei Shinjuku Line

42

41

Kiyomizu Moat

To Ichigaya
(400m)

Sanbanchō

Kitanomaru-kōen

48

Hanzōmon Line

46

49

Takebashi

401

44

47

51

50

Area not open
to public

Fukiage
Imperial
Gardens

Higashi Gyoen

85

45

C1

Area not open
to public

Shinjuku-dōri

Hirei Moat

Uchibori-dōri

Shimo-dōkan
Moat

86

87

89

To Nagata-chō
(300m)

To Aoyama
(2km)

Sakurada
Moat

Area not open
to public

To Roppongi
(1.5km)

Kami-dōkan
Moat

90

88

Imperial Palace
Outer Garden

Imperial Palace
Plaza

Map 7

To Hongo
San-chome
(400m)

Tokyo Medical &
Dental University

Kanda
Myōjin
Shrine

8

Ginza Line

Chūō-dōri

1

Hibiya Line

17

7

Ochanomizu

Yamanote & Keihin-Tōhoku Lines

North-bound Shinkansen Line

Chiyoda Line

Akihabara

Ochanomizu

6

Ochanomizu

Electronics
Neighbourhood

9

10

11

Asakusabashi

Sōbu Line

31

5

Nichidai
Hospital

32

12 Akihabara

Meiji
University

Chūō Line

Akihabara

Kanda-gawa

33

Shin-Ochanomizu

30

28

14

13

29

26

Sporting Goods
Neighbourhood

25

27

Toei Shinjuku Line

Iwamotochō

34

24

Yasukuni-dōri

22

23

Ogawamachi

Awajichō

21

Kanda

15

Iwamotochō

Kodenmachō

Kanda
Nishikichō

20 19

Kanda

4

18

Kanda

Kodenmachō

17

Kanda

Kodenmachō

16

Chūō-dōri

Shuto Expressway Loop Line

Sōbu Line

Hibiya Line

C1

Marunouchi Line

56

Shin-Nihombashi

Nihombashi-Muromachi

52

Toei Mita Line

Chiyoda Line

53 54

Ginza Line

Shuto Expressway No 1

55

Mitsukoshi Mae

57

Ōtemachi

Hanzōmon Line

Ōtemachi

Ōtemachi

84

Eitai-dōri

Ōtemachi

58

To Asakusa-bashi
JR Station

83

Mitsukoshi Mae

59

60

To Suitengumae
Station (450m)

Ōtemachi

82

61

Tōzai Line

Nihombashi

Shuto Expressway No 6

Wadakura
Square

Marunouchi

Sōbu Line

Sotobori-dōri

Tokyo

Tokyo
Stock
Exchange

75

Tokyo

Marunouchi
Central Exit

76

Nihombashi

63

Nihombashi

74

73

64

To Tokyo City
Air Terminal
(TCAT)
(450m)

Tokyo

77

72

Hibiya Line

Nijū-bashi-mae

81

Tokyo

66

65

Chūō-dōri

Yaesu
Central
Exit

Yaesu

67

62

80

79

78

71

68

Toei Asakusa Line

Kayabachō

70

69

To Tokyo International
Forum (250m)

To Southbound
Shinkansen

0   100   200m
0   100   200yd

MAP 8 – KANDA, TOKYO STATION AREA, IMPERIAL PALACE

PLACES TO STAY

3 Tokyo International
Youth Hostel
東京国際ユースホステ
ル

4 YMCA Asia Youth
Center
YMCAアジア青少年
センター

5 Yama no Ue Hilltop
Hotel
山の上ホテル

13 Akihabara Washington
Hotel
秋葉原ワシントン
ホテル

17 Central Hotel
セントラルホテル

18 Grand Central Hotel
グランドセントラル
ホテル

19 New Central Hotel
ニューセントラル
ホテル

25 Tokyo Green Hotel
Ochanomizu
東京グリーンホテル
御茶ノ水

29 Hotel New Kanda
ホテルニュー神田

30 Tokyo Ochanomizu
Hotel Juraku
東京御茶ノ水ホテル
聚楽

72 Yaesu Terminal Hotel
八重洲ターミナル
ホテル

75 Yaesu Ryūmeikan
八重洲龍名館

76 Hotel Kokusai Kankō
ホテル国際観光

81 Tokyo Station Hotel
東京ステーション
ホテル

82 Tokyo Marunouchi
Hotel
丸ノ内ホテル

83 Palace Hotel
パレスホテル

PLACES TO EAT

6 Pronto Coffee
プロントコーヒー

8 Jangara Rāmen
じゃんがらラーメン

15 Doutor Coffee

20 Taiwan Yatai
台湾屋台

22 Starbucks

24 Botan
ぼたん

26 Kanda Yabu Soba
神田やぶそば

34 Hisago
ひさご

38 Mandala
マンダラ

39 Muang Thai Nabe;
Muito Bom; Menam no
Hotori
ムアンタイなべ；
ムイトボン

56 Maromachi Sunaba
砂場

60 Starbucks

67 Nanban-tei
南蛮亭

68 Banya
番屋

73 Becks Coffee; Berlitz

79 Starbucks

OTHER

1 Institute Franco-
Japanais du Tokyo
日仏学院

2 British Council

7 Yushima Seidō
湯島聖堂

9 Tokyo-Mitsubishi Bank
東京三菱銀行

10 LAOX Electronics Store
ラオックス電化店

11 Akihabara Eki-mae
Commons
秋葉原駅前広場

12 Akihabara Department
Store
秋葉原デパート

14 Mansei-bashi Bridge
万世橋

16 Kinko's

21 Kinko's

23 Matsuya
まつや

27 Transportation
Museum
交通博物館

28 Kanda Post Office
神田郵便局

31 Hitachi Building
日立製作所

32 Nikolai Cathedral
ニコライ堂

33 Mitsui Kaij Insurance
Building
三井海上ビル

35 Tuttle Bookshop
タトル書店

36 Issei-dō Bookshop
一誠堂書店

37 Jimbōchō Post Office
神保町郵便局

40 Tayasu-mon Gate
田安門

41 Nihon Budōkan Hall
日本武道館

42 Indian Embassy
インド大使館

43 Yasukuni-jinja
靖国神社

44 Irish Embassy
アイルランド大使館

45 UK Embassy
イギリス大使館

46 Chidorigafuchi Water
Park
千鳥ヶ淵水上公園

47 Kōgeikan Craft
Museum
工芸館

48 Kagaku Gijitsukan
Science Museum
科学技術館

49 Tokyo Kokuritsu Kindai
Bijutsukan
国立近代美術館

50 Kitahanebashi-mon
Bridge/Gate
北桔橋門

51 Hirakawa-mon Gate
平川門

52 Tokyo Immigration
Bureau
東京入国管理局

53 Federation of
Economic
Organisations
経団連

54 Nippon Keizai Shimbun
(Nikkei) Head Office
日本経済新聞

55 Tokyo International
Post Office
東京国際郵便局

57 Bank of Japan
日本銀行

58 Bank of Tokyo-
Mitsubishi
東京三菱銀行

59 Mitsukoshi Department
Store
三越百貨店

61 Nihombashi Bridge
日本橋

62 Yamatane Bijitsukan
Art Museum
山種美術館

63 Kite Museum
凧の博物館

64 Haibara Japanese
Paper Store
はいばら和紙店

65 Takashimaya
Department Store
高島屋百貨店

66 Maruzen Bookshop
丸善

69 Yaesu Underground
Arcade
八重洲地下街

70 All Nippon Airways
(ANA)
全日空

71 TCAT Airport
Limousine Bus Stop
ＴＣＡＴ空港リムジン
バス停

74 Post Office
郵便局

77 Daimaru Department
Store
大丸百貨店

78 JR Highway Bus
Terminal
ＪＲ高速バス
ターミナル

80 Tokyo Central Post
Office
東京中央郵便局

84 Ōte-mon Gate
大手門

85 Site of Edo-jō Castle
江戸城跡

86 Imperial Household
Agency
宮内庁

87 New Palace Building
(Imperial Palace)
新宮殿

88 Nijū-bashi Bridge
二重橋

89 Kokuritsu Gekijō
Theatre (National
Theatre)
国立劇場

90 Supreme Court
最高裁判所

CHRIS MELLOR

Higoshi Gyoen, also known as the Imperial Palace East Garden, is a pleasant refuge from the busy city.

MAP 9 – UENO, ASAKUSA

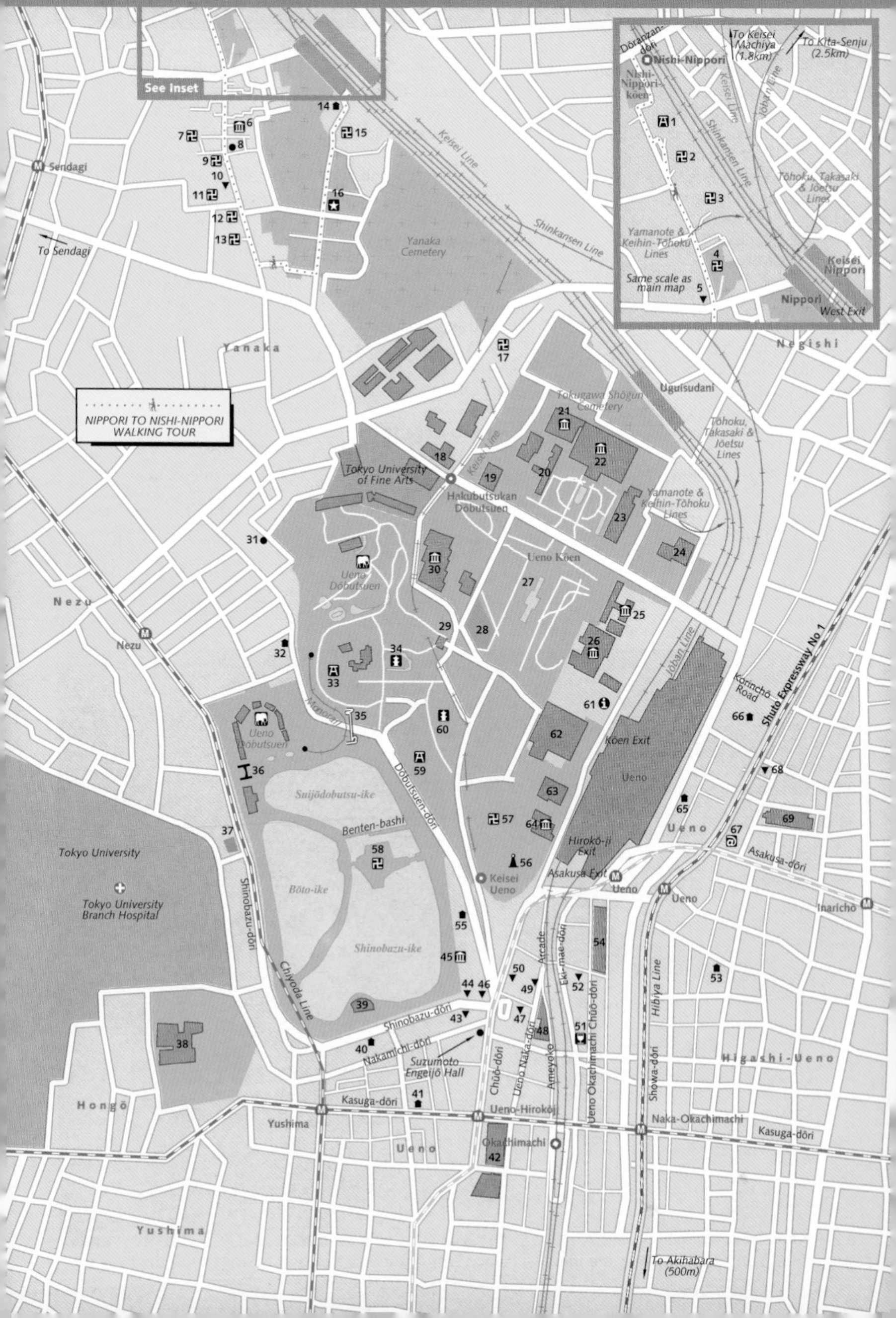

See Inset

To Keisei
Machiya
(1.8km)
To Kita-Senju
(2.5km)

Dōzaezaka-
dōri

Nishi-Nippori

Nishi-
Nippori-
kōen

Keisei Line

Jōetsu Line

Tōhoku, Takasaki
& Jōetsu
Lines

Yamanote &
Keihin-Tōhoku
Lines

Same scale as
main map

Keisei
Nippori

Nippori
West Exit

Sendagi

Keisei Line

Shinkansen Line

Yanaka
Cemetery

To Sendagi

Negishi

NIPPORI TO NISHI-NIPPORI
WALKING TOUR

Uguisudani

Tōhoku,
Takasaki &
Jōetsu
Lines

Yanaka

Tokugawa Shogun
Cemetery

Tokyo University
of Fine Arts

Hakubutsukan
Dōbutsuen

Yamanote &
Keihin-Tōhoku
Lines

Ueno Kōen

Nezu

Ueno
Dōbutsuen

Nezu

Jōban Line

Shuto Expressway No 1

Korinchō
Road

Ueno
Dōbutsuen

Dōbutsuen-dōri

Suijōdobutsu-ike

Kōen Exit

Ueno

Chiyoda Line

Benten-bashi

Ueno

Tokyo University

Bōto-ike

Hirokō-ji
Exit

Tokyo University
Branch Hospital

Asakusa-dōri

Shinobazu-ike

Inaricho

Shinobazu-dōri

Keisei
Ueno

Asakusa Exit

Ueno

Ueno

Arcade

Ueno

Higashi-Ueno

Hibiya Line

Nakamichi-dōri

Shinobazu-dōri

Chūō-dōri

Ueno-Naka-dōri

Ameyoko

Ohi-mae-dōri

Ueno Okachimachi Chūō-dōri

Showa-dōri

Suzumoto
Engeijō Hall

Hongō

Kasuga-dōri

Yushima

Ueno

Nakamichi-dōri

Chūō-dōri

Ueno-Hirokō

Okachimachi

Naka-Okachimachi

Kasuga-dōri

Yushima

To Akihabara
(500m)

Minowa

To Hotel New Koyo

Kokusai-dōri

Senzoku

Ryūsen

Taito-ku

Hashiba

Imado

Iriya

Asakusa

Kita-Ueno

SHITAMACHI WALKING TOUR

Kappabashi-dōri

Taito-ku

Kappabashi-hon-dōri

Kototoi-dōri

Asakusa

86

85

84

83

82

81

80

79

78

Nishi-Asakusa

Shin-Nakamise-dōri

Ginza Line

72 73 74

70

71

75

76

77

Kaminarimon-dōri

Tawaramachi

Asakusa-dōri

Moto-Asakusa

Kototoi-dōri

Kokusai-dōri

Hisago-dōri

Rokku-Broadway-dōri

Dempō-in

87

88

89

90

91

92

93

94

95

96

97

98

99

100

101

102

103

104

105

106

107

108

109

110

111

112

113

114

115

116

117

Asakusa-kōen

Umamichi-dōri

Hanakawado

Nakamise-dōri

Metro-dōri

Kaminarimon

Ginza Line

Kotobuki

Asakusa

Komagata-bashi

Edo-dōri

Sumida-gawa

Shuto Expressway No 6

Torigoe

To Asakusabashi
(1.5km)

Toei Asakusa Line

Kappabashi-dōri

Asakusa-dōri

Orange-dōri

Chūō-dōri

Sumida-gawa
River Cruise Route

Tōbu Nikkō Line

To Nikkō

Tōbu
Asakusa

Sumida-kōen

Azuma-bashi

Azumabashi

MAP 9 – UENO, ASAKUSA

PLACES TO STAY
14 Suzuki Ryokan
鈴木旅館
32 Suigetsu Hotel Ōgai-sō
水月ホテル鴎外荘
37 Hotel Sofitel Tokyo
ホテルソフィテル東京
40 Hotel Parkside
ホテルパークサイド
41 Hotel Pine Hill Ueno
ホテルパインヒル上野
53 Ueno Terminal Hotel
上野ターミナルホテル
55 Kinuya Hotel
きぬやホテル
65 Hotel New Ueno
ホテルニューウエノ
66 Hotel Green Capital
ホテルグリーン
キャピタル
72 Taito Ryokan
台東旅館
77 Hotel Top Asakusa
ホテルトップ浅草
85 Asakusa View Hotel
浅草ビューホテル
98 Ryokan Shigetsu
旅館指月
99 Ryokan Mikawaya
旅館三河屋
110 Asakusa Plaza Hotel
浅草プラザホテル
113 Capsule Hotel Riverside
カプセルホテル
リバーサイド

PLACES TO EAT
5 Darjeeling Restaurant
10 Matsujuan Restaurant
松寿庵レストラン
43 Izu-ei Honten
伊豆栄本店
44 Kameya Issui-tei
かめや一睡亭
46 McDonald's
47 Samrat
サムラート
49 Maharaja
50 Ganko-zushi
がんこ寿司
52 Ueno Yabu Soba
上野藪そば
68 Maguroyāsan
まぐろ家さん

75 Tenya
天屋
76 Owariya
尾張屋
78 Rāmen-tei Hanayashiki
ラーメン亭花やしき
79 Edokko
江戸っ子
82 Raishūken
来集軒
83 Asakusa Imahan
浅草今半
84 Akiyoshi Yakitori
秋吉やきとり
97 Daikokuya
大黒屋
101 Tonkyu
とんきゅ
102 Capricciosa
105 McDonald's
106 Real Italian Gelato
108 KFC
115 Komagata Doj
駒形どじょう
116 Asahi Beer Building;
La Ranarata
アサヒビールビ；
ラ・ラナラータ
117 River Pier
Azumabashi; Asahi
Beer Flamme d'Or
リバーピア吾妻橋

OTHER
1 Suwa-jinja
諏K神社
2 Senkōji
浄光寺
3 Yōfuku-ji Temple
養福寺
4 Keiō-ji Temple
経王寺
6 Asakura Chōso
Museum
朝倉彫塑館
7 Ryūsen-ji Temple
龍泉寺
8 Sandara Kōgei Basket
Store
さんだら工芸屋
9 Kaizō-in
海蔵院
11 Kannon-ji Temple
観音寺

12 Chōan-ji Temple
長安寺
13 Jōzai-ji Temple
常在寺
15 Tennō-ji Temple
天王寺
16 Police Box
交番
17 Kanei-ji Temple
寛永寺
18 Tokyo National
Cultural Property
Research Center;
Kuroda Memorial Hall
東京国立文化財研究所
19 Gallery of Hōryū-ji
Treasures
法隆寺宝物館
20 Hyōkeikan Hall
表慶館
21 Heiseikan
平成館
22 Tokyo National
Museum
東京国立博物館
23 Gallery of Eastern
Antiquities
東洋館
24 Rinnō-ji Temple
輪王寺
25 Kokuritsu Kagaku
Hakubutsukan
Museum
国立科学博物館
26 Kokurutsu Seiyō
Bijitsukan Museum
国立西洋美術館
27 Great Fountain
28 Children's Playground
こども広場
29 Ueno Zoo Main
Entrance
上野動物園表門
30 Tokyo Metropolitan
Museum of Art
東京都美術館
31 Rokuryū Onsen
六竜温泉
33 Tōshō-gū Jinja Shrine
上野東照宮
34 Five Storey Pagoda
五重塔
35 Aesop-bashi Bridge
いそっぷ橋

A restaurant sign on the street in Ueno – a great hunting ground for cheap Japanese food

PAUL DYMOND

MAP LEGEND

CITY ROUTES

Freeway .... Freeway
Highway .... Primary Road
Road .... Secondary Road
Street .... Street
Lane .... Lane
.... On/Off Ramp
.... Unsealed Road
.... One Way Street
.... Pedestrian Street
.... Stepped Street
.... Tunnel
.... Footbridge

REGIONAL ROUTES

.... Tollway, Freeway
.... Primary Road
.... Secondary Road
.... Minor Road

BOUNDARIES

.... International
.... Provincial
.... Disputed
.... Fortified Wall

HYDROGRAPHY

.... River, Creek
.... Canal
.... Lake
.... Dry Lake; Salt Lake
.... Spring; Rapids
.... Waterfalls

TRANSPORT ROUTES & STATIONS

.... JR Train Line
.... Shinkansen Line
.... Private Line
.... Metro
.... Cable Car, Chairlift
.... Ferry
.... Walking Trail
.... Walking Tour
.... Path
.... Pier or Jetty

AREA FEATURES

.... Building
.... Park, Gardens
.... Market
.... Hotel
.... Beach
.... Cemetery
.... Campus
.... Plaza

POPULATION SYMBOLS

CAPITAL .... National Capital
CAPITAL .... Provincial Capital
CITY .... City
Town .... Town
Village .... Village
.... Urban Area

MAP SYMBOLS

.... Place to Stay
.... Place to Eat
.... Point of Interest

.... Airport
.... Bank
.... Bus Terminal/Stop
.... Cave
.... Church
.... Cinema
.... Cycling
.... Embassy
.... Gate
.... Golf Course
.... Hospital
.... Internet Cafe
.... Lookout
.... Monument
.... Museum
.... National Park
.... Pagoda
.... Parking
.... Police Station
.... Post Office
.... Pub or Bar
.... Shopping Centre
.... Swimming Pool
.... Taxi
.... Telephone
.... Temple/Shrine
.... Tourist Information
.... Zoo

Note: not all symbols displayed above appear in this book

LONELY PLANET OFFICES

Australia
Locked Bag 1, Footscray, Victoria 3011
☎ 03 8379 8000 fax 03 8379 8111
email: talk2us@lonelyplanet.com.au

USA
150 Linden St, Oakland, CA 94607
☎ 510 893 8555 TOLL FREE: 800 275 8555
fax 510 893 8572
email: info@lonelyplanet.com

UK
10a Spring Place, London NW5 3BH
☎ 020 7428 4800 fax 020 7428 4828
email: go@lonelyplanet.co.uk

France
1 rue du Dahomey, 75011 Paris
☎ 01 55 25 33 00 fax 01 55 25 33 01
email: bip@lonelyplanet.fr
www.lonelyplanet.fr

World Wide Web: www.lonelyplanet.com *or* AOL keyword: lp
Lonely Planet Images: lpi@lonelyplanet.com.au